LOL
(RD)

CU00733449

TURKEY'S RELATIONS WITH THE WEST AND THE TURKIC REPUBLICS

In Memory of My Father

Ahmet Bal
(1934 - 25th April 1997)

Turkey's Relations with the West and the Turkic Republics

The rise and fall of the 'Turkish Model'

DR İDRİS BAL
Police Academy, Ankara, Turkey

Ashgate

Aldershot • Burlington USA • Singapore • Sydney

© İdris Bal 2000

All rights reserved. No part of this publication may be reproduced, stored in a retrieval system or transmitted in any form or by any means, electronic, mechanical, photocopying, recording or otherwise without the prior permission of the publisher.

Published by
Ashgate Publishing Limited
Gower House
Croft Road
Aldershot
Hampshire GU11 3HR
England

Ashgate Publishing Company
131 Main Street
Burlington VT 05401-5600 USA

Ashgate website: http://www.ashgate.com

British Library Cataloguing in Publication Data
Bal, İdris
    Turkey's relations with the west and the Turkic Republics:
    the rise and fall of of the 'Turkish model'
    1. Turkey - Foreign relations - 1980 -
    I. Title
    327.5'61

Library of Congress Control Number: 00-134010

ISBN 0 7546 1408 5

Printed in Great Britain by
Antony Rowe Ltd, Chippenham, Wiltshire

Contents

List of Tables

Preface

In this book I have sought to analyse the relations between Turkey, the West and the newly independent Turkic Republics, in the context of the 'Turkish Model' proposed and supported by the West as a possible model for development in the Turkic Republics. It summarises the Turkish Model of development as applied in Turkey, and its shortcomings and discusses the role of Turkey in the area after the collapse of the Soviet Union, from the point of view of both the West and Turkey itself. It analyses the possible reasons why the Turkish Model was proposed and how the Turkic Republics received it, and why it declined from favour in such a short period of time.

This book is a revised version of the thesis submitted to the University of Manchester for the degree of Ph.D. in 1998. Several people helped me in the preparation of this study and I am grateful to all of them. My thanks are due in the first place to Dr. Çiğdem Balım, Dr. Edmund Herzig and Dr. Şaziye Gazioğlu for their guidance and assistance. In Britain, my thanks are due to Chris Binns, Professor William Hale, Dr. Marie Bennigsen Broxup, and to Dr. Andrew Mango, all of whom answered my questions and gave me valuable ideas.

In Turkey, several people, including politicians, academics and my relatives, helped me. My mother and father gave me invaluable help while I was conducting a survey among Turkish people, and several other relatives helped me in delivering and collecting the questionnaires during my first survey. My thanks also go to my brother-in-law Selim Kireç, who delivered and collected the questionnaires of my second survey, among Turkic students in Turkey.

Secondly I would like to thank Kamran İnan (former minister of foreign affairs, minister of state and currently an MP), Namık Kemal Zeybek (former minister of state), Abdülkadir Aksu (former minister of interior affairs), Cemil Çiçek (former minister of state), Acar Okan (advisor to the prime minister Tansu Çiller), Prof. Yusuf Hallacoğlu (head of the Institute of Turkish History and Language), Ertuğrul O. Çırağan (foreign policy advisor of the Democratic Left Party), Necati Bilican (former Head of the Turkish Police Forces), Yaşar Toga (deputy president of the Turkish International Co-operation Agency), Mustafa Çalık (General Director of the Journal 'Türkiye Günlüğü') and Selçuk Alkın (a member of the administrative committee of the Society of Azerbaijan Culture). Professors Mehmet Saray, Hasan Köni, Ayşe

Ayata, Nadir Devlet, and Seyfi Taşan (editor of the Journal 'Foreign Policy', published in Ankara) also receive my thanks for accepting to see me and answering my questions.

My thanks are also due to representatives of the Turkic republics in Turkey. In particular I would like to thank ambassadors: Mehmet Nevruzoğlu Aliyev, (Azerbaijan); Nurmuhammad Hanammov, (Turkmenistan); Dr. Anvarbek Mokeev, counsellor at the Embassy of Kirgizstan in Ankara; İsmail Yolcuoğlu, former counsellor at the Embassy of Azerbaijan in Ankara; Zakir Haşimov, counsellor at the Embassy of Azerbaijan in Ankara; Annaguli Nurmemedov, counsellor at the Embassy of Turkmenistan in Ankara; Doulat Kouavychev, third secretary at Kazakstan's Embassy in Ankara, responsible for political affairs; and Kayrat Sh. Sarıbayev, third secretary at Kazakstan's Embassy in Ankara, responsible for cultural affairs.

Finally, I have to thank my wife, Hülya Deniz, for her unfailing encouragement and unstinting support and understanding.

İdris Bal

List of Abbreviations

ASSR	: Autonomous Soviet Socialist Republic
BP	: British Petroleum
BSEC	: Black Sea Economic Co-operation (Karadeniz Ekonomik İşbirliği Teşkilatı - KEİB)
CIS	: Commonwealth of Independent States (Bağımsız Devletler Topluluğu - BDT)
CSCE	: Conference on Security and Co-operation in Europe
DEİK	: Turkish acronym for the Foreign Economic Relations Council (Dış Ekonomik İlişkiler Konseyi)
DİE	: Turkish acronym for the State Statistics Institute (Devlet İstatistik Enstitüsü)
DLP	: The Democratic Left Party (Demokratik Sol Parti)
DP	: The Democrat Party (Demokrat Parti)
EC	: European Community
ECO	: Economic Co-operation Organisation
EEC	: European Economic Community
EFTA	: European Free Trade Association
EU	: European Union
HADEP	: Turkish acronym for the Peoples' Party of Democracy (Halkın Demokrasi Partisi)
HEP	: Turkish acronym for the People's Work Party (Halkın Emek Partisi)
IHT	: International Herald Tribune
IMF	: International Monetary Fund
JP	: The Justice Party (Adalet Partisi)
KGB	: Soviet Secret Service
KOSGEB	: Turkish acronym for the Centre to Develop and Support Small and Medium Scale Industry (Küçük ve Orta Ölçekli Sanayiyi Geliştirme ve Destekleme Kurumu)
MEI	: Middle East International
MP	: The Motherland Party (Anavatan Partisi)
MPs	: Members of Parliament
NAP	: The National Action Party (Milliyetçi Hareket Partisi)
NATO	: North Atlantic Treaty Organisation
NDP	: The Nationalist Democracy Party (Milliyetçi Demokrasi Partisi)

NLP	: The Nationalist Labour Party (Milliyetçi Çalışma Partisi)
NP	: The Nation Party (Millet Partisi)
NSP	: The National Salvation Party (Milli Selamet Partisi)
OECD	: Organization for Economic Co-operation and Development
PFA	: Popular Front of Azerbaijan
PKK	: Turkish acronym for the Kurdish Workers Party
PP	: The Populist Party (Halk Partisi)
PTT	: Turkish acronym for the Turkish Post Telephone and Telegraph Organisation (Posta Telefon Telgraf)
RDP	: The Reformist Democracy Party (Islahatçı Demokrasi Partisi)
RPP	: The Republican People's Party (Cumhuriyet Halk Partisi)
SCSE	: State Committee for the State of Emergency
SDP	: The Social Democrat Party (Sosyal Demokrat Parti - SODEP).
SDPP	: The Social Democrat Populist Party (Sosyal Demokrat Halkçı Parti)
SEAP	: South-East Anatolian Project (Güneydoğu Anadolu Projesi - GAP)
SEE	: State Economic Enterprise
TICA	: Turkish International Co-operation Agency (Türk İşbirliği ve Kalkınma Ajansı - TIKA)
TMB	: Turkish acronym for the Union of Turkish Constructors (Türk Müteahhitler Birliği)
TOBB	: Turkish acronym for the Union of Turkish Chambers and Bourses (Türkiye Odalar ve Borsalar Birliği)
TPAO	: Turkish acronym for the Turkish Petrols Joint-Stock Company (Türk Petrolleri Anonim Ortaklığı)
TPP	: True Path Party (Doğru Yol Partisi)
TRT	: Turkish acronym for the Turkish Radio and Television Corporation (Türkiye Radyo ve Televiziyon Kurumu)
TSE	: Turkish acronym for the Turkish Standards Institute (Türk Standartları Enstitüsü)
UK	: United Kingdom
UN	: United Nations
US	: United States (of America)
USSR	: The Union of Soviet Socialist Republics (Sovyet Sosyalist Cumhuriyetler Birliği - SSCB)
WP	: The Welfare Party (Refah Partisi)

Introduction

Following the collapse of the USSR, Turkey and Iran were considered as the rival powers which would fill the power vacuum in Central Asia and the Caucasus created by the former superpower and which would be imitated by the newly independent states in their search for a political model, nationhood and identity. During the early days of this competition, the West (including US) was seen as supporting Turkey. The 'Turkish Model' was forwarded as an ideal Muslim democracy, and a model of development especially for Kazakstan, Kirgizstan, Uzbekistan, Turkmenistan and Azerbaijan, which are Muslim in religion and have ethnic and linguistic ties with Turkey. After a meeting with the Turkish Prime Minister Süleyman Demirel in Washington on 13 February 1992, US president George Bush pointed to Turkey '...as the model of a democratic, secular state which could be emulated by Central Asia' (Rashid, 1994, p.210). On the other hand, it was believed that Iran was the representative of fundamentalist Islam and oppression, and it was feared that Iran sought to export its regime to this unstable area of the world using its historical, geographical and religious ties. Robins (1994, p.63) summarises the situation when he says

> When the Soviet Union formally broke up, exaggerated claims were immediately made as to the role, which Turkey could play in Central Asia. Such claims owed more to ideology than to practicality. The major proponent of such a view was the United States, which feared that a political vacuum had been created in Central Asia and that it would be filled by Iran and its revolutionary brand of Islam.

In fact, soon it became apparent how difficult it was to simplify the complex relations of the republics of Central Asia and Azerbaijan and as reflected in their more recent works, academics and analysts began to point out the European, American, Japanese, Israeli, Saudi Arabian, Pakistani, Indian, Chinese and, more importantly, Russian interests in the area.[1] The Western knowledge of the region increased and in turn the West reconsidered their initial assumptions and policies and ended their support for the Turkish model. Although the Turkish model of a democratic, secular state, Westernised with a market economy and close to the West yet Islamic and Turkic, has been mentioned by many researchers (Mango, 1993; Rashid, 1994; Akiner, 1993; Smolansky, 1994; Hostler, 1993; Henze, 1992, p. 35; Sander,

1

1994; Aybet, 1994; Söylemez, 1992; Demirel, 1992; Winrow, 1992; Yalçın, 1992; Israeli, 1994; Apostolou, 1992; Saivetz, 1994; Parsons, 1993; Karasik, 1993), outside Mango's article titled 'The Turkish Model' (Middle Eastern Studies, Vol.29, No.4, October 1993, pp.726-757), there are no studies devoted entirely to the details of the 'Turkish model' and its proposal as a model for the Turkic Republics. Therefore, the present study intends to take a close look at the state of the Turkish Model at a time when it was proposed to the Turkic states of the former Soviet Union, and while doing so it wants to shed light on Turkey's domestic politics and foreign policy following the break up of the Soviet Union. Hence, on the one hand it aims to explore Turkish foreign policy in the early 1990s and the shaping of the Turkish public opinion, and on the other hand it wants to explore the attitudes of the West and the Turkic republics towards Turkey.

The study is divided into five chapters. In chapter one, the Turkish Model is explored. Its birth and development is presented. Economic, political and legal aspects of the model are introduced and its achievements are discussed. In the second part of chapter one, the major shortcomings of the Turkish model are also discussed. These are singled out as the military interventions and the Kurdish and Alawite minority issues. These problems are also diagnosed as the most serious domestic problems of contemporary Turkey. Chapter two focuses on Turkish politics and policy making after the collapse of the Soviet Union. In the first part of this chapter the factors that affected Turkish reaction to the collapse of the USSR and emergence of the Turkic republics are outlined and reactions of parties, politicians, intellectuals, media, public opinion are discussed. In the second part of the chapter, the change in Turkish foreign policy style after 1980 is emphasised and developing relations with Turkic republics are outlined. In chapter three, the promotion of the Turkish Model by the West and the reasons behind the proposal are discussed. This chapter also dwells on the possible reasons which led to the decline of Western support for the Turkish model. In chapter four, the Turkic Republics are discussed with respect to their relations with Turkey and their reactions to the Turkish Model. In chapter five, there is a general conclusion summarising all the discussions taking place through the book and giving concluding remarks.

In this book, the term 'Turkic Republics' is used throughout to mean the following republics: Azerbaijan, Kazakstan, Kirgizstan, Uzbekistan and Turkmenistan.

The study is based on primary and secondary written sources in English and Turkish and interviews with Turkish politicians, officials and academics who are considered as policy makers, with representatives of Turkic republics in Ankara, and with British academics. The results of two surveys carried out by the author among Turkish citizens and students from Turkic Republics are also presented.

Note

1. For example, see M.B. Olcott, (1996), *Central Asia's New States*, United States Institute of Peace Press, Washington; E. Herzig, (1995), *Iran and the Former Soviet South*, The Royal Institute of International Affairs, London; G. Bondarevsky and P. Ferdinand, (1994), 'Russian Foreign Policy and Central Asia', in P. Ferdinand, (ed.), *The New Central Asia and Its Neighbours*, Pinter Publishers, The Royal Institute of International Affairs, London; J.B.K. Lough, (1993), *Russia's Influence in the 'Near Abroad': Problems and Prospects*, Conflict Studies Research center, The Royal Military Academy Sandhurst Camberley, Surrey; J. Lough, (1993), 'Defining Russia's Relations with Neighbouring States', *RFE/RL Research Report*, vol.2, no.20; O.M. Smolansky, (1994), 'Turkish and Iranian Policies in Central Asia', in H. Malik, (ed.), *Central Asia: Its Strategic Importance and Future Prospects*, Macmillan Press, London; R. Israeli, (1994), 'Return to the source: the republics of Central Asia and the Middle East', *Central Asian Survey*, vol.13, no.1; Y.V. Gankovsky, (1994), 'Russia's Relations with the Central Asian States Since the Dissolution of the Soviet Union', in H. Malik, (ed.), Central Asia: Its Strategic Importance and Future Prospects, *op.cit.*; G.E. Fuller and I.O. Lesser, (1993), *Turkey's New Geopolitics*, Westview Press, Oxford; M.I. Abramowitz, (1993), 'Dateline Ankara: Turkey After Özal', *Foreign Policy*, no.91; B.P. Henze, (1992), *Turkey: Toward the Twenty-First Century*, Rand Corporation, Santa Monica.

1 The Turkish Model of Development

Introduction

After the disintegration of the former USSR, several politicians, academics and media commentators mentioned the 'Turkish Model' as a feasible model of government and development for the newly independent Turkic States. After a meeting with the Turkish Prime Minister Demirel in Washington on 13 February 1992, President Bush pointed to Turkey '...as the model of a democratic, secular state which could be emulated by Central Asia' (Rashid, 1994, p.210). Similarly, in June 1992, Mme Catherine Lalumiére, the Secretary General of the Council of Europe, a body dedicated to the defence and propagation of European concepts of humans rights, visited the Central Asian Republics, and declared that '...Turkey provided a valid model of development for many a newly independent country in Asia' (Mango, 1993, p.726). Mohammed Salih, the leader of Uzbek opposition party, the Erk, said 'We are a Turkic people and Turks have never been fanatics. I think religion should not intervene in politics and the only possible model is Turkey' (Sander, 1994, p.40). Uzbek President also said 'I announce to the whole world that my country will go forward by the Turkish route...'.[1] In fact, initially all the leaders of Turkic republics regarded Turkey as a model for their own development.[2] According to Mango (1993, p.726), the usual implications appears to be that 'the republic of Turkey is a model of secular, democratic, Muslim country, aiming to achieve Western standards, in partnership with the West, by applying liberal free-market policies'. Israeli (1994, p.19), pointed out that after the collapse of USSR Turkic republics looked up to Turkey as a model, and in his view Turkey 'is ethnically and linguistically close to them (with the exception of the Tajiks who are Iranian), to provide both an example of a secular-minded Islamic country developing in close collaboration with the West'. Winrow (1992, p.107), put forward similar arguments as well. In his view,

The United States and other Western states have acknowledged that ideally the ex-soviet Turkic republics should adopt the Turkish model of development - namely, a reasonably well-functioning liberal democracy supported by a free market economy in a secular Muslim populated state.

A Turkish diplomat portrayed Turkish model as,

> The Turkish model helps explain how a nation is built in a very central region of the World, how independence is won and maintained, how contemporary values and democracy are established and kept and how a liberal economy is achieved through gradual transformation of institutions (Aybet, 1994, p.27).

Turkish academic Oral Sander (1994, p.40) also regarded Turkey as a model and argued that 'Kemalism (Turkish Model) is likely to be a better model for the Turkic republics than fundamentalism in view of their manifest aspirations for organic ties with the West and for political and economic modernisation'.[3] On the other hand, Akiner (1993, p.56), argued that

> Turkey and Iran are in fact being used as symbols. When the message is decoded, what is actually being asked is the following: do the Central Asians intend to follow the path of Islamic fundamentalism or of secularism; do they intend to move to a market economy; do they intend to adopt a western democratic form of government.

The common desirable achievements of the model as defined by various sources were a secular state (in a country where the majority of the population is Muslim), a multi-party system, co-operation with and closeness to the West, and a market economy. The fact that Turkey which had risen from the ashes of an Islamic Empire had succeeded in achieving some form of democracy and had been able to set up a market economy, and most importantly had done all this very recently was important. What is more, Turkey was the closest in terms of its culture and language to some of the newly independent states of the former Soviet Union. If one did not scrutinise the ideological and cultural basis of this model of development and its cycle of maturation over the years, and the problems that the model brought to its country of origin, it did indeed look like a quick answer to the problems that the new states faced after the disintegration of the Soviet Union. The Turkish Model could be used as a 'transitional' model for development.

This chapter first outlines the experiments in Westernization during the Ottoman period and the formulation of the Turkish Model by Kemal Atatürk between the years 1923 and 1938. Second, it gives the development of the Turkish model from 1938 to the early 1990s when the struggle for democracy continued, and Turkey's closeness to the West was strengthened by its membership of major Western institutions such as NATO, Council of Europe, and its economic transformation from a centrally controlled economy to the market economy took place. While the chapter summarises the development of the features of the Turkish Model chronologically, it does not aim to discuss ideological basis of the Model in depth. Military coups, Kurdish separatism and Alawite discontent will be outlined as the outstanding problems of the Turkish model.

The Formulation of the Turkish Model during Atatürk: 1923-1938

The development of the Turkish Model has its roots in the Ottoman period, when European style bureaucracy and institutions for administration were put into place. After failing to conquer Vienna in 1682, the Ottoman Empire began to question the efficiency of its army, education and all administrative structures, and taking Europe as its example, it began to restructure itself from the last decade of the 18th century onwards. Similar to Western models, the Ottoman Empire created ministries of interior affairs, foreign affairs and education. In 1835 the Ministry of Interior Affairs and the Ministry of Foreign Affairs became separate ministries; from 1838 onwards, committees which constituted the origins of the Ministries of Agriculture, Trade, Industry and Public Works were established. In 1834, a postal administration was established and the first telegraph lines started functioning in 1855. In 1840, inspired by the administrative system of France, the law on the administration of 'Vilayet's (provinces) was adopted, and governors who received their salaries from the central administration were appointed. During the same year, a code of Criminal Law also inspired by the French criminal law, was adopted. In 1841, trade laws were adopted from various Western countries. In 1840, a state bank, 'Osmanlı Bankası' (Ottoman Bank) was established and the first banknotes were printed. In 1858, trade courts were reorganised and Land and Sea Trade Laws (resembling French laws) came into force, accompanied with amendments to the Land and Criminal Laws in 1861. In 1863, 'Şura-i devlet' (the Administrative Court) was established in order to deal with administrative cases. In 1870, the first part of 'Mecelle-i Ahkam-ı Adliye' (the modified Civil Law) was published. In 1863, Galatasaray Lycée, and Robert College, where French and English were the languages of instruction respectively, opened. New railway lines were constructed in the European and Anatolian parts of the Empire, and the first railway line started to function between İzmir and Aydın in 1867. In order to encourage trade, private banks and insurance companies were established.

After the First World War and the foundation of the Turkish Republic (1923), Mustafa Kemal[4] took into his close circle those intellectuals who were pro Western, and their presence helped him to accelerate, and in some cases to finalise the reforms which had already started during the last years of the Ottoman Empire (Vali, 1971, p.10; Söylemez, 1992, p.49).[5]

Social and Legal Reforms after 1923

The social and legal reforms of Mustafa Kemal[6] and his colleagues were concerned with separating religion and state on all fronts. This was necessary in order to create a civic society resembling that of Western democracies and to this aim the Sultanate was abolished in November 1922 followed by the Caliphate in 1924. The new Constitution of 1924 ratified by the Grand National Assembly, declared Turkey a Republic and sovereignty as belonging unconditionally to the nation. Although the 1924 version of the Constitution accepted Islam as the state religion, this article was revoked in 1928. The principle of secularism was inserted into the Turkish Constitution with an amendment made in 1937.[7] Meanwhile, religious courts were abolished, Islamic law was abandoned, religious orders were outlawed, religious schools were closed, and the entire education system was placed under the supervision of the Ministry of Education. Western legislation was introduced in all fields drawing on the Swiss civil code, the German criminal law of procedure, and the Italian penal and commercial codes. The Family Code adopted in 1926 made marriage a civil agreement between two consenting individuals and gave women the same rights as men. The lunar calendar of Islam was replaced by the Gregorian calendar and the weekend holiday was moved from the Islamic holy day of Friday to the Christian Sunday. During the reforms, the symbolic importance of clothing for Islam did not go unnoticed, and the 'fez', worn by Turkish Muslims as a symbol of their loyalty to the caliph, was forbidden; European clothing was generally recommended and brimmed hats for men became mandatory. In 1928 a Latin based alphabet was introduced to replace the Arabic alphabet as a part of the language reform which intended to cleanse Turkish of Arabic and Persian syntactic structures and words. In 1932, all prayers, including the call from the mosque, had to be recited in Turkish and not in Arabic, the language of the Koran. In 1934, the law requiring everyone to adopt a surname was passed. Mustafa Kemal himself became Mustafa Kemal Atatürk, 'Father of Turks'.[8]

Definition of 'Turkishness'

During the 19th century when it became clear that the empire was collapsing, the Ottoman elite began to search for a 'unifying element' to cease the dispersion of the Empire. Their efforts gave birth to three ideologies; Pan-Ottomanism, Pan-

Islamism, and Pan-Turkism.[9] The aim of pan-Ottomanism was to save the Empire by uniting numerous nations under the name of Ottomanness or Osmanlı (Akçura, 1991, p.19). Non-Muslim nations would be free in their belief and language as usual, but they would enjoy equal rights with the Muslim population of the empire and they would be represented in the parliament. The goal of Islamism was to unite Islamic peoples of the empire both socially and politically under a single Muslim community (Sindi, 1978, p.100). Pan-Turkism on the other hand aimed at the unity of people of Turkic origins (Hostler, 1993, p.143).

During the Tanzimat period (1839-1876,) Ottomanism became state policy. However this policy failed to satisfy the non-Muslim nations of the empire who continued their separatist activities and demanded their independence. Therefore after Abdülhamid II (1876), pan-Islamism was adopted as the state policy with the aim to salvage at least the Muslim part of the empire. Yet the rise of nationalism among the Muslim people of the empire, was unstoppable as well. Lastly pan-Turkism emerged in the empire[10], and during the First World War, it also was tried as the state policy.

After the collapse of the Ottoman Empire, the First World War and the establishment of the Turkish Republic, the population was far more homogenous than the population of the Ottoman Empire. However, there were still some religious minorities, such as various groups of Christians and Jews. Within the Muslim population of Anatolia, there were ethnic differences (for example Turks, Kurds, Circassians etc.) and differences of sect. Whereas religion united the Sunni Muslim population during the Ottoman Empire, and the absence of a cultural and a religious policy eased the differences between the peoples most of the time, in the new Republic religion and state were separated, and religion, the importance of which was reduced in the state and society, could no longer be a unifying power. Atatürk's solution to the problem was to define an entity called 'Turkishness' and urge the citizens to unite around it.[11]

Although Mustafa Kemal was a nationalist, his nationalism was not based on race, but limited by the boundaries of Turkey and open to all citizens (Robins, 1991, p.4). It was a quick and practical solution to the problems created by the objective to create a new identity and a culture which would cut its ties with the undesirable sections of its past. Now the peoples of the new Republic had to unify around 'Turkishness' which, as defined by Atatürk, emphasised the centrality of a being a Turkish citizen, and took no account of the origins of its constituent people. Anyone, who carried a Turkish passport and called Turkey his/her homeland, was a 'Turk'. Hence being a Turk was a question of citizenship rather than race[12], and in theory, Atatürk's nationalism disregarded differences in race and religion. 'Proclaiming oneself a Turk thus became a badge of pride and the key to full membership of the state, rather than the social stigma it had been under the Ottomans' (Robins, 1991, p.5) and the founder of the Republic called himself Atatürk, 'Father of Turks', and cemented nationhood with the phrase 'Ne Mutlu Türküm Diyene' ('Happy is he/she who can call himself/herself a Turk'), a phrase still to be found on the walls of important official buildings (Hindle, 1993, p.59).

Attempts at a Multi-Party System

Although the Cumhuriyet Halk Partisi (Republican People's Party- RPP), which was established by Mustafa Kemal in 1923, remained as the only political party until 1945, during Atatürk's rule other short-lived political parties were established such as Terakkiperver Cumhuriyet Fırkası (the Progressive Republican Party) and Serbest Fırka (the Free Republican Party).

When Atatürk began his reforms after the establishment of the new republic, these were not realised without the opposition of his former colleagues. During the Lausanne peace negotiations (20th November 1922 - 24 July 1923), the first uprising against Atatürk took place in Parliament. In order to have a more 'friendly' Parliament during these turbulent times, Atatürk asked the Parliament to dissolve itself on 1 April, 1923.[13] In the new Parliament which replaced the old one, supporters of Mustafa Kemal outnumbered the opposition, and this ensured a suitable basis for the ratification of the Lausanne Peace Treaty (23 August 1923), the declaration of the Republic (29 October 1923) and the abolition of the Caliphate (3 March 1924) without much discussion. Under these conditions, Atatürk's colleagues Kazım Karabekir Pasha, Ali Fuat (Cebesoy) Pasha, Refet Pasha, Rauf (Orbay) and Adnan (Adıvar) left the RPP and on 17 November 1924 established the Terakkiperver Cumhuriyet Fırkası (the Progressive Republican Party). This party had a liberal-democratic program and criticised the authoritarian administration of the Kemalist cadre. On 1 February 1925, the Sheikh (Şeyh) Said revolt took place. Following the accusations that the Terrakkiperver Cumhuriyet Fırkası had supported this Kurdish uprising which wanted an Islamic rule, the party was closed on 5 June 1925 and its members were taken off to court (Erdoğan, 1992, p.112).

A second attempt at a multi-party system took place in 1930, and in contrast to the previous one, this time Atatürk played a vital role in the establishment of an opposition party. Mustafa Kemal had his reasons for creating an official opposition. Firstly, in the Western democratic countries, as Kinross (1993, p.450) points out, 'Turkey's one-party system was seen as a sign of her inferiority to the West. He [Atatürk] had been stung by the criticism of European writers that the Turkish system, though Western in form, was Eastern in practice'. It was naturally disturbing for a man who advocated democracy to be criticised for being anti-democratic. Atatürk is reported to tell his friend Fethi (Okyar), 'I do not want to die without bringing the regime of personal rule in Turkey to a close. I want to create a liberal Republic' (Kinross, 1993, p.450). Atatürk claimed that the administrative tradition of the Turks was familiar with democracy. İnan (1971, p.69) cites him as saying

> In the early history of the Turkish nation, through their famous councils and electing heads of the states in these councils, Turks proved that they were strongly attached to democratic ideas. However, in the later period of our history, Padişahs headed Turkish states and they left these (democratic) principles and became despotic.

He also criticised anti-democratic ideologies and underlined the superiority of democracy in several of his speeches, for example, 'According to us, in our understanding, popular governmental administration is possible through democracy (İnan, 1971, pp.74-77). Secondly, in the 1930s, opposition to Atatürk's reforms was increasing and discontent was not helped by economic stagnation. The opposition had to be kept under control and under these circumstances, Atatürk asked his friend and Prime Minister, Fethi (Okyar), to establish an opposition party (Erdoğan, 1992, p.112; Kinross, 1993, pp.450-451) and Serbest Cumhuriyet Fırkası (Free Republican Party) was established on 12 August 1930 under the spiritual protection of Mustafa Kemal. However, the life of this party was to be short. It was wrongly perceived as a truly opposition party and the citizens of Turkey rushed to support it. Although support came from all sections of the society, the presence of a large conservative mass among its members was significant. To complicate matters, members of the Republican People's Party tried to create the impression that their colleague Fethi Okyar was in actual opposition to Mustafa Kemal. Okyar unwillingly closed his party on 7 November 1930 (Erdoğan, 1992, p.112). This was the last attempt at a multi-party system during the life of Atatürk.

Foreign Policy During Atatürk[14]

Although the Ottoman empire was weakened at the beginning of the twentieth century, it was still one of the big powers, and the new Republic had to learn to adjust itself to being a secondary power after an Imperial past. Also, in contrast to the Ottoman Empire, it had defined itself as a part of the Western civilisation. Hence, the desire to be a part of the Western scheme of things, while accepting a less glorious role in international affairs began to shape the foreign policy of Turkey after 1923 (Deringil, 1992, p.1).

During the 1930's, there were other one-party regimes and leaders like Atatürk but there were significant differences between Atatürk's foreign policy and theirs. Unlike Hitler, Mussolini and Stalin's policies, Kemalist foreign policy was essentially pacifist, nourishing non-territorial or political ambitions at any other country's expense. As Kinross (1993) points out, peaceful co-existence, 'Peace at home and peace in the world' were Mustafa Kemal's watchwords. Atatürk had no plans to reconquer former Ottoman lands and his foreign minister defined his country's policy, by stating: 'Turkey does not desire an inch of foreign territory, but will not give up an inch of what she holds' (Kinross, 1993, p.458). The main desire of Turkey was only its territorial integrity and freedom (Kinross, 1993).

The resolution of 'not giving up an inch' of what Turkey holds was an important feature of Turkish foreign policy. Its origins are in the resolution of 'Misak-ı Milli' (the National Pact of 1920) an oath taken by the members of the last Ottoman parliament to protect the borders of the Ottoman Empire as of 17 February 1920 including Mosul and Aleppo (Haleb), which were within the borders of the Ottoman Empire. There would be plebiscite for Kars, Ardahan and Batum. The Pact also decided that Istanbul, as the capital city of the Islamic Caliphate and the Ottoman Empire had to be under full security and the rights given to minorities would be adjusted according to the right given to the Muslim minorities in other countries. The National Pact was issued during the Erzurum Congress of the Turkish nationalist resistance movement between 23rd July and 6th August 1919 under the presidency of Mustafa Kemal and it was rectified during the Sivas Congress between 4th and 13th September 1919 (Kösoğlu, 1990, pp. 733-734; Tunaya, 1986, p.300). However, after the Lausanne treaty (24 July 1923) Hatay (Alexandretta), Mosul and Kirkuk were left outside the borders of Turkey. In 1924, the Sheikh Said revolt (11th February-12th April 1925) hindered Mustafa Kemal's plans to reunite Mosul with Turkey but Hatay was reunited with Turkey in 1939, one year after Atatürk's death (Armaoğlu, 1988, pp.3, 48-351; Güzel, 1995, p.121). In other words, 'Peace at home, peace in the world' was not a passive policy; it meant that there would be peace after the borders decided by the 'Misak-ı Milli' were achieved although this did not necessarily mean armed struggle and peaceful solutions were to be preferred. And indeed, the Montreux Treaty (20th July 1936) which changed the status of the straits; boundary treaties with the USSR; attempts to balance Hitler and Mussolini in the West with the Balkan pact (9th February 1934) and in the East with the Saadabad Pact (9th July 1937) were the important achievements of the new foreign policy during the time of Atatürk.

Economic Reforms

It is apparent that Atatürk was well aware of the importance of economy in safeguarding the sovereignty of a state. This stance is clearly indicated by some of his statements. For example,

> A nation's absolute independence can only be achieved through a combination of sovereignty of the nation with that of the economy. ....However grand political and military victories may be, they do not make an impact if they are not merged with economic ones. ...We have to give absolute priority to the economic matters of our newly born Turkish republic, if we desire to reach the level of contemporary civilisation. This age, no doubt, is an age of economy (Kartay, 1989, p.62).

During Atatürk's rule, the economic policy of the state changed twice. Between 1923 to 1930, Atatürk followed a more liberal economic policy and main economic decisions were aimed at spreading private ownership of land, appropriating land for landless farmers and migrants, extending state credit for capital accumulation in agriculture, promoting private enterprises, protecting domestic production by customs policies and refraining from external borrowing. Alongside new legislation such as the industry promotion law, the law protecting the value of the Turkish currency and the Civil and Trade Codes, organisations like the Central Bank (Merkez Bankası), Agricultural Bank (Ziraat Bankası), Business Bank (İş Bankası), Industry and Mining Bank (Sanayi ve Madencilik Bankası), Chambers of Trade and Commodity Exchanges and Agricultural Credit Co-operatives were established, and agricultural, industrial and population censuses were carried out. The building of railways was given priority and the total length of the rail networks rose from 4,138 km to reach 5,638 km by 1930. During this period, agricultural output increased by 58% and in 1930, for the first time, foreign trade yielded a surplus.[15]

Despite these positive developments of the first period, during the 1930s, private enterprise was unable to speed up the industrialisation process (Kartay, 1989, pp.64-65). There was an insufficiency of capital accumulation and a lack of initiative and management ability in the private sector. The fact that the farmers were not trained and willing to abandon traditional ways of production did not help the situation (Okyar, 1993, p.27). Moreover, the world economic crisis that erupted in 1929 reduced the prices of Turkey's main products, (such as wheat, cotton, tobacco and other agricultural produce) which in turn led to a reduction in income for large masses of the population. In order to combat poverty, public institutions were established to buy up the agricultural produce, and by doing so to stabilise the prices. Although Atatürk tried to promote the idea that industrialisation was the key to catching up with the developed states, the private sector was not able to achieve this aim in the period until 1930. The solution was for the state to come to the aid of the private sector. Some economists, for example Okyar (1993, pp.26-27), claims that in Atatürk's thoughts, etatism (state control) was a temporary instrument of economic policy in order to save Turkey from the negative effects of the 1929 world economic crisis, and to speed up economic development. For whatever the reason, a mixed economic policy, which placed considerable emphasis on the role of the state was adopted, where the state institutions would act as if they were private companies seeking benefit However, the public sector and the command economy would later become persistent and it would continue until the 1980s with the will of those who gained political and bureaucratic benefits from it.

After the adoption of a mixed economic system, five-year plans, which covered only industry were prepared. The first five-year industrial plan, which was in force in 1934, aimed to design industrial operations in accordance with local and natural resources, basic consumer needs, raw material availability and manpower resources. For the duration of the plan, the growth rate was 9%. Although a second five-year plan was introduced in 1939, the Second World War hindered its application. In summary, from the beginning of the Turkish Republic to the death of Atatürk in 1938, around seventeen industrial establishments were built, such as paper, iron and steel mills and in particular facilities for producing sugar, cloth and thread. Also, in order to improve the transport network within the country, new railway lines were constructed, and this was not an achievement to be undermined in such a short period of time (Kartay, 1989, pp.64-65).[16]

Development of the Turkish Model after Atatürk

Passage to a Multi-Party System

Atatürk attempted to establish a democratic republic based on what he perceived to be Western values (Altuğ, 1991, pp.25-39). In this context, Robins (1991, p.4) points out that 'Atatürk had a strong vision of what the values and norms of that state should be: it should be independent, modern, industrialised, Europe-oriented, secular, Turkish and based almost exclusively on the territory of Anatolia'. He was adored by the masses as a hero, the Father of the State, and the strong hold of the state silenced the displeased who were dispersed and unorganised. It was not possible to think of the new Turkish State and any of its institutions as separate from Atatürk. Immediately after Atatürk's death (1938), his former lieutenant,

İsmet İnönü, became the president until 1946. During this period, Turkey entered Western organisations partially because of the post-war Soviet threat and partially because Westernization was the aim of the new Republic. This approach to the West had implications for Turkey's domestic politics, because Turkish membership of the Western organisations encouraged a domestic change towards a more Western liberal democracy (Lewis, 1951, p.320). For example, Louis (1984, p.79) points out that following the second World War, Britain urged Turkey to reform its political system with a more democratic constitution.

There was also strong domestic opposition to one-party rule, and İnönü and the leaders of the RPP had to seek the possibility of establishing an amicable opposition party. In 1946, the Demokrat Parti (Democrat Party- DP) was formally established by Bayar, Menderes and their friends who were members of the Republican People's Party (Timur, 1991, p.16). Some other members of RPP established the liberal-conservative Millet Partisi (Nation Party- NP) under the leadership of Fevzi Çakmak (retired Field Marshall) in 1948 (Erdoğan, 1993, p.116).

The RPP and the DP shared a belief in Kemalism in principle but the DP advocated a more liberal interpretation of Kemalism and was supported not only by conservatives but, also by the liberal and leftist opposition who were dissatisfied with the 'oppression' of the one-party rule. Elections were held on 21 July 1946 during which RPP won 395 and DP 66 seats; but the principles of secret balloting and judicial supervision of elections were not in force. It is widely agreed that the election results were distorted by state suppression, and were not a just reflection of public opinion (Erdoğan, 1993, p.114). The Democrat Party pressed for a new election law which would require secret balloting, open counting and judicial supervision of elections and May 14, 1950 elections were held according to the new law. The Democrat Party won an important victory over the Republican People's Party, the party of Atatürk and İnönü, which had been in power since the Republic was founded in 1923. The level of participation in the election, at 89.3%, was very high. A total of 487 members of Parliament were elected; the DP won 408 seats, the RPP only 69 seats, and the NP won 1 seat. Nine seats went to independents. Although this was an unexpected result for the RPP, it ceded power to the DP peacefully and Bayar became the president (the first president who did not have military origins) and Menderes the Prime Minister on 22 May 1950 (Koçak, 1992, pp. 153-154; F. Ahmad and B. T. Ahmad, 1976). The victory of the DP over RPP was perceived as the victory of the conservatives and traditionalists over the new Republican elite and the army officers. Thus, the multi-party system became an important characteristic of the Turkish model despite the military coups, which were to follow in later years.

Turkey as a Part of the Western Bloc

That Turkey did not enter the Second World War is seen as İnönü's most important achievement after Atatürk's death. Turkey was neither economically nor militarily ready for a war in 1939 (Deringil, 1989, p.3), but there were additional reasons behind the Turkish decision not to enter the war. Because of the traumatic experience of the War of Liberation (1919-1923), Turkey was very sensitive about its freedom and independence, and Turkish decision-makers who had experienced the First World War and the War of Liberation played a vital role in the decision not to enter another war (Sadak, 1949, p.451; Deringil, 1989, p.58). Atatürk's statement 'Peace at home, peace in the world' was used as the principle motto of Turkish foreign policy and neutrality became the best way of securing Turkish interests. Despite the provocations, both domestic and external, Turkey managed to stay out of the war.[17]

Following the emergence of two superpowers, the United States and the Soviet Union at the end of the war, Turkey was to choose the side of the United States and the West in the new bi-polar system. There were good reasons for this choice. Although Turkey did not enter the Second World War, Turkey's fear of war did not cease when the war ended in 1945. This was mainly because of the Soviet Union who did not want to renew the Treaty of Neutrality and Non-Aggression of 1925 unless its demands were answered positively. The Soviet Union demanded four concessions from Turkey in any new treaty. First, Kars and Ardahan, Ottoman territories near the Soviet-Turkish border in the northeast of Turkey, which had been ceded to Russia in 1878, had to be returned to Soviet control. These areas had been recovered by the Turks after the Russian Revolution in 1917, and a treaty had been signed between the Soviet Union and Turkey in 1921. The second Soviet demand was for military bases on the Bosphorus and the Dardanelles; the third was for a revision of the Montreux Strait Convention; and the fourth, for a revision of the Thracian border in favour of the communist-dominated Bulgaria (Vali, 1971, p.34; Timur, 1991, pp.42-47; Mcghee, 1954, pp.615; Sadak, 1949, p.453; Altuğ, 1988, p.10; Kuniholm, 1980, p.219; Lenczowski, 1980, p.135).[18] The Soviets were serious in their demands; Soviet troops were massed on the Turkish-Bulgarian border in the frontier region of Thrace, and in Moscow and Sofia a hostile propaganda campaign against Turkey had begun (Kuniholm, 1980, pp.257-58; Karaosmanoğlu, 1988, p.295). Furthermore, these developments indicated that 'Moscow's final objective was not simply revision of the Montreux Convention and territorial adjustment, but that the Soviet Union wanted to reduce Turkey to the position of a satellite'(Vali, 1972, p.76). Obviously this was a major threat to Turkey's sovereignty, and Turkey refused to make any concession to the Soviet demands (Satterthwaite, 1972, p.77). Because of the expansionist policies of the Soviet Union, Turkey's political agenda was entirely dominated by this issue (Bilge, 1983, p.36; Bowder, 1977, p.164), and this is seen as the main reason which led to Turkish application for membership of NATO (Vali, 1971, p.34; Orhonlu, 1992, pp.526-27; Tuncay and others, 1992, pp.138-139; Barchard, 1985, p.44; Sander, 1993, p.45). As Baharçiçek, (1993, p.106) pointed out, naturally there were other reasons that encouraged Turkey to make this application:

> Firstly, Turkey was eager to enter a prestigious club. Secondly, the desire to become a westernised society was another factor, which had an important impact on Turkey's willingness to integrate with NATO. Westernization and modernisation formed an implicit link between strategy and other aims held in common with her new Western identity. But at the same time the ideological aspiration to become an integral part - at least in terms of military alliance - of the Western world without any doubt played a decisive role in Turkey's decision.

Thus, Westernization, indicating co-operation with the West, became the leading philosophical principle of Turkey's foreign policy in the real sense, and developments since the Second World War indicate that Turkey has been following the principle of Westernization in foreign policy. For example, in the early post-war period Turkey demanded assistance from the West against the Soviet threat, and was supported by the West through the Truman Doctrine and the Marshall Plan. Turkey became a founder member of the Council of Europe and joined the North Atlantic Pact. It applied to the European Community for membership in 1959 and the Ankara agreement was signed in 1963 with the objective to make Turkey a full member. In 1987 Turkey applied for full membership[19], and to fulfil the conditions which would ease its acceptance, in January 1988, it gave its citizens the right to make individual applications to the European Human Rights Commission, and signed the Council of Europe Convention against Torture and Inhuman and Degrading Treatment, becoming the first country to ratify this. Closeness to and co-operation with the West, one of the features of the Turkish model, therefore became more apparent in the foreign policy of Turkey.

Passage to Market Economy

State-controlled economy in Turkey persisted until 1980. An exception to this was the period between 1950 to 1960 when following the 1950 elections the DP introduced a liberal economic program, the main economic principles of which were the gradual privatisation of state enterprises; the withdrawal of the state from areas such as manufacturing while retaining involvement in the infrastructure; and the limitation of state intervention in foreign trade to a very low level (Okyar, 1993, pp.27-28). During the first three years, the results of this liberal economic policy were very positive; there was a revival in the agricultural sector, assisted by the use of machines and artificial fertilisers, and also by good weather conditions. The revival led to an increase in agricultural output, and Turkey became a wheat-exporting country. Positive developments were also seen in the industrial and mining sectors. Because of the Korean War and the rebuilding of Europe, the demand for Turkish exports, particularly agricultural ones, increased rapidly and thus considerable growth was seen in the volume of foreign trade. In this period, new investments in basic industrial fields were made by both private and public sectors. The Turkish Industrial Development Bank (Türkiye Sanayi Kalkınma Bankası) was founded to give credit to private sector investments, and State Economic Enterprises (SEEs) (which were to create immense problems in later decades) were established.[20] New measures were introduced to encourage the inflow of foreign capital and thirteen Turkish-foreign partnerships were issued with oil exploration licences and a high growth rate of 12% was achieved in this period. Yet, after 1954, increase in imports of industrial and consumer goods had a negative impact on the balance of payments leading to an economic bottleneck. Measures similar to those of the war years were reintroduced, and the Turkish currency was devalued in 1958. Thus in the period 1954-58, growth rates started to decline and fell to 2-3%. Then, after 1958, new economic measures were introduced to delay liberal principles (Okyar 1993, pp.27-28)[21], and soon after these measures a revival were seen in the economy.

After the military coup in 1960, the 1961 constitution made economic planning a legal requirement. The new government turned from liberalism to a centrally controlled economy. Between 1960-1976 the real average growth of the Turkish economy was 6% and the return to a state-controlled or planned economy could not save Turkey from entering another economic bottle-neck in the late 1970s: the economy suffered from severe foreign exchange shortage, external debts, a high inflation rate, public finance deficits and rising unemployment. Between 1975-80, too much state intervention resulted in an increase in the losses of the SEE's which in turn led to rising inflation.[22]

Amid all these, positive developments had also taken place in Turkey since the 1920s. Hale (1981, p.256) summarises the positive developments of the Turkish economy as follows:

Since the foundation of the republic, Turkey's economic life has been transformed. At the beginning of the 1920s she had virtually no mechanised industry and few modern communications. All but a fraction of her people were illiterate... by 1980 the population had increased more than threefold and the national income almost fourteen fold over the levels of 1927.

In 1980, it became apparent that although Turkey was not a socialist state, the public sector played too great a role: 60% of the economy belonged to the State Economic Enterprises (SEEs) which did not function according to price mechanisms. SEEs did not have the right to decide on their production, investment, employment or the price of their products (Togan, 1992, p.96). With a decree on 24 January 1981, Turgut Özal's government brought an end to the strategy of import substitution as a means of industrialisation, and adopted free market mechanism as a principle of the economy (Togan, 1992, p.97). Özal, later described the new policy as:

> Trade and exchange regulations have been liberalised, quotas and import deposits have been abolished, quantitative restrictions on imports and agricultural subsidies have been removed. Liberal foreign investment legislations have been introduced, price controls have been discontinued, positive interest rates and realistic exchange rates were adopted.[23]

By 1991, state intervention in the economy was reduced and the economy was opened to outside market forces. In 1988, the ratio of exports within the national income had increased to 16.5% from 5% in 1980, and although the inflation was still high and the state still supported most of the products in the public sector, (in particular agricultural products) it was now a market economy. In terms of the composition of the national income, the agricultural sector was no longer the largest sector of the economy as it was 20 or 30 years ago. In the early 1990's, while the ratio of agriculture within the national income declined to 20-30%, the ratio of industry increased to 40-50%. Turkey officially entered a new era in its struggle for development with its open economy, and this openness became a characteristic of the Turkish Model (Yalçın, 1993a, p.12).

Problems for the Turkish Model

Military Coups

Although it is comforting to notice that in developing countries the military inclines to intervene in domestic politics, and that Turkey as a developing state has not been an exception to this rule (Turan, 1986, p.273), the role of the Turkish army as an integral part of the Turkish Model is more complicated than this general statement implies. The Republic was established by Generals (Atatürk and his colleagues) then it was ruled by another General, İnönü, until 1950, and most of the Turkish presidents have been of military origins. Since 1950, the process of democratisation in Turkey was interrupted three times during its short history, namely in 1960, 1971 and 1980. Yet, in 1990s, Turkey enjoyed a multi-party democracy, a market economy, and was, in general, proud of its armed forces.

The reasons given by the military for interventions have been similar in nature. In 1950, the power was transformed to the opposition (Democrat Party) peacefully and for a while it looked as if the multi-party democracy had become a part of the Turkish Model. However, the 1960 military coup overthrew the Menderes government. The army claimed that Menderes government had abandoned its main aim by using religion as an instrument for party politics thus making citizens enemies of each other, and by establishing domination of a class over the others (a serious offence according to Turkish Constitution) (Öztürk, 1993, p.70). After the coup, a new constitution was accepted with the aid of the intellectuals and judges who were mostly proponents of the Republican People's Party, which strengthened the role of the army. Between 1961 and 1972, nine governments were established. All of the governments established between 1961 and 1965 elections were coalitions. Süleyman Demirel's Adalet Partisi (Justice Party) which was seen as a continuation of the Democrat Party, won the 1965 and 1969 elections and established governments. Then on 12 March 1971, Demirel's government was forced to resign by the Generals who accused the government of not controlling terrorism, and failing to provide economic and political stability in the country (Turan, 1986, p.274). This was not an actual coup but a military intervention in civilian affairs. On 12 September 1980, again during a time when Süleyman Demirel was the Prime Minister, another military coup took place. The reasons given for the latest coup were similar to previous coups; that is, unending terrorism, activities of the political parties, Turkish Grand National Assembly failing to fulfil its duties (Öztürk, 1993, p.86) and the economic crisis that the country was in. Democracy was delayed from 1980 until 1983, when after the formation of new political parties, elections took place and the Anavatan Partisi (Motherland Party- MP) came to power.

The involvement of the Turkish Army in domestic politics has been encouraged by several factors. Firstly, Turkish military tradition encourages the army to intervene in politics, which stems from Turkish state tradition and the understanding of the rights of the individuals in the state. Going back to recent history, during the Ottoman empire, there was never a clear distinction between the military and civilian sections of state administration. Therefore, the same person could serve in his lifetime as a military commander, a provincial governor, and finally resume an army command. In the Ottoman empire, for long periods, the army (and most notably the Janissaries, followed by the Young Turks) virtually took over the state, and therefore in reality the Sultans became no more than puppets in their hands (Hale, 1990, p.55). With the establishment of the Turkish Republic this tradition did not end, and in fact was strengthened by the fact that the national hero Atatürk was a General.

Secondly, the Turkish army strongly believes that it represents enlightenment, secularism and modernism, an image which also comes from the Ottoman legacy because reform movements, which emerged in the Empire during the nineteenth century were led by the military. Reform in education in particular, started in the army and in return, graduates of new military schools began to see themselves as the vanguards of enlightenment, committed to political reforms as well as technical innovation. The fact that the Republic, a secular state, was designed by the military intelligentsia made this claim stronger. The Turkish army believes that their mission is to defend the state (which they have set up) not only from external threats but also from what they would regard as internal threats. The continuation of the state despite the individual was, and is the motto of the Turkish military, and also a very important part of Turkish democracy and nationalism. The military regards itself as the guardians of democracy and the civilians, which need to be cared for and guided. Related with this argument former president and 1980 coup leader Evren stated; 'The Turkish armed forces are devoted to democracy and they are its indestructible guards' (Brown, 1989, pp.400-401).

Thirdly, an additional factor that strengthens the mission of being vanguards of modernism and being superior in some way to the civilians, is the homogenous lifestyle of the Turkish army officers. They are isolated from the rest of the people from a very early age, beginning with their education in the military high schools where they live and work apart from the rest of society. This isolation results in group solidarity among the officers. Orhan Erkanlı, a former member of the National Unity Committee of 1960, wrote in 1973:

> Besides being a professional group, the officers are also a class. In Turkey, there is a military class, just as there is a workers' and a peasants' class. The military class lives an enclosed life, and its contacts with its civilian surroundings are slight. All the officers spend their lives between their homes and barracks where home is basically an extension of the barracks. They spend all twenty-four hours of the day in the same environment, and in the company of the same people this way of life draws them into exactly the same ideas, opinions, complaints and results (Hale, 1990, p.54).[24]

Since the continuation of the state is the ultimate aim, in this struggle they regard the civilians with suspicion. Political parties are not an exception and they are usually regarded by the army officers as gatherings of undisciplined individuals. Although the officers share the view that a multi-party system is an integral element of democracy, they also believe that 'political parties must not divide the nation into different groups and provoke an interest conflict, but must contribute to the welfare of the people and development of the country' (Birand, 1986, p.119). Furthermore, in fulfilling this task of 'uniting the people', political parties must act in conformity with Kemalism and with a view to safeguarding national independence and territorial integrity of the country. Even the opposition parties must also act 'constructively'. In his memoirs, General Kenan Evren, former President of the Republic (1983-9) and leader of 1980 military coup, strongly indicates his discontent with the political parties, and complains about those expressing disagreement for its own sake: 'I have never seen an opposition party approving a governmental policy or decision' (Karaosmanoğlu, 1993, pp. 26-27).

Fourthly, the regulations of the armed forces, the Constitution and the administrative structure of the Turkish state, encourage the army to intervene in politics. Article 35 of the Turkish Armed Forces Internal Service Code states: 'the duty of the Armed Forces is to protect and safeguard Turkish territory and the Turkish Republic as stipulated in the Constitution'. This was cited by General Kenan Evren after the coup of 12 September 1980 as the legal basis for the argument that the armed forces had the ultimate duty of taking over the government, because the state would otherwise have collapsed (Hale, 1990, p.56).

In the administrative structure of the Turkish state[25], armed forces are not under the control of the civilian governments, but directly connected to the Prime Minister. However, this was not always so. With a law accepted on 30 May 1949, the statute of Office of the Chief of General Staff (Genel Kurmay Başkanlığı) was changed. With this change Office of the Chief of General Staff was placed under the Ministry of National Defence hence similar to Western countries, the army (at least in appearance) was put under the control of the government (Öztürk, 1993, pp.65-66). But with the 1961 constitution this was changed and Office of the Chief of General Staff was again directly connected to the Prime Minister disregarding the Ministry of National Defence.

Again due to the administrative structure of the Turkish State, military coups are not the only way that the Turkish military can intervene in civilian life. With the 1961 constitution, following the coup, the Milli Güvenlik Kurulu (National Security Council) was created. This is an important institution with which the Turkish Army sends its messages to the civilians and it is composed of the

President, the Prime Minister, the Chief of General Staff, the Ministers of National Defence and Foreign Affairs and the Commanders of the Army, the Navy, the Air Force and the Gendarmerie Forces. It meets periodically under the chairmanship of the President. As the formation of the Council suggests, the representatives of the Turkish Armed Forces (five members) outnumber the civilian representatives (four members). In addition to this, with the exception of Turgut Özal and Süleyman Demirel, all other Presidents have had military origins. The Council is responsible for the formulation of the policy for the security of the state and its application, and presents these to the Council of Ministers in order to be executed.[26] In other words, the National Security Council provides a legal forum for the armed forces to convey their views to civilian politicians, and to voice the concerns of the military regarding domestic politics and foreign relations (Brown, 1989, pp.389-400). For example, in 1997, the army believed that TPP (True Path Party)–WP (Welfare Party) coalition Government prepared a suitable base for Islamic radical movements to flourish and through the National Security Council (with 28 February decisions) forced this government to resign. Then, a new coalition government was established between DLP (Democratic Left Party), MP (Motherland Party) and DTP (Democratic Turkish Party). WP was closed down by the Constitution Court and members of this party formed a new party, 'Virtue Party'. However, there is a case in the Constitution Court against Virtue Party and it is highly likely that this party will be closed down by the court as well unless a surprise development, such as, an amendment in the Turkish constitution that makes closing a political party very difficult, takes place.

Fifthly, from time to time, civilians, including politicians, intellectuals, elite and the media encourage the army to intervene. This lack of belief in democracy and the incapability of the civil society to solve its own problems, is related to the military interventions themselves. It can be argued that the military has not allowed democracy to mature by accepting a more humble role in the society. For example, a significant event that encouraged the army for the 1960 coup was that, with the Democrat party rule the army had lost its prestigious place within the state, as aptly summarised by an officer after the 1960 coup. 'The prestige of the army was declining. ... An officer no longer had status in society. ... It was not that we needed money, for officers had always been ill paid, but we had honour and respect in the past. Now it has gone' (Brown, 1989, p.388). The 1960 coup might have returned the honour of the army, but democracy was undermined. Civilian politicians lost their courage to speak up against the Generals, thus the civilians lost faith in their politicians and in democracy. They manifestly began to regard the Generals as their 'big brothers', and began to complain about each other to them. This went as far as the civilians encouraging the military to intervene when things did not work in their favour. For example, before the 1980 coup, some civilians, members of the parliament and even some ministers were known to have visited the Generals to ask for military intervention (Öztürk, 1993, p.85).

In general, military coups have undermined Turkey's process of democratisation and have become a part of the Turkish Model, which in itself, to a large degree was created by the military itself. During the coups the representatives of the people lost their seats, and sometimes they were hanged (as in the case of Prime Minister Menderes, Foreign Minister Fatin Rüştü Zorlu and Interior Minister Hasan Polatkan after the 1960 coup). Military coups banned parties and imposed restrictions on the freedom of speech, but they had another major effect. The political parties had supporters in all regions of the country from all groups, and played a major part in maintaining social unity and the balance of power. For example, as Robins (1991, p.32) points out, in the 1950s and 1960s, there was an effort on the part of the Turkish state to co-opt Kurdish notables into the political process. The Kurds responded positively to the first free general election in 1950, supporting the Democrat Party. After the elections, many of the Kurdish notables became Members of Parliament and some even became Ministers, thus taking part in democracy and the administration of the state. Every military coup brought with it a more nationalistic trend, which resulted in the minorities to regard as Turkey belonging solely to citizens of Turkic origin. Therefore it is possible to argue that every military coup accelerated the separatist activities in SouthEast Anatolia (Yılmaz, 1993, p.16). Although after every coup the Generals always gave way to democracy and the multi-party system took over with new parties, or with old parties under a different name (Karaosmanoğlu, 1992, p.32). Nevertheless the construction of a civil society took great blows. Hence, military interventions were an integral part of the history of Turkish Republic.

Separatist Activities in South East Anatolia

The outstanding problem of Turkey in the late 1980's and through 1990's was the Kurdish terrorist activities mainly in SouthEast Turkey[27] carried out by the Kurdish Workers Party, PKK.[28] A survey conducted in 1992 by the Sociology Department of Selçuk University, suggested that Turkey's gravest current crisis was terrorism despite high inflation and unemployment.[29] The situation has deteriorated since then and public reaction to the crisis has therefore increased. The cost of stopping PKK activities grows more expensive by the day for the Turkish Republic. Moreover, on the international arena Kurdish separatist movements have formed a barrier to Turkish foreign relations in general, relations with EU in particular.

The number of Kurdish people living in Turkey is a debatable issue. Different sources suggest different figures sharply affected by the ideological beliefs of the authors. The PKK and Kurdist writers tend to talk about 20 million Kurds in Turkey. Rouleau (1993, p.122) suggested that Turkey had about 10 million Kurds, or about 17% of the total population; he also suggested that anywhere between half and two-thirds of this Kurdish population lived outside the South-Eastern provinces, or in what he called Turkish Kurdistan.[30] Since the Kemalist doctrine proposes that nationhood and citizenship are one, there is no distinction between Turks and Kurds in government records. Therefore, it can be said that no one knows the exact size and geographic distribution of the Kurdish population (Rouleau, 1993, p.122). The issue is complicated by the difficulty in establishing a criteria for Kurdishness. What is the criteria for being a Kurd? Is it language, race, or geography...? For one, Kurds are not concentrated in SouthEast Anatolia, but are spread throughout the whole of Anatolia. For example, in 1993, a survey found that while four percent of the citizens of Istanbul considered themselves to be Kurds, another four percent described their parents as Kurdish but thought of themselves as Turks.[31] Also, other ethnic groups, for example the Arabs, also inhabit SouthEast Anatolia. Therefore to accept the whole of the population of the region as Kurdish and to call the place Kurdistan would be questionable as far as the Turkish authorities are concerned.

It was claimed that PKK activities did not have economic, cultural or social reasons, and that there was no relationship between the PKK and poverty, backwardness, democratisation and human rights (Yalçın, 1993b, p.3). The PKK is a terrorist organisation but it is difficult to agree with this claim. For example, in a survey conducted by the Intelligence Office of the General Directorate of Security, 14% of the respondents gave ethnicity, as the reason for supporting the PKK.[32] Marxism, the ideology on which the PKK was established, was seen as an important factor in determining who supports the PKK, as it aims to establish a socialist state. After the apparent victory of capitalism over communism, it was argued that the communists in Turkey recast their struggle in the form of a Kurdish uprising and that communists, whether Turks or Kurds, always support (at least passively) the PKK; it was even claimed that there were non-Kurdish leftist militants in the PKK camps (Turgut, 1992, p.45). On the other hand, it can be argued that non-communist Kurdish elite, whether conservative or social democrat (such as the former Minister of Internal Affairs Abdülkadir Aksu, a conservative from Diyarbakır, and the former Minister of Foreign Affairs Hikmet Çetin, a Kurdish social democrat) usually dislike the PKK.

Although the Turkish Model could not have done much to prevent Marxism, the loss of the Islamic culture because of the Model, is seen as an important factor which contributed to separatism. Conservative intellectuals and Kurdish politicians such as Abdülkadir Aksu, pointed out that Islam used to serve as a unifying factor above all ethnic differences, and that the Ottoman period was an example of this unity.[33] Islamic political parties in Turkey argue that the forceful pragmatism and modernisation of Kemalism which undermined the place of religion within the system, has encouraged ethnic differences and led to separatist activities and because of lack of common, unifying factors the Kurds identified themselves in a different way than the rest of the citizens of Turkey (Yılmaz, 1993, pp.19-20).

In a provocative development with regard to separatist uprisings, the military rulers of Turkey enacted a law in 1983, which banned the use of the Kurdish language. Although this ban was lifted in 1991, it played a significant role in the development of Kurdish separatism, justifying the aim of the separatists and giving them an effective weapon. The situation was not helped when some Turkish academics began to argue that Turks and Kurds come from the same origin, and that Kurds are Turks or Turks are Kurds.[34] Especially after the 1980s, the Kurdish elite in Turkey began to emphasise the differences between Kurdish people and the Turkish majority. Kurdish nationalists, as with all nations struggling to prove their identity, strive to create an elaborate Kurdish history, culture, religion and language.[35]

It has been claimed that the Turkish governments have neglected SouthEast Anatolia economically, and kept it underdeveloped (Fuller, 1993, p.111). Indeed the National income is at its lowest level in the region, which is not economically united with the rest of the country (Yılmaz, 1993, p.17; Robins, 1991, p.29). However at the other extreme, Turkish governments have also tended to see the problem only as one of economic backwardness, believing that once this problem is solved the whole issue would be eliminated. Hence, the state has been attempting to develop the region by spending much more than its income from the region by undertaking giant projects (in particular SEAP: the South-East Anatolian Project - GAP: Güneydoğu Anadolu Projesi). According to the survey of the Intelligence Office of the General Directorate of Security, 33% of the respondents gave economic factors as the determining cause of the problem[36], and independent Piar-Galup research suggested that 32.1% of the Turkish elite regarded the region's economic backwardness as a cause of the problem. Yet, only 14.3% of ethnic Turks overall and 8.2% of ethnic Kurds agreed with the statement.[37]

The bulk of the problem may lie in the fact that the Turkish Model stresses the word 'Turkishness', and 'Kemalism' and the statements of Atatürk have been used liberally by the state. That is, it is not clear that 'Turkishness' (as defined by Atatürk) has been perceived by the people as denoting citizenship only. The frequent use of his statements such as 'Ne Mutlu Türküm Diyene' ('Happy is he/she who can call himself/herself a Turk'), 'Türk övün çalış güven' ('Oh Turk, be proud, work and trust'), 'Bir Türk Dünyaya bedeldir' ('A Türk is equivalent to the World'), etc. have had negative effects and have provoked ethnic separatism. It is argued that these statements have disturbed even what had once been the most loyal Ottomans: the Kurds. Without doubt nation-based symbols have strengthened ethnicity-based separatism (Yılmaz, 1993, p.20; Yetkin, 1993, p.55). The PKK claims that Kurds have been forced to be Turks and have not been given political, cultural and normative rights as Kurds. It is only when Kurdish people accept that they are Turks that they can enjoy normal rights like other Turkish citizens.[38] In a parallel way, Fuller (1993, p.111) claimed that Turkey has been the most repressive country in terms of its cultural policy towards the Kurds because their existence as a separate nationality within Turkey was denied until very recently. He accepted that Kurds in Turkey could and regularly did rise to the highest position within the state - however, he added that they did so 'on the condition that they ignore their Kurdish heritage and accept assimilation as Turks'.

Another flaw of the Turkish Model has been in its understanding and application of democracy. It can be argued that the banning of socialist, communist and radical parties in the Turkish democratic system might have helped ethnic separatism in Turkey. Educated young people of the region tend to support communist or socialist parties, and the banning of these parties nationally has prevented these voters from uniting with the rest of the population of Turkey. And that especially after the collapse of communism, these voters have started to defend ethnic separatism (Yılmaz, 1993, pp.16-17). Although the current existence of Birleşik Sosyalist Parti (United Socialist Party)[39], İşçi Partisi (Labour Party)[40], and Halkın Demokrasi Partisi (Peoples' Party of Democracy- HADEP) as Socialist representative parties undermine the argument at present, it may have been too late to change the course of earlier trends.

To sustain security in the region and to fight against the PKK, the Turkish government has been spending a significant part of its income to finance around 120,000 soldiers in SouthEast Anatolia. Moreover, during the armed struggles buildings and villages have been destroyed, half the region's population has moved or been moved to other areas in order to prevent the possibility of the villages acting as hiding places for the PKK. Within the region, people from remote mountain villages have moved to cities such as Diyarbakır, creating additional burdens on the economy of the region, which is already failing.

The Turkish media often claims that terrorism is supported and financed by external sources[41] and name several states as supporters of the PKK.[42] For example, Syria is accused of using the PKK against Turkey in order to bargain for more water from Turkey, which is getting scarcer due to the SEAP (South East Anatolian Project - GAP). Robins (1991, p.31) points out that the PKK has its main training bases in Syria, the no-man's-land in northern Iraq and Lebanon.[43] Apart from Syria and Iraq, Armenia and Armenians[44], Greece[45], Russia[46], Germany (Demirer, 1994, p.31), Italy[47] and several other states have been mentioned as supporters of the PKK. The Turkish public opinion regards external support for the PKK as the main reason behind growing terrorist activities in Turkey. For example, 45% of the respondents to a survey by the Intelligence office of the General Directorate of Security pointed to external support as the major reason of the problem, and 51% underlined the importance of external support for terrorism.[48] Turkish politicians believe that external support for the PKK should be seriously taken into consideration in order to solve the problem.

Separatism has limited Turkish foreign policy in several ways.[49] Firstly, it has diverted attention from foreign affairs to domestic disputes. Even during most important foreign relations events, the PKK has managed to steal the show. For example, on the day of the opening of the Hasret Bridge between Turkey and Nahcevan (28 May 1992), two important events took place. First, 290 signatures were collected from people, including Halkın Emek Partisi (People's Work Party) members, complaining about Turkey to the UN and to other international institutions. Second, the PKK attacked a police station near the bridge (Igdır-Gürgüre).[50] The impression that Turkey had internal problems and would be incapable of helping to solve the Azeri-Armenian problem or in establishing close relations with the Turkic republics was created.

Secondly, Turkish relations with the EU have been harmed by separatism, and Turkish attempts at a military solution to the problem have been severely criticised.[51] The EU considers the problem in terms of human rights violations, and regards it as a barrier to Turkish membership of the EU (Kuniholm, 1991, p.45). For example, Fuller (1993, p.117) suggested that

> Persistence in the military option sets a course that will severely damage Turkey's standing in the West. While Ankara's human rights record is high by regional standards, if Turkey wishes to gain entry into the EU, its human rights must improve to meet European standards.

Separatism forms a new problem for Turkey's relations with the World in general and with its neighbours in particular. It is difficult to regard Turkey's relations with its neighbours as perfect; Turkey has serious problems with Greece, Syria, Iraq, Iran and Armenia. Turkey's relations even with Bulgaria is questionable. Because of the Bulgarian administration's ill treatment of Turkish minority, Turkey and Bulgaria had cool relations in 1980s and this crisis resulted in migration of hundreds of thousands of Turkish minority to Turkey. Therefore, Turkey's already poor relations with its neighbours have been affected negatively as Turkey usually accuses its neighbours for aiding PKK. On the other hand, rise of separatism in Turkey provided with a new form of foreign policy instrument to those who want to weaken Turkey.

Kurdish separatism forms the most important challenge to the Turkish Model because it illustrates that the Model can't cope with, and in fact might have worsened the problems of 'ethnicity'. There is a serious fear that the problem may give rise to further disputes between Kurds and Turks, because it should be borne in mind that the Kurdish population in Western Anatolia and Central Anatolia are greater than that in South East Anatolia. When the PKK kills a soldier, the burial ceremony turns into a big anti-PKK and anti-Kurdish demonstration.[52] Any news about terrorism has the potential danger of fostering feelings of hatred and bitterness towards the Kurds, and there is also the danger of the spread of terrorist attacks to major cities (Kuniholm, 1991, p.45). Briefly, it may be said that Kurdish separatism increasingly overshadows domestic politics, weakening the credibility and stability of the governments. Rouleau (1993, p.122) argued that the sharp increase of the PKK separatist movement in early 1990s indicated the possibility of a Yugoslav-type civil war. This would mean the destruction of the Turkish Model and the Turkish Republic. However, since then, Turkish armed forces had successful operations and some of the leaders of the PKK, such as Abdullah Öcalan and Şemdin Sakık, were captured. Öcalan, leader of the PKK, forced to leave his traditional hiding place in Syria because of Turkish pressure on Syria and then he was captured. PKK also failed to get enough support from the people of Kurdish origin. Therefore, in the year 2000, to make emphasise on the possibility of civil war can easily be regarded as an exaggeration, but the PKK continues to overshadow and undermine Turkey's domestic policy as well as foreign policy.

Alawite Discontent[53]

The name Alawite describes a wide variety of Shiite and dervish sects. According to Mcdowall (1992, pp.57-58), it is used more specifically

> To describe the mixture of Shiite Islam, Persian Mazdeism, Christianity and possibly Central Asian ideas adopted by the Turkmen and Kurdish tribes who inhabited parts of eastern Anatolia at the beginning of the 16th century, before the Ottomans had extended their control to the area.

This definition however, does not make enough emphasis on Islamic core for the Alawites. More simpler and reliable definition for Alawites is that the Alawites are followers of Ali as their name suggests and they are within the circle of Islam and they interpret Islam according to their own methods. Therefore, before becoming anything else, Alawitism or Alavilik is an Islamic sect. The Alawites, also known as 'Kızılbaş'[54], had supported the Shiite Persian Empire against the Sunni Ottomans. However, when the Ottomans defeated the Persian empire in 1514, the Alawites were unwillingly incorporated into the Ottoman Empire (Mcdowall, 1992, p.58). It may be said that since 1514, the Alawite-Sunni dispute has persisted in Turkey, and the secularism of the Turkish Model has not been able to resolve the issue.

The Alawites obey the five fundamental principles of Islam and practice them according to their own interpretations: the shada (statement of faith), the performance of prayer five times daily, alms-giving, fasting in Ramadan, and the Hajj (the pilgrimage to Mecca). According to the Alawites, the state of the heart and mind is more important than visible rituals. They worship in mosques but Cemevis (community houses) where social and religious activities took place are also important for Alawits. Alawites, like many other minority sects, sometimes practise dissimulation (taqiyyah[55]) in order to avoid discrimination and as a method of survival in a Sunni world (Mcdowall, 1992, p.58). By means of Taqiyyah, they can cover their identity and increase their chances of social and professional success.

The real level of the Alawite population in Turkey is debatable as there is no reliable statistical evidence. Because of the 1925 legislation against the Tarikat, or religious orders, there are no official figures concerning the size of the Alawite population (Robins, 1991, p.8). Some Alawite sources claim that they form up to 40 per cent of the Turkish population (Lewis, 1974, p.213). However, it is widely accepted that Alawites form somewhere between 15 and 20 per cent of the Turkish population.[56] The situation is also complicated by the fact that the Alawites are not a homogenous group; there are ethnic and linguistic divisions, for example, different language groups can be found among them such as Turkish, Arabic, and different Kurdic languages (Zaza and Kurmanci) (Mandel, 1990, p.170).

The Alawites overwhelmingly support Atatürk's secularising reforms and tend to vote for centre-left political parties.[57] For example, the success of the Sosyal Demokrat Halkçı Parti (Social Democratic Populist Party) in the 1991 election was particularly marked in Erzincan and Tunceli, where Alawite Kurds formed the majority of the population (A. Ayata, 1993, p.44). It may be said that the Alawites are almost totally committed to the left, often to the extreme left. On the other hand, in the areas where the sectarian confrontation is the sharpest, the Sunnis are concentrated on the extreme-right (Mackenzie, 1981, p.22). The demands of Alawites within the Turkish Model was one of the important issues on the Turkish political agenda during the early 1990s. For the first time their demands from the state, their place within Islam and their dispute with the Sunnis were discussed by the media and openly by the governments.[58] The demands of Alawites from the state and their problems can be grouped into five categories.

Firstly, in the Turkish Model, according to the Constitution, the state should remain above all religious affairs by safeguarding the equality of the different religious beliefs in the country.[59] Alawites claim that the government is secular but 'Sunni Islam remains perceived as the established religion' (Mcdowall, 1992, pp.60-61) and the state only recognises Sunnis because it opens only mosques and pays the salaries of imams (Sunni clerics). They accuse the state of not financing their Cemevis and not paying the salaries of their clerics.[60]

Secondly, the state opens religious schools to train imams for the mosques. In these schools Sunni thought (Hanafi Fiqh) is taken as the basis for religious education. Alawites want either their beliefs to be taught as well, or to have separate schools where they can teach their beliefs. This dispute is not helped by the fact that after the 1980 military coup, in order to prevent the spread of communist movements, the military government passed an act in 1981 which made religious education compulsory for all students (including Muslims and non-Muslims) in primary and secondary schools (S. Ayata, 1993, p.60; Özgüden, 1988, p.52; Barchard, 1990). After lobbying by the French, non-Muslim students were excluded from these classes in 1990.[61] However, Alawite pupils still have to take this course because they are not recognised as a separate ethnic or religious group.[62] Although Alawites oppose religious education classes which follow a Sunni syllabus and seek religious education which fit the teachings of their sect, Alawite intellectuals do not agree among themselves on the place of their sect within Islam, the role of the Koran and the Prophet, and indeed on the main principles of their sect.

Thirdly, it is argued that the Directorate of Religious Affairs fulfils the needs of Sunnis but not of Alawites. The Alawites have no representation within the Directorate of Religious Affairs, and official authority on religious affairs in Turkey is given to the Sunni sect (Özgüden, 1988, pp.18-19). Therefore, Alawites want to be represented in this institution in order to fulfil the needs of their sect.

Fourthly, Alawites claim that they have consistently been suppressed, during both the Ottoman Empire and the Turkish Republic. Especially after the 1960's, an Alawite-Sunni dispute took place in the form of left versus right or communism versus nationalism dispute. During the 1970's, open clashes between the Sunnis and the Alawites took place in which several hundred people died; for example, 107 people died in Kahramanmaraş on 23 December 1978 (S. Ayata, 1993, p.65; Özgüden, 1988, pp.35-36).[63] Although at the time the Ecevit government and some commentators described the incident as a Sunni massacre of Shiites (Pevsner, 1984, p.74). Kenneth Mackenzie (1981, p.8) reports that

Provocations were many-sided: Sunni Muslims and Shiite Muslims, Turks and Kurds, right-wing agitators and Marxist agitators were sucked into the imbroglio. The leftists, being in the minority, took a battering but the casualties included rightists as well.

After the incident, martial law was announced in 132 provinces, journalist Savaş Ay, describing the situation after a visit to Tokat, said:

> The people were selling their furniture and their animals and the young girls were selling their gold in order to buy a gun and thus provide themselves with security. In short, a dreadful armaments race was being carried out by both the leftist (Alawites) and the rightist (Sunnis) circles.[64]

After Kahramanmaraş similar incidents took place in Çorum, Ordu, Ankara, Urfa, Adana, Gaziantep, Samsun, Bursa, Diyarbakır and Mardin (Özgüden, 1988, p.45). The latest incident of this kind took place in Sivas where 37 people died on 2 July 1993.[65] Apart from the Dersim revolt (1936), there has been no visible state involvement in the disputes; on the surface civilians have caused the conflicts, usually in the form of a right versus left dispute, and both sides bear some responsibility for the incidents. The exception to this is the Alawite claim that the Turkish state burned Alawite villages (in the Eastern Anatolia) in 1994, in order to force the inhabitants to leave. Former State Minister Azimet Köylüoğlu, who was responsible for Human Rights Affairs, claimed that the state burned villages[66] in Tunceli[67], and the former deputy chairman of the Grand National Assembly, Kamer Genç, a representative from Tunceli, supported this claim.[68] Such claims from high-level politicians may indicate the extent of the problem. In fact, the SDPP (Social Democrat Populist Party) was a coalition partner at the time, and these accusations against the state were made by members of the SDPP itself.

Fifthly, extremist Alawite groups are seeking to establish a separate state. One of the most extreme groups the Kızıl Yol (Red Path), based in Germany and defends the idea of the founding of a nation of Alawites. They take Kurdish separatism as a model for their movement (Mandel, 1990, p.166).

As yet, the Turkish state has not been able to fulfil the demands of the Alawites. The state and the Sunnis still claim that without a clear definition of Alawitism and clear answers to principal questions such as the position of the Koran and the tradition of the Prophet in the Alawite sect, it will be difficult to fulfil any demands. Undoubtedly the result of this issue will affect Turkish internal policy as well as its foreign policy. Hohmann (1993, p.162) argued that European support for Turkey was tied in with these issues, and that 'Of course, the Europeans could justify giving such backing to Turkish ambitions only if Ankara abides by its commitment to respect human, civil and minority rights, and especially those of its Kurdish population group'.

Conclusion

The process of Westernization, which began during the Ottoman Empire in the shape of legal and social reforms, formed the basis for Atatürk and his intelligentsia to develop what is known as the Turkish Model. The Turkish Model was initially designed by Atatürk between 1923-1938. The new state was established on a secular basis, and various social, cultural and legal reforms were introduced to ensure the Westernization of both the administrative structures of the state and of the social framework. 'Turkishness' was introduced and the teachings of Atatürk were used in the struggle to create a new identity and ideal for the peoples of the young Republic. The transition to a multi-party system did not happen until 1946. After 1950 elections Democrat Party came to power bringing an end to the one-party rule, which had prevailed in the country since the establishment of the Republic in 1923. After the Second World War, Soviet demands pushed Turkey to make a real choice in its foreign policy, and Turkey joined NATO, and Turkish membership of Western institutions such as the Council of Europe, the OECD and her associate membership of the EU, reinforced Turkey's closeness to the West. The transition to a market economy took a long time, and the change did not follow a straight line of development. Between 1923-1930 a liberal economic policy was followed; in 1930 a mixed economic policy placing considerable emphasis on the role of the state was adopted, and it continued until 1980s with the exception of the Democrat Party's attempts at liberalisation. In 1981, the strategy of import substitution as the means towards industrialisation was abolished. Turkish economy transformed from being a closed, agricultural and non-competitive economy to being market-oriented and liberal, and the Turkish experience in economic transformation and a market economy constituted another important characteristic of the Turkish model. Thus, in the early 1990's, the Turkish Model came to mean a secular state where the majority of the population was Muslim, with a multi-party system, and which was close to and co-operates with the West, and had a market economy.

Although the Turkish model was proposed for the newly independent Turkic republics, in reality this model was not without its problems in its homeland. It was not able to cope with ethnic, religious, democratic and human rights issues. These outstanding problems of the Turkish Model are 'military interventions', 'Kurdish separatism' and 'Alawite discontent'.

Although Turkey transformed its single-party system to a multi-party system peacefully in 1946, the Turkish multi-party system was interrupted three times by military interventions (1960, 1971 and 1980). The Turkish Army's involvement in domestic politics was encouraged by several factors. Firstly, Turkish military tradition of interfering with the civil rule encourages the army to intervene in politics. Secondly, the Turkish army strongly believes that they represent enlightenment, secularism, Kemalism and modernism. This sense of being vanguards of the state has lasted from the Ottoman times to the present. Thirdly, the homogeneous lifestyle of the Turkish army officers distances them from the civilians. They do not trust the civilians and regard them as unruly and not dependable when it comes to state affairs. Fourthly, the status of the Turkish army in the Turkish system encourages the army to intervene in civil politics. Fifthly, because of the deficiency of democratic traditions and values, sometimes civilians, politicians and the media encourage the generals to intervene, strengthening their belief that they are the protectors of the Turkish people and Turkish state.

The role of the Army in the Turkish Model, is engrained within the structure of the Model and in fact the understanding of democracy that the Model brings has in many ways been designed by the Army itself. The inability of the Turkish Model to construct a civil society, undermines the position of Turkey as a Western democratic state and the Turkish Model's supposed main characteristic   as a 'multi-party system'.

The Turkish Army has been directly and indirectly responsible for the escalation of the minorities' problem in Turkey. One example is the Kurdish separatist movement, which has involved Turkey in an undeclared war within its own territory since 1984. Although in theory, Kemalism and therefore the Turkish Model, identifies Turkishness as 'citizenship' and as a unifying factor, it is not perceived by Kurdish people as such. The military coups and the abolishing of political parties by the military frequently, have not allowed the Kurds and the Turks (or any other minorities) to form long lasting political relationships through the membership of these parties, and have not allowed the differences to be melted towards the construction of a healthy civil society. In contrast, after each coup, the importance of 'Turkishness' has been stressed. Especially after 1980, Kurdish intellectuals have openly identified themselves as different from ethnic Turks. To tackle the problem, Turkish governments have encouraged investments in East and SouthEast Anatolia on the one hand and have denied the existence of a separate identity for the Kurds on the other. Finally by the 1990's, the state recognised a separate Kurdish identity, and the ban on the Kurdish language imposed by Kenan Evren's military regime was lifted.

Kurdish separatism dominates Turkish domestic policy and it has significant effects on Turkish foreign policy. The fact that Turkey is unable to resolve the problem of ethnic minorities, weakens the adoption of the Turkish Model by the newly independent Turkic Republics, who have ethnic minority problems themselves. Moreover, because the struggle against a Kurdish uprising uses Turkey's financial resources, Turkic Republics know that they can not expect much from Turkey in terms of financial support.

The dissatisfaction of the Alawite religious minority also appears to be a potential cause of crisis for Turkey and for the Turkish Model. Alawites as a religious minority group seek to be recognised as a separate group from that of the Sunni majority and ask financial support for their Cemevis and clerics, and want religious education, which fit their beliefs. Alawites want to be represented in the Directorate of Religious Affairs in order to fulfil the needs of their sect. They claim to have been consistently suppressed during both the Ottoman Empire and the Turkish Republic. Continuing discontent of Alawites suggests that as yet, the state has not been able to fulfil the demands of the Alawites. Although without a clear definition of Alawitism or Alawism, it will be difficult for the state to know exactly what to do, nevertheless it is apparent that although the secular Constitution of Turkey guarantees freedom of belief for its citizens, Turkish model has not been capable of maturing on this front since 1923.

Notes

1   *Independent*, 21 December 1991.
2   For further statements and discussions on Turkish Model see following Chapters.
3   See also O.M. Smolansky, (1994), 'Turkish and Iranian Policies in Central Asia', in H. Malik, (ed.), *Central Asia: Its Strategic Importance and Future Prospects*, Macmillan Press, London, pp. 292-293, 299, 305; W.C. Hostler, (1993), *The Turks of Central Asia*, Praeger, London, p. 161; B.P. Henze, (1992), *Turkey: Toward the Twenty-First Century*, Rand Corporation, Santa Monica, p. 35; Y. Söylemez, (1992), 'Turkey: Western or Moslem', *Turkish Review*, Autumn, p. 55; S. Demirel, (1992), 'Newly-Emerging Centre', *Turkish Review*, Winter, pp. 5-6; A. Yalçın, (1992), *Türkiye Modeli ve Türk Kökenli Cumhuriyetlerle Eski Sovyet halkları*, Yeni Forum Dergisinin 16-19 Eylül tarihinde düzenlediği sempozyuma sunulan bildiriler, Yeni Forum A.Ş., Ankara.
4   For more information about Atatürk, see P.Kinross, (1993), '*Atatürk The Rebirth of a Nation*', Weidenfeld & Nicolson, London; H.C. Armsttrong, (1939), '*Grey Wolf*', Penguin Books, Harmondsworth.
5   Also, see A. Yalçın, (1993), 'Türk modeli kavramı ve Türkiyenin iktisadi kalkınmasındaki bazı özellikler' in *Türkiye-Azerbaycan ve Orta Asya Cumhuriyetlerinde Demokrasi ve Piyasa Ekonomisine Geçiş Süreci*, Yeni Forum Uluslararası 2. Sempozyumu 16-23 November 1992, Baku, Azerbaycan, Yeni Forum A.Ş. Ankara, pp. 9-11. For further details of Westernization in the Ottoman Empire, see E. Kalaycıoğlu and Y. Sarıbay, (ed.) (1986), *Türk Siyasal Hayatının Gelişimi*, Beta Basım Yayım Dağıtım A.Ş., Istanbul.
6   For Kemalism, see W.M. Hardman, (1990), *Kemalism: Evolution or Revolution*, A Dissertation

Submitted to the Faculty of the School of Arts and Sciences of the Catholic University of America in Particular Fulfillment of the Requirements for the Degree Doctor of Philosophy, Washington.

7   Directorate General of Press & Information of the Turkish Republic, *Turkey*, 1993, Ankara, p. 35.

8   For a more detailed account of the social and legal reforms of Atatürk, see for example; Kinross, *op.cit.;* P.Robins, (1991), *Turkey and the Middle East*, Pinter Publishers, London; A.S. Weekes and R.V. Weekes, (1978), 'Turks, Anatolian' in R.V. Weekes, (ed.), *Muslim Peoples*, Greenwood Press, London.

9   For these ideologies see, Y. Akçura, (1991), *Üç Tarz-ı Siyaset*, Türk Tarih Kurumu Yayınları, Ankara; S. Hilov, (1992), 'Düşünce Tarihi 1908-1980', in M. Tuncay, C. Koçak and others, (eds), *Türkiye Tarihi, Çağdaş Türkiye Cilt.4,* Cem Yayınevi, Istanbul; E. Kuran, (1992), 'Osmanlı İmparatorluğunda Yenileşme Hareketleri' in *Türk Dünyası El Kitabı Cilt.1*, Türk Kültürünü Araştırma Enstitüsü, Ankara; A. Özcan, (1992), *Pan-Islamism; Osmanlı Devleti Hindistan Müslümanları ve İngiltere 1877-1914*, Isam Yayınları, Istanbul; H. İnalcık, (1992), 'Osmanlı İmparatorluğu'nda Kültür ve Teşkilat', in Türk Dünyası El Kitabı Cilt.1, *op.cit.*; L. Rasonyi, (1988), *Tarihte Türklük*, Türk Kültürünü Araştırma Enstitüsü, Ankara; C. Eraslan, (1992), 'İkinci Abdül Hamit'in İslam Birliği Siyaseti ve Eğitime Etkileri', in *İkinci Abdülhamid ve Dönemi Semposyum Bildirileri*, Seha Neşriyat ve Ticaret A.Ş., Istanbul; M. Hülagu, (1993), 'İngiliz Belgelerinde Pan- İslamism ile ilgili Bir Rapor', *Türk Dünyası Araştırmaları*, no. 85, Original source is: India Office Library and Records (London), (IOR): L/P&S/20/G 77; Z. Kurşun, (1992), *Yol Ayırımında Türk-Arab İlişkileri*, İrfan Yayınevi, Istanbul; A. Rustow, (1976), 'İkinci Meşrutiyette Meclisler', *Güney-Doğu Avrupa Araştırmaları Dergisi*, no. 4-5; N.Z. Zeine, (1966), *The Emergence of Arab Nationalism*, Khayats, Beirut; N.Z. Zeine, (1958), *Arab-Turkish Relations and the Emergency of Arab Nationalism*, Beirut; A.M. Sindi, (1978), *The Muslim World and Its Efforts in Pan-Islamism*, A Ph.D. Dissertation Presented to the Faculty of the Graduate School University of Southern California; H. Algül, (1991), *Bir fazilet Devletinin Kuruluşu*, Nil Yayınları, İzmir; Sultan İkinci Abdülhamid, (1984), *Siyasi Hatıratım*, Istanbul; J.M. Landau, (1990), *The Politics of Pan-Islam*, Clarendon Press, Oxford; B. Bozgeyik, (1993), *İslam Birliği Üzerine Oynanan Oyunlar*, Timaş, Istanbul; İ.S. Sırma, (1990), *İkinci Abdülhamid'in İslam Birliği Siyaseti*, Beyan Yayınları, Istanbul; F. Sümer, (1993), 'Osmanlılar ve Türkler', *Türk Dünyası Tarih Dergisi*, no. 75; G. Antonius, (1938), *The Arab Awakening*, Hamilton, London; C. Küçük, (1992), 'İkinci Abdül Hamit'in Dış Politikası', in İkinci Abdülhamid ve Dönemi Sempozyum Bildirileri, *op.cit.*; E. Kedourie, (1966), *Afghani and Abduh*, Frank Cass & Co. Ltd., London; N.R. Keddie, (1972), *Sayyid Jamal ad-Din 'al-Afghani'*, University of California Press, London; M. Saray, (1987), *Gaspıralı İsmail Bey*, Türk Kültürünü Araştırma Enstitüsü, Ankara; A. Haurani, (1970), *Arabic Thought in the Liberal Age*, London; Ö.F. Akun, (1992), 'İkinci Abdülhamit'in Kültür Faliyetlerine Bazı Dikkatler' in İkinci Abdülhamid ve Dönemi Sempozyum Bildirileri, *op.cit.*; Ş. Hanioğlu, (1986), *Osmanlı İttihat ve Terakki Cemiyeti ve Jön Türkler 1889-1902*, Istanbul; Ş. Mardin, (1989), *Jön Türklerin Siyasi Fikirleri 1895-1908*, İletişim Yayınları, Istanbul; F. Ahmad, (1969), *The Young Turks: The Committee of Union and progress in Turkish Politics 1908-1914*, Oxford; S.G. Haim, (1976), *Arab Nationalism*, London; C.E. Down, (1986), *The Origins of Arab Nationalism*, Middle East Institute, Columbia University; S. Kocabaş, (1993), 'Birinci Dünya Harbinde Araplar Üzerine İngiliz Oyunları', *Türk Dünyası Tarih Dergisi*, no. 74; W.C. Hostler, *op.cit.*; B. Lewis, (1961), *The Emergence of Modern Turkey*, London; Kinross, *op.cit.*; H.C. Armstrong, *op.cit.*; S. Zenkovsky, (1960), *Pan-Turkism and Islam in Russia*, Harvard University Press, Cambridge; F.Ç. Derin, (1992), 'Osmanlı Devletinin Siyasi Tarihi', in Türk Dünyası El Kitabı Cilt.1, *op.cit.*; U. Heyd, (1950), *Foundations of Turkish Nationalism*, Luzac & Compony Ltd. and The Harvill Press Ltd, London; H. Tuncay, (1978), *Ziya Gökalp*, Toker Yayınları, Istanbul; Z. Gökalp,

(Translated by Robert Devereux), (1968), *The Principles of Turkism*, E.J. Brill, Leiden; G. Fraser, (1988), 'Enver Pasha's Bid for Turkestan 1920-1922', *Canadian Journal of History*, vol. 23 no. 2; İ. Bal, (1996), 'Yusuf Akçura, Üç Tarz-ı Siyaset ve Üç Tarz-ı Siyasetteki Türkçülük' ün Varsayımları Üzerine Yorumlar', in A. Yuvalı, M. Ergunşah, M. Keskin and A. Öztürk, (eds), *Türkiye Cumhuriyeti Devletinin Kuruluş ve Gelişmesine Hizmeti Geçen Türk Dünyası Aydınları Sempozyumu Bildirileri (23-26 Mayıs 1996)*, Erciyes Üniversitesi Türk Dünyası Araştırmaları Merkezi Yayınları, Kayseri; J. M. Landau, (1981), *Pan-Turkism in Turkey*, C. Hurst & Company, London.

10   For reasons which caused the rise of Turkish nationalism see for example; Ç.F. Derin, *op.cit.*

11   For the intellectuals who affected Atatürk's thoughts, see Heyd, *op.cit.*; Kuran, *op.cit.*; Rasonyi, *op.cit.*; Tuncay, *op.cit.*; Gökalp, *op.cit.*; Kinross, *op.cit.*

12   Atatürk has been accused of hidden racism and the official argument used by the state against those who accuse him of racism is that, Turkishness in Atatürk's sense was never related to race because two important figures in the foundation of Turkish nationalism who inspired Atatürk were racially non-Turks, namely Ziya Gökalp (ethnically Kurdish) and Tekin Alp (Moiz Kohen; ethnically Jewish). For a sample of this official argument, see Ç. Yetkin, (1993), 'Atatürk milliyetçiliği ve terrör', *Yeni Forum*, vol. 14, no. 286, pp. 55-56.

13   For opposition to Atatürk during the First Parliament, see for example; C. Koçak, 'Siyasal Tarih', in M. Tuncay, C. Koçak and others, (eds), Türkiye Tarihi, Çağdaş Türkiye Cilt.4, *op.cit.*; M. Erdoğan, (1993), 'Türkiye'de Demokrasiye Geçiş Deneyimi (1945-1950)', in *Türkiye-Azeraycan ve Orta Asya Cumhuriyetlerinde Demokrasi ve Piyasa Ekonomisine Geçiş Süreci*, (Yeni Forum Uluslararası 2. Sempozyumu 16-23 Kasım 1992, Baku, Azerbaycan, Yeni Forum A.Ş., Ankara.

14   For the details of Turkish Foreign Policy between the years 1919 to 1939 see, for example; F. Armaoğlu, (1988), *20.Yüzyıl Siyasi Tarihi 1914-1980*, Türkiye İş Bankası Kültür Yayınları, Ankara, pp. 307-360.

15   'Turkish Republic on its 70th anniversary', *Turkish Review*, Summer 1993, vol. 7, no. 32, pp. 15-16.

16   For the Turkish economy from the beginning to 1980s see; O. Okyar, (1980), *Cumhuriyet Dönemi Türkiye Ekonomisi*, Akbank Yayınları, Ankara.

17   During the 1930s, there was a lot of sympathy for Germany among the intelligence and the Generals in Turkey. See for example; Landau, Pan-Turkism in Turkey, *op.cit.*

18   For Soviet demands also see İ. Soysal, (1991), '70 Years of Turkish Soviet Political Relations', *Turkish Review*, vol. 5, no. 24; F.A. Vali, (1972), *The Turkish Straits and NATO*, Hoover Institution Press, California, p. 59; W. Taubman, (1982), *Stalin's American Policy, From Entente to Detente to Cold War*, W.W. Norton and Company, New York, pp. 108-109; O. Sander, (1993), 'Turkish Foreign Policy: Forces of Continuity and of Change', *Turkish Review*, Winter; C. Orhonlu, (1992), 'Türkiye Cumhuriyeti Tarihi', in Türk Dünyası El Kitabı, Cilt. 1, *op.cit*, pp. 526-527.

19   Turkey was not accepted as a full member, but it achieved a Customs Union with the European Union in 1996. For Turkey's relationship with the European Union, for example, see İ. Bal, (1996), 'European Union, Turkic Republics and Turkish Dilemma', *Pakistan Horizon*, vol. 49, no. 1, pp. 69-88; M. Müftüler, (1993), 'Turkey and European Community: An Uneasy Relationship', *Turkish Review*, Autumn, pp. 38-39, and for the Western European Union, see S. Duke, (1996), 'The Second Death (or the Second Coming?) of the WEU', *Journal Of Common Market Studies*, vol. 34, no. 2.

20   Examples of State Economic Enterprises were; Makina Kimya Endüstrisi (Machinery and Chemicals Industry), Et ve Balık Kurumu (Meat and Fish Board), Türkiye Çimento Sanayi (Cement Industry), Azot Sanayi (Nitrogen Industry), Türkiye Petrolleri Anonim Ortaklığı

(Turkish Petroleum Corporation), Türkiye Kömür İşletmeleri (Coal Works), SEKA (Paper Industry) and Demir ve Çelik Sanayii (the Iron and Steel Industry).

21   Directorate General of Press & Information of the Turkish Republic, Turkey, *op.cit.*, pp. 77-78.

22   In 1991, reflecting on the past, Turgut Özal described the situation of the Turkish economy in the 1970s as resembling the 'socialist economies of the East European countries. In fact, we were even lagging behind those countries. We had long queues, a black market, several exchange rates, enormous subsidies, etc. We had to establish a free market economy ... Our exports at the beginning of the last decade were a mere 2.2 billion dollars. Our oil imports alone added up to 3.4 billion dollars. Our economy was suffering from a chronic account deficit'. (President Turgut Özal's address at the 'European Studies Centre Global Panel', 9 April 1991, see for the document; *Turkish Review*, Spring 1991, vol. 5, no. 23, pp. 109-118).

23   President Turgut Özal's address at the 'European Studies Centre Global Panel', 9 April 1991, *Turkish Review*, Spring 1991, vol. 5, no. 23, pp. 109-118.

24   For Orhan Erkanlı's ideas see; O. Erkanlı, (1973), *Anılar... Sorunlar... Sorumlular*, Baha Matbası, Istanbul.

25   For the description of the Turkish state structure see; Directorate General of Press & Information of the Turkish Republic, Turkey, *op.cit.*, pp. 23-58.

26   *Ibid.*, p. 33.

27   For example, E. Rouleau, (1993), 'The challenges to Turkey', *Foreign Affairs*, vol. 72, no. 5, p.122; F. Eroğlu, (1994), 'Güneydoğuda Siyasi çözüm arayışlarının ideolojik kökenleri', *Türk Yurdu*, vol. 14, no. 78, pp. 34-35.

28   The formal establishment of the PKK by Abdullah Öcalan took place in 1979. The organization has a pan-Kurdish vision, and aims firstly to gain regional autonomy with the separation of South East Anatolia from Turkey, and the establishment of a Marxist-Leninist Kurdistan. (See, C. Akyol, (1993), 'Terrörle mücadelede yapılan yanlışlar ve doğrular', *Yeni Forum*, vol. 14, no. 295, p.55). Ultimately to create a greater Kurdistan uniting the Kurdish areas of Turkey, Iraq, Iran and Syria. (See, G. Rowley, (1993), 'Multinational and National Competition for Water in the Middle East: Towards the Deepening Crisis', *Journal of Environmental Management*, vol. 39, no. 3, 1993, p.195.). It is a heavily ideological, utopian Marxist-Socialist organization (See, G. Fuller, (1993), 'The fate of the Kurds', *Foreign Affairs*, vol. 72, no. 2, p. 116).

29   140 people took part in this survey - 78 (55.7%) males and 62 (44.3%) females.

30   For different claims about the number of Kurdish people, see, T. Hindle, (1993), 'Young Turks', in *The World in 1994*, The Economist Publications, London, p. 59. Where the Kurdish population is cited as 12 million. According to 'Denge Kurd' Newspaper (a PKK source) published in Baku (October 1993), the population of Kurds living in Turkey is more than 20 million (*Yeni Forum*, vol. 15, no. 298, March 1994, p.5). Again, according to Kurdist writer Beşikçi, there are 20 million Kurds in Turkey. See also O. Türkdoğan, (1993), 'Türkiye'de Etnik Gruplar', *Türk Dünyası Tarih Dergisi*, vol. 7, no. 78; who claims 7 percent of Turkey's population to be of Kurdish origin. At the other extreme Mehmet Turgut estimates 4,500,000 Kurds in Turkey in 1992; see M. Turgut, (1992), 'Kürtçe Konuşan vatandaşlarımızın Sayısı meselesi', *Yeni Forum*, vol. 13, no. 277, pp. 43-45.

31   See, *Milliyet*, Konda Büyük Araştırması, 2 March 1993.

32   *Hürriyet*, 12 July 1993.

33   *Personal Interview with Abdülkadir Aksu*, Ankara, 1995.

34   On this claim, see A.B. Ercilasun, (1992), 'Resmi Dil Türkçedir', *Türk Kültürü*, vol. 30, no. 348, pp. 194-195; İ. Parmaksızoğlu, (1983), *Tarih Boyunca Kürt Türkleri ve Türkmenler*, Ankara; Ş.K. Seferoğlu, (1983), 'Türkmen ve Kürt Türkleri', *Türk Kültürü*, no. 243; F. Kirzioğlu, (1968), *Kürtlerin Türklüğü*, Ankara); Rasonyi, *op.cit.*; M. Risvanoğlu, (1994), *Saklanan Gerçek vol. 1*

and 2, Tanmak Yayınları, Ankara; H. Başbuğ, (1984), *İki Türk Boyu, Zaza ve Kurmançilar*, Ankara; A. Turan, (1992), 'Kürt Tarihi ve Uygarlığı', *Yeni Forum*, vol. 13, no. 273, pp. 54-66; M.Ş. Sekban, (1970), *Kürt Sorunu*, İstanbul. Although Sekban is a Kurdish, he claims in his book that Kurds are Turks. See also, T. Erer, (1990), *Kürtçülük Meselesi*, Istanbul; M. Keskin, (1990), 'Güneydoğu Anadoluda Türk devletleri', *Türk Yurdu*, vol. 10, no. 37, pp. 28-30; M. Aksoy, (1993), 'Kalkınma ve Kürtçülük meselesi', *Yeni Forum*, vol. 14, no. 289, 1993, pp. 64-66; N. Göyünç, (1992), 'Türk-Kürt ilişkileri', *Yeni Forum*, vol. 13, no. 274, p. 37; H.N. Orkun, (1987), *Eski Türk Yazıtları*, Ankara, p. 591; Y. Gürler, (1992), 'Kürtlerin Türk Kültürü İçindeki Yeri', *Yeni Forum*, vol. 13, no. 274, pp. 61-62; Türkdoğan, 'Türkiye'de Etnik Gruplar', *op.cit.*, p. 11; Ercilasun, *op.cit.*, p. 195; A. Turan, *op.cit.*, p. 58; Z. Gökalp, (1992), 'Türkler'le Kürtler', *Küçük Mecmua*, no. 1, Diyarbakır, p. 11. For sources which do not accept Kurdish as a language in its own right, see T. Gülensoy, (1994), 'Türkiyede Kürdoloji Araştırmaları', *Azerbaycan*, vol. 43, no. 296, 1994, pp. 19-20; Y. Gürler, (1992), 'Kürtlerin Türk Kültürü İçindeki Yeri', *Yeni Forum*, vol. 13, no. 274, p. 62; Ş.K. Seferoğlu, (1994), 'Hocam Fındıkoğlu ve Bölücülük-3', *Yeni Forum*, vol. 15, no. 299, p. 31.

35 Researchers such as C. Bender, İ. N uri, İ. Beşikçi, etc. have stressed that Kurds are a minority in Turkey and are suppressed by the Turkish authorities (For example, see C. Bender, (1991), *Kürt Tarihi ve Uygarlığı*, Kaynak Yayınları, İstanbul; İ. Nuri, (1977), *Kürtlerin Kökeni*, İstanbul; İ. Beşikçi, (1990), *Bir aydın, Bir Örgüt ve Kürt sorunu-Belgeler*, İstanbul. This movement has been headed by M. Anter, K. Burkay, T.Z. Ekinci, M.A. Arslan, M.A. Eren, Ş. Elçi, etc. (*Yeni Forum*, vol. 13, no. 276, May 1992, p. 8). To prove that Kurds are different from Turks racially, culturally, linguistically and historically, Kurdish scholars attempt to find a separate national history, and contacts with Turks are usually disregarded (Gürler, *op.cit.*, p. 62).

36 *Hürriyet*, 12 July 1993.

37 *Sabah*, Piar-Galup Araştırması, 9 July 1992.

38 *Yeni Forum*, vol. 15, no. 298, March 1994, p. 5.

39 The leader of this party is Prof. Dr. Sadun Aren. For his opinions about the future of the world and socialism, see S. Aren, (1995), 'Yeni Bir Dünya Yeni Bir Sosyalism', *Yeni Türkiye*, vol. 1, no. 3, pp. 146-148.

40 Leader of this party is Doğu Perinçek. For his political views, see D. Perinçek, (1995), 'Güneyli Diş Politikası', *Yeni Türkiye*, vol. 1, no. 3, pp. 127-145.

41 For example, see *Hürriyet*, 5 May 1993; *Cumhuriyet*, 18 July 1993; *Milliyet*, 30 May 1993.

42 For example, see A. Yalçın, (1992), 'Ülkenin ve devletin bölünmezliği', *Yeni Forum*, vol. 13, no. 276, p. 4; *Yeni Forum* vol. 13, no. 276, May 1992, p. 8; M. Öztürk, (1992), 'Doğu Anadolu meselesinin tarihi boyutları Üzerine bazı görüşler', *Türk Yurdu*, vol. 12, no. 55, p. 10; also, see *Hürriyet*, 5 May 1993; *Cumhuriyet*, 18 July 1993; *Milliyet*, 30 May 1993.

43 See also, *Newspot*, no. 15, 19 August 1994, p.3 and O. Türkdoğan, (1993), 'Terrör olayının sosyo-pskolojik nedenleri', *Türk Yurdu*, vol. 13, no. 71, p. 5.

44 About Armenian support, see *Forum*, vol. 13, no. 282, 1992, p.13; Yalçın, (1993), 'Terrörle mücadelede doğru teşhis ve strateji', *YeniForum*, vol. 14, no. 295, p. 3; *Yeni Forum*, vol. 11, no. 291, August 1993, p. 11; *Yeni Forum*, vol. 15, no. 300, May 1994, p. 10; A. Yalçın, (1992), 'Ülkede iç savaş ortamı varmı?' *Yeni Forum*, vol. 13, no. 275, p. 5.

45 This support has been ratified by some Greek members of parliament who attended the congress of the PKK sympathizer Democracy party (DEP) who openly talked of their support for the PKK (*Milliyet*, 27 November 1993). *Cumhuriyet* reported that Greece gives 10,000,000 dollars to the PKK annually, and Iran also gives financial support, weapons and logistics (*Cumhuriyet*, 17 July 1993).

46 The connection between Russia and the PKK is a growing concern for the Turkish governments.

A Kurdish conference took place in Russia in April 1994; see *Yeni Forum*, vol. 15, no. 300, May 1994, p.10; A.J. Wohlstetter, (1994), 'Rus emparyalizmi hortlarken Batı bocalıyor', *Yeni Forum*, vol. 15, no. 298, p. 9.

47   After Abdullah Öcalan, leader of PKK entered Italy in late 1998, Turkish public and media accused Italy for supporting PKK and people protested Italian goods and Italian treatment of Öcalan.

48   *Hürriyet*, 12 July 1993.

49   Doğu Perinçek underlines the Kurdish problem as a mortgage on Turkish Foreign Policy. He explains that if this problem ends the money spent to fight against PKK can be used for the benefit of the people. See Perinçek, *op.cit.*, p. 142.

50   *Yeni Forum*, vol. 13, no. 277, June 1992, p. 18.

51   *Guardian*, 3 April 1992.

52   For example, as a reaction to a PKK attack in Erzurum, the conservative people of Erzurum were on the verge of attacking Kurdish minorities in Erzurum (in 1994); the authorities and the police barely managed to restrain them through Sheyh Nazım (a religious leader).

53   For the first version of 'Alawite Discontent' see: İdris Bal, (1997), 'The Turkish Model: the place of the Alawites', *Central Asian Survey*, vol. 16, no. 1, pp. 97-102.

54   For the early history of the Kizilbaşs, see M. Moosa, (1988), *Extremist Shi'ites: The Ghulat Sects*, Syracuse University Press.

55   For Taqiyyah, see H. Enayat, (1982), *Modern Islamic Political Thought*, Macmillan, London, pp. 175-181.

56   See, D. Barchard, (1985), *Turkey and the West*, Routledge & Kegan Paul, London, p. 25; The Economist Intelligence Unit, *Turkey, Country Profile 1993-1994*, London, 1993, p. 16; The Economist Intelligence Unit, *Turkey: Country Report 4ᵗʰ quarter 1993*, London, 1993, p. 13; Robins, *op.cit.*, p. 8; D. Özgüden, (1988), *The Extreme-Right in Turkey*, Info-Turk, Brussels, pp. 18-19; *Financial Times*, May 21 1992.

57   See; A. Mango, (1993), 'The Turkish Model', *Middle Eastern Studies*, vol.29, no. 4, p. 736; *Financial Times*, May 21 1992; L.W. Pevsner, (1984), *Turkey's Political Crises*, Praeger, New York, pp. 34,45,59; P.Bumke, (1989), 'The Kurdish Alevis- boundaries and perceptions' in A. Andrews, (ed.), *Ethnic Groups in the Republic of Turkey*, Weiesbaden.

58   On 24 September 1994 on ATV (a Turkish TV channel) the first TV programme concerning the Alawites, focusing on their demands from the state and the place of Alawites within Islam was broadcast. (ATV, 24 September, 1994; Siyaset Meydanı (directed by Ali Kirca)). Then, During the October 1994 a TV series prepared by Zülfü Livaneli (for ATV Channel) concerning Alawite people and their demands was broadcast. After the incidents in Istanbul, media and politicians began to mention the issue more frequently. For example, see *Radikal Gazetesi*, 'Alavilik', 18,19,20 December 1996.

59   Özgüden claims that respect for the equality of beliefs never existed in Turkey, and the neutrality of the state with regard to different religions does not exist (Özgüden, *op.cit.*, pp. 18-19).

60   *Financial Times*, 21 May 1992.

61   *Financial Times*, 21 May 1992.

62   *Ibid.*

63   The Economist Intelligence Unit, Turkey, Country Profile 1993-1994, *op.cit.*, p.16.

64   *Newspot*, 4 June 1981.

65   The Economist Intelligence Unit, Turkey: Country Report 4th quarter 1993, *op.cit.*, p.13; *Independent*, 6 July 1993.

66   Turkish security forces claimed that the Alawite villages were used as a base by the PKK.

67   *Yön*, vol. 1, no. 20, 16 October 1994, p.7.

68   Ibid., pp. 8-10.

Library and Information Services
University of W:... ...itute, Cardiff
Colchester Avenue
Cardiff
CF23 7XR

2 Turkish Reaction to the Emergence of the Turkic Republics

Introduction

The end of the Cold War and of the Soviet Union had a great impact on Turkey because although Turkey lost its strategic position from the Western point of view as a bulwark against the Soviet Union, new opportunities were opened for her. In six of the newly independent states of the former Soviet Union, the majority of the population was Muslim and five of these republics (Azerbaijan, Kazakstan, Kirgizstan, Turkmenistan and Uzbekistan) were regarded as Turkic Republics. This new situation affected Turkish politicians, elite and the public deeply for a variety of reasons.

The present chapter will dwell on the Turkish reaction to the emergence of the Turkic Republics, and the promotion of the Turkish model, and how Turkey developed relations with the new Turkic Republics during the early days of their independence. To this end, first the main factors that affected the reactions and decisions of Turkey will be outlined. Second, the attitudes and reactions of Turkish politicians, political parties, elite, the media and the public will be discussed. Third, Turkish foreign policy style, and Turkish policy towards the Turkic Republics will be discussed.

Factors that Affected Turkish Reactions

There are two main reasons for Turkey's interest in Central Asia and the Caucasus (especially in Azerbaijan). The first and most important one includes cultural issues such as ethnicity, religion, history and language. It answers the question whether Turkey would be so interested in this part of the world if these Republics were not Muslim in religion and Turkic in origin. The second reason includes security issues and Turkey's international relations in general.

It is commonly accepted in Turkey that Turks in Turkey and Turks in the Turkic Republics of the former Soviet Union have the same ethnic origins, and the

43

Turks of Turkey are accepted as having migrated to Anatolia from Central Asia.[1] Mainly because of common heritage, 'Anatolia is the motherland for us, while Kazakstan is the land of our ancestors', said Turgut Özal, the late president of Turkey, in a speech given during his second and final official visit to Kazakstan in April 1993 (Hyman, 1994c, p.11). Demirel, Turkey's current president, also underlined the importance of sharing the same history, saying

> It is quite natural that Turkey acts by taking into account its national interest in terms of its security, its economic and social relations. However, Turkey, which considers its national interests in this issue, has some moral responsibilities. These moral responsibilities come from Turkey's history ... It is impossible to isolate yourself from your history ... History offers opportunities as well as responsibilities and difficulties.[2]

When Azeris, Uzbeks, Kazak, Kirgizs and Turkmens are regarded as being from the same origin[3], ethnicity cannot be separated from political and economic relations either at the level of the nation state or internationally as Frank (1992, pp.22-23) points out. Therefore 'ethnicity' affected the reactions of Turkish people generally in favour of the newly independent Republics.

Religion is an important part of the common culture between Turkey and the Turkic Republics. Islam was the unifying factor in the Turkic world (D'encausse, 1988, p.1; Zaim, 1993, pp.9-10), and it is still possible to say that Islam is the common religion of the Turkic people; Islamic moral values are still important and Islam is regaining its strength. The fact that nearly all Turkic people (except two-thirds of Azeris) follow the Sunni sect of Islam, constituted an additional reason which encouraged Turkish people to welcome the new developments and the emergence of the Turkic Republics with great enthusiasm.

Languages of the same family are spoken by Turkic peoples. However, the division between Turkish and European views on this subject should not be forgotten. While the majority of Turkish specialists consider Turkic languages as 'dialects' of one another, European academics consider these as independent languages (Zenkovsky, 1960, pp.3-8).[4] For the purposes of this chapter, the important thing is the popular Turkish perspective and image, rather than the reality. Therefore, according to popular Turkish assumption, a common Turkish language is another important factor that unifies Turkic peoples. As Devlet (1993, pp.21-22) suggested, whether we regard these languages as dialects or independent languages, there are strong links between these languages which allow us to assert that this kinship is another factor that should unify the Turkic world. The Minister of Culture Fikri Sağlar pointed out in 1992 that 'the Turkish Language has been the most important unifying factor for the Turkic people who have been separated several centuries ago'.[5] It is asserted by Turkish authors that after the break-up of the USSR, 'Turkic' has taken its place among the six most used languages in the world in terms of number of speakers (Duman, 1993, p.1).

The attitudes at all levels of Turkish society -parties, intellectuals, the media, public opinion- were effected by the belief that these newly independent Republics were supposed to share a common culture, history and religion with the people of Turkey.[6] It is possible to argue that, if it were not for the existence or supposed existence of these ties, Turkish people (in general) would not be so interested in the region and welcome developments with great enthusiasm.

The second main reason for Turkey's interest in Central Asia and the Caucasus is connected with security issues and Turkey's position in the World politics. Turkey shared a common border with the USSR and as a member of NATO it defended thirty-seven percent of the common borders with the communist block (Warsaw Pact) and had the second-largest army in NATO (İnan, 1995a, p.96). In the case of an actual war, it would have been the first country to confront the Soviets. Following the collapse of the USSR, Turkey's importance for the West seemed to decline. The possibility of a confrontation between the Western and Eastern blocks no longer exists, former Socialist countries started to reform their old systems by adopting market economies and multi-party systems with the assistance of the West and old hostilities motivated by ideological and military competition were replaced by new friendships. This new situation meant that Turkey was no longer an important partner for the West (including the US) as a buffer against the Soviet Union (Hunter, 1994, p.243). However, for Turkey the threat from the 'East' did not disappear and Turkey felt its position becoming more vulnerable as the support of the West declined. Historically Russia had claims on the Straits and the eastern provinces of Turkey, and had wanted to penetrate the South and reach the Mediterranean Sea. Therefore, Turkish politicians felt (and still feel) that in spite of the death of communism, no one could be sure that Russia had given up their expansionist ideas. Later, the rise of Zhirinovsky confirmed Turkish worries, which was best expressed by President Süleyman Demirel's words in 1994:

> Will Russia re-create the Russian empire? There is the phenomenon of Zhirinovsky, which brings this doubt to mind. ... If it is true that one in every two people in Russia thinks like Zhirinovsky, it becomes clear that this problem is more serious than the Zhirinovsky phenomenon....[7]

Turkish politicians felt that the West would be reluctant to help Turkey in the case of any dispute because the West did not presently regard Russia as the enemy. As Hale suggested, Turkey's political leadership wanted to convince the Western powers that although the Cold War had finished, Turkey still occupied an important strategic position in global politics and was still important to the West. Turkey needed to find some arguments with which it could approach the Western powers.[8]

Turkey's active support of the Western coalition against Saddam Hussein during the Gulf War was an attempt to convince the West that Turkey was still important in global politics and also to persuade the European Union to admit it as a member.[9] Turkey's effective closure of the Iraqi pipeline to the Mediterranean (through which Iraq exported fifty four per cent of its oil, or approximately 1.5 million barrels a day); extension until December 1991 of the Defence and Economic Co-operation Agreement which gave the US access to military bases in Turkey, deployment of over 100,000 troops along the Iraqi border, and its allowing the use of NATO air bases such as İncirlik, played a vital role in the success of the anti-Iraqi coalition (Kuniholm, 1991, pp.36-37; Aybet, 1992, p.102). At the expense of its economy, Turkey abides by UN sanctions on Iraq and this helps the rise of inflation in Turkey.[10] Turkey's effective role in the Gulf War was appreciated by US President Bush. In his speech at Ankara Esenboğa Airport, said:

> When Saddam Hussein invaded Kuwait, Turkey acted courageously to ensure that aggression would not stand. And as the whole world knows, the international coalition could not have achieved the liberation of Kuwait without Turkey's pivotal contributions.[11]

Yet, in contrast to Turkey's expectations, Turkish support for the anti-Iraq coalition did not bring enough backing from the West for Turkey's position in terms of its relations with the EU and its problem with terrorism in South East Anatolia. The belief in Turkey that Turkey is without support and is 'lonely' in international relations may be worth emphasising here as a potentially important factor affecting its reactions and decisions. In the 1990's, in spite of Turkey's close relations with the West, the West did not support her on crucial issues such as Kurdish separatism, the disputes with Greece,[12] the Cyprus problem and the water dispute in the Middle East.[13] Turkey was punished with regards to these issues in the past. For example, the US and the West because of Turkish intervention in Cyprus in 1974 punished Turkey.[14] Turkey's position on Kurdish separatism in SouthEast Anatolia is not supported either because the US and Western states have been supporting a political solution to the dispute and pressing Turkey towards this.[15] Similarly Turkey's position on the water dispute in the Middle East is not supported. Turkey, Iraq and Syria are involved in the water dispute (Rowley, 1993, p.188),[16] with Iraq and Syria opposing Turkey's South East Anatolian Project (SEAP-GAP), claiming that Iraq's share of the Euphrates would decline from 30 billion cubic meters to below its minimum need, and that 50% of Syria's 31.8 billion cubic meters annual Euphrates supply would be cut off.[17] Hence, it is argued that after the end of the Cold War the major threat to Turkey now comes from the South East, namely from Iraq and Syria and that this shift would be reflected in Turkey's new defence strategy (Kuniholm, 1991, p.40). Especially, Syria has been an important source of anxiety on the part of Turkey, because

> Syria was for a long time perceived as a source of threat due to its military association with the Soviet Union. A treaty of assistance between the two and the flow of sophisticated Soviet weaponry to Syria, together with the presence of the Soviet navy in the eastern Mediterranean, gave rise to a feeling of having been encircled by Soviet power to the north and the south (Sezer, 1992, p.234).

After the collapse of the Soviet Union, although the Soviet-Syrian connection was broken, there was a proliferation of sophisticated weaponry - ballistic missiles, chemical weapons –'and of nuclear weapons capability in the immediate neighbourhood of Turkey' (Sezer, 1992, pp.234-235).[18] In general, since the First World War, Turkey's relations with the Middle Eastern Arab countries have been cool. Recognition of the Turkish Republic of Northern Cyprus (1983) internationally was a test case for Turkey and when it was not able to draw enough support from the Arab states, this was understood as a clear sign that they were not 'friends' of Turkey.

The dispute over Cyprus with Greece has been one of the most serious problems for Turkish foreign policy because it has become a dispute between Turkey and the European Union. It is highly likely that other Turco-Greek disputes, such as those over the islands in the Aegean Sea, will become disputes between Turkey and the EU, and it is clear that Turkey will be under more pressure in the future (Bal, 1996a, p.77).

In post-Cold War era, Turkey needed allies, and in this respect the emergence of the Turkic Republics was important; it was hoped that because of their common culture, ethnicity and history, these Republics, who were regarded as natural allies, would support Turkey in the international arena. Therefore, Turkey's main objective was to see these new Turkic Republics gain and keep their independence. This tendency was later illustrated by the fact that the Turkish Republic of Northern Cyprus was also invited to some of the meetings that took place among the Turkic Republics and Turkey.

In the case of Turkey's relations with the EU, it is obvious that they were far from being perfect in early 1990's. Especially after the Turkish application for full membership of the EC in April 1987, it was realised to a significant extent that Turkish attempts to integrate with Europe would end in despair (at least in the short term). Because this application was rejected and there was no indication that Turkey would be accepted as a full member in the near future (Laffan, 1992, p.202; Müftüler, 1993, p.40). Luxembourg summit (in December 1997) had demonstrated that Turkish membership to EU was not possible in the near future. İnan (1993, p.70), a former Ambassador and Turkish Foreign Minister, argued that the possibility of joining the EU in the future was diminishing because of developments in Eastern Europe, and argued that Europe was giving priority to Eastern European states rather than Turkey for cultural reasons. Developments in post-Cold War era ratified these claims and Turkey which has been waiting for full membership since 1959, was put behind ex-Communist Eastern European states. Although Turkey has been recognised as an official candidate for the full membership of the EU in Helsinki summit (in 1999), Turkey will be able to gain a full membership after Eastern European countries become full members. There is also no timetable for Turkish membership and no one knows when Turkey will be a full member.

The importance of the cool relations between Turkey and the EU for this study is that negative developments have been pushing Turkish public opinion away from the West and urging Turkish decision-makers to search for more creative foreign relations policies.[19] While relations between Turkey and the EU were reaching a crisis point, in 1991, the USSR collapsed opening a window of opportunity for Turkey. However, although the collapse of the USSR radically improved the strategic position of Turkey, and provided new opportunities, this did not alter Turkey's pro-Western policy (Hale, 1992, p.680).[20] Therefore, Turkey set out to fulfil its ambitions with regards to the West while making use of the opportunities that the New World Order presented. In the early 1990s Turkey began to consider several potential structures: the Black Sea Economic Co-operation (BSEC), a free trade agreement with the United States, and the Balkan Co-operation Council. In addition to these, new opportunities appeared, such as the Economic Co-operation Organisation (ECO) and co-operation with the Turkic Republics (Connelly, 1994, p.32).[21]

Another issue which may be worth underlining is that Turkey's position in the early 1990's, while the USSR was collapsing and the new Turkic Republics emerging as independent states, was much better than it had been in the past in every respect - economy, international relations, etc. Hence, Turkey was in a position to take an interest in the new states and seek possible ways of co-operation. Also, by the 1990's, a new Turkish elite and a new group of entrepreneurs had developed, which were in a position to be able to take on new challenges outside Turkey. Civil institutions and the private sector were able to invest in and seek co-operation with the Turkic Republics. Therefore, whereas

Turkey once avoided relations with Turkic peoples outside Turkey, the disintegration of the USSR in 1991 provided a suitable base for an enthusiastic welcome from Turkey and Turkish people.

It may also be suggested that the collapse of the USSR and the emergence of the Turkic Republics provided an opportunity for the Turkish government to divert the attention of the public from domestic and international crises such as economic problems, terrorism and cool relations with the EU. [22]

There is no doubt that the exaggerated claims that Turkey was becoming a great state and that there was an area open to Turkish influence, (from the Balkans to the Great Wall of China) also affected the sentiments of the Turkish people and that these claims were made by the international press boosted the Turkish ego. Therefore, the proposal of the Turkish Model to the Turkic Republics by some Western decision-makers was influential on the reactions and decisions of Turkey. All these encouraged the Turkish side to welcome the new developments in the Nort East even more enthusiastically.

Attitudes and Debates

It is important to stress that although academics were discussing the possible collapse of the USSR in the early 1980s (Rupert, 1992, p.177), Turkey was unprepared for the emancipation of the Turkic Republics as independent states (Mütercimler, 1993, p.12; İnan, 1993, p.71; Karamısır, 1994, p.217; Baharçiçek, 1993, p.260).[23] In the first meeting of the Slavic Republics in Minsk on December 8, 1991, the Commonwealth of Independent States (CIS) was established which marked the end of the USSR. The first meeting of the expanded CIS in Alma Ata on December 21 1991 declared the former Soviet Republics as sovereign and independent, and each Republic as having full control of its own natural and local economic enterprises (Olcott, 1992, p.108). Although President Demirel referring to the establishment of the Turkic Republics, pointed out that this development had been expected for a century and that Turks were waiting for this moment[24], on another occasion he admitted Turkey's unreadiness for the emancipation of these Republics, saying

> While the 1990's approached, no one could have imagined that the Soviet Union would disintegrate, and that out of it a Georgia, an Azerbaijan, a Turkmenistan, an Uzbekistan, a Kirgizstan, a Tajikistan and Armenia would become independent.... disintegration of the Soviet Union was a surprise for everybody. No one was prepared for an event of this kind. Including the Republics, which emerged out of this empire, no one was prepared for this.[25]

Turkish unreadiness may be explained by three factors. First, because of the Cold War and the fear of Soviet expansionism, Turkey never wanted to provoke the Soviet Union, as they had common borders and the Soviet Union was militarily superior to Turkey. Second, after the first World War Turkish decision-makers and intellectuals generally refrained from dealing with other Turkic people who were known in Turkey as 'dış Türkler' (outer Turks). The term 'pan-Turkism' was regarded dangerous and a threat to world peace. Third, Turkish decision-makers and analysts did not have much information about the USSR and were not able to predict the sudden collapse of the Soviet Union. For example, even in 1991 Vahit Halefoğlu (1991, p.30) (Minister of Foreign Affairs, 1987-1989) argued in an article that 'the referendum held on 17 March in the Soviet Union on the subject of the new forms of links to be established between the Federal Republics and the Union, brought to light the desire of the Turkic peoples to stay attached to the Soviet Union'. However, once the Soviet Union collapsed Turkey was eager to get involved. Demirel underlined the importance of the event by saying 'The collapse of communism was a great thing for us'.[26]

Politicians and Parties

When Turkic republics became independent, Turgut Özal was the President (since 9 November 1989), and Süleyman Demirel was the Prime Minister of Turkey. Later after the sudden death of Özal in April 1993, Demirel replaced him in the presidency. President Özal welcomed the developments with great enthusiasm and he changed the style of Turkish foreign policy by pushing Turkey to play a more aggressive and active role. His proposal of the Black Sea Economic Co-operation (BSEC) and his role in the Gulf War[27] are examples of this. During the Gulf War he actively supported the US and tried to use this war as an instrument to solve Turkey's international problems. Within a few months, two interior ministers and one head of the Turkish Armed Forces resigned because they did not agree with Özal's policies (Yerasimos, 1991, p.190). It may be suggested that the Turkish failure to join the EU was an important factor that lay behind Özal's initiatives, however, it is difficult to explain all the statements and decisions of Özal through this; rather, his style, ideas and character should be taken into account.

Even before the formal end of the USSR, Özal visited Azerbaijan in March 1991 (Yerasimos, 1991, p.192) and wanted Turkey to act quickly to develop relations with Turkic Republics because otherwise the opportunities might be lost.[28] The leaders of Turkey, Azerbaijan, Kazakstan, Kirgizstan, Turkmenistan and Uzbekistan met in Ankara in 1992, in the first of a series of summits between Turkey and the Turkic Republics. At this summit, Özal pointed out that the

'Turkish world' had a rare opportunity, and that if they used this opportunity in the right way, the twenty-first century would belong to the Turks. After explaining the brotherhood among the Turkic world and pointing out the strength of solidarity and co-operation among Turkic people, he added,

> If this is so, I can see no valid reason not to establish regional co-operation among our countries. ..... Our peoples are expecting this kind of co-operation because we are from the same origin. We are branches of the same great tree and we are a big family. Naturally we are keen on each other, and we will be keen on each other. Our co-operation is to the benefit of our peoples and regions.[29]

Although Özal was trying to co-operate with the newly independent Turkic states, he was aware of the limitations of Turkey and the difficulties involved, but he intended to use these to the advantage of Turkey. He wanted to cooperage with the West and the US, and use Turkey as a bridge between the West and these countries. He summarised the situation by saying that it would take 'years for these countries to understand how to operate democracy and a market economy' and that 'Turkey will do what it can to help, but we have our own problems and we will need support. We will expect the European Community and the United States to give us that backing'.[30] Özal's ambitions did not end here, he regarded the Turkish Model (liberal, democratic and secular) as an example to the entire Islamic world. He kept on underlining the position of Turkey as a bridge between the East and the West.[31]

During Özal's presidency, Süleyman Demirel was Prime Minister and the leader of the right-of-centre Doğru Yol Partisi (True Path Party - TPP). A veteran politician, who had been the Prime Minister six times before and was twice overthrown by military coups (the last coup took place in 1980), Demirel also welcomed the developments with great enthusiasm, and made statements similar to Özal's. For example: after a visit in April 1992 to the Central Asian Republics, he talked grandly of a 'Turkish-speaking community of states stretching from the Adriatic to the Great Wall of China'.[32] On another occasion, he said 'Turkey is prepared to take upon itself the responsibility for the state of affairs in the region stretching from the Adriatic Sea to the borders of China' (Smolansky, 1994, pp.282-284). Demirel argued that 'Turkey's position is more important than before. A new window of opportunity has opened for us with the Turkic Republics'.[33] Similarly, he accepted Turkey's historical and cultural responsibilities and emphasised the brotherhood among Turkic peoples. However, Özal's and Demirel's attitudes differed. Demirel was a typical Turkish Cold War decision-maker who did not want to disturb neither the US nor the USSR or become involved in international debates. This was confirmed by his own words:

There are different interpretations about how the politics will be established, how stability will be obtained. Eventually, Turkey will adjust its policy by taking into account these obscure balances and sensitivities and by abstaining from creating hostilities and abstaining from creating problems.[34]

Therefore, the enthusiasm of Demirel towards the new Republics was limited and his difference of opinion with Özal became apparent on several occasions, for example: during the time when there was public pressure on the Turkish government to intervene in the Azeri-Armenian dispute on the side of Azerbaijan.[35] During an official visit to Turkic Republics in the spring of 1993, President Özal declared 'What can the Armenians do if shots happen to be fired? ... march into Turkey?'. Meanwhile his rival in Ankara, Prime Minister Demirel, took a different view: 'We shall not attack Armenia. If we attack, others on the other side will also attack' (Yılmaz, 1994, p.95). Demirel described this pressure as: 'We are being pushed, and we are under pressure from the pro-Azerbaijani public opinion. People say we should intervene. Actually we can intervene, but that won't be the end of the problem. Maybe the problem will start when you intervene'.[36] Demirel also underlined the danger of 'a conflict between Muslims and Christians that will last for years' (Pipes and Clawson, 1993, p.136). All in all, in his reaction to the collapse of the Soviet Union Demirel was more cautious than Özal. Also, he was deeply worried because of the problems created by the disintegration of the Soviet Union: 'Now, a disputed Caucasus and a disputed Balkans are added to a disputed Middle East' (Demirel, 1995, p.6). However, Demirel was as happy as Özal for Turkey to be shown as a role model for the newly independent states. He insisted that 'it is in Europe's interests to see that a modern, secular and democratic Turkey is seen as the role model for the ex-communist countries in the region'.[37] By claiming this, Demirel meant that Europe needed Turkey much more than it did before - as much as Turkey needed Europe. It may be suggested that he also wanted to use Turkey's importance as a role model in order to ease entry to the EU and to show that Turkey was still important for the West because of ideological competition in the region.

After his tour of the Central Asian capitals, Özal died suddenly in April 1993[38] and Prime Minister Demirel was elected President in May 1993. He declared: 'in Central Asia we are the emissaries of Europe. We are the Europeans who are taking European values to Central Asia... We want to remain Europeans'. Evidently repudiating the ultra-nationalist vision of a Turkish 'empire' in Turkestan, Demirel stated: 'pan-Turkism, the goal of uniting all Turkic speaking nations, is utopia' (Hyman, 1994c, p.16). After Özal, Turkey's Central Asian policy was revised and a more cautious policy began to be followed.[39]

After 1991 general election, during the emergence of the Turkic Republics, the Doğru Yol Partisi (True Path Party - TPP), the Ana Vatan Partisi (Motherland Party - MP), the Sosyal Demokrat Halkçı Parti (Social Democratic Populist Party - SDPP), the Refah Partisi (Welfare Party - WP), the Milliyetçi Çalışma Partisi (Nationalist Labour Party - NLP) and the Demokratik Sol Parti (Democratic Left Party - DLP) were the main parties represented in the parliament. The political developments after the 1980 military coup are important to understand the parties and politics in Turkey. Following the coup, a new constitution was issued in 1982 by the regime and accepted by a national referendum in November 1982. In the same national referendum, General Evren who led the coup, was elected president for the next seven years. A new electoral law and a law on political parties were issued in the Spring of 1983. Pre-coup parties were not allowed to re-establish themselves officially and about seven hundred politicians, including Süleyman Demirel (leader of the Justice Party), Bülent Ecevit (leader of the Republican People's Party), Alparslan Türkeş (leader of the National Action Party) and Necmettin Erbakan (leader of the National Salvation Party) were banned from returning to formal political activity. Under the new rules fifteen new parties were founded; but only three of them were allowed to enter the general election in November 1983. These parties were the Milliyetçi Demokrasi Partisi (Nationalist Democracy Party - NDP), the Halkçı Parti (Populist Party - PP) and the Anavatan Partisi (Motherland Party - MP) which won the election. Sources cite that after 1983, Turkey moved towards an open, more liberal political system, although civil rights were somewhat more restricted than in most Western democracies (Finkel and Hale, 1990, p.104).[40]

The Motherland Party (MP) was founded by Turgut Özal, who had served as the deputy Prime Minister between September 1980 and July 1982. The MP won two general elections in 1983 and 1987 and one local election in 1984.[41] The 1987 election was a real test for the MP, as it was contested by the descendants of Adalet Partisi (Justice party - JP) which now operated under a new name, the Doğru Yol Partisi (True Path Party - TPP) and the Cumhuriyet Halk Partisi (Republican People's Party - RPP) which took the name, the Sosyal Demokrat Halkçı Parti (Social Democratic Populist Party - SDPP) (A. Ayata, 1993, p.42).[42]

The rise of the MP was unquestionably the most important aspect of Turkish party politics in the 1980s, which is interpreted differently by different researchers. The first group views the MP as an extension of the 1980 coup government. According to them, the party is corporatist in nature, an instrument in integrating the Turkish economy into world markets, essentially conservative and supported by religious and nationalist groups, an executive committee of the Turkish bourgeoisie and a reflection of the rise of the new right in Turkey.[43] According to the alternative view, however, the MP is seen as the 'initiator' of liberal revolutions, anti-bureaucratic, pluralist, modern and able to bring together a coalition including a wide range of ideological groups'.[44] The MP claimed no descent from any of the pre-1980 political parties. Instead, the party began to introduce an alternative viewpoint -a 'synthesis' of the pre-1980 ideological strands of liberalism, social democracy, nationalism and conservatism (A. Ayata, 1993, p.33).

Like other pre-coup parties, the Republican People's Party (RPP) was closed down after the 1980 coup. After the coup two new parties, the Sosyal Demokrat Parti (Social Democrat Party - SDP) and the Halk Partisi (Populist Party - PP), tried to become the heir of the RPP inheritance. This process ended up with integration, and the SDP and the PP merged to form the Sosyal Demokrat Halkçı Parti (Social Democrat Populist Party - SDPP) on November 3, 1985. The leader of the pre-coup RPP, Bülent Ecevit, became the leader of a new party- the Demokratik Sol Partisi (Democratic Left Party - DLP). In reality the RPP inheritance was divided between these three parties (A. Ayata, 1993, pp.42-43).

Demirel's pre-coup Justice Party (JP) was re-established as the True Path Party (TPP), Erbakan's Milli Selamet Partisi (National Salvation Party - NSP) as the Refah Partisi (the Welfare Party (WP) and Türkeş's Milliyetçi Hareket Partisi (National Action Party - NAP) as the Milliyetçi Çalışma Partisi (the National Labour Party - NLP). The TPP managed to enter Parliament in the 1987 elections, the WP and NLP failed to pass the national threshold, and were thus unable to send MPs to Parliament. Therefore, until the 1991 election, only three parties were represented in the Parliament: the MP, the TPP, and the SDPP.

Table 2.1   Turkish Parties Contesting the 1991 Election, and Distribution of Valid Votes and Seats

Parties	Distribution of Votes	Seats
True Path Party	6,600,726 (27.03%)	182
Motherland Party	5,862,623 (24.01%)	115
Social Democratic Populist Party	5,066,571 (20.75%)	88
Welfare Party	4,121,355 (16.88%)	62
Democratic Left Party	2,624,301 (10.75%)	7
Socialist Party	108,369 (0.44%)	-
Independents	32,721 (0.14%)	-

Source: Directorate General of Press and Information, (1993), *Turkey*, Ankara, p.39 and *Official Gazette,* 17 November 1991. TBMM.

Following a referendum on September 6, 1987, Demirel, Ecevit, Erbakan, Türkeş and about hundred other pre-coup politicians gained the right to be elected. Özal became President in 1989, and thereupon first Yıldırım Akbulut (November 1989 - June 1991) and then Mesut Yılmaz (June - November 1991) became the leaders of the MP and consequently Prime Ministers. However, Özal was the charismatic factor in getting votes for the MP and when he left the party leadership in order to become the president, the MP lost the 1991 early general election to the True Path Party. During the election campaign, both the True Path Party and the Social Democrat Populist Party promised to liberalise the constitution and the political system. At any rate, much of their economic agenda was effectively set for them by Turkey's pressing economic problems, in particular the soaring rate of inflation. A coalition government was formed by Demirel (the leader of TPP) and İnönü (the leader of SDP) in November 1991.[45]

Table 2.2 Distribution of Seats in Turkish Parliament as of January 1993

Parties	Seats
True Path Party	182
Motherland Party	94
Social Democratic Populist Party	52
Welfare Party	40
Republican People's Party	21
People's Work Party	18
Nationalist Labour Party	13
Great Unity Party	7
Democratic Left Party	3
Nation Party	2
Independents	18

Source: Turkey, Ankara: Office of the Prime minister Directorate General of Press and Information, February 1993, p.39.

The 1991 election is important because it gives a true representation of how complicated the political scene in Turkey was at the time. Six political parties contested the October 20, 1991 general elections however, under the banner of the Welfare Party, three political parties - the Welfare Party, the National Labour Party and the Reformist Democracy Party - joined forces, called themselves an alliance and entered the election. Therefore the votes and the seats won in the Parliament by the Welfare Party in 1991, in fact belonged to three parties. Another alliance was formed between the radical Kurdish politicians and the SDPP. After the general elections these alliances were broken, some new parties were established and some of the deputies resigned from their parties. The Halkın Emek Partisi (People's Work Party - HEP) was created by the radical Kurdish deputies of the SDPP. These deputies were believed to be PKK supporters and with the establishment of these new parties, the parties represented every strand, from radical Kurdish minority to Islamists and extreme nationalists.[46]

Following the general election in 1991, veteran politicians who were banned from politics after the 1980 military coup returned to Parliament. Demirel, a former centre right Prime Minister; Bülent Ecevit, the former socialist Prime Minister; Alparslan Türkeş, leader of the extreme right-wing groups; and Necmettin Erbakan, a veteran Islamist politician and leader of the Welfare Party, were among the most notable. There were also new faces, including the radical Kurdish deputies who entered the Parliament under the banner of the SDPP (Brown, 1992). While the results of the October 1991 general elections reconfirmed the strength of the conservative vote in Turkish politics, and the weakness of the left in Turkey, neither of the conservative parties were able to form a government on their own. The main centre-left party, the Social Democratic Populist Party, welcomed Demirel's offer to form a coalition. The alliance between the TPP and the SDPP in Parliament surprised several people; even former SDPP critics were impressed. 'I cannot believe my eyes and ears', one of them wrote (Laber, 1992).

While the collapse of the USSR and of the largest communist regime damaged left-wing parties worldwide, leaving them struggling to produce new economic thoughts and reorganise themselves, in Turkey the SDPP and DLP moved towards the centre. On the other hand the MP and TPP moved towards the centre as well, and the differences between them therefore became very slight. The establishment of a coalition government between the SDPP and the TPP became possible mainly because the gap between these two parties narrowed, and both of them approached the centre of the political spectrum. The left started to modify its ideas to the new situation and adopted some liberal and nationalist ideas (Karamısır, 1994, pp.80-81). This helped the emergence of a consensus in Turkish politics generally, and particularly in the coalition government which promised the most radical reform programme since Atatürk founded the republic in the 1920's.[47] However, the presence of Özal as President was a major obstacle for the government. Özal was critical of the government on economic issues, he halted civic appointments; and he advised the opening of a television channel broadcasting in the Kurdish language as a solution to 'the Kurdish problem'.[48]

Social class, religion, ethnicity and urban-rural differences are the major determinants of electoral behaviour in Turkish politics. In general it is argued that the traditional urban middle classes (small businessmen, shopkeepers, artisans) as well as the peasants are more inclined to vote for the right, while the organised working class and the new middle classes (professionals, civil servants, and so on) tend to vote for the left. Also, the Alawites, who generally backed Atatürk's secularising reforms, overwhelmingly support the leftist parties, while Sunnis overwhelmingly support the political right (A. Ayata, 1993, p.46; S. Ayata, 1993, p.65; Mango, 1993, p.736; Pevsner, 1984; Bumke, 1989, pp.511-518).[49] Since the 1950's, around 50-60 percent of the Turkish electorate has consistently voted for parties of the moderate right; hence, any party, which manages to dominate this area of the political spectrum, has had an excellent chance of winning.

After 1991 election, the centre right was divided between the Motherland and True Path parties. Both the MP and the TPP support free enterprise and the market economy, but accept the need for some government intervention and limited public ownership. They follow a moderate conservative line on social and cultural issues. Ideologically, there is little to choose between them, although the TPP seems to be slightly more aligned with small rather than big business, compared with the MP.[50]

Following the collapse of the USSR, the MP welcomed the new developments, and before transferring the power to the coalition government, all of the fifteen new Republics were recognised by Turkey on 16 December 1991 (Andican, 1993, p.24). Trends in the foreign policy of the MP can best be illustrated through the views of its prominent policy makers. Cem Kozlu (1995, pp.83-86), deputy president of the MP, regarded the Central Asian Turkic Republics as an instrument to develop Turkey's relations with Far Eastern countries such as Japan, Singapore, Thailand, Malaysia, South Korea, Taiwan and Hong Kong. Instead of promoting the Turkish Model to other countries, he advocated that the experiences of Far Eastern countries were useful for Turkey as there were similar social and cultural conditions in those countries.[51] He wanted Turkey to cooperage with Far Eastern Asian countries and make joint investments in Central Asia. In return, he argued, Turkey's relations with Far Eastern countries would develop, and because of the harsh competition for markets internationally, he wanted Turkey to consider all alternatives (Kozlu, 1995, p.86).

Kamran İnan (1993, p.71; 1995a, p.96), ex-ambassador and ex-Foreign Minister, regarded the collapse of the USSR and emergence of the Turkic Republics as historical luck, and he was critical of the style of Turkish foreign policy after 1991, and accused it of being passive and reactionary. After the emergence of the Turkic Republics, according to İnan, Turkey kept a distance between herself and the new states. An obvious example of this was, according to

İnan (1995a, p.96), the Karabakh case. In his view, instead of stopping Armenia, Turkey encouraged the Armenian occupation by offering wheat aid, opening her land and air fields to send aid to Armenia, and signing an agreement to sell energy to Armenia which was cancelled because of pressure in Turkey (İnan, 1995a, p.96). He argued that after the end of the Cold War the West and the US did not need Turkey any more, and therefore the Turkish position has been undermined in NATO; Turkish membership of the EU was abandoned, and instead Eastern European states have been given priority. On the other hand, in his view, Turkish foreign policy was passive and needed to be reformulated according to the new situation. Because of the new developments (primarily the end of the USSR), relations between the West and Russia have increased, and therefore Turkey has been left alone against the Russian threat (İnan, 1995a, pp.96-98).

The views of Agah Oktay Güner (1995, pp.152-157), a member of the Central Decision Committee of the MP, represent the more nationalist wing of the party. He underlined the importance of pan-Slavist ideology for Russia, claiming that Russia still followed this policy and thus still constituted an important threat for Turkey. Therefore, according to him, for the future of Turkish foreign policy, the importance of pan-Slavism should be taken into account.

The second party of the centre-right, the True Path Party (TPP), based its foreign policy on Atatürk's famous principle: 'Peace at home, peace in the world', and to its literal application. Until the death of Özal, Süleyman Demirel was the leader of the TPP and the Prime Minister. The attitude and reaction of Demirel as Prime Minister to the collapse of the USSR and the emergence of the Turkic Republics was summarised above. Tansu Çiller (1995, p.102), Minister of State responsible for economy (1992), and the Prime Minister after 1993, asserted that there was no place in the TPP's foreign policy for 'adventurism'. The TPP advocated the Customs Union and full membership of the EU. However, the TPP had more - right of the centre elements as well. Ayvaz Gökdemir (1995, pp.48-50), a member of the TPP and Minister of State in Demirel cabinet, regarded the end of the Soviet Union and the emergence of the Turkic Republics as a gift of destiny. He advocated the establishment of close cultural and economic relations, and warned against missing this opportunity. Similarly, Köksal Toptan, a member of the TPP and the Minister of Education in 1992, welcomed the emergence of the Turkic Republics enthusiastically, and emphasised their cultural and ethnic connections with Turkey and the necessity of establishing co-operation with them. As an initial objective, he highlighted the necessity of a common language.[52]

During Demirel and İnönü's coalition government, the MP continued to advocate Turkey's active involvement with the Turkic states, especially in the Azeri-Armenian conflict over Karabakh. Prime minister Demirel's reaction was 'If the opposition wants a military solution, they [the opposition] should go to Nahchevan and fight' (Doğan, 1993a, p.5). After the death of Özal, when Demirel became President and Tansu Çiller took his place as the Prime Minister and party leader, she claimed that the Turkish Customs Union and Turkey's efforts towards membership of the EU did not mean that Turkey turned her back on the Turkic Republics; instead, Turkey would become a gate or bridge between the Turkic Republics and the EU.[53] However, it was a cautious policy as illustrated by Çiller's own words (1995, p.121). After praising Azerbaijan and the cultural and historical ties of Turkey with the region, she added

> We do not regard Tsarist Russia or the USSR and present Russia as the same. We do not want our memories of unpleasant events that took place during Tsarist Russia and the USSR, to overshadow our friendship with Russia with which we have evolved close relations. We regard Russia, like Turkey, as a future part of the EU. We will not fight with Russia any more.

In brief, although the centre-right parties, the TPP and the MP, welcomed the emergence of the Turkic Republics, and underlined the new opportunities for Turkey, the TPP was more cautious in getting actively involved in any dispute which might endanger Turkey's security. Also, it can be added that by the end of 1993, the early euphoria about the Turkic Republics was dying away.

After the 1980 coup, the left in Turkey became very fragmented which translated to the fragmentation of the thirty to forty percent of the Turkish voters. The supporters of the banned Republican Populist Party (RPP) divided into the Populist Party (PP) and the Social Democrat Party (SDP). The division within the social democrats got worse as Ecevit established another party on the RPP's political base, the Democratic Left Party (DLP). In the 1983 election, the PP became the second majority party, however in the local elections of 1984, the SDP received more votes and as mentioned above, this forced the two parties to unite and form the Social Democrat Populist Party (SDPP) on November 3, 1985. Ecevit's DLP did not want to integrate with the other two parties and thus, the centre left ground now was occupied by two parties, the DLP and the SDPP. After the 1991 election, the SDPP became a coalition partner. When the ban on pre-coup parties was lifted, the Republican People's Party (RPP) was re-established on 9 September 1992 thus dividing the votes of the left once more.

After 1991 election, there were two parties dominating the centre left; the SDPP, under the leadership of Erdal İnönü, and the DLP, under the leadership of Bülent Ecevit; but, as mentioned above, the RPP was established by Deniz Baykal in September 1992. It is worth noting that on 18 February 1995, the SDPP and the RPP united under the banner of the RPP. All these parties claimed to favour moderate social democratic policies although Ecevit backed a more Turkish nationalist line (for instance on the Kurdish question) than the other two leftist leaders.

The SDPP claimed that integration with the EU was its aim. In its view the EU, which represented an integration of the principles of complete democracy and an organised, competitive market economy, was a social democratic project, and the customs union was a step towards integration with the EU.[54] Although the SDPP advocated full Turkish membership, it accused the EU of not obeying the treaties signed between Turkey and the EU and criticised the EU on the subjects of free movement of labour, the fourth financial protocol, rights granted to Turkey by the Ankara Treaty and on additional protocol principles.[55]

The SDPP accepted Atatürk's principal 'Peace at home, peace in the world' as the main basis for its foreign policy, which was later reflected in the foreign policy of the RPP (former SDPP and RPP). The party accuses the Western world and international institutions of double standards related to the Bosnian conflict; it wanted Armenia to withdraw from Azeri occupied territory, and peaceful solutions to the Karabakh problem and other problems in the Caucasus.[56]

The Initial reactions of the SDPP at the end of the Soviet Union and the emergence of the Turkic Republics were cool because the party regarded dealing with outer Turks as dangerous and unnecessary, and also because ideologically they had some sympathy for the USSR and were forced by its demise to reconsider their thinking and move towards the centre of the political spectrum (Karamısır, 1994, p.80). However, as Ayata pointed out, after being faced with the reality of the Turkic Republics, the cool attitude was replaced by a warm welcome.[57] For example, as noted above, Hikmet Çetin, a member of the SDPP and Foreign Minister in 1992, said that it was natural for Turkey to seek close co-operation with the Muslim Republics because of a shared history, religion, ethnic ties and language (Smolansky, 1994, p.283), and that Turkey supported Azerbaijan and did not accept the changing of borders by means of forceful occupation (Çetin, 1995, pp.56-57).

Like Çetin, Murat Karayalçın, a member and later leader of the SDPP, argued that after the end of the Cold War there were new opportunities as well as new risks (the conflicts in Bosnia and Karabakh) for Turkey. He also underlined that Armenia was the aggressor and that if Armenia withdrew from Azerbaijan good relations between Turkey and Armenia could be re-established (Karayalçın, 1995, pp.46-47).

Although after the 1995 elections the DLP became the largest centre left party, furthermore, largest political party of Turkey following 1999 general elections, during the 1991-1995 period it was weaker than the SDPP, (represented by seven deputies in Parliament). According to its leader Ecevit, 'to give extensive freedom to religious beliefs' was a necessity of pluralist democracy as well as of secularism.[58] Hence, one of the differences between the SDPP and the DLP was that the latter promised to put secularism into real action and guaranteed freedom for different religious beliefs.[59] Ecevit drew attention to an interesting point when he said: 'if we became friends and allies with those countries which occupied our country seventy years ago, why should not we become friends within ourselves?'.[60] He was of course talking about the religious minorities in Turkey, specifically about the Alawi-Sunni dispute. The DLP wanted Turkey to use all its potential to be a regional power and follow a region-oriented foreign policy, and it criticised close relations between Turkey and the US. For example, Turkey's support for the US in the Gulf War was criticised by the DLP, which argued that Turkey had problems with its region and thus should have not used its influence in the war. According to the DLP, because of the deficiency of this policy, Turkey was unable to use the opportunities created by the end of the USSR.[61]

Ecevit's foreign policy adviser Ertuğrul O. Çırağan emphasised that in the 1987 election report, Ecevit asserted that the USSR would disintegrate, and that he wanted to initiate relations with the Turkic Republics even then. Çırağan also explained that the DLP did regard the end of the USSR as the disappearance of a threat to Turkey. Although he underlined the new opportunities created by the end of the USSR, he criticised the claim that 'a Turkish world from the Adriatic to the Great Wall of China' was born because this claim was used as an instrument in domestic politics and it had an effect on the rebirth of pan-Turkic ideology.[62]

In general, left-wing parties were initially reluctant to deal with the 'outer Turks' and they tended to criticise those who dealt with them and they were not terribly impressed when the Turkic Republics declared independence. A former academic and a leftist MP[63] argued in a speech in Parliament that 'there are too many little Enver Pashas around'.[64]

The cool initial reaction of the left changed gradually. Ministers of the SDPP and the leftist parties in general became interested in the collapse of the Soviet Union and again, the leader of the DLP Bülent Ecevit led the way. He wanted the government to form a special ministry responsible for the 'outer Turks' (Devlet, 1993, pp.5-6). He also argued that Turkey must involve itself more actively in the Karabakh conflict. This angered the pan-Turkists. A deputy of the National Labour Party (NLP) Oktay Öztürk said: 'Those who once had us tortured in prisons because we were Turanists, now do not regard the measures taken by the state as sufficient, and they hold press conferences and declare the necessity of the establishment of a ministry for outer Turks' (Anadol, 1995b, p.316).[65]

After 1991 election, the main parties of Islamic and Ultra-nationalist Right in

Turkey were Welfare Party and Nationalist Labour Party. Until the 1995 general election, ten to twenty percent of Turkish electors supported the Islamic and extreme-nationalist right. However, support for these parties increased sharply in 1995 general election. Support for the Welfare party was 7.1% in 1987, which increased to 16.9% in the 1991 elections. However, it must be noted that, as mentioned above, in the 1991 election the National Labour Party (NLP) and the Reformist Democracy Party (RDP) entered the election under the banner of the Welfare Party, and therefore this support was in fact for all these parties. Support for the Welfare party increased to 21.1% in 1995 general election and became largest political party in Turkey. The Welfare Party was closed down by the decision of Turkish Constitution Court in 1998, as the Court believed that Welfare Party's activities violated principle of Secularism in Turkish Constitution (Article 2). Then Virtue Party (Fazilet Partisi) was established as a successor to the Welfare Party. The support for the new party was 18% in 1999 general election. However, there is a case in the Constitution Court against Virtue Party (Fazilet Partisi) and some circles claim that this party will be closed down by the court as well.

In 1990s, the main Islamist party of Turkey was the Welfare Party, the successor to the National Salvation Party (NSP), led by Necmettin Erbakan. However, this does not mean that only this party took Turkey's Muslim votes; in fact other centre-right and right wing parties have always enjoyed considerable support from the more religious voters. At the same time, since around ninety-nine percent of Turkey's population is Muslim, it is not strange to see a person who prays five times a day giving his vote to a centre-left party, and apart from small far left-wing parties, all other parties take (especially) Sunni Muslim feelings into account.

The Welfare Party[66], differed from the others in that it advocated spiritual development as a means to general development[67] and what it called a 'just economic system', in which there is no place for interest rates.[68] The Welfare Party claimed that it would make Turkey a leader state not a 'satellite', and that the European Union was established with the advice of Pope Pius XII, and that therefore the place of Turkey was not in the EU but in the unity of Muslim countries.[69] The Welfare Party also advocated a United Nations of Muslim Countries, an Islamic alliance similar to NATO and Common Market, a common currency for Muslim countries, and a Cultural Co-operation Institution of Muslim countries (Brown, 1992).[70] Thus, the emergence of the Turkic Republics presented a suitable new target for the Welfare Party in its attempts to draw together the Islamic world. It saw good relations with the Turkic Republics as an important step towards the final objective: Islamic unity. The WP urged the government to be more active, and in the case of the Karabakh conflict, it wanted direct intervention.[71]

After the 1980 military coup, the main ultra nationalist party in Turkey was the Nationalist Labour Party. When the ban on pre-coup parties was lifted the name of this party was changed to National Action Party (NAP) led by retired Colonel Alparslan Türkeş until his sudden death on April 1997. Following the death of Türkeş, Devlet Bahçeli became leader of this party in 1997. In early 1990s, support for this party has increased to some nine percent. But the main increase took place in 1999 general election and the support to this party reached to 21% and this party became second largest political party after DLP. This result was determined by several factors: Firstly, the activities of the PKK caused an increase in national feelings, which made the NAP popular. Secondly, the end of the USSR and the emergence of the new Turkic Republics was seen by some to confirm the pan-Turkist ideas of Türkeş. Finally, Bahçeli's moderate interpretations of Turkish nationalism and pan-Turkism helped the people to welcome this ideology. It was reported that 'before the outlawing of various warring political parties during the martial law take-over in 1980, Ülkücüler [the supporters of pan-Turkism] were... certainly the largest 'rightist' unit in the nation' (Copher, 1992). The main objective of Türkeş and the several political parties he had founded had been 'the protection of Turkish values and the spread of pan-Turkism' (Copher, 1992). For example, the early political speeches by Colonel Türkeş called for the 'liberation' of the 'captive Turks' in places like the Thrace, Iraq, Bulgaria and Soviet Central Asia. Even in 1944, Alparslan Türkeş, while defending himself before the court, confirmed that he supported the idea of uniting all Turks under a single banner (Türkeş, p.276).[72] In general, Türkeş saw the US forces in Turkey as assisting the struggle against communism, and as Copher pointed out, Turkey's need for self-sufficiency and military/economic strength put Türkeş in the position of supporting the active recruiting of foreign investors and industrial interests (Copher, 1992, pp.42-43).

Like Erbakan, Türkeş underlined a spiritual crisis as the main problem of Turkey: 'not even one nation can survive without spirituality' (Türkeş, 1995, p.10). He also opposed the use of foreign languages in universities and singled out sexism as a barrier to the development of Turkish youth (Anadol, 1995b, p.337). Türkeş also made statements similar to those of Erbakan. For example, on the Gulf War Türkeş said 'Allah is one and likes oneness, therefore as an Islamic world we should act for unity', but he stressed the important position of Turks within the Islamic world as a defender of the rest of the Islamic World - like an armour. He pointed out that although Islamic countries had valuable resources, at present they constituted a market for the West (Anadol, 1995b, pp.342-343). Türkeş's claim that Turkey's spiritual crises was one of the main problems of the country is very similar to the Welfare Party's spiritual development program; maybe because of these common objectives, these parties managed to enter the 1991 election together under the banner of the Welfare Party.

Recalling Erbakan's 'Milli Görüş' (National View), Türkeş proposed 'Dokuz Işık' (Nine Lights) as a doctrine for development. According to Türkeş, this doctrine is national, one hundred percent local, and tied to Turkey's religion, Islam, and it sees Islam as its basis and is respectful to national culture, tradition and history, while also regarding modern science as a guide (Türkeş, 1995, p.16).[73] Türkeş criticised other parties on the subject of the outer Turks: 'when we talked about outer Turks, they used to accuse us of being pan-Turkist and fascist. However, now (after the end of the USSR) everyone has seen the reality...'(Anadol, 1995a, p.277).

The similarities between the WP and the NAP suggest that there is not a sharp distinction between nationalism, Islamism, Turkism or Turanism in Turkey. Turkism does not mean pure racism, in fact this movement advocates Islam and Turkish culture and regards Islam as a basic factor in Turkish culture. While the NAP tries to base its ideology partially on Islam, the WP was not purely a pan-Islamist party. They both regard Turkey as the leader of the Islamic world rather than its follower, they both advocate Turkish culture and Islam in similar ways. Maybe the most important distinction between the two parties is with respect to their attitudes towards secularism. While the WP claimed that secularism as a principle was an unnecessary article of the Turkish constitution[74], Türkeş believed in its necessity: 'Sharia is a big threat for Turkey. Therefore, all citizens should embrace secularism tightly. The principle of secularism should be kept in all circumstances. All of us are Muslims, therefore we should not allow religion to be used'.[75]

Türkeş wanted the Turkish government to improve relations with the Turkic Republics on all fronts, and warned that if this were not the case, the gap could be filled by Iran and Saudi Arabia. He emphasised that a careful policy should be followed towards Armenia defending the Azeri case in the Karabakh conflict. He claimed that the collapse of China as well had begun with events in Tianmen Square, and that Marxism as a system had collapsed (Anadol, 1995b, p.326).

In an interview with Komsomolskya Pravda, after claiming that his party was nationalist but not racist, and therefore its nationalism was acceptable in Islam, Türkeş said: 'we do not want to unite all Turks under the one state but we want all Turks to live under the guarantee of human rights. We want people to be free. The NAP wants peace and brotherhood, not conflict in the international arena' (Anadol, 1995b, p.329). He then underlined that they were interested in the problems of Turks wherever they lived (Anadol, 1995b, p.334).

After the collapse of the Soviet Union, in a conference speech delivered to students at Konya Selçuk University, Türkeş reiterated his statement about Turkish unity, saying

Of course, Turkish unity will take place one day ... Turkey's leadership of the newly established Central Asian Republics in all issues is very important ... Of course, Turkish unity will take place one day but imperialists and foreign powers which oppose this brought the Kurdish problem, the PKK, in front of Turkey. Kurds are our brothers. We have been living together for nine hundred and twenty years. Kurds are a clan of the Turks. We should be aware of this separatism trick (Anadol, 1995b, p.299).

This statement suggests that although Türkeş sometimes claimed that his party was not trying to unite all Turks under the banner of one state, in reality this (pan-Turkism) constituted a main characteristic of his party.

In Turkey's relations with the Turkic Republics, Türkeş underlined the common alphabet as an important factor for the future of relations (Anadol, 1995b, pp.357-358). Like Ecevit, he emphasised the need for a special ministry for the 'outer Turks'. According to him this ministry should deal with all Turks living outside Turkey, from Australia to the US (Anadol, 1995b, p.359).

During Demirel's government, although the NAP was not a coalition partner, it was acting as if it were. Türkeş supported the government's policy towards the Turkic Republics and in return, the government asked Türkeş for his opinion, especially on subjects related with the Turkic Republics. Türkeş was sometimes used in formulating the Turkish foreign policy, for example, before the elections in Azerbaijan, Elchibey was supported by Türkeş on the request of the Turkish government (Anadol, 1995a, p.76). During his trip to Azerbaijan and Central Asia with Prime Minister Demirel (1992) Türkeş was welcomed warmly in Azerbaijan (Anadol, 1995b, p.301). According to the leader of the Azerbaijan Mehebbet Partisi, Cumsud (Iskenderov) Abdullahoğlu, 1,200,000 people gathered in Azadlık Square in Baku on 3 May 1992; this crowd welcomed and clapped Elchibey and Türkeş with enthusiasm, and in his speeches, Türkeş urged Azeris to support Elchibey (Anadol, 1995b, pp.303-304, 309). Copher claimed that at the age of 75, Türkeş was stronger in the Muslim Central Asian Republics than he ever dreamed he would be in his own homeland (Copher, 1992, p.43).

In brief, for Turkish politicians, the meaning of the collapse of the Soviet Union was much more than the collapse of communism. After the collapse, with the exceptions of the Kurdish left and Marxist left[76], all the main parties, even those who had criticised dealings with the 'outer Turks' in the past, began to take an interest in the Turkic Republics as these developments were seen as creating new opportunities for Turkey. With the end of the Soviet Union the issue of 'outer Turks' started to occupy the political agenda, and Turkish politicians in general welcomed the creation of a 'Turkish world from the Adriatic to China' with enthusiasm. Demirel and his ministers, regardless of their parties (SDPP-TPP), reacted positively to the collapse of the Soviet Union and underlined the new opportunities it created. They also stated that it was natural for Turkey to establish close relations with these republics because of their common cultural values, ethnicity and history. Turkish officials believed that Turkey was the leader of the Turkic world, and must therefore show the true path to the other Turks (Toker, 1992, pp.166,175,181). The common positive reaction to the emergence of the Turkic Republics was epitomised by Türkeş, the leader of the NAP, who had pushed this issue since the 1940's and therefore had become a figurehead.

Elite and Intellectuals

Kemalist Turkey defined itself as part of the Western civilisation. However, 'despite strenuous efforts to reject their Ottoman past, the Turkish elite remained undeniably Ottoman in outlook and upbringing' (Deringil, 1992, p.1). The first cracks in the superficial unity of the Turkish elite came to surface in the post-1946 era with the beginning of the multi-party system. 'It is around this time that the 'identity crisis' relating to Turkey's role in the world would emerge. The resurgence of Islam and the Democratic Party's concessions to conservative feeling, such as the return of Arabic in the daily call to prayer, would be the beginning of serious soul searching' (Deringil, 1992, p.7) but, the critical break in the pattern did not appear until the mid-1980s, when for the first time a Turkish Prime Minister (i.e. Özal) openly attended Friday prayers and performed the pilgrimage to Mecca (Deringil, 1992, p.8). Özal, who was a liberal politician in economic issues, had some relations with and sympathy towards the Nakşibendi tarikat and in the 1980's and 1990's the importance of tarikats increased in parliament and the administration and generally in the society.

Before the 1980 military coup, roughly speaking, Turkish intellectuals were divided as leftists and rightists in varying degrees, or according to how they perceived communism. Following the shock of the military coup, the collapse of the USSR in 1991 had great impact on the Turkish elite, because it indicated the victory of capitalism over communism. While the Turkic Republics were gaining their independence, the formation of the Turkish elite changed from being generally bipolar, divided between anti-communism and pro-communism, to being multipolar and adopting more liberal and nationalist lines with the exception of a small group of hard-core Marxist intellectuals. Meanwhile, the nationalist and pro-

Sunni attitudes were openly expressed, which in return contributed to the rise of ethnic and religious minority problems. Alawites turned to the defence of their sect and began to make demands from the state and the Kurdish left dedicated themselves completely to separatism.

Turkish intellectuals and higher bureaucrats stressed the political and economic advantages of the new developments for Turkey. For Seyfi Taşan (head of the Foreign Policy Institute) and Bilal Şimşir (Ambassador and Foreign Ministry Director-General of Relations with the CIS), Turkey was transformed from being marginal to Western security interests to being a central power in the region and that the Western democracies should inject large amounts of economic aid into the new Republics using Turkey as an intermediary. In saying so they regarded Turkey as a natural broker in the region.[77]

In the same manner, Ambassador Umit Arık, (President of Turkish International Co-operation Agency (TICA)), regarded Turkey as a window from the Turkic Republics to the world, and vice versa. Apart from BSEC and the ECO, he also underlined the necessity of creating a co-operation zone which he called 'The Co-operation Region of Caucasian and Inner Asian Turkic States' (Kafkasya ve İç Asya Türk Devletleri işbirliği Bölgesi) among the Turkic Republics, including Turkey.[78]

The economic benefits of the new developments began to occupy the agenda immediately. Memduh Hacıoğlu, President of the Council of Istanbul's Association of Manufacturers, argued that the Turkic Republics created a suitable market for Turkish industry - more so than Western markets. On the other hand, he singled out certain fields such as space technology and medical technology, which was more advanced in the Turkic Republics than in Turkey. Therefore in this case, according to him, the Turkic Republics could be of assistance to Turkey (Hacıoğlu, 1992, p.3).

At the third İzmir Economy Conference (4-7 June 1992)[79], Turkey's relations with the Turkic Republics were discussed. While Nihat Gökyiyit, President of the Turkish-CIS Work Council, stressed the importance of small and medium-sized enterprises in developing economic relations with the Turkic Republics, Erol Manisalı, President of the European and Middle Eastern Studies Association, proposed the establishment of a 'Türk Cumhuriyetleri Ekonomik Bölgesi' (Economic Zone of Turkic Republics), and suggested that it would be desirable for the public and private sectors to act on this. In general it was emphasised at this conference that co-operation with the Turkic Republics, which were rich in natural resources, would provide political and economic opportunities for Turkey.[80]

In an interview, Gültekin Köksal (President of the Executive Committee of Pet Holding), expressed how they regarded the post-Soviet situation as having great potential for Turkish businessmen, and generally as a historical opportunity. He also advised Turkish businessmen to act quickly, as other states and their companies were interested in investing in the Turkic Republics. He advised the Turkish businessmen to choose their areas of investment carefully, maintain stability and not to undermine Turkish credibility, which he claimed was very high in these Republics.[81]

The general feeling in Turkey was that the economic structures of Turkey and the Turkic Republics were such that they could complement each other, but Turkish assistance was necessary in their transformation to market economy. The establishment of an economic co-operation zone and/or loose integration without violating present treaties with the EFTA and EU, and the establishment of a free trade zone similar to the EFTA were suggested (Karluk, 1992, pp.20-24).[82]

The Turkish elite was not blind to the problems the new situation presented. They emphasised the continuing importance of Russia and the Turkic Republics' dependence on it. More importantly, Turkey had a weak economy and a secret war in South East Anatolia, and without solving these problems it would be difficult for Turkey to function in the former Soviet Union (Baykara, 1992).

Even those who stressed Turkey's status as a role model, argued that the CIS might survive for some time because of the dependence of the Republics' economies on each other but that political divisions would eventually appear followed by demands for economic independence, and this could cause the emergence of politically and economically independent Republics (Güvemli, 1992, pp.12-16). Others talked of the superiority of a centrally controlled socialist system in terms of equal opportunities in education and a high literacy rate, skilled workers, infrastructure (roads, metros, water supplies, sewage systems, parks), and balance in the population between urban and rural habitants; and that the presence of large, organised agricultural enterprises was an advantage for those countries, since divided land could cause a decline in productivity (R. Bozkurt, 1992, pp.25-28). Meanwhile, Marxist intellectuals felt the need to re-examine their stance. For example, in the İktisat Dergisi (April 1992), published by the Association of the Graduates of the Faculty of Economy, Marxist intellectuals Metin Çulhaoğlu, Zülfü Dicleli, Ender Helvacıoğlu, Ertuğrul Kürkçü, Ömer Laçiner, Saruhan Oluç and Sungur Savran discussed the future of socialism and its validity. They all underlined that socialism had not died, and resolved to work for socialism and be patient in their cause. It was noted that the presence of Cuba and China should not be forgotten.[83]

Table 2.3 Central and West Asian Countries Assessment Survey
(All points over 10)

Questions / Countries	Kazakstan	Kirgizstan	Uzbekistan	Turkmenistan	Azerbaijan	General
Interest in Turks	3.70	5.9	7.9	7.2	8.6	6.6
Comprehension of Turkish	2.6	3.9	6.0	6.3	8.8	5.5
Awareness of Independence	3.9	4.7	6.6	5.7	8.7	5.9
Degree to which Turkic-origin people control government	3.5	4.5	6.0	5.8	7.6	5.5
General level of welfare	5.7	5.0	6.5	4.6	6.1	5.6
General potential for investment	4.4	4.3	6.6	5.2	6.9	5.6
Efficiency of communication	1.6	1.0	2.5	2.0	4.8	2.5
Efficiency of transportation	2.9	2.5	3.6	3.0	6.1	3.6
Ease of finding responsible authority	3.0	3.0	5.5	4.9	6.1	4.6
Closeness to Turkish culinary traditions	3.5	4.4	5.6	5.2	6.9	5.1
Efficiency of hotels	4.0	4.1	5.8	2.6	4.4	4.2
Cultural closeness to Turkey	3.3	5.0	7.1	6.9	8.0	6.1
Degree of modernisation and urbanisation	6.9	6.7	7.7	6.0	7.4	6.9
Availability of goods	4.2	4.3	5.3	3.9	5.4	4.6
Potential for 'suitcase trade'	3.2	3.3	4.3	3.4	5.3	3.9
Degree of ethnic integration	5.1	4.9	5.4	5.2	4.9	5.1
Affinity to old regime	6.1	5.6	4.6	5.2	2.9	4.9
Degree of religious feeling	3.0	3.6	5.7	4.9	5.3	4.5
Comprehension of market economy	3.4	3.5	4.9	3.6	6.0	4.3
Development of private sector	3.0	2.8	3.8	2.5	5.0	3.4
Potential for small businesses	4.2	4.3	5.5	4.4	6.3	4.9
Suitability for long-term investment	4.2	4.1	5.7	4.2	6.4	4.9
Potential for joint ventures with native companies	3.9	3.9	5.7	4.4	6.4	4.9
Suitability for immigration from Turkey	3.5	3.6	5.5	4.0	6.5	4.6
Degree of freedom of thought	3.7	3.9	5.2	4.2	6.5	4.7
General	3.9	4.2	5.6	4.6	6.3	

Source: 'TOBB Türk Cumhuriyetleri İnceleme ve Araştırma Gezisi' (12-21 April 1992), an unpublished report prepared by TOBB.

Turkic Republics were visited by hordes of Turkish elite, bureaucrats and businessmen. As Ayata argued, these visits affected the Turkish left in a positive way because they realised that people there spoke similar languages and had positive feelings about Turkey. This led them to take an interest in the issue and change their initial cool reaction. On the other hand these visits and meetings with Turkic peoples negatively affected the Turkish right, especially the extreme right. They realised that the people of the Turkic Republics had been deeply affected by seventy years of Communist rule, that they were not good Muslims and the languages were not that similar. In other words, the emotions and the high expectations of the right declined; on the other hand the cool reaction of the Turkish left was replaced by a positive image of Turkic people, and the left adopted nationalist feelings.[84]

A survey conducted by Türkiye Odalar ve Borsalar Birliği, TOBB (Union of Turkish Chambers and Bourses) among the intellectuals, bureaucrats, businessmen and press members who took part in a visit to the Turkic Republics (12-21 April 1992) organised by TOBB showed that Azerbaijan and Uzbekistan were seen as the countries most suited to co-operation with Turkey. The TOBB survey report suggested that a co-operation or common economic field project similar to the BSEC should be developed.[85]

The Turkish elite was aware of Turkey's fragile position in the area. The multi-faceted aspect of Turkey's position was summarised in the words of a Turkish industrialist: 'When we pray we Turks face south to Mecca. When we do business we face West to Europe. When it comes to politics we may now start facing east to the rediscovered Turkic World'.[86]

The Media

In the 1990's, the total circulation of all the national dailies in Turkey averaged three million, and nine of these newspapers have an average daily circulation of over 50,000. The majority of the dailies have their headquarters in Istanbul and are distributed nationally. Aside from the nationally circulated newspapers there are more than 700 local newspapers with circulations varying from 500 to 10,000. The circulation of weekly political magazines varies from between 10,000 to 50,000. Satirical magazines are also very popular with a total weekly circulation of around 600,000.[87]

Table 2.4 Turkish Newspapers with Daily Circulations of over 50,000 (as of September 1992)

Newspaper	Daily Circulation
Sabah	722,950
Hürriyet	619,579
Milliyet	394,598
Türkiye	312,771
Bugün	179,188
Zaman	122,457
Cumhuriyet	62,081

Source: Directorate General of Press and Information, (1993), *Turkey*, Ankara, p.184.

Turkish TV, which started in 1968 in black and white as Turkish Radio and Television (TRT) under state control, went over to colour in July 1982 and since then not only the number of channels offered by TRT increased but also the state monopoly was raised. There are a total of 261 TV channels (16 of them broadcast nation-wide) and 1201 radio stations (36 of them broadcast nation-wide) in Turkey.[88] Among the most interesting developments is the TRT AVRASYA channel, which began to broadcast via satellite to the Turkic Republics in 1992.

The Turkish media was not ready for the 'emancipation' of the Turkic Republics in 1991, however it welcomed the new developments and began to send correspondents to the area, and frequently provided news from the Turkic world. For example, in 1992 Sabah newspaper issued an introductory booklet for each Republic, in what was called the 'Turkic Republics Series'.[89] Almost all the newspapers published a series of articles about the Turkic Republics. For example, the DLP leader Bülent Ecevit prepared a series of articles (called 'Hazardan Tiyenşan'a') about the Turkic Republics for the Yeni Günaydın newspaper, published between 1-12 February 1992.[90] In this publication, Ecevit underlined Turkey's position as a secular democratic model for the new Turkic Republics.[91] In a similar way, Yeni Hafta newspaper gave its readers introductory information about the Republics in a series called 'Mercek'. Not only the Turkic Republics but other Turkic people in the Russian Federation were introduced, and general information was given. Also Yeni Hafta supplied introductory information about the Saha (Yakut) Autonomous Republic.[92] On the other hand, Zaman, an Islamic-nationalist newspaper, welcomed the collapse of the USSR and the emergence of the Turkic Republics, and it even began to be published in the Turkic Republics. Nationalist magazines such as Türk Tarih Dergisi, Türk Kültürü, Türk Yurdu etc., and the nationalist liberal Yeni Forum, welcomed the developments and several articles were devoted to the subject in each issue. Türk Dünyası Tarih Dergisi, Türk Dünyası Araştırmaları (periodical), Doğu Türkistan'ın Sesi (periodical), Türk Yurdu Dergisi, and the Turkish Review (a government publication) published articles on the Turkic world. Meanwhile new periodicals and magazines came into existence, such as Eurasian Studies (Avrasya Etüdleri) and Avrasya Dosyası (Eurasian File) published by TICA, İpek Yolu (in Russian and in Turkish), Türk Dünyası (published by the Turkish Ministry of Culture), all subsidised by the Turkish state.

While the new opportunities were underlined by all the printed press and broadcasts, liberal and right wing media urged the governments to take a more active role in the Turkic Republics.[93] Although the left-wing media in general was interested in the issue, there were also unwelcoming responses to the new developments. For example, 2000'e Doğru magazine that represented the Marxist stance, criticised the emergence of the Turkic Republics.[94]

A conference titled 'The Role of the Media in Developing Ties with the Turkic Republics' (Türk Cumhuriyetlerinin Tanışmasında ve Yakınlaşmasında Basının rolü) organised by TICA took place between 20-21 October 1993 in Istanbul. At this conference the need for an international news agency of Turkic Peoples was stressed because news circulation in the world was controlled by international news agencies which reported the news in a way to fit their own views.[95] The Turkish press (especially the economic press) was urged to help the media of the Turkic Republics, and the need for every newspaper to have a specialist on the area and a correspondent in these Republics was underlined. At the end of this conference it was decided to establish the Eurasia Press Organisation (Avrasya Basın Birliği).[96]

Turkish Public Opinion

The feelings of the Turkish public for the Turkic Republics were initially surprise, like finding long lost relatives. The Karabagh conflict was the only test case which showed how strongly the Turkish people felt for fellow Turkic peoples [although it is true that Turks feel a particularly strong sympathy for Azerbaijan (Pipes and Clawson, 1993, p.135)], and there was public pressure on the Turkish government to intervene on the side of Azerbaijan.[97] When the Turkish media portrayed Turkish-speaking Azeris as victims of highly trained and well-armed Armenians, and showed Azeris begging for help in a language which everyone understood, Turkish people began to advocate sending weapons and troops to assist their poorly-armed Turkic cousins, so much so that after demonstrations in Ankara and other cities urging Turkish military support for the Azeris, Prime Minister Demirel angrily commented 'We are not going to be run by the street'.[98] Later, he admitted to President Bush: 'I am under very heavy pressure. There are meetings and demonstrations, and they even call on the government to resign. This is a democratic country and, at some point, we won't be able to resist public opinion. It might become a conflict like the Arabs and Israelis'.[99] One may argue that because of this public opinion, during an official visit in the spring of 1993, President Özal declared that Turkey could interfere in the conflict on the side of Azerbaijan and that 'there is a need to scare the Armenians a little bit' (Yılmaz, 1994, p.95). These remarks were pushed aside by his Prime Minister Demirel who regarded them as 'completely irresponsible', and insisted in the interview that the policy of his government was to stay out of the conflict and use diplomatic means to try to halt the fighting.[100] There have been no other cases of conflict in the Turkic Republics where the Turkish public has felt so emotional about.

Table 2.5 Survey Among Turkish People (İzmir-Manisa-Edremit, May-July 1993); Distribution of People According to Cities and Professions

Professions	İzmir	Manisa	Edremit	Total
Workers	109	32	-	141
Traders	82	5	5	92
Student	30	5	32	67
Civil Servant	37	8	22	67
University student	58	-	-	58
House wife	34	4	-	38
Driver	25	3	-	28
Pensioner	17	1	1	19
Unknown	6	-	-	6
Farmer	-	3	-	3
Total	398	61	60	519

Although it is commonly agreed that the Turkish public has sympathy towards the Turkic Republics mainly for cultural and ethnic reasons, I wanted to reassess Turkish public opinion by conducting a modest survey of my own during May-June 1993 which involved 519 people living in İzmir, Manisa and Edremit (see Table 2.5). To this end, I prepared ten questions, assessing the reactions and attitudes of Turkish people to the emergence of the Turkic Republics.

In the first question it was attempted to have the answer of the question that although it was reality that the people of Turkey and peoples of post-Soviet Turkic states are from the same origin, do Anatolian Turks think in this way and what is their concept of the Turkic World? 506 participants answered this question. Out of this number, 484(95.652%) participants answered first question by choosing option 'a' which emphasises that Azeries, Kirgizes, Kazaks, Turkmens, etc. and Turks of Turkey are from the same origin and race sharing the same culture. Only 22(4.347%) participants answered this question by choosing 'b' which emphasises that only Turks of Turkey are real Turks, and others are different.

In the second question, it was attempted to find that although ethnicity, religion, language, tradition are underlined as important factors that bound Turks of Turkey and people of Turkic republics, which factor was the most important one? Participants were asked what was the most important unifying factor for Turkic World. Six different options were given; race (a), religion(b), tradition (c), economic interest (d), military (strategic) interest (e), language (f). It should be noted here that people were having difficulty in answering this question. Although one answer was preferred, some participants chose more than one option. 273 (46.428%) participants out of 588 chose religion as the most important unifying factor for Turkic people. 223 (37.925%) out of 588 participants chose race as the unifying factor. Answers to this question suggested that religion and race were most important factors.

In the third and sixth questions, it was attempted to get expectations of Turkish people from the relations between Turkey and Turkic republics. To this end in the third question it was asked that 'do you believe that there would be a close relation between Turkey and Turkic republics; to extend that economic co-operation and later even a political unity would take place'. 508 participants answered this question. 93 (%18.3) participants chose option 'a' that was 'No, I do not believe. It is impossible to talk about integration as all Turkic republics are independent states; each of them will continue its own way'. 369 (%72.6) participants chose option 'b' that was 'Yes, I believe and want that there will be such unity. However, naturally there will be some difficulties'. 46 (%9) participants chose option 'c' that was 'I do not know'. The sixth question was similar to third question, and aimed to establish the long-term expectations (if there were any) of Turkish people. It was asked that 'Will Turkey and the Turkic republics, by means of integration, establish a strong Turkish unity that will be an important state in the next century?' 512 participants answered this question. 97 (18.95%) participants chose option 'a' which was 'No, such thing can not take place'. On the other hand, 415 (81.05%) participants chose option 'b', which was 'Yes I believe so, and I want this'. These answers suggested that in 1993, Turkish public opinion was very enthusiastic, and Turkish people had long-term expectations such as Turkish unity. One can argue that the statements made by politicians, including Turkish presidents, such as 'The next century will belong to the Turks', 'A Turkish world from the Adriatic Sea to the Great Wall of China was born', and others along similar lines, were adopted by the public which regarded these statements as realities. In fact, these statements were usually made for domestic political reasons and as Taşhan points out, were disturbing to Turkey's allies,[101] but the Turkish public believed these statements and wanted the Turkish governments to take active measures in this direction.[102]

In the fourth question, it was asked that 'do you believe that Turkish language (Anatolian Turkish) would be a single language of Turkish world?' 514 participants answered this question. 393 (76.46%) participants chose option 'a' which was 'Yes, it will be so', 121 (23.55%) participants chose option 'b' which was 'No, it can not be so'. These answers given to this question can be regarded also as a good indicator of Turkish public's enthusiasm. However, it should not be forgotten that other factors that shaped Turkish public opinion such as, culture, media, statements of politicians should be taken in to account as well.

In the fifth question it was asked that 'Do you believe that close relations between Turkey and Turkic republics will provide economic interest for Turkey and Turkic republics?' 507 participants answered this question. 464 (91.52%) participants chose option 'a' which was 'Yes, it will provide economic interest for both side'. 43 (8.48%) participants chose option 'b' which was 'No, it will not be economically beneficial for both side'.

Although as mentioned above there was a public pressure on Turkish government to intervene to the Azeri Armenian conflict on the side of Azerbaijan, in the seventh question, it was attempted to get a more sophisticated reaction of the Turkish people to the Azeri-Armenian war. Answers to this question ratified public pressure on the Turkish government: it was found that 191 participants, nearly 38 (37.74%) per cent of the surveyed people wanted Turkey to intervene in the Azeri-Armenia conflict on the side of Azerbaijan immediately (option-a). 245 participants, nearly 49 (48.41%) per cent of others wanted Turkey to use economic and political instruments, then, if these are not enough, to intervene in the war on the side of Azerbaijan (option-b). Only 70 (13.8%) participants agreed with the statement that Azerbaijan and Armenia are independent states and they should solve their problems themselves (option-c).

In the eight question, it was asked that 'In the future, by integrating with Russians and other minorities, Turkic republics will be under Russian sovereignty similar to the USSR'. 511 participants answered this question. 192 (37.57%) participants chose option 'a' which was 'It is impossible that such a thing can happen'. 32 (6.26%) participants chose option 'b' which was 'Yes, Turkic republics will be under Russian sovereignty again'. 287 (56.16%) participants chose option 'c' which was 'If Turkic republics do not develop their relations with each others and with Turkey and weaken their states, such danger always exist'. This result suggested that although Turkish people welcomed the emergence of the Turkic republics and they were enthusiastic, nearly 63 (62.42%) per cent of the surveyed people had some doubts about future of the Turkic republics. They consider Russia as a threat to the independence of the Turkic republics unless they develop their relations with each other and Turkey. Therefore, in this case it is possible to regard Turkish public opinion as realist rather than visionary.

In the ninth question, it was attempted to get the attitudes of Turkish people towards EU and Turkic republics. Therefore it was asked that 'Which foreign policy principle given below do you favour?'. 497 participants answered this question. 105 (21.12%) participants chose option 'a' that was 'Turkey should try to enter EU with her all strength and in order not to shadow her relations with EU, she should limit her relation with Turkic republics'. 261 (52.51%) participants chose option 'b' that was 'Turkey should try to establish a Turkish Community with Turkic republics and she should abandon trying to enter EU'. 131 (26.35%) participants chose option 'c' that was 'Turkey should be bridge between the East and West and therefore she should gave up the idea of entering EU and establishing a Turkish Unity. With such an independent policy, Turkey can became more efficient state'. This survey suggested that although to enter EU is one of the main objectives of Turkish foreign policy, Turkish public is not that much enthusiastic about entering EU. 78.86% of the surveyed people did not want to Turkish entrance to the EU. While 26.35% of surveyed people favour an independent policy and want Turkey to be a bridge between East and West instead of trying to enter EU or trying to create a Turkish unity, 52.51% of the surveyed people favoured to establish close relations with Turkic republics, further more they favour trying to establish Turkish Community. If we attempt to find the reason of this trend, it can be suggested that after the recent developments, Turkey's refusal by the EC in 1989 and collapse of the USSR, a shift of interest has been seen in the Turkish public opinion as only 21% of the surveyed people gave priority to the EU and wanted Turkey to enter the EU (option-a). On the other hand, surprisingly, more than half of surveyed people gave priorities to the Turkic republics and wanted Turkey to foster its relations with the Turkic republics. In this shift of public support, apart from the reasons mentioned above, the role of media and enthusiastic statements of the Turkish politicians should be underlined.

In the tenth question, it was asked that 'During the known history of the Turks, what was the weakest aspect of them that led them (their states) to collapse'? 532 participants answered this question; 185 (34.77%) participants chose option 'a', 'Economic weakness'. 13 (2.44%) participants chose option 'b', 'military weakness'. 327 (61.46%) participants chose option 'c', 'lack of co-operation and unity'. 7 (1.32%) participants chose option 'd', 'lack of population'. The answers to this question suggested that Turkish people gave priority to co-operation and unity, and economic issues. Therefore, one can suggest that in terms of relations with the Turkic republics, Turkish people support close co-operation.

This survey suggested that Turkish public opinion welcomed the end of the USSR and the emergence of the Turkic republics enthusiastically; and that for cultural reasons, and because of the media and statements of politicians, the Turkish public had enthusiastic expectations about the future of the Turkic world, such as the creation of a Turkic Community.

Turkish Policy Towards the Turkic Republics

Some right-wing politicians regarded the Turkish foreign policy style before the 1980s as being passive and reactionary. For example: Kamran İnan (1993, pp.44-45; 1995a, p.95) argued that after the rule of Atatürk, Turkey adopted a passive foreign policy style, and did not want to be active in international relations. The accusation is that also during this period, Turkey also turned its back on the Turkic world, and that this passive policy worsened Turkey's image in international relations.[103] The exception to this passive policy was the 1950's, during the rule of the Democrat Party and its celebrated Foreign Minister Fatin Rüştü Zorlu.[104] However, analysts such as Deringil label the same period as 'non-adventurist'. Deringil claimed that

> It is only since the mid-1980s and early 1990s that foreign policy has moved away from the basic premises guiding it since 1923, and that occurred despite the best efforts of the professional diplomats of the Foreign Ministry, and was due to the direct intervention in foreign affairs by non-experts in various Motherland Party governments. Since 1983 Turgut Özal and the Motherland party increasingly diverted from the traditional non-adventurist line of Turkish foreign policy (Deringil, 1992, p.5).

In the 1990's, Turkish decision-makers started to be more active, searching for possibilities of co-operation in the region. There was considerable change in Turkish foreign policy style; the traditional Turkish policy of non-interference with the Turks living outside of Turkey changed (Hostler, 1993, p.162). Özal who advocated an active, if not aggressive, Turkish image initiated this change. For example, during the Gulf War, he actively supported the international coalition against Saddam Hussein, a policy which dismayed the Foreign Ministry and the chief of staff, who later resigned. Another example was Özal's declaration to a Greek newspaper in May 1991 that 'the Dodecanese Islands were never Greek, they belonged to the Ottoman Empire. If I had been in İsmet İnönü's place [in 1944] I would have gone in and taken them. Turkey committed a historic error in this case' (Deringil, 1992, p.6). He also proposed the Black Sea Economic Co-operation, advocated active support for Azerbaijan, and even mentioned military intervention against Armenia.

Although Özal's active foreign policy understanding and his charismatic leadership was important in this changing style of Turkish foreign policy, there were other factors which forced Turkey to be active and look for possible alternative co-operations. As briefly discussed at the outset of this chapter, with the end of Cold war, the importance of Turkey for the West declined in terms of East-West confrontation and Turkey was trying to find new arguments to prove that she was still important in global politics and for Europe. Secondly, cool relations between the European Community and Turkey played a role in Turkey's search for alternative areas of co-operation and relations with new partners. Thirdly, lack of support for Turkish position in international circles on crucial issues such as the Cyprus issue, Separatism in South East Anatolia and the water conflict with Syria and Iraq, encouraged Turkey to look for new allies in the international community.

During the same period, one of the contemporaneous worries on the part of the Western powers was what was going to happen in the Caucasus and Central Asia. Western policy-makers worried that with the dissolution of the Soviet Union a power vacuum had been created in Central Asia, which might be filled by radical Islamic fundamentalism sponsored by Iran, if the West did not take measures to prevent this. Western promotion of the Turkish Model[105] provided Turkey with new instruments; it meant a ratification of Turkey's strategic position in the region after the Cold War, enabling Turkey to claim that it was still important for the West and world politics. Thus, Turkey was happy with the Western promotion of the Turkish Model.[106]

Turkish decision-makers welcomed the emergence of the Turkic Republics enthusiastically. Whether Islamist or advertly Pan-Turkist, the nationalist backgrounds of the majority of the politicians of the time increased their enthusiasm. Now they could not only promote a Turkic World, but also do it with the approval of the world media and without being accused of pan-Turkism, an accusation which in the past could lead to persecution even in Turkey. While the Turkish side (in general) tried to find new arguments and formulate a Turkish policy towards the Turkic Republics, Western (especially US) promotion of the

Turkish Model gave an opportunity to the Turkish government and everybody in Turkey who wanted to deal with the Turkic Republics. For a short period of time, dreams of a United Turkic States led by Turkey, all represented in the international arena began to look possible even to the most cautious. The new situation offered a solution to the problem of finding an overall framework for Turkish foreign policy. On the other hand, the leftist coalition partner of the government was well aware that democracy was the key to becoming a role model in the region. 'We have to produce democracy in our own country in order to point the way', said Minister of Culture Fikri Sağlar on one occasion (Laber, 1992). Officially, the main objective of Turkish policy, as Acar Okan pointed out, was to help the Turkic Republics to gain and keep their independence.[107] There is no denial that Turkey, which needed support on crucial issues such as Kurdish separatism, the Cyprus issue and the water conflict with Syria and Iraq over the rivers Fırat (Euphrates) and Dicle (Tigris), assumed that the new Turkic Republics would be its natural allies in international organisations, and therefore regarded their full independence as being in its interests.

Even before the end of USSR, Turkey had taken positive steps to develop relations with the USSR and the Turkic republics. Although hostility between Turkey and the USSR generally continued until the disintegration of the latter, economic relations between the two countries increased, especially after 1985. Turkey started to import Soviet natural gas, and Turkish firms entered the Soviet market (Barchard, 1985, p.44). Soviet-Turkish trade was 411 million dollars in 1985 and reached 1.8 billion dollars by 1990 (Ataöv, 1992, p.92). President Özal visited the Soviet Union between 11-16 March 1991, the first visit at presidential level for twenty-two years. Özal's visit coincided with the seventieth anniversary of the Soviet-Turkish Treaty of Friendship and Fraternity (16 March 1921). A large Turkish delegation of officials and businessmen travelled with Özal to Moscow, Kiev, Alma Ata and Baku, and during the visit new agreements were signed, the most important being the treaty of friendship, good-neighbourliness and co-operation (12 March 1991). Later, treaties were signed also with Ukraine, Kazakstan and Azerbaijan (Ataöv, 1992, p.92). President Özal visited Baku, which led to the opening of a Turkish General Consulate in the Azerbaijani capital, the signing of a protocol and the announcement of a joint communiqué (Ataöv, 1992, p.103). Kazakstan was the only Central Asian Republic that President Özal visited in early 1991. A protocol defining future relations was signed during Özal's visit to Alma Ata (15 March 1991). It referred to an expansion of relations in all fields, especially direct contacts between business firms as well as between governments (Ataöv, 1992, p.104). In November and December 1991, the Presidents of Uzbekistan, Turkmenistan and Kirgizstan were welcomed by Özal in Ankara, and

Turkey promised to give support to these new Republics at all levels (Henz, 1992, p.33). Things had never looked so good for Turkey on the international relations front.

Table 2.6 Turkey's Trade with Former USSR between 1988 and 1991 (Million $)

Year	Exports	Imports	Balance	Capacity
1988	271.408	442.619	-171.211	714.027
1989	704.772	596.710	+108.062	1301.482
1990	531.100	1271.400	-740.300	1802.500
1991	610.600	1089.800	-479.200	1700.400

Source: Prepared by İdris Bal by using following sources; An unpublished note on the Soviet economy at the beginning of 1990 prepared by Şevket Özügergin, Consultant responsible for Trade and Economy at the Turkish Embassy in Moscow, April 1990; DEİK Bülten September 1992, p.2.

Political and Economic Relations

After the independence of the Turkic Republics, Turkey became the first country to recognise the Turkic Republics. Turkey also helped the acceptance of these Republics as full members to International institutions such as the United Nations (UN) and the International Monetary Found (IMF), World Bank (Çarıkcı, 1997, p.770). Turkey's quick recognition of these Republics and its help in their struggle to integrate with the World can be interpreted as Turkey's belief that if these republics integrated with the World, their independence would be strengthened and Russian domination would be reduced.

After the emergence of the Turkic Republics as independent states several official and unofficial Turkish visits to Azerbaijan and Central Asia took place. The first major visit to the Turkic Republics took place between 28 February and 6 March 1992. The Turkish Minister of Education Köksal Toptan, Foreign Minister Hikmet Çetin, State Minister Şerif Ercan, officials from the Ministry of Education and Foreign Ministry, businessmen and members of the Turkish press participated in the visit; a total of a hundred and fifty people. They visited Azerbaijan, Kazakstan, Uzbekistan, Turkmenistan, Kirgizstan, Tajikistan and Ukraine with the aim to observe the needs of these countries on the spot and obtain information for future projects.[108] During this visit, agreements were signed to develop cultural-educational relations (for example: eight different agreements were signed in Uzbekistan).[109] After the end of this comprehensive visit, Foreign Minister Hikmet

Çetin claimed that Turkey could play a very important and effective role in the region. Noting that they were not competing with anybody concerning relations with the CIS, and that the visit had been very positive and warm, he said that the atmosphere showed that Turkey could be a model country for these Republics. Çetin said: 'These countries want to benefit from Turkey's experience while opening up to the outside world and they want a relationship that is based on equality'.[110] On the other hand, State Minister Ercan pointed out that 'the most important element which will strengthen our ties over the years is language'.[111]

Enthusiastic Turkish efforts to establish close relations were positively answered by the Turkic Republics. A significant development on the road to close co-operation was the Ankara Meeting which took place among the presidents of the Turkic Republics on 30-31 October, 1992, involving the leaders of Turkey, Azerbaijan, Kazakstan, Kirgizstan, Turkmenistan and Uzbekistan after which a declaration was announced emphasising common cultural values, and the intention to recreate common cultural factors including language.[112] Foreign newspapers commented on the meeting. Le Figaro said that with this meeting the Turkish world was about to be officially born, and indicated that it was the first time a meeting had taken place among Turkic states in history. Nezavisimaya argued that the Ankara meeting was an indicator of the Central Asian states' decision to choose Turkey rather than Iran as a partner.[113] As will be discussed in the next chapter although a race between Turkey and Iran was constantly mentioned, neither Turkey nor Iran openly admitted to this race and in contrast they stated that they were not competing with any country in the region. Although there are ideological differences and there were elements of competition between Iran and Turkey, common interests generally proved stronger than differences. Both of them are members of ECO, they have common borders and Iran strategically occupies an important place between Turkey and the Turkic Republics. These factors encouraged Turkey and Iran for co-operation rather than confrontation.[114]

Turkey attempted to help Turkic Republics in their transformation from centrally controlled economy to market economy and from a one-party system to multi-party democracy. Turkey's intention of helping Turkic Republics in these issues was normal as Turkey regarded itself as a model for the newly independent Turkic Republics. Demirel, Prime Minister in 1992, declared that 'Turkey is committed to being a model of democracy, rule of law, tolerance, respect for human rights and economic liberties'.[115] A Turkish International Co-operation Agency (TICA) was established in Ankara which was planned to provide 'assistance to these countries in developing their independent state structures, drafting their laws, and solving problems related to banking, insurance, foreign trade, budgets and tax systems during the transition to a free market economy' and the new directorate was planned to promote 'economic, commercial, technical, social and educational co-operation with developing countries on the basis of projects which will contribute to the development of these countries'.[116] This same objective was reflected by Prime Minister Demirel during its opening ceremony in 1992: 'In fact these countries (new Republics) have great resources... If these societies manage to develop these resources by science, technology, and initiative, they can easily join the most advanced and richest countries within ten years. So it is necessary to help them in this direction...'.[117]

Turkey sent experts to the Republics in order to help them in their struggle to transfer their economies to market economy, and to establish free trade regions (zone). In order to develop banking services, Turkish public banks such as Ziraat Bankası established co-partner banks and they opened branches (Çarıkcı, 1997, p.770; Yusuf, 1997, p.780). Turkish institutions such as the Turkish Standards Institute (Türk Standartları Enstitüsü - TSE), the State Statistics Institute (Devlet İstatistik Enstitüsü - DİE), TICA, and the Centre to Develop and Support Small and Medium Scale Industry (Küçük ve Orta Ölçekli Sanayiyi Geliştirme ve Destekleme Kurumu - KOSGEB) began to offer training, technical and consultancy services. Also diplomats from Turkic republics attended courses organised by Turkish Foreign Ministry. A technical co-operation agreement was signed between TSE and the standardisation institutions of Azerbaijan, Bashkiria, Chuvashistan, Kazakstan, Kırgizstan, Mongolia, Uzbekistan, Tatarstan, Turkmenistan, Kabardino-Balkaria Republics, Moldova, and Bosnia, also 'Bölgeler arası standardizasyon Birliği' (Unity of Standardisation between Regions) was established among Turkey and the Turkic Republics (Yusuf, 1997, p.783).

Turkey was enthusiastic in help the new Republics to modernise their telecommunications and transport networks; Turkish, Indian and Pakistani companies helped the Central Asian Republics to modernise and improve the poor telephone system inherited from the USSR (Hyman, 1994c, p.12). The Turkish Communications and Transport Minister Yaşar Topçu went to the Turkic Republics accompanied by fifteen deputies and a large number of bureaucrats and journalists, and inaugurated a 2500-line capacity digital telephone exchange established by the Turkish PTT in Kazakstan, Uzbekistan, Kirgizstan, Türkmenistan and Azerbaijan.[118] During his tour of the region (April 1992), Prime Minister Süleyman Demirel offered some one billion dollars worth of loans and export credits.[119] According to 1999 figures, export and project credits opened by Turkey (by means of Türk-Eximbank) to the Turkic Republics reached approximately 1.1 billion US dollars, 70% of which was used by the Turkic Republics (see Table 2.7).

Table 2.7 Credits Opened by Turk-Eximbank to the Turkic Republics until 21 April 1999 (Million $)

Country name	Country Limit (Amount of Credit)	Used for Goods	Used for Projects	Total
Azerbaijan	250.00	59.60	28.58	88.18
Kazakstan	240.00	40.05	173.07	213.12
Kirgizstan	75.00	35.76	12.37	48.13
Uzbekistan	375.00	124.58	201.38	325.96
Turkmenistan	163.26	74.99	29.35	104.34
Total	1103.26	334.98	444.75	779.73

Source: Türk İşbirliği ve Kalkınma Ajansı, (1999), *Türkmenistan Ülke Raporu*, Ankara, p.29.

In addition, many private Turkish companies began to invest and trade in the region. The first joint venture registered in Uzbekistan, for example, was by a Turkish company in the cotton sector (Hyman, 1994c, p.14). According to the Union of Turkish constructors (Türk Müteahhitler Birliği -TMB) which has 45 member firms, members of TMB had investments in thirteen CIS countries. Total value of the contracts they had taken on was around 8.7 billion US dollars and only 20.3% of this, 1.8 billion US dollars were from the Turkic Republics. However, apart from the members of TMB, Turkish private sector invested especially in the textile sector. Therefore the responsible ministers state that Turkey's investment reached six billion US dollars in Turkic Republics by the end of 1996 (Çarıkcı, 1997, p.769). An indication of the attitude of the Turkish private sector was the statement of Sultan Sirkeci, owner of Şiral İnşaat: 'We went to Libya and Iran in order to earn money. However, we should go to these places (the Turkic Republics) to help ... we should go to these Republics as Turkish builder-contractors, but our first objective should not be earning money'.[120]

On the other hand, Turkey aimed to develop its economic relations through the Economic Co-operation Organisation (ECO), initially established by Turkey, Iran and Pakistan in 1964. The aims of the organisation are to lift, in the course of time, customs barriers among member countries, establish an investment and development bank, develop regional tourism and work towards more effective transport and communications system. At the Ashkabad meeting (May-1992) of the heads of state, all sides agreed that they wished to expand economic and political co-operation.

Table 2.8   Volume of the Jobs Taken by Members of Unity of Turkish Constructors in the Turkic Republics and Turkey's Direct Investments in these Republics between the Years 1991-1996 (Million $)

Country	Total number of contrasts	Complete jobs (million $)	Continued jobs	Total (Million $)	Direct Investment (Million $)
Azerbaijan	15	49.2	235.1	284.3	25.5
Kazakstan	33	228.4	420.9	649.3	29.9
Kirgizstan	4	34.8	72.9	107.7	11.1
Turkmenistan	47	299.7	223.4	523.1	3.4
Uzbekistan	9	27.6	203.5	231.1	4.9
Total	108	639.7	1155.8	1795.5	74.8
CIS Total	397	4768.5	3815.3	8683.8	

Source: TMB Dökümanı, April 1997, Hazine Müsteşarlığı Dökümanları, March 1997.

The final document, signed by the presidents of Iran, Kazakstan, Kirgizstan and Uzbekistan and the Prime Ministers of Turkey and Pakistan, expresses the confidence that the widening and deepening of co-operation in economy, trade, science, culture, technology and other social areas will substantially contribute to progress and promote the improvement of the world situation (Baharçiçek, 1993, pp.281-182).

The importance of establishing and expanding air services, railways and sea transport was stressed and to implement bilateral and multilateral projects for these purposes was agreed on. Another important suggestion was the implementation of new projects related to the construction of gas and oil pipelines, oil extraction and construction of refinery (Baharçiçek, 1993, p.281). An important session of the ECO Council of Ministers took place in Islamabad, Pakistan, on 28 November 1992 and seven new members joined the organisation - Azerbaijan, Kirgizstan, Kazakstan, Turkmenistan, Uzbekistan, Tajikistan and Afghanistan - bringing the total number of members to ten.[121]

After the independence of the Turkic Republics, rich petrol and gas fields of the region opened to the World. Along with big US, European and Russian companies, Turkish Petrol Joint-Stock company (TPAO), started to search for oil and natural gas in the Turkic Republics. In Kazakstan, 'Kazaktürkmunay' company was established by TPAO and the Geology Ministry of Kazkstan, which started work on three wells. TPAO has a 6.75% share in the Azerbaijan International Operating Company Consortium (Aydın, 1997, p.871). Also a protocol of co-operation was signed for the oil in the Caspian Sea (Shakh Deniz

Prospect) between BP/Statoil, Socar, and TPAO. The share of the TPAO is 9% (Yusuf, 1997, pp.781-782). The transportation of oil and gas became an important issue.[122] Russia proposes the route of Baku-Novorossisk, a harbour of Russian Federation in the Black Sea. Turkey on the other hand, opposes the Russian project and claims that if oil is transported by sea through the Dardanelles and the Bosphorus, it will cause serious problems of pollution, and will not allow them to go through the straits. Turkey advocates and proposes Baku-Ceyhan oil pipeline project (Aydın, 1997, pp.780-781; Doğan, 1997, p.806). Turkish proposal of Baku-Ceyhan pipeline project has been backed by US and an accord setting out terms for seeking commercial investment in the proposed 1,600-kilometres pipeline from Baku, the capital of Azerbaijan, to the Turkish Mediterranean port of Ceyhan has been signed in the summit of the Organisation for Security and Co-operation in Europe (OSCE) in Istanbul on 18th November 1999.[123] Similarly, Turkmen natural gas is planned to be brought to Turkey by a pipe line from which Turkey plans to get gas for her domestic consumption, the rest will be exported to the West (Yusuf, 1997, p.781).

Table 2.9 Turkey's Trade With the Turkic Republics in the Years Between 1992-1997 (Million $)

Country		1992	1993	1994	1995	1996	1997
Azerbaijan	Export	94.2	68.2	132.1	161.3	216.3	319.7
	Import	25.5	33.9	8.9	21.8	39	58.3
Kazakstan	Export	13.7	67.8	131.7	150.8	164	210.6
	Import	8.8	43.7	32.3	86.6	93.7	165.3
Kirgizstan	Export	1.8	17.0	17.0	38.2	47.8	49.4
	Import	1.3	3.5	4.3	5.5	5.9	7.6
Uzbekistan	Export	36.6	213.5	64.6	138.6	229.9	210.6
	Import	20.3	31.9	78.6	61.5	56.5	94.8
Turkmenistan	Export	7.3	83.9	84.3	56.3	99.9	117.5
	Import	17.8	76.9	65.6	111.8	64.8	73.5
Total	Export	153.6	440.4	429.7	545.2	757.9	907.8
	Import	73.7	189.9	189.7	287.2	259.9	399.5
Export+Import		227.3	630.3	619.4	832.4	1017.8	1307.3
Export-Import		79.9	250.5	240.0	258.0	498	508.3

Source: Prepared by İdris Bal.

In 1996, 3.3% of Turkey's total export was with the Turkic Republics.

Industrial products such as iron-steel construction spare parts, construction equipments, hygienic installation equipments, motor vehicles and spare parts, electronic goods, telecommunication equipment, and foodstuffs take priority in the exports. Turkey imports mainly, cotton and cotton thread, raw and processed leather, wool, phosphate fertilisers and various metals (Çarıkcı, 1997, p.769).

Trade with the Turkic Republics has not been as easy as it was envisaged in 1992. The biggest problem of Turkey's trade with the Turkic Republics is transportation. For land transportation there are three possible routes: over Georgia, over Iran or over Armenia. Iran causes bureaucratic problems to Turkish vehicles and the railway from Iran is under-used for the same reason. War and cold relations between Turkey and Armenia render this route useless as well. Although Turkish vehicles prefer it, the Georgian route is not safe and the roads are not good. For the present time, air transport is better in comparison with land and rail transportation (Yülek, 1997, pp.756-757; Coşkun, 1997, p.762; Yusuf, 1997, p.783). Apart from this major barrier, there are problems within the new Republics of banking and insurance, domestic and external trade laws (Çarıkcı, 1997, p.771).

In general, it is possible to point out the lack of co-ordination and organisation in Turkey's policy towards Turkic republics. There are several units belong to different ministries such as TICA, Foreign Economic Relations Council (DEİK), and TOBB. Therefore, one can argue that if a special ministry responsible for Turkey's relations with the Turkic Republics and controlling all these separate units, is established, Turkey's relations with the Turkic Republics can be further developed in all fields.

Cultural Relations

Although Turkish leaders constantly stressed that their country had neither the ability nor the desire to act alone in the region, Turkey was active in wooing the Turkic Republics in the cultural field.[124] Following independence, a revival of Islam had occurred in the Turkic Republics. They needed books on religion, and their mosques needed repairing (Toker, 1992, pp.154-156). Although their aims were different, Turkey, Iran and Saudi Arabia began to send Korans and other religious books to the Republics, and experts were sent to teach Islam. Iran's distribution of tens of thousands of copies of the Koran - especially in Azerbaijan, where a majority of the population is Shiite - can be regarded as evidence of this eager help.[125] According to Arif Soytürk, who was the head of the Foreign Relations Department of the Presidency of Religious Affairs at the time, Turkish aid to 'outer Turks' began in 1990.[126] In Ramadan 1990, the Turkish Presidency of Religious Affairs sent four imams to the USSR. In Ramadan 1991, their number was increased to ten; four of them to Azerbaijan, four of them to the Russian Federation (Tatarstan), one to Yugoslavia, and one to Mongolia. In 1992, Turkey sent thirty-seven specialists to the Muslim Republics of Central Asia (including Azerbaijan). It was also arranged to send fifty more imams to the Muslim republics for a longer period. After 1991, students from Muslim Republics came to Turkey for religious education in the Koran schools.[127]

Apart from educating these students, the Presidency of Religious Affairs helped Turkic people to make their Hajj journeys. For example, in 1991 expenses of 225 Azeris were paid by the Turkish Presidency of Religious Affairs. In addition to this, Turkey sent tens of thousands of books to the Muslim Republics. The Ministry of Religious Affairs also planned to support mosque construction, for example; the foundations of the Ashkabat-Turkey mosque were laid on January 12, 1993.[128] Not only the Turkish State but also the Turkish private sector was involved; businessmen provided books on religion and Turkish culture. This effort for religious education did not go unnoticed without criticism. Some Turkish elite was angered, they claimed that the Turkic people needed technology and modern science rather than religious propaganda.[129]

Table 2.10 Imams Sent by the Turkish Presidency of Religious Affairs to the Turkic World in Ramadan 1992

Country	Number of Imams Sent
Azerbaijan	8
Turkmenistan	7
Kirgizstan	4
Uzbekistan	7
Tajikistan	4
Kazakstan	7
Yugoslavia	5
Ukraine	3
Georgia	4
Russian Federation (Tatarstan)	10
Albania	9
Total	68

Source: 'Bugüne Kadar Başkanlığımızca Soydaşlarımıza Sunulan Hizmetler', An unpublished document prepared by the Presidency of Religious Affairs.

Table 2.11   Distribution of the Students Who Came to Take Religious Education in Turkey Between the Years 1991-1993 (According to Their Places of Origin)

Place of Origin	Number of Students
Mongolia	77
Kazakstan	57
Bulgaria	70
Chechnya	30
Azerbaijan	6
Daghestan	13
Georgia	56
Uzbekistan	7
Tatarstan	15
Romania	22
Karachai	5
Turkmenistan	58
Meskhetian Turks	1
Bosnia-Herzegovina	5
Kirgizstan	6
Macedonian	7
Russia (Ufa-Kazan region)	87
Albania	85
Total	607

Source: 'Bugüne Kadar Başkanlığımızca Soydaşlarımıza Sunulan Hizmetler', An unpublished note prepared by the Presidency of the Turkish Religious Affairs.

Apart from religious aid, the Ministers of Education of the Turkic Republics and Turkey met at the 'First Conference of Ministers of Education of Turkish Republics' (Türk Cumhuriyetleri Eğitim Bakanları Birinci Konferansı) between 16-23 May 1992 in Ankara. At this conference, apart from emphasising student exchanges and cultural activities, the ministers agreed the creation of a common Turkish language.[130] The Second Conference of Ministers of Education of Turkish Republics took place in Bishkek between 29 September and 3 October 1992. The conference decided to prepare a 'Common Program of History and Literature in the Turkish World' (Türk Dünyasında Tarih ve Edebiyat Ortak Programı), and a commission met in Yalova on 3 December 1992 to make initial preparations. During the conference, because of Kazak opposition the decision for the adoption of a common Latin alphabet could not be taken, but the Azeri Minister declared that they would adopt a Latin alphabet. The Kazak Minister also refused to accept the independence of the Turkish Republic of Northern Cyprus.[131] However, it was agreed that the Republics should begin preparations to adopt the Latin alphabet, which was seen as an important instrument for the unification of the Turkic world.[132]

Another significant development in 1992 was the opening of Turkish schools in the Turkic Republics.[133] In 1996, the number of schools opened by the Turkish Ministry of Education were: one school in Azerbaijan, two schools in Kirgizstan, eight schools in Uzbekistan, and three schools in Türkmenistan (Uzun, 1996, p.154). Turkish foundations and private firms also started to open schools in the Turkic Republics and in regions of the Russian Federation in which Turkic peoples live.[134] In particular, private schools opened in the Turkic Republics by the followers of Fetullah Gülen (Fethullah Hodja) should be highlighted. Gülen and his supporting businessmen have been more active than the Turkish State itself, or rather, their efforts have been welcomed by the state. Gülen is the charismatic leader of a Nurcu order and the Turkish schools under his supervision are duplicates of the ones, his order opened in Turkey. The education in these schools advocates Kemalism, secularism, excellence in science and languages, and they are English medium schools. The national history and the language of the countries they operate in are taught by the local teachers, and the schools have one Turkish and one native director. The education they offer is above the regional average, and they select their students through nationally held examinations (Uzun, 1996, pp.147-162). These schools advocate Turkish state policy of moderate Islam and modern science, and no doubt it is hoped that the students will help their countries to adopt the Turkish Model and prepare a suitable basis for relations between Turkey and the Turkic world. Since students attending these colleges learn the Latin alphabet and English, as well as Turkish and Turkish culture, it can be assumed that they will grow closer to Turkey, the West and the Latin alphabet. Private schools of Gülen do not receive financial help from the Turkish government, and they are probably the most effective tools of influence for the future.

Apart from private schools, educational exchanges between Turkey and the Turkic Republics constituted an important step in cultural relations.[135] Turkic students from the Russian Federation as well as from the Turkic Republics were invited to Turkey. Following the official visit of Prime Minister Demirel to the Turkic Republics between 27 April and 3 May 1992, Turkey invited 2000 students from each Republic between the years 1992 to 1993. These students learned Turkish in their first year, and the following year started to attend Turkish universities and colleges (see Table 2.12). A major problem in the education exchange program occurred when Uzbekistan called its students back to Uzbekistan because the Uzbek government believed that some students in Turkey held meetings with members of the Uzbek opposition in Turkey (Mohammed Salih). In the 1992-93 academic year, 1120 students, and in 1993-94, 244 students were called back to Uzbekistan. In 1997, only 438 Uzbek students are registered at Turkish schools (see Table 2.13) (Çarıkcı, 1997, p.767).

Table 2.12 Distribution of Students Who Came to Turkey for Education During the Period 1992 to 1993

Country	Higher Education	Secondary Education
Azerbaijan	1,293	310
Kazakstan	1,109	169
Kirgizstan	384	344
Uzbekistan	1,124	270
Turkmenistan	1,185	519
Other Turkic Groups	408	24
Total	5,095	1,634

Source: Ali Arslan, (1994), *Türk Cumhuriyetleri ve Türk Topluluklarından Türkiye'ye Gelen Öğrenciler (1992-93)*, Yay Ofset, Istanbul, p.5.

Table 2.13 Distribution of Students Who Came to Turkey for Education During the Period 1996 to 1997

Country	Secondary Education	Language Course	Pre-Under Graduate	Under Graduate	Master	Doctorate	Total
Azerbaijan	16	110	159	1495	12	1	1793
Kazakstan	7	126	157	826	33	29	1178
Kirgizstan	29	59	147	500	28	41	804
Uzbekistan	-	29	61	324	23	1	438
Turkmenistan	349	147	677	1031	11	11	2226
Total	401	471	1201	4176	107	83	6439

Source: Prepared by İdris Bal by using E. Çarıkçı, (1997), 'Türk Cumhuriyetlerinde Ekonomik Gelişmeler ve Türkiye'nin Katkıları', *Yeni Türkiye*, no.15, p.767.

Important steps were also taken in the field of broadcasting. Turkish Radio and Television Corporation (TRT) INT-Avrasya TV Channel began broadcasting to the Turkic Central Asian states and Azerbaijan on April 27, 1992, the day that the Turkish Prime Minister started his visit to the Turkic Republics. The Turkish Minister of Communications, Yaşar Topçu, claimed that 'the TV broadcasts beamed to the Turkish Republics of Central Asia are a source of joy for the whole Turkish community'. Prime Minister Demirel boasted that 'once the connections are completed, TRT will have the second largest coverage in the world, after CNN'.[136] Avrasya TV was described as cementing 'still further the existing cultural and social ties with these countries and formed a solid bridge'.[137] As Baharçiçek (1993, p.285) put it, this was an important move that could develop closer cultural relations and understanding among the people of the region and contribute to Turkish political influence.

The alphabet reform was another area that Turkey was keen to promote. In contrast to Iran, who also believed that the Cyrillic alphabet should not be used by the new Republics, Turkey advocated the Latin alphabet rather than the Arabic alphabet (Copher, 1992, p.44). In the Turkish view, the use of a Latin alphabet would ease written communications between the Republics and the world, and the use of a common Turkic alphabet within the Turkic World would be even better. The Latin alphabet would help them to adopt the Turkish Model, and 'in September 1991 the Turkish Standards Institute began a series of meetings intended to co-ordinate work on agreeing a common alphabet for all the Turkic-speaking nationalities' (Hyman, 1994c, p.15). The Turcology Research Institute of Marmara University organised a symposium between 18-20 November 1991 in Istanbul, titled the International Symposium of Contemporary Turkish Alphabets (Milletlerarası Çağdaş Türk Alfabeleri Sempozyumu). Around thirty academics participated in this symposium which stressed the need to prepare a common Latin alphabet, since 'the Latin alphabet was the most suitable alphabet for Turkic peoples and Turkic languages' (Devlet, 1993, pp.27-30).[138] The Turkish Ministry of Culture organised a Standing Committee of Turkish Language as a preparation for the Conference on Turkish Language and Latin alphabet to take place on 17-25 June 1992. During the 1992 Conference, which was attended by the Ministers of Culture of the Turkic Republics, not only the Turkish side but also the participants from the Turkic Republics expressed the need to use the Latin alphabet and achieve a common written language. Azeri academic Kamil Veliyev argued that without a common language and common alphabet, it would be impossible to solve major problems. He said that Azerbaijan had adopted the Latin alphabet, and advocated that Anatolian Turkish (the Turkish spoken in Turkey) should be the common language for the Turkic peoples.[139] Tünegün Kasymbegov, advisor to the

Kirgiz President and head of the Commission on Culture to the Kirgiz Assembly, said: 'We [Turkic peoples] used to have one common language', and stressed that the reason why there was currently no common language was because some Turkic peoples were subject to Russia, China and Iran. He talked about the will of Kirgizstan to adopt the Latin alphabet and reminded the audience that the Kirgiz President had established a commission in the Kirgiz parliament to administer the adoption of the Latin alphabet.[140] Azerbaijan, Turkmenistan and Uzbekistan indicated that they were planning to abandon the Cyrillic alphabet, similar sentiments were expressed by the Kazak representative, although he said that the conversion to Latin alphabet would take some time because of the large Russian minority in Kazakstan.[141] To promote the adoption of a common Latin alphabet, Minister Toptan promised to publish the necessary books in Turkey and send them to the Republics.[142] During the same conference, the delegates tried to agree on the details of a common Latin alphabet for the Turkic languages. The following year, at another meeting in Ankara, on 8 March 1993, it was accepted that each Turkic Republic would prepare its alphabet using the common Turkic alphabet consisting of 34 letters.[143]

Turkey strongly advocated the creation of a common written language, almost like the Modern Standard Arabic. All the Turkologists, who were traditionally members of the NAP in their youth and well known for their pan-Turkist inclinations now were on the stage. To this end, a new institute was established in Istanbul to create a form of Turkish that would be comprehensible by all the Turkic-speaking nations.[144] The acceptance of the Latin alphabet could be regarded as a significant step towards achieving a common written language and the Turkish side suggested that the Turkish spoken in Turkey should be taken as the base for this new written Turkic language (Karaörs, 1994, p.63). Bilal Şimşir who was responsible for the CIS desk at the Turkish Foreign Ministry, advocated this idea and said: 'Turkmenistan, Kirgizstan, Uzbekistan, Kazakstan, Tajikistan and Azerbaijan all have Turkish speaking populations. Many have relatives in Turkey and (it would be easy for them to) adapt to the Turkish dialect'.[145] In this statement lies the denial of the fact that Turkic languages are languages on their own right, and the presumption that after all they are dialects of modern Anatolian Turkish. This heavy-handed approach to language and culture, which denied all history and scientific reality, very soon contributed to pushing the Turkic Republics away from Turkey.

In brief, after the end of the Soviet Union, Turkey made great progress in establishing cultural relations in a short time. Religious aid (which started even before the end of the USSR), Turkish schools, educational exchanges and TV broadcasting, desire to create a common written language and to use a common

(Latin) alphabet were aimed to strengthen the cultural connections between Turkey and the Turkic Republics; and these in return, according to Turkish policies, were to encourage the Turkic Republics to adopt the Turkish Model and a way of life similar to the one in Turkey.

Test Case in Relations

When the Turkic Republics gained their independence, their ruling elite were former communists who claimed to have adopted liberal and nationalist values. On the other hand, there were nationalist oppositions, which did not have significant impact on their countries and were controlled by the former communist ruling classes. Turkey's energetic promotion of substantive democratic reforms in these newly independent Republics was creating problems for the heavy-handed ruling regimes, which usually preferred to use the traditional communist strong-arm tactics against dissidents or opposition sympathisers. Hyman (1994c, pp.16-17) claimed that

> These regimes seem just as willing to resort to coercion and control as was the case before independence and are, in turn, suspicious of Turkey's democratic rhetoric.... For the Turks, the dilemma is to what extent they should be seen to be dealing with the old elite, and to what extent they should be trying to second-guess regime change.

Apart from Azerbaijan, oppositions to the regime in the Turkic Republics were not strong. In Azerbaijan, after the Soviet intervention of January 1990 the power of the pro-Turkic, nationalist Azerbaijan People's Front increased and it was backed by Turkey. Ataöv (1992, p.102) pointed out the importance of Azerbaijan for Turkey:

> Among all the Turkic Republics of the CIS, it may be said that Turkey has a 'special relationship' with the Azeris, who live in Azerbaijan and in some adjacent areas and whose dialect is closest to the Turkish spoken in contemporary Asia minor and Thrace. In the North Eastern corner of Turkey, there are still families or their descendants who have migrated from Azerbaijani lands. The Turks and Azeris were at all times conscious of this kinship.

In fact, not only for Turkey but also for Iran, relations with Azerbaijan are arguably of greater importance than with any other Republic of Central Asia. Geographically, Azerbaijan is in a strategic position for both Iran and Turkey, but for Turkey this importance is greater as Azerbaijan 'lies much closer to Turkey than does Central Asia, with Nakhichevan, an Azeri enclave on the border of Armenia, being the sole point at which a narrow land border (and a newly-built bridge, of some symbolic importance) exists with Turkey' (Hyman, 1994c, p.12).

During the presidential elections of 7 June 1992 in Azerbaijan, Turkey did not support Deputy President Yakup Memedov, but preferred to see the leader of the Azerbaijan People's Front, Ebulfez Elchibey, as President. However, there was division within the People's Front and Itibar Memedov, who accused Elchibey of being a liberal democrat and called himself a nationalist democrat, also became a candidate for the presidency. It was obvious that Yakup Memedov would benefit from this development. Turkey needed to convince Itibar Memedov to withdraw his candidacy, or it would be necessary to announce to the nationalist voters in Azerbaijan that Turkey supported Elchibey and not Memedov. In his tour of the Turkic Republics, Demirel took the NAP leader Alparslan Türkeş, who had no official status but who was popular in Azerbaijani pan-Turkist circles, with him. Demirel conveyed the Turkish preference through Türkeş who underlined Turkey's and his own support for Elchibey in his speech in Azerbaijan. Later, Turkey achieved her objective and Elchibey became the President of Azerbaijan (Anadol, 1995b, pp.310-311).

Turkey supported Azerbaijan in her struggle against Armenian invasion, and regarded the disputed region of Nagorno-Karabakh as an integral part of Azeri land.[146] Following the Armenian attacks on Nakhichevan, Nakhichevan appealed for Turkish intervention. Turkey wanted Armenia to stop its aggression and claimed that it had the right to intervene in Nakhichevan since the 1921 Treaty of Kars between Ankara and Moscow gave Turkey this right in case of any change in the status of Nakhichevan.[147] Again because of this treaty, President Turgut Özal recommended the Turkish government to send troops to defend Nakhichevan.[148] He was not alone in his request, as Ecevit, leader of the Democratic Left Party, and Türkeş, the leader of the Nationalist Action Party, also urged Turkey to intervene militarily if Armenia attacked Nakhichevan.[149] Following Özal's statement, Russian Marshal Yevgeny Shaposhnikov, head of the armed forces of the Commonwealth of Independent States, said that 'such an intervention could create a third world war'.[150] At home, Prime Minister Demirel, who approached the conflict more cautiously, did not welcome President Özal's call. When Kelbajar was occupied by Armenians, Özal wanted action against Armenia, but Demirel brushed him aside by saying 'the government makes the foreign policy. We will act with the world on the issue of Azerbaijan' (Çandar, 1993a). Demirel argued that although Azerbaijan was in the right, any Turkish intervention might be considered provocative by the world opinion. He warned that 'sentiment can be instrumental in solving big problems, but I believe that only justice will lead to a

solution'. Demirel also warned that 'if the United States and Western countries
back Armenia in this conflict, then we will have to stand by Azerbaijan, and this
will turn into a conflict between Muslims and Christians that will last for years'
(Baharçiçek, 1993, p.254). Hence although Turkey helped the Azeris to organise
their armed forces,[151] it did not get involved officially. The Turkish government
was accused by the Turkish press of helping Armenia by allowing the West to send
help to Armenia through Turkish territory, and that this Western help included
military equipment.[152] Yalçın Doğan, writing in Milliyet, argued that by supporting
Armenia, Turkey undermined the prestige of Elchibey in Azerbaijan (Doğan,
1993a). Due to pressure from Russia combined with Prime Minister Demirel's
cautious policy, Turkish help to Azerbaijan in the Karabakh conflict was limited.
For example; Elchibey told members of the Turkish press that when Kelbecer was
besieged by Armenians he had asked for helicopters from Demirel to evacuate the
civilians but the helicopters were not given to Azerbaijan.[153] As the position of
Azerbaijan in the war weakened, it contributed to a decline in the popularity of
Elchibey's regime.

Elchibey was an open supporter of Turkey and a pan-Turkist, and mainly for
this reason, he was not welcomed by Russia or Iran.[154] When Suret Huseinov, a
former KGB member who was removed from office together with defence
minister Rahim Gaziyev started a revolt in Ganje,[155] Elchibey escaped to
Nakhichevan, his birthplace, as he did not feel secure in Baku. Turkish press
reported that when the revolt started in Ganje red flags were in the air.[156] When
Aliyev and Huseinov cancelled oil contracts signed with America, the UK and
Turkey,[157] the Turkish press claimed that this revolt was planned and supported by
Russia.[158] Aliyev retained power, since Elchibey did not return to Baku. Iran was
very happy with this development; and the Iranian media welcomed it, claiming
that Elchibey's pro-Turkish politics had created this revolution, and that it was an
indication of the failure of the Turkish model.[159] After this incident, Elchibey
accused Turkey of leaving him alone, and regarded Turkey's reaction to the revolt
as even less supportive that of the US.[160]

Turkish and foreign press speculated about the revolt, for example: Le
Monde claimed that Russian and Iranian ethnic groups living around Lenkoran
supported the revolt.[161] On the other hand, Turkish media criticised the Turkish
government and regarded the decline of Elchibey's regime as a fiasco for Turkey's
Central Asian policy, as Yalçın Doğan (1993b) argued in Milliyet. Cengiz Çandar
(1993a) claimed in his column in Sabah newspaper that on 7 June 1993 an action
plan was prepared by the Turkish Foreign Ministry, but was not followed, and that
if Turkey had acted in time, this revolt in Ganje could have been controlled; for
example a delegation could have been sent to Baku at an early stage to show that

Turkey was behind Elchibey. Turkey, however, sent a delegation on 15 June 1993 - too late, as Huseinov was only seventy kilometres away from Baku. According to Çandar (Çandar, 1993a), there was a faction in the Turkish Foreign Ministry which wanted to cooperage with Russia, therefore, instead of supporting an alternative democratic administration in Azerbaijan which would be opposed to Russia, they preferred Aliyev. Çandar also asserted that Elchibey represented Turkey against Russia and Iran, and was an extension of the influence of Turkey in petrol-rich Azerbaijan. In this respect, the Elchibey regime became a dangerous example for the Central Asian states, and it had to be removed by Russia and Iran.

Another argument was that since Turkey was not able to fulfil Azeri expectations and stop the Armenians, Azerbaijan turned to Moscow. By this time it was becoming clear that Moscow, not Ankara, was the external determining factor (Yılmaz, 1994, p.96). Opposers of the foreign policy of Demirel claimed that after the revolution in Azerbaijan it became clear that Turkey was not an alternative to Russia, as Turkey appeared to have limited power and no courage. The Turkic Republics were then obliged to turn towards Russia as the only reliable and powerful state, because Turkey was in a dilemma as to whether to support the opposition or the former communists. In the case of Azerbaijan it supported the opposition, but even this support was not that clear as Turkey watched the collapse of Elchibey's administration rather then helping him. Yalçın (1993b, pp.6-7) claimed that after this incident everybody learned that Turkey was untrustworthy.[162] Ambassador Şükrü Elekdağ (1993) pointed out in Milliyet that Turkey was too passive and had encouraged Armenia in its assault by opening its airfields, signing an energy agreement and stating that Turkey could not intervene in the conflict alone. He claimed that the fall of Elchibey undermined Turkey's policy in Eurasia, and pointed out that the Turkic Republics as well as the West would reformulate their policies after this event. The Turkish press believed that Elchibey was at the head of a regime that represented the future for the Turkic Republics. Çandar (1993b) argued that Turkey should have worked with people similar to Elchibey but not with Communist nomenclature. Foreign media made similar claims as well. For example: the New York Times underlined that the fall of Elchibey, who was elected democratically and represented the Turkish sphere of influence, would weaken the influence of Turkey in the other Republics. It was claimed that after the incidents in Azerbaijan, no one could claim that Turkey would be a major player elsewhere.[163] These arguments were not mere speculation; in fact, as will be seen in the following chapters, they showed the limits of Turkey's power, and this played a role in the decline of the popularity of the Turkish Model in the Turkic Republics.

Conclusion

The Turkish side welcomed the end of the USSR and the creation of the Turkic Republics. This reaction was strongly affected by the fact that the Turks in Anatolia and the populations of the Turkic Republics are accepted to be of the same origins, and that there are cultural and linguistic connections. Turkey's position in the post-Cold War era affected Turkish reactions as well; mainly, the cool relations between Turkey and the EU, isolation on crucial issues like Cyprus and Kurdish separatism, and attempts to find new arguments to prove that Turkey was still important for the West and global politics, played vital roles in the enthusiastic Turkish reaction to the emancipation of the Turkic Republics. Turkey regarded the Turkic Republics as natural allies who could support the Turkish position on international issues. At the same time, promotion of the Turkish Model that was readily accepted by the West became an instrument through which Turkey could show its continuing importance for the world politics in general.

Turkish politicians, parties, intellectuals, the media and public welcomed the end of the USSR. Although the Turkish left was sceptical at first, later on they also welcomed the developments although the Marxists and the Kurdish left were the exceptions to this enthusiastic welcome. Turkish Marxists adhered to their cause, claiming that although the Soviet model had collapsed, communist ideology had not, and underlining the continuing presence of China and Cuba as socialist states. On the other hand, after the end of the USSR, the Kurdish side turned completely towards separatism. The reaction of different levels of Turkish society - parties, elite, the media and public - affected one another, for example: the enthusiastic statements of the Turkish leaders about the Turkish world affected public opinion, and therefore Turkish people started to believe that a Common Market or Community of Turkic states would be established. On the other hand, the proposal of the Turkish Model by the West, and statements by the foreign media to the effect that a 'new Turkic world is born' or that 'Turkey is becoming a superpower' encouraged them even more.

More or less all levels of the Turkish society agreed that the Turks of Turkey and the populations of the Turkic Republics came from the same origin, shared the same religion, languages of same family and traditions. The official statements stressed that these peoples were the brothers and sisters of Anatolian Turks, and that the Anatolian Turks welcomed their independence and would like to support them to be independent forever. However it is difficult to claim that there was a consensus that a political Turkic Union should be established as soon as possible, or an economic co-operation of Turkic people similar to the EC should be established and so on. The Turkish left and more liberal nationalists opposed these utopian claims.

After the end of the USSR, Turkey started to take active steps and recognised the Turkic Republics - becoming the first country to do so. Although Turkey promised financially and economically more than it could provide and effort, some projects did come true such as the modernisation of telecommunication systems in some of these Republics. However, the most important developments took place in the field of cultural relations. Turkey welcomed 6729 Turkic students in 1992; Turkish AVRASYA TV started to broadcast to the Turkic Republics; the Turkish Presidency of Religious Affairs sent books and İmams to the Turkic Republics and students from the Turkic world came to Turkey for religious education. Turkey advocated the adoption of a common Latin alphabet and the creation of a common Turkish language to aid the adoption of the Turkish Model, and also no doubt a Turkish way of life.

Notes

1   For the history of Turkic peoples, see D. Avcıoğlu, (1989), *Türklerin Tarihi*, 5 Volume, Tekin Yayınları, Istanbul; N. Kösoğlu, (1990), *Türk Dünyası Tarihi ve Türk Medeniyeti Üzerine düşünceler*, Ötüken Neşriyat, Istanbul; F. Sümer, (1992), *Oğuzlar*, Türk Dünyası Araştırmaları Vakfı, Istanbul; Z. Kitapçı, (1988), *Türkistanda İslamiyet ve Türkler*, Nur Basımevi, Konya.

2   TIKA, *Cumhurbaşkanı Sayın Süleyman Demirel'in Türk İşbirliği ve Kalkınma Ajansı'nın Üçüncü Çalışma Yılının Başlangıcında 'Günümüzde Avrasya' Konulu Toplantıda Yaptıkları Konuşma, (14 September 1994)*, pp. 5-6.

3   In a personal interview, Annaguli Nurmemedov, Under-secretary at the Turkmen Embassy in Ankara (1993), expressed the view that 'Tajiks are people who speak Iranian language and are of Turkic origin. They join the group of Turkic people naturally and historically. Their tradition and culture is the same as our tradition, but there is Iranian civilisation in their language. In the past there were Arabic and Iranian effects on our culture as well. But in the case of the Tajiks this effect was greater and the Iranian language remained as the people's language'.

4   Marie Bennigsen Broxup criticised Turkish view and underlined languages of the Turkic Republics as independent languages and not as dialects of Turkish (*Personal Interview with Maria Bennigsen Broxup*, London, 1995).

5   D.F. Sağlar, (1992), 'Kültür Bakanı Durmuş Fikri Sağlar' in *Sürekli Türk Dili Kurultayı*, (Ankara, Kültür Bakanlığı Yayınları, no. 1413, 1992), p. 6.

6   President Süleyman Demirel, at a meeting 'Eurasia Today' organised by Turkish International Co-operation Agency (TICA) on 14 September 1994 said: 'No one can deny history. Let me express openly that Turkey is after neither pan-Turkism nor pan-Islamism. In this region there are people who share the same history, same religion and same customs with us. With these peoples our tales are the same, our lullabies are the same, our epics, our language, our religion and our sentiments are the same. If we call them our brothers and sisters, no one should wonder why. How else can you define brothers and sisters?' (TIKA, *Cumhurbaşkanı Sayın Süleyman Demirel'in Türk İşbirliği ve Kalkınma Ajansı'nın Üçüncü Çalışma Yılının Başlangıcında*

'*Günümüzde Avrasya' Konulu Toplantıda Yaptıkları Konuşma (14 September 1994)*, Ankara.

7   TIKA, *Cumhurbaşkanı Sayın Süleyman Demirel'in Türk İşbirliği ve Kalkınma Ajansı'nın Üçüncü Çalışma Yılının Başlangıcında 'Günümüzde Avrasya' Konulu Toplantıda Yaptıkları Konuşma (14 September 1994)*, Ankara, p. 10.

8   Personal interview with William Hale, SOAS, London, 1995.

9   Turkey's Middle East policy, and the dispute over water should be considered as additional factors that encouraged Turkey to support the Western coalition against Saddam. Iraq and Syria opposed to the South East Anatolian Project (SEAP-GAP), and tried to stop the building of dams for GAP. For example, former President Özal pointed out at a meeting of regional directors of the Turkish State Water Administration that the construction of the Atatürk Dam on the Fırat (Euphrates) would not have been possible if the Iran-Iraq war had not diverted attention away from the issue. He added that 'They [Iraq and Syria] would now be doing their utmost to prevent us from building this dam had we not started its construction during this period [the war]'. As Özal's statement suggested, Turkey considered Syria and Iraq as potential enemies. See S. Bölükbaşı, (1993), 'Turkey Challenges Iraq and Syria: The Euphrates Dispute', *Journal of South Asian Middle Eastern Studies*, vol. 16. no. 4, pp. 9-32.

10   *Newspot*, no. 15, 19 August 1994, p. 5; Turkey lost forty billion dollars because of the UN embargo against Iraq according to August 1994 figures.

11   See, 'President George Bush's Speech at Ankara Esenboğa Airport, 20 July 1991', *Turkish Review*, vol. 5, no. 25, Autumn 1991, p. 104.

12   For Greek-Turkish relations, see T. Veremis, (1992), 'Greek-Turkish Relations and the Balkans', in *The Southeast European Year Book 1991*, Hellenic Foundation for Defence and Foreign Policy, Athens.

13   On the handicaps of Turkey in general, see E. Rouleau, (1993), 'The Challenges to Turkey', *Foreign Affairs*, vol. 72, no. 5; G. Aybet, (1992), 'Turkey in its Geo-Strategic Environment', in *Rusi & Brassey's Defence Yearbook 1992*, Royal United Services Institute, London; A. Mango, (1992), 'European Dimensions', *Middle Eastern Studies*, vol. 28, no. 2.

14   For the Turkish Cypriot's perspective on the Cyprus issue, see R. Denktaş (President of the Turkish Republic of North Cyprus), (1995), 'Kıbrısta Son Durum', *Yeni Türkiye*, vol. 1, no. 3, pp. 18-20.

15   For the Kurdish separatism see Chapter One; also see M. Gunder, (1994), *The Changing Kurdish Problem in Turkey*, Research Institute for the Study of Conflict and Terror, London.

16   For Turkey's Peace Pipeline project as a solution to the conflict, see C. Duna, (1988), 'Turkey's Peace Pipeline', in J.R. Starr and D.C. Stoll, (eds), *The politics of scarcity*, Westview Press, London, pp. 119-124.

17   *Economist*, 18 June 1987, pp. 52-58.

18   Turkish authorities single out three major problems between Turkey and Syria: first, Syrian support for the PKK; second, Syria's dissatisfaction with the amount of water Turkey has released from its dams on the Fırat (Euphrates) river; and third, Syrian claims on the Turkish province of Hatay - (the speech by the Head of the Foreign Policy Institute, Seyfi Taşhan, delivered at the meeting organised by the Royal Institute of International Affairs on 13-14 January 1992, 'Turkey from marginality to centrality', *Turkish Review*, vol. 6, no. 27, Spring 1992, p. 53.) Also see Bölükbaşı, *op. cit.* pp. 9-32; and K. İnan, (1989), 'The South-East Anatolian Project: A Perspective for Future Investors', Turkish Review, vol. 3, no. 15, p. 45; Directorate General of Press & Information of the Turkish Republic, (1990), 'Southeastern Anatolia Project (GAP)', *Turkish Review*, vol. 4, no. 20, p. 53.

19   For relations between Turkey and the EC, see N. Yalçıntaş, (1990), 'Turkey and the European Community', in H. Korner and R. Shams, (eds), *Institutional Aspects of Economic Integration of Turkey in to the European Community*, Verlag Weltarchiv Gmbh, Hamburg; M.A. Birand, (1990), *Türkiye'nin Ortak Pazar Macerası, 1959-1990*, Milliyet Yayınları, Istanbul; M.T. Uzunyaylalı, (1990), *Avrupa Topluluğu Islam ve Türkiye*, Doğu Ajans Yayınları, Istanbul; A. Eralp, (1993), 'Turkey and European Community', in A. Eralp, M. Tunay and B. Yeşilada, (eds), *The Political and Socioeconomic Transformation of Turkey*, Praeger, London, pp. 193-214; T.C. Başbakanlık Hazine ve Dışticaret Müsteşarlığı, Avrupa Topluluğu Koordinasyon Genel Müdürlüğü, (1993), *Avrupa Topluluğu ve Türkiye*, Ankara; M. Müftüler, (1993), 'Turkey and European Community: An Uneasy Relationship', *Turkish Review*, Autumn; T. Özal, (1991), *Turkey in Europe and Europe in Turkey*, K. Rustem & Brother, Nicosia; D. Arter, (1993), *The Politics of European Integration in the Twentieth century*, Dortmonth Publishing Company, Hants; V. Bozkurt, (1992), *Türkiye ve Avrupa Topluluğu*, Ağaç Yayıncılık Ltd. Şti., Istanbul; A. Eralp, (1993), 'Turkey and the European Community in the Changing post-war international system', in C. Balkır and A.M. Williams, (eds), *Turkey and Europe*, Pinter Publishers Ltd, London; E. Gerger, (1989), *Tanzimattan Avrupa Topluluğuna Türkiye*, İnkilab, Istanbul.

20   Turkey entered the Customs Union with the EC without becoming a full member in 1996. Although Turkey wants to see the Customs Union as a first step of the full membership, there is no such automatic established procedure.

21   See also, F. Şen, (1993), 'Black Sea Economic Cooperation: A Supplement to the EC?', *Aussen Politik*, vol. 44, no. 3.

22   *Financial Times*, 21 May 1992.

23   Ayvaz Gökdemir, MP from Gaziantep and a former State Minister, expressed this issue as; 'This fact (independence of the Turkic Republics), which we never expected or hoped for, never prepared for, and faced suddenly, inspired our spirits to make great efforts'. [A. Gökdemir, (1995), 'Yirmibirinci Asrın Milletimize Vaad Ettiği İmkanlar', *Yeni Türkiye*, vol.1, no.3, pp. 48-50].

24   *Sabah*, 3 February 1992.

25   TIKA, *Cumhurbaşkanı Sayın Süleyman Demirel'in Türk İşbirliği ve Kalkınma Ajansı'nın Üçüncü Çalışma Yılının Başlangıcında 'Günümüzde Avrasya' Konulu Toplantıda Yaptıkları Konuşma (14 September 1994)*, Ankara, pp. 7-8.

26   *The Washington Post*, 9 February 1992.

27   About Gulf War see, K. Matthews, (1993), *The Gulf Conflict and International Relations*, Routledge, London.

28   *Türkiye Günlüğü*, Summer 1992, p. 12.

29   *Dünya*, 6 November 1992.

30   *Guardian*, 3 April 1992.

31   *Time*, 13 May 1991, p. 23.

32   *Middle East*, July 1992, no. 213, p. 5.

33   *Time*, 10 February 1992.

34   TIKA, *Cumhurbaşkanı Sayın Süleyman Demirel'in Türk İşbirliği ve Kalkınma Ajansı'nın Üçüncü Çalışma Yılının Başlangıcında 'Günümüzde Avrasya' Konulu Toplantıda Yaptıkları Konuşma (14 September 1994)*, Ankara, p. 7.

35   *Jane's Defence Weekly*, 18 April 1992.

36   *Financial Times*, 7 May 1993.

37   *Guardian*, 3 April 1992.

38   His wife, Semra Özal, some of his relatives and some people in Turkish media claim that Özal did not die but he was killed. However, there is no published evidence that proves this allegation.

39   In a personal interview, Kamran İnan claimed that after Özal, Turkey returned to her classic passive policy in international relations. Similarly Kurtcebe Alptemoçin, former Foreign Minister, asserted that 'Everybody related with foreign policy in Turkey is pro-status quo... Especially after Özal, Turkey gave up the tradition of determining the foreign agenda', (*Yeni Hafta,* 4-10 October 1993).

40   The Economist Intelligence Unit, (1993), *Country Profile, Turkey 1992-93,* London p. 3; and The Economist Intelligence Unit, (1994), *Country Profile, Turkey, 1993-94,* London, p. 6.

41   For details of the 1987 general elections see A. Finkel and w. Hale, (1990), 'Politics and Procedure in the 1987 Turkish General Election', in A. Finkel and N. Sırman (eds), *Turkish State, Turkish Society,* Routledge, London.

42   The Economist Intelligence Unit, (1993), *Country Profile, Turkey 1992-93,* London, pp. 5-6.

43   See B. A. Yeşilada, (1988), 'Problems of Political Development in the Third Turkish Republic', *Polity,* vol.21, no.2, pp. 345-372; Zaralı, (1986), *Anap Üzerine Tezler, 11.Tez,* no. 2; M. Tunay, (1993), 'The Turkish New Right's Attempt at Hegemony', in A. Eralp, M. Tunay and B. Yeşilada, (eds), *The Political and Socioeconomic Transformation of Turkey,* Praeger, London, pp. 11-30.

44   See chapters by Ergüder, Heper, Rustow, and Karpat in M. Heper and A. Evin, (1988), *State, Democracy, and the Military: Turkey in the 1980s,* Gruyter, New York.

45   The Economist Intelligence Unit, (1993), *Country Profile 1992-93,* London, pp. 5-6.

46   *Financial Times,* 21 May 1992.

47   *Financial Times,* 21 May 1992.

48   Ibid.

49   *Financial Times,* 21 May 1992.

50   The Economist Intelligence Unit, (1994), *Country Profile: Turkey, 1993-94,* London, p. 7.

51   For his detailed research about Far East models see C. Kozlu, (1994), *Türkiye Mucizesi için Vizyon Arayışları ve Asya Modelleri,* Türkiye İş Bankası Kültür Yayınları, Ankara.

52   Milli Eğitim Bakanlığı Yurtdışı Eğitim Genel Müdürlüğü, (1993), *Milli Eğitim Bakanlığı ve Türk Dünyası,* Ankara, pp. 8-9.

53   Başbakanlık Basın Merkezi, (1995), 'Tansu Çiller'in Rektörler Toplantısında Yaptığı Konuşma, (19 March, 1995)', in *Avrupa ile Bütünleşiyoruz, Gümrük Birliği,* Ankara, p. 72.

54   *Cumhuriyet Halk Partisi Çalışma Raporu,* 27. Olağan Kurultay 9-10 September 1995, Ankara, p. 39.

55   CHP Yayınları, *CHP-SHP Bütünleşme genel Kurulu, Ana İlkeler ve Temel Hedefler Bildirgesi,* 18 February 1995, Ankara p. 27.

56   *Ibid.,* pp. 28-29; Cumhuriyet Halk Partisi Çalışma Raporu, *op. cit.,* p. 20,22.

57   *Personal interview with Ayşe Ayata,* Professor of Political Science, Middle East Technical University, Ankara, 1996.

58   *Güvercin,* DSP Genel Merkezi Haber Bülteni, 5 August 1994, p. 3; see also, B. Ecevit, (1993), 'Türk Halk Tasavvufu İnanç Özgürlüğü ve Laiklik, *Çağrışım Dergisi,* June.

59   For example, see DSP Yayınları, (1995), *Demokratik Sol partinin 1995 Seçim Bildirgesi Özet,* Ankara, p. 3.

60   *Sabah,* 18 August 1993.

61   Demokratik Sol partinin 1995 Seçim Bildirgesi, özet, *op. cit.,* p. 16.

62   *Personal interview with Ertuğrul O. Çırağan,* Ankara, 1996.

63   Most probably Mümtaz Soysal, a member of the SDPP.

64   *Yeni Forum,* June 1992, p. 18.

65   The nationalism of Ecevit should not be confused with pan-Turkism and racism. In an article published in a weekly magazine *Nokta,* he summarised his view on nationalism and explained

that his nationalism was in fact the nationalism of Atatürk. See B. Ecevit, (1984), 'Türk Milleti ve Türkiye', *Nokta Dergisi*, 11-17 June, pp. 20-24.

66   The Welfare Party was closed down by the decision of Turkish Constitution Court in 1998 as the Court believed that Welfare Party's activities violated principle of Secularism in Turkish Constitution (Article 2). Then Virtue Party (Fazilet Partisi) was established.

67   Refah Partisi Yayınları, *Milli Görüşün İktidardaki Hizmetleri (1974-1978)*, Ankara.

68   See, N. Erbakan, (1991), *The Just Economic System*, Refah Partisi Yayınları, Ankara; See also, Refah Partisi Yayınları, *21 Soruda Adil Düzen*, Ankara

69   Refah Partisi Yayınları, *24 December 1995 Refah Partisi Seçim Beyannamesi (Özet)*, Ankara, p. 29.

70   Refah Partisi Yayınları, (1995), *24 December 1995 Seçimi Refah Partisi Sloganları*, Ankara, p. 5.

71   On Necmettin Erbakan's view, see N. Erbakan, (1995), 'Türkiye'nin Dış Politikası Nasıl Olmalı', *Yeni Türkiye*, vol. 1, no. 3.

72   A. Türkeş, (no date), *Temel Görüşler*, Bizim Ocak Kitap kulübü, Ankara, p. 276.

73   See also, A. Türkeş, (1985), *Dokuz Işık*, Burç Yayınları, Eskişehir.

74   Instead the meaning of secularism, if it is to be retained in the constitution, should be defined; see Refah Partisi Yayını, *Refah Partisinin Anayasa Değişikliği Uzlaşma Teklifi*, (Ankara: Refah Partisi Yayını).

75   *Yeni Yüzyıl*, 26 December 1996; In this context it is necessary to point out that NAP had an Islamic faction led by Muhsin Yazıcıoğlu, Muharrem Şemsek and colleagues. The differences were deeply rooted even before 1980. The Islamic faction left the NAP (*Cumhuriyet*, 6,9,14 July 1992, *Milliyet*, 9 July 1992, *Hürriyet*, 14 July 1992) and later established a party called Büyük Birlik Partisi (the Great Unity Party).

76   The Marxist left is represented in Turkey by Doğu Perinçek and his party 'İşçi Partisi (Workers Party)'. For the opinion of Doğu Perinçek on International relations, see D. Perinçek, (1995), 'Güneyli Dış Politikası', *Yeni Türkiye*, vol. 1, no. 3, pp. 127-145. Sadun Aren and his 'Birleşik Sosyalist Parti (United Socialist Party)' is also a representative of the Marxist left. For Aren's view on the future of Socialism see; S. Aren, (1995), 'Yeni Bir Dünya Yeni Bir Sosyalism', *Yeni Türkiye*, vol. 1, no. 3, pp. 146-148.

77   *Jane's Defence Weekly*, 18 April 1992.

78   Ambassador Ümit Arık, head of TICA (Turkish International Cooperation Agency), '*Yeni Uluslararası Düzen, Türk Dış Politikası, Bağımsız yeni Türk Devletleri ve Türk İşbirliği Kalkınma Ajansı*', an unpublished document from the archives of TICA.

79   For a brief introduction to the Third İzmir Economy Conference see, K. Atasayar, (1992), '3. İktisat Kongresinin Ardından', *İşveren*, no. 6.

80   *İşveren*, no. 6, June 1992, p. 29.

81   *İşveren*, no. 6, June 1992, pp. 26-28; H. Gültekin Köksal, President of the Administrative Committee of ROSTURK, made similar statements on other occasions; see Hazine ve Dış Ticaret Müsteşarlığı İhracatı Geliştirme Etüd Merkezi, Dış Ticaret Elemanı Eğitim Programı 2-10 March 1992, 'Yeni Türk Cumhuriyetleri ile Ticari İşbirliği Olanakları' by H. Gültekin Köksal.

82   Rıdvan Karluk was advisor to the Prime minister related with co-ordination of the economic relations between Turkey and Turkic Republics in 1992. In his article he analysed economic problems of the Turkic Republics. See, 'Yeni bağımsızlığını kazanmış Türk Cumhuriyetlerinin serbest piyasa ekonomisine geçişinde alınması gereken tedbirler ve öneriler', *Istanbul Sanayi Odası Dergisi*, vol. 27, no. 315, 22 May 1992.

83   *Yeni Forum*, June 1992, pp. 13-14; For details of these discussions see articles by Metin Çulhaoğlu, Zülfü Dicleli, Ender Helvacıoğlu, Ertuğrul Kürkçü, Ömer Laçiner, Saruhan Oluç and

Sungur Savran in *İktisat Dergisi*, April 1992.

84 *Personal interview with Ayşe Ayata*, Ankara, 14 May 1996.

85 *TOBB Türk Cumhuriyetleri İnceleme ve Araştırma Gezisi*, an unpublished report prepared by TOBB.

86 *Guardian*, 3 April 1992.

87 Directorate General of Press and Information, (1993), *Turkey*, pp. 184-185.

88 The numbers were taken from the High Council of Radio Television (RTÜK) on 7 April 1997. However the number of private TV channels and Radio stations increases every year.

89 *Sabah* also gave its readers a booklet on Bosnia, which is also regarded as a Turkic Republic.

90 Ecevit's articles were published in *Yeni Günaydın* on 1, 2, 6, 8, 10 and 11 February 1992. On 7 and 12 February 1992, Ecevit and Ardan Zentürk published joint articles.

91 *Yeni Günaydın*, 1 February 1992.

92 *Yeni Hafta*, 27 September - 3 October 1993.

93 For example, see *Yeni Forum*, June 1992, pp. 9-10; *Yeni Hafta*, 11-17 October 1993; *Sabah*, 22 June 1993; *Zaman*, 4 July 1993.

94 See *2000'e Doğru*, July 1992.

95 See TIKA, (1994), *Türk Cumhuriyetlerinin tanışma ve yakınlaşmasında basının rolü konferansı*, 20-21 October 1993, Istanbul, Türk İşbirliği ve Kalkınma Ajansı Yayınları, no. 10, Konferanslar Dizisi. 4, pp. 18-20. For Umit Arık's statements see; pp. 21-22.

96 See *20-21 October 1993 Turk Cumhuriyetlerinin Tanışması ve Yakınlaşmasında Basının rolü Konferansı Sonuç bildirgesi.*

97 *The Wall Street Journal*, 13 March 1992; *Jane's Defence Weekly*, 18 April 1992 and *The Washington Post*, 19 March 1992, p. 17.

98 *International Herald Tribune*, 13 March 1992.

99 *The Washington Post*, 19 March 1992, p. 17.

100 *The Washington Post*, 19 March 1992, p. 17.

101 The head of the independent Foreign Policy Institute, Seyfi Taşhan, underlined that 'with the statement "A Turkish world will be established from the Adriatic to the Great Wall of China", we made several states hostile to us. Also this statement of Demirel's became meaningless later'. See *Yeni Hafta*, 23 September - 3 October 1993.

102 The results of this survey also suggested a shift of interest in Turkish public opinion, as only 21% of those surveyed gave priority to the EU and wanted Turkey to enter it, whereas surprisingly, around 52% gave priority to the Turkic Republics and wanted Turkey to foster its relations with them.

103 Also see his book, K. İnan, (1995), *Hayır Diyebilen Türkiye*, Timaş Yayınları, Istanbul.

104 F.R. Zorlu was Foreign Minister in the Democrat Party government until the 1960 military coup, following which he was hanged.

105 It must be noted that on some occasions before the collapse of the USSR, Turkey's successful economic transformation was mentioned by some circles as a model for the Eastern European states, which were struggling to transform their centrally planned economies to open market economies. For example; Özal mentioned the Turkish experience as a model for the rest: see Ataöv, (1992), 'Turkey's Expanding Relations with the CIS and Eastern Europe', in C.H. Dodd, (ed.) *Turkish Foreign Policy*, Eothen Press, Huntington, p. 89.

106 *Guardian*, 3 April 1992.

107 *Personal interview with Acar Okan*, adviser to the Prime Minister, Ankara, 1993.

108 *Newspot*, 12 March 1992, p. 1.

109 Milli Eğitim Bakanlığı Yurtdışı Eğitim Genel Müdürlüğü, (1993), *Milli Eğitim Bakanlığı ve Türk Dünyası*, Prepared by Zeki Alan, Ankara, p. 14.

110 *Newspot*, 12 March 1992, p. 7.

111 *Ibid.*

112 *Dünya*, 6 November 1992; *Ankara Declaration (Ankara Bildirisi)*, Ankara, unpublished, Foreign Ministry, 1992.

113 *Dünya*, 6 November 1992.

114 For the competition and Iran's policy towards Turkic Republics see Chapter Three.

115 *Newspot*, 9 April 1992, p. 2

116 *SWB*, ME/1290, A5, 29 January 1992.

117 'Cumhurbaşkanı Sayın Süleyman Demirel'in Türk İşbirliği ve Kalkınma Ajansı'nın Üçüncü Çalışma Yılının Başlangıcında 'Günümüzde Avrasya' Konulu Toplantıda Yaptıkları Konuşma', *op. cit.*, p. 14.

118 *Newspot*, 3 December 1992.

119 *Financial Times*, 21 May 1992.

120 Interview with Sultan Sirkeci, *Tim-se*, no. 103, March 1992.

121 *Newspot*, 3 December 1992.

122 For this issue see A. Aydın, (1997), 'Orta Asya Petrolü Üzerine Zor Bir Senaryo: Hazar – Akdeniz Mega Projesi', *Yeni Türkiye*, vol. 3, no. 15.

123 *TRT Avrasya TV*, News at 6.00 p.m., 18.11.1999.

124 *Financial Times*, 21 May 1992.

125 *Financial Times*, 21 May 1992.

126 *Personal Interview with Arif Soytürk*, Ankara, 21 June 1993.

127 462 of these students were placed in Istanbul, 65 in Trabzon, 58 in İçel, and 22 in Konya.

128 *Bugüne Kadar Başkanlığımızca Soydaşlarımıza Sunulan Hizmetler*. An unpublished note prepared by the Presidency of Religious Affairs, p. 34.

129 *Dünya*, 27 April 1992; See article by Taylan Erten in *Dünya*, 27 April 1992.

130 Milli Eğitim Bakanlığı ve Türk Dünyası, *op. cit.*, p. 35.

131 *Sabah*, 17 October 1992.

132 Milli Eğitim Bakanlığı ve Türk Dünyası, *op. cit.*, p. 54

133 *Tercüman*, 28 September 1992; *Sabah*, 15 October 1992; *Sabah*, 17 October 1992.

134 Milli Eğitim Bakanlığı ve Türk Dünyası, *op. cit.*, p. 11.

135 *SWB*, SU/1322, A4/1, 6 March, 1992.

136 *Newspot*, 7 May, 1992, p. 3; See also, T. Karasik, (1993), *Azerbaijan, Central Asia, and Future Persian Gulf Security*, Rand, Santa Monica, p. 39.

137 Turkey, *op. cit.*, p. 190.

138 For a list of participants in this symposium, see N. Devlet, (1993), Çağdaş Türkiler, Ek Cilt, Doğuştan Günümüze Büyük İslam Tarihi, Çağ Yayınları, Istanbul, pp. 28-29.

139 For Azeri Linguist Kamil Veliyev's speech, see Kültür Bakanlığı, *(1992)*, *Sürekli Türk Dili Kurultayı*, Ankara,), pp. 14-17. Similarly, Azeri linguist Bekir Nebiyev mentioned Turkish unity and expressed his positive attitude towards Turkey. For his speech, see Sürekli Türk Dili Kurultayı, *op. cit.*, pp. 20-26.

140 For the speech of Tünegün Kasymbegov, adviser to the Kirgiz president, see, Sürekli Türk Dili Kurultayı, *op. cit.*, pp. 18-20.

141 For the speech of the Kazak representative see, Sürekli Türk Dili Kurultayı, *op. cit.*, pp. 29-30.

142 *Tercüman*, 1 February 1992.

143 *Newspot*, 11 March 1993, p. 3.

144 *Guardian*, 3 April 1992.

145 *Jane's Defence Weekly*, 18 April 1992.

146 *SWB*, SU/1346, C1/2, 3 April 1992.

147   *The Times*, 26 May 1992.
148   *The Christian Science Monitor*, 15-21 May 1992, p. 10A.
149   *Milliyet*, 20 May 1992.
150   *The Independent*, 25 May 1992.
151   *Cumhuriyet*, 21 September 1992. Although Turkey denied the accusation, it has been claimed that Turkey sent special forces and tanks to Azerbaijan.
152   *Zaman*, 24 December 1991.
153   *Yeni Forum*, July 1993, p. 10.
154   *Ibid.*, pp. 8-9.
155   *Sabah*, 23 June 1993.
156   *Milliyet*, 12 June 1993.
157   *Milliyet, Hürriyet, Cumhuriyet*, 28 June 1993; *Cumhuriyet*, 22 June 1993.
158   *Cumhuriyet*, 20 June 1993; *Milliyet* 24 June 1993; For this claim see Y. Aslan, (1993), 'Azerbaycan'da Sovyet Oyunu', *Yeni Forum*, July, pp. 17-19. Similarly, Dr. Timur Kocaoğlu underlined in *Yeni Düşünce* newspaper that Turkey should have interfered in the developments in Azerbaijan (the fall of Elchibey) for its own security, not only for reasons of humanitarianism or Azeri brotherhood. He claimed that Russia and Iran co-operated in overthrowing Elchibey who was following pro-Turkish policies (*Yeni Düşünce*, 10 September 1993).
159   *Cumhuriyet*, 20 June, 1993; *Sabah*, 22 June 1993.
160   *Yeni Forum*, July 1993 p. 10.
161   *Le Monde*, 17 June 1993.
162   In a personal interview, Cemil Çiçek made similar claims.
163   Zaman, 7 August 1993

3 The Rise and the Fall of the Turkish Model in the West

Introduction

As it is stated at the outset of chapter one that President Bush (Rashid, 1994, p.210) and Mme Catherine Lalumiére, the Secretary General of the Council of Europe, pointed out Turkey as a model for newly independent Central Asian republics. During her visit to the Central Asian Republics, Lalumiére declared that 'Turkey provided a valid model of development for many a newly-independent country in Asia' (Mango, 1993, p.726). Mango (1993, p.726) and Yalçın (1992d, p.22) referred to the statement of Mme Catherine Lalumiére and argue that this was the first time the West proposed the Turkish Model to the Turkic Republics.[1] On the other hand, there were some people who were not sure about who first proposed the Turkish Model to the Central Asian Republics. For example: William Hale thought that the initiative might have come from both sides at the same time.[2] However even if Turkey had proposed its model for the Turkic Republics first,[3] the support of the West was crucial for the popularity of the proposal. In this study although European States and US are referred as 'the West' in general, it is necessary to make a clear distinction between US and European states in terms of their support to the Turkish model. Although European states favoured the Turkish model and want to see Turkish model being adopted by newly Turkic republics, as Robins (1994, p.63) pointed out, the major proponent of such a view was the United States, which feared that a political vacuum had been created in Central Asia and that it would be filled by Iran and its revolutionary brand of Islam. This chapter seeks the possible reasons behind the Western support for the Turkish Model and how this support has declined. In the course of the discussion, a major emphasis will be made on the period 1991-93 because it was in this period that Turkish model was proposed and the term 'Turkish Model' occupied newspapers in Turkey and in the West. However, reference will be made to events outside the period in order to give a clearer picture of the Western policies towards the area at a later date.

Western Promotion of the Turkish Model

Turkey had joined the Western security system after the Second World War because of the Soviet threat, and within that system it played a vital role. Thirty-seven percent of the common borders between the Western block and the Eastern block were protected by Turkey, and with the exception of the US, Turkey had the largest army (İnan, 1995b, p.12). However, Turkey's Western allies looked upon it essentially as a rampart against Soviet military expansion, rather than as an equal partner sharing their own democratic principles and traditions. In the post-Cold War situation, Turkey's international credibility could no longer be based mainly on its former Cold War role as an anti-Communist bastion and defender of NATO's South East flank (İnan, 1995b, p.12; Ahrari, 1994, p.531).[4] Thus, with the end of the Cold War, Turkey's geopolitical importance to the West was in doubt. Therefore, apart from the obvious economic reasons and benefits, it was argued that Ankara promoted the Black Sea Economic Co-operation (BSEC) with the expectation that by leading the Black Sea states - some of which, like Russia, Ukraine and Romania, are major regional players - in a pact to encourage development and stability, the US and Europe would be persuaded of Turkey's continued significance in a potentially explosive area.[5] Briefly, it was seen as an instrument by which Turkey could persuade the West that it was still important to them.

However, in general, Western intellectuals and strategists underlined that there were new opportunities and new roles for Turkey in the region. It was argued that with the destruction of the Iron Curtain, the importance of Turkey had increased.[6] Some analysts pointed out the importance of Turkey by declaring that 'Turkey is at the absolute geopolitical centre of a newly emerging world' (Hostler, 1993, p.162)[7] and that Turkey had become an important regional power (Abramowitz, 1993, pp.164-167; Hostler, 1993, p.162). Henze (1992, p.1) claimed that Turks were increasingly realising that their country need no longer be a merely passive element in international political and economic life, but could influence the world, not only its own neighbourhood. The Turkish proposition of BSEC was singled out as an important development and an indicator of Turkish influence in the region (Arter, 1993, p.232). The collapse of the USSR in mid-December 1991 and the creation of fifteen independent states, according to Hiro (1994, p.68), 'led to the rise of Turkic nationalism in Azerbaijan and the five Republics of Central Asia, and opened up vast economic, diplomatic and cultural possibilities for Turkey at official and private levels'.[8] This suggested that Turkey's advantage in terms of its relations with the Turkic Republics lay not only in its geopolitical position but also in the ties of kinship, common culture, language and history between the Anatolian and Central Asian Turks. It was even pointed out how difficult it was to distinguish politics from ethnicity (Frank, 1992, pp.22-23).[9] It was argued that Turkey's importance for the West had increased, as Turkey was usually regarded as a gateway to the new republics of the Caucasus and Central Asia because of its potential for helping the West to establish relations with those areas (Henze, 1992, p.v).

Some of the claims made for Turkey, especially by the Western media, were exaggerated. For example, The Daily Telegraph described the position of Turkey as 'An old empire rising again'.[10] Jane's Defence Weekly stressed the importance of Turkey using the headline 'Turkey: growing power in a region of change'[11], while the Economist wrote that 'Turkey is the Star that shows Turkic countries the way'.[12] German radio claimed that the Turkic Republics and Turkey were trying to establish economic co-operation. German newspaper Frankfurter Rundschau, under the headline 'Big revenge', wrote: 'Russia and England had divided inner Asia between them and destroyed the sick man of the straits, the Ottoman Empire, 100 years ago. Today, the revenge for that old game has been played, and in this game Turkey, being the main actor, is taking her revenge' (Toker, 1992, p.255). Die Welt claimed that Turkey could govern Central Asia, and went on to suggest that the Turkish formation of BSEC was 'the indicator of Turkish power' (Toker, 1992, p.256). The French Paris Match claimed that a new Ottoman Empire was born: 'Turkey, whose application to unite with Europe was refused by the EC, is awakening. The Turkic Republics have turned to Ankara. Turkey is a superpower in the region' (Toker, 1992, p.256). Der Standart from Austria pointed out that 'a Turkey stretching from the Adriatic to the Great Wall of China has been born... Turkey is becoming a big power....' (Toker, 1992, p.256). Certainly these were exaggerated claims, but the common point underlined by these media commentaries was the existence of new opportunities and new horizons for Turkey.[13] Frank (1992, p.23) summarised these opportunities; 'Ever since Atatürk, Turkey itself seems to prefer becoming the last wagon on the European train. But if Europe now closes off that option, perhaps Turkey will opt for becoming the locomotive on a Pan-Turkist Asia instead'.

Therefore, the end of the Cold War, far from robbing Turkey of its strategic importance as once seemed likely, promoted it to the very eye of the storm. Some American strategists even argued that 'Turkey replaced Germany as the US's most important ally'.[14] This encouragement by the West boosted the national pride of the Turkish officials. Maybe because of the realisation of Turkey's new leadership role in Central Asia and Balkans[15], Hikmet Çetin (1992, p.11), the Turkish Foreign Minister in 1992, pointed out that 'in the current era of transition and ferment, Turkey has a greater stake than ever in the preservation of stability in Europe'. It was interpreted that 'after years spent at the fringe of Western clubs such as the EEC and NATO', Turkey had begun to flex its regional muscles. Related with this, a Turkish academic, Professor Hasan Koni at Ankara University, said, 'We are no longer asking ourselves, whether we are European, Middle Easterners or both. We have come to terms with our own identity. We are Turks and we like it'.[16]

The Western support of Turkey as a model for the rest of the Turkic world[17] was ratification of Turkey's importance for the West in the post-Cold War era and in the early 1990s the Turkish model became popular and was regarded as an ideal path for the Turkic Republics, in fact for all the Muslim Republics, of the former Soviet Union. This was not because the Model was perfect, in fact it had significant problems.[18] Turkish democracy was interrupted three times; in 1960, in 1971 and most recently in 1980, and its economy was weaker than those of the European powers. But more importantly, the model's main problems were related to ethnic (Kurdish) and religious minorities (Alawite). Despite its flaws, the model became popular in the early 1990's because of three main reasons: first, the Turkish Model was secular and democratic (or had experience of turning a single party system into a multi-party system) in essence and it was close to the West; second, there was a supposed common culture, religion and linguistic affinity between Turkey and the Turkic Republics; and third, the Turkish Model had a recent experience in transforming a centrally planned economy into a market economy. Although the West knew that the formation of a civil society and democracy in Turkey were not perfect in comparison to the Western standards, perhaps this was a positive ingredient for the Model rather than a negative point, because the adoption of the Model would ease the passage to Western style democracy in the future rather than to hinder it.

Secularism and Democracy

After the end of the communist system, Muslim peoples as well as members of other denominations had started to revive their religion. Mosques began to be reopened and new ones built. Briefly, Islam was beginning to emerge in the region very quickly. The unknown factor in the West was what these developments might lead to, and that Iranian-type regimes might be established in these Muslim Republics was a real worry.[19] As Malik (1992, p.35) pointed out,

> Following the collapse of the Soviet Union, the fear of the 'evil Empire' has given way to the fear of the 'Islamic Empire'[20] stretching from North Africa in the West to Central Asia in the East. The return to Islam by the peoples of Central Asia has been the most significant development of the past few years.

Huntington (1993), in his well-known article 'Clash of Civilisations' claimed that the new confrontation will be between the West and Islam. Some sources went as far as stating that if in the near future (the next 20 years) the confrontation is between Islam and West, then Turkey's role model was important not only for the new Muslim Republics of the former Soviet Union, but also for the entire Muslim World.[21] The possibility of the strengthening of an Islamic-based influence in the region made the West nervous because it could mean the creation of an anti-Western, fundamentalist bloc in the Middle East reaching to the borders of China (Xiaodong, 1992, p.12).

In Turkey, the opinion was divided. While Turkish secularism combined with Islam was seen as the best model, the more Islamic and conservative states-people of Turkey claimed that the West was scared of Islam with the fear of losing its own influence in the world.[22] The leftist parties in Turkey singled out (and still do) Islamic fundamentalism and especially Iran as a danger to the whole area including Turkey.[23]

The West worried about the possibility that Central Asian states joining the Iran- Algeria group, because if radical Islam was adopted by the newly independent states in the Caucasus and Central Asia, the region could pose a threat to the West because of its geographic position and natural resources. Therefore, the Muslim states of the former Soviet Union were to be discouraged from adopting the 'Iranian Islamic model' (Ahrari, 1994, pp.530-531). It was assumed that if the Muslim states of the former USSR adopted Islamic-oriented governments, this would automatically lead to anti-Americanism and anti-Westernism because one of the main characteristics of the Iranian model is its anti-Americanism. For the West, Islamic resurgence meant extremism and anti-Westernism. It was also assumed that Iran's involvement in the Muslim republics was inherently destabilising (Ahrari, 1994, pp.531-532).[24]

These concerns of the West were supported by geopolitical factors. Iran was in a key strategic position as it had common borders with Azerbaijan and Turkmenistan and therefore could easily develop its trade with the area. It also had cultural connections especially with Tajikistan who spoke an Iranian language and it had historical connections with the whole area; moreover two-thirds of the Azeri population were Shiite, which could prepare a suitable base for any Iranian influence. In brief, there was a Western fear that the power vacuum created by the end of the USSR could be filled by Iran, and the Iranian model could be adopted by the Muslim states of the former USSR (Robins, 1994, p.63).

The rise of Iran and Turkey as the new players in the Caucasus and Central Asia because of their historical, geographical and cultural closeness to the region seemed inevitable. Turkey and Iran were seen as rival powers (Gharabaghi, 1994, p.115). Hence, overwhelming attention has been paid to an ideological competition between Iran and Turkey by the media, as well as by several Western academic publications.[25] It was expected that after the end of the USSR, Iran would try to export its regime to its newly independent Muslim neighbours (G. Kut, 1994, p.17; Israeli, 1994, pp.20-21). Especially for this reason the West supported the Turkish Model. The Turkish Republic was established on secular bases; the Sultanate and Caliphate were abolished and European laws were adopted instead of Islamic law. The principle of secularism was in the constitution since 1937. Turkish state modelled itself after the European states and the European civilisation. In this sense Turkey was a European state, which aimed to cooperate with the West and aimed to reach the level of the West in technology and civilisation. Although Turkish one party rule continued until 1946, and although Turkish democracy was not perfect, in the early 1990's Turkey was a sample of democracy and secularism in its region. Also there was a similarity between Turkey and Turkic Republics as Turkey was a theocratic state which had become a democracy. Similarly Turkic people of Central Asia were governed as theocratic states until when they were faced with one-party rule during the former USSR. After the independence, apart from other aspects of the Turkish Model, democracy (multi-party) experience of Turkey could be helpful for these new Republics. Therefore, the Turkish Model was the best choice in the area as a counter model against Iran.

Common Origins and Cultural Affinity

In the early 1990s, the West (and indeed the World) did not know much about the Muslim republics of the former Soviet Union. The closest affinity of their origins and cultures (as history showed) would be either with Turkey or with Iran. The Central Asians mostly had Turkic origins, and the assumption was that probably years of communism had not drastically altered these Turkic origins and cultures and that it would be easier for the Muslim republics to follow the path of a country with which they felt close to and shared a common heritage.

Mainly because of the common origins of the peoples of Turkey and the Turkic Republics (Frank, 1992, pp.22-23),[26] public opinion towards Turkey in the Turkic Republics was assumed to be positive.[27] Turkish observers consistently pointed out that the people of the Turkic Republics saw the people of Turkey as their kin and Turkey as a strong relative state that would show the 'true path' to the new Turkic Republics.[28] It can be argued that the possibility of the existence of positive feelings between the peoples of Turkic origin encouraged the West to put forward the Turkish Model for the newly independent Turkic Republics of the ex-Soviet Union.

Turkish Experience in Economic Transformation

During the USSR, the economies of the Turkic Republics were controlled by the centre and detailed plans were applied to their economies. The scope for lower levels of government to choose their own priorities was very limited. As White pointed out, the all-union ministries situated in Moscow produced 57% of industrial output, and the union-republic ministries based partly in Moscow produced a further 37%. Only 6% of the industry was wholly regulated at the level of the Republics (White, 1991, pp.139-140). Soviet industrial policies led to mass wastage which could not be sustained and the absence of competition in the economy, the determination of the prices by the centre but not in the market resulted in wastage and corruption (Ergun, 1992, p. 109).

After the collapse of the USSR, the independent Republics attempted to transform their economies from the centrally controlled, inefficient communist system to market economy; but this was a difficult task. One of the candidates for the presidency in the Russian Republic in 1991, Vadim Bakatin, described the difficulty as 'It is easy to make the transformation from capitalism to socialism. It looks like making an omelette by breaking eggs. But it is not easy to produce a Capitalist regime from Socialism. It looks like trying to make fresh eggs out of an omelette' (Ergun, 1992, p.109). A market economy has requirements such as private ownership, suitable legal bases (commercial laws, and other legal controls), low inflation rates, a tax policy that suits the price system, free interest rates, prices to be determined by the market and not by the state, the presence of a banking system and a capital market (Togan, 1992, pp.89-95). At the same time people need to be trained in order to be able to function in a market economy. However, there was no unwillingness on the part of Turkey to take on the responsibility of helping other countries to make the transition. One of the most outstanding characteristics of the Turkish Model was its performance in economic transformation, in other words its success in transforming its centrally controlled economy to a liberal economic system. In fact, Turkish analysts were convinced that Turkey was suitable for the position of a leader, because

> Turkey did a decade ago what the CIS and the Eastern European countries are now trying to do. These former socialist countries look at Turkey as a country, which transformed itself from a closed, to an open economy. Their representatives frequently state that they study the 'Turkish Model' (Ataöv, 1992, p.89).

One can argue that if for the newly independent states the experience of another country which had made a similar transformation to market economy was needed, then the Turkish Model would be the best choice because it had the additional advantage of having originated from a country with ethnic and cultural affinities with the region, and Turkey had made the transition recently.

Grooming the Turkish Model

After it was more or less agreed that Turkey was a successful example of a democratic secular state with a liberal economic system and an Islamic culture (Olcott, 1992a, p.265), its promotion went ahead full speed. Turkey was the only Muslim state which could integrate with the West, as several secular institutions had been developed in the Western style,[29] more importantly the origin of the Turkish model was in the Western democracies (especially the French model[30]). Prime Minister Demirel, while visiting Britain in 1993, stated 'We will bring European values to the region', meaning that Turkey represented Europe and European values in the region.[31] Turkey needed this role in the region. It had to prove that it was still important even after the Cold War or perhaps anxious to try to find an agenda with which it could approach the post-Cold War situation in general. In this sense, the end of the Soviet Union provided a new instrument for Turkey, and a new area was opened to Turkish influence in the shape of the Turkic republics of the former USSR, and the instrument was the Turkish model in which Turkey and the West, including the US, found a new basis for strategic co-operation.

The Turkish government immediately underlined its secular image, and proposed itself as the obvious choice as opposed to Iran. For example, in an interview in Istanbul, Prime Minister Demirel told the journalists that 'We are the only Muslim country defending secularism, and we believe that being Muslim is not a handicap to being part of the Western world'.[32] He emphasised that 'Turkey is committed to being a model of democracy, rule of law, tolerance, respect for human rights and economic liberties'.[33] Furthermore, Demirel argued in his Davos visit (at the beginning of 1992), and later in his formal US visit, that the Turkish model was a suitable model for the newly independent Muslim Republics of the Caucasus and Central Asia. In the post-Cold War situation, with the uncertain search for a New World Order, Demirel's proposition was welcomed and supported by the West (G. Kut, 1994, p.14).

Turkey was actively encouraged by America in offering itself as a role model to Central Asia and Azerbaijan (Hiro, 1994, pp.68-69). The Bush administration underlined that by using the common ethnic variable Turkey should persuade Central Asian states to adopt the Turkish secular model of government (Ahrari, 1994, pp.530-531). During Prime Minister Demirel's US visit, the Bush administration announced its support for Turkey and the Turkish model with respect to the Turkic republics.[34] After a meeting with the Turkish Prime Minister Demirel in Washington on 13 February 1992, President Bush pointed to Turkey 'as the model of a democratic, secular state.... In a region of changing tides, Turkey endures as a beacon of stability', Bush said. US companies were encouraged to find Turkish partners for joint ventures in Central Asia, and 'US diplomats encouraged Central Asian politicians and bureaucrats to travel to Turkey to see a modern country at work' (Rashid, 1994, p.210; Kesic, 1995). US foreign minister Baker gave similar messages, suggesting Turkey as an ideal model for their development to the leaders of the Muslim republics of the former Soviet Union in his Central Asia visit.[35] It was assumed that adoption of the Turkish Model by the Central Asian states would enable them to avoid political instability, and the spread of radical Islam (Winrow, 1992, p.107).

Western support for the Turkish model meant, at the same time Western support for Turkey in its competition with Iran.[36] The Turkish model was emphasised as an ideal Muslim democracy, as opposed to the Iranian regime. NATO chief Manfred Woerner said in Moscow in February 1992 that Islamic fundamentalists were becoming increasingly strong in the Muslim Republics and that this did not conform to NATO interests. NATO looked to Turkey to redress the balance (Rashid, 1994, p.210). William Taft, the US representative in NATO, also argued that 'Turkey constitutes a good model for the Muslim countries in the transition to a democratic, secular system'. Furthermore, he also highlighted necessity that Turkey should be supported by Western countries in its efforts to help the Muslim Republics of the former Soviet Union.[37] A similar statement by Mme Catherine Lalumiére, the Secretary General of the Council of Europe, has been cited at the beginning of this chapter (Mango, 1993, p.726).

Even one section of the Russian elite looked favourably on the idea that the Turkish model should be adopted by these new Muslim Republics and that Turkey should play a vital role in the region. They did not want to see instability in the region, and was especially concerned about the rise of Iranian-originated religious radicalism. Russia would be affected directly by developments in the region mainly because of the ethnic Russians living in the area and through its own Muslim population. Therefore they supported the Turkish attempt to reconcile with the Muslim population of the area and the institution of secular and democratic states (G. Kut, 1994, pp.14-15).

The Decline of the Popularity of the Turkish Model

By the end of 1992, the popularity of the Turkish Model, or at least the support of the West for this Model, began to decline, and by the end of 1993 it ended almost completely. This is mainly because firstly, a few years after the collapse of the USSR it was clear that the influence of Iran in the region was limited and that there was no concrete danger that the Central Asian Republics would adopt the Iranian model. Secondly, with its 'near abroad' policy, Russia attempted to control the political developments within the lands of the former USSR, and the West remained passive in the face of this development. Furthermore there was no great power vacuum as Russian influence declined but never collapsed completely. Thirdly, there was a fear of pan-Turkism because of the increasing relations between Turkey and Turkic Republics, which exceeded the boundaries of the Turkish Model. Finally, problems within Turkey (problems related to ethnic and religious minorities) played their roles in the decline of Western support for the Turkish Model.

The Realisation of the Limits of Iranian Influence

Western assumptions about the future of Central Asia after the end of the USSR were based on limited information (Hunter, 1992, pp.57-58). However, after independence, Western knowledge about them increased quite rapidly, and most of the obscurer aspects of the Republics in terms of politics, economics, culture and public opinion became clearer to the West. Therefore, the West reconsidered its initial assumptions about the region, and altered its initial policies.

Iran has an advantage over Turkey in the region firstly because of its geographical situation. Turkey does not share land borders either with the Central Asian states or with Azerbaijan. The exception to this is Turkey's common border (around 10 km) with Nakhichevan, a province of Azerbaijan isolated from the main Azeri land. Iran has common borders with Turkmenistan, Azerbaijan and with the Azeri enclave of Nakhichevan. Ashkhabad, the capital of Turkmenistan, lies near the border of Iran and is connected with it by road and by railway (Ali, 1993, p.63). Only forty kilometres separate Ashkhabad from Iran which also enjoys the advantage of a long coastline on the Caspian Sea. By means of the Caspian Sea, Iran has proximity to Kazakstan and naval access to Azerbaijan, Turkmenistan and Kazakstan. One could argue that the proximity of Afghanistan to the region could also be regarded as an advantage for Iran. Afghanistan has common borders with Turkmenistan, Uzbekistan and Tajikistan. At the same time Afghanistan has common borders with Iran, and these countries can therefore be regarded as the gateway to the Middle East from the Central Asian Republics (Israeli, 1994, p.20).

Although Iran has a geo-strategic advantage, it had disadvantages in the economic field as the capability of Iranian economy was limited and it therefore could not give economic support to the Muslim Republics of the former Soviet Union, whose economies urgently needed capital investment. The Iranian economy was too weak to meet the demands of the Muslim Republics of the ex-Soviet union, having been weakened by the Islamic revolution in 1979 and after that by the war with Iraq, which lasted for eight years (1980-88). Although around ninety percent of its revenues came from oil, as Ahrari (1994, pp.528-529) pointed out, 'Iran has been operating in an environment of depressed oil prices throughout the 1980s, even in the 1990s, international oil prices are not much better while its oil income is down'. Iran also faced significant economic problems at home. However, Iran's main obstacle was its Shiite character which does not suit the Sunni Muslim population of Central Asia, with the exception of Azerbaijan (two-thirds of the Azeri population is Shiite). Indeed, there has always been a degree of hostility between the two sects, and it was quickly realised that in the Muslim Republics of Central Asia, where a majority of the population belonged to the Sunni sect, Iran's effect would always be limited. As Sardar Assef Ali, the Pakistani Minister of State for Economic Affairs, who headed the Pakistani delegation to the Central Asian Republics in December, 1991, put it: 'They (Central Asian Republics) have problems with Iran. Besides the bitter legacies of the past, a majority of people living in Central Asia are Turks. Also 95% of them are Sunni Muslims of the Naqashbandi order. So they are uneasy with Iran because of these factors' (Hussain, 1992, p.3). Nurmemedov, under-secretary of Turkmenistan's Ambassador in Ankara, raised this issue by saying: 'Iranian fundamentalism cannot come to us, their people are Shiite, our population is Sunni. Our people do not trust their Mullahs'.[38] In Azerbaijan, however, although two-thirds of the Azeri population is Shiite, it was difficult to regard this as an advantage for Iran, and Shiism in Azerbaijan did not pose a problem for Turkey because Azeris had a strong ethnic affinity and preference for Turkey.[39] Furthermore, there were hostile attitudes towards Iran because of the Azeri minority in Iran, and 'the ethnic affinities on both sides of the Iranian border pose a serious threat to Iran's stability and already conjure up a 'greater Azerbaijan' notion that can only be unsettling for Tehran' (Israeli, 1994, pp.20-21).

Therefore Iran could compete only in Tajikistan, the only Persian-speaking population in Central Asia (Shameem, 1994, p.19). But even in Tajikistan, despite the ethnic and cultural affinities, the Shiite-Sunni divide could not be bridged by Iran despite its best efforts. The Islamic opposition in Tajikistan should not be confused with Iranian Shiism, as the Tajik Islamic militants are Sunnis (Effendi, 1994, p.576). Although it is claimed by some authors that 'Iran does send in hundreds of Mullahs to run the mosques of Central Asia as well as thousands of Korans to uplift the spirits of the believers' (Israeli, 1994, p.25), as Yahya Effendi (1994, p.575) pointed out, 'how and where can a Shiite Mullah run a Sunni mosque in a Sunni area'? It is as misleading as saying that 'the Church of England is sending in hundreds of vicars to run churches in Roman Catholic Spain'. Therefore, 'any suggestion that Iran is capable of destabilising that region is as preposterous as the one that was in vogue in the 1980's - that Iran was capable of exporting its revolution to the neighbouring states of the Persian Gulf' (Ahrari, 1994, p.533). Because of the Shiite character of Iran, its model of revolution was not exportable to the Persian Gulf states in the 1980s and after the collapse of the Soviet Union, in a similar way, it would be difficult to export the Iranian model to the Central Asian states because of the unsuitable cultural base.

More over, the evidence showed that after Ayatollah Khomeini, Iran become more moderate and ceased its attempts to export its regime to the Sunni Muslim countries. This represents a realisation of the limitations of Shiite Iran in a Sunni world. The policies of President Ali Hashemi Rafsanjani clearly appeared to be more moderate and pragmatic than those of Khomeini. The main objective of Iranian policy in the Caucasus and Central Asia was not to export its regime, as was assumed by the US and the West; instead Iran, which was to a significant extent isolated by the international community because of its radicalism, aimed to find a new basis for co-operation in the region. As Herzig (1995, p.4) emphasised;

> The Iranian government has made considerable efforts to reduce its international isolation by convincing other states that Iran is a 'normal' state, committed to upholding international law and maintaining the norms of international conduct, a potential partner rather than a threat.

After the new formations in the region, Iran also wanted to prevent developments, which could threaten the integrity of Iranian territory and the Iranian regime. Azeri and Turkmen people constituted an important section of the Iranian population. When Azerbaijan and Turkmenistan were established as independent states after the collapse of the Soviet Union, Iran wondered about the possible sympathy of its own population for these new Republics. In addition to this, certain statements of the 'Azerbaijan People's Front' about the future of Iran were alarming to Iran in terms of the intentions of Azerbaijan and the Azeri population in Iran. Therefore, Iran supported the opposition in Azerbaijan, which favoured closer relations with Iran and Russia as opposed to Elchibey's pan-Turkist policies. Iran also approached Russia. Despite the disappointment of Azeri Muslims, Iran did not take their side in the conflict with Armenia over the Karabakh region, but attempted to act as a mediator between Azerbaijan and Armenia. Even in 1990, Iran maintained her silence during the massacre in Baku, and thereby lost a certain amount of Azerbaijani loyalty.[40] Furthermore, Iran became the first Muslim state outside the CIS to establish diplomatic ties with Armenia (Ahrari, 1994, pp.528-533). It can be claimed that Iran did not want to see a stable, strong Azerbaijan on its doorstep as this would encourage irredentist tendencies among Azeri Iranians. In other words, as Hiro (1994, p.74) put it; 'Iran chose to put national interests above any purely ideological consideration of unequivocally helping fellow Muslims in Azerbaijan', and Iranian policy towards the Muslim Republics of the former USSR was oriented towards the attainment of goals that had more to do with national interest than ideological commitment (Herzig, 1995, p.56). However, one result of this policy was that it provided an instrument for President Elchibey to justify his policy of strengthening ties with Turkey.

Thus, in contrast to Western assumptions, Iran was looking for co-operation in political and economic fields but not attempting to export its religion and ideology. In fact Iran was developing its relations in these fields (Hyman, 1994c, p.13), trying to establish good economic relations not only with the Muslim Republics of Central Asia but with other former Soviet Republics as well. For example, in January 1992 Iran signed a trade accord worth up to $7bn with Ukraine, and Russia was becoming a big trading partner (Hyman, 1994c, p.11). Because of realistic and pragmatic Iranian policies, the West and the US, which had based their policies on the assumption that there was a danger of Islamic radicalism and Iranian-type regimes in the Central Asian Republics and in Azerbaijan, changed their policies. The danger of Islamic radicalism was misleading. On the other hand, although there were problems with their democracies, these new Republics had some degree of stability, which was sufficient to create suitable conditions for Western and US companies (G. Kut, 1994, p.18). When the West and the US began to adjust their policies according to the new realities of the situation Western support for the Turkish Model declined as quickly as it had appeared. However, Russia's role in the whole affair should not be underestimated.

The Russian Factor

It was at first assumed that the collapse of the USSR had created a power vacuum in the area[41], but a few years later it became clear that this was an exaggeration, and although the Russian power had declined, its influence in Central Asia and the Caucasus did not collapse. During the first years after the dissolution of the Soviet

Union, the main focus of attention for president Yeltsin and his colleagues was the future shape of the political system in the Russian Federation, and they were more concerned with purely domestic affairs such as Yeltsin's battle with Khasbulatov, the leader of the Russian parliament. During these first two years Russia gave priority to domestic issues. Yeltsin was concerned with transforming the Russian economy into a genuine market economy; more importantly, as Bondarevsky and Ferdinand (1994, p.41) pointed out, Russia assumed that

> Central Asian dependency upon Russia would persist for a whole host of reasons; their own country's industrial might, the dependence of the Central Asian Republics upon innumerable economic links with Russia; preponderance of Russian engineers and technicians in the Central Asian economies, and of Russian administrators in government service; the various social and ethnic contradictions within and between the republics; lack of their own armed forces and the stationing there of units from the Turkestan and Central Asian military regions; and, finally, the fact that the Republics lacked their own foreign policy apparatus.

Therefore Russia gave the appearance that it was not interested in the region, which was wrongly interpreted, and a power vacuum was envisaged. Later, it became obvious that although the USSR had ended, Russia's hegemonic ambitions in the region remained little changed. On this issue, opposing groups - neo-fascist elements, neo-communists and hard-line advocates of Russian nationalism and great power ideology - were united (Sagadeev, 1993, pp.172-173). Moscow's policy towards the former Union Republics, according to Rywkin (1994), has a remarkable similarity to America's Monroe Doctrine; admitting no foreign interference within its sphere of influence. He claimed that a traditional policy of 'divide and rule' is being applied in the Caucasus by utilising Armenia as Russia's main regional ally. The geopolitical significance of Russia's security policy for the adjacent region is very important and notwithstanding enormous domestic difficulties, Russia intended, both in theory and practice, to remain a major actor in Central Asia (Mesbahi, 1993, p.120).

In 1992, Russia gave priority to domestic affairs; however after mid-1992 and throughout 1993 this policy changed. One reason for this change was that certain circles in Russia, who were not happy with the political reforms and saw the new regime as responsible for the problems brought about by economic reforms, began to support conservatives and nationalists who opposed the reformist leaders. Interestingly, the supporters of the old Communist party and the new ultra-nationalists achieved a red-brown unification in the 1993 election. This meant that the opposition was uniting and the reformists were losing public support. In addition, the dissatisfaction of the Russian army with Russia's position in world politics must be noted. The USSR used to compete with the US, but the Russian Federation was asking for help from the West to carry out its reforms and this was difficult to accept. Because of these pressures Yeltsin began to change his policy, and the significance of moderates in his administration declined. In order to carry out reforms, Yeltsin wanted to compromise with the opposition. On his way back from a visit to Japan, Turkish Prime Minister Demirel visited Moscow and met with Russian Foreign Minister Kozyrev, who underlined that the Russian interest in Caucasus was not over at this stage (G. Kut, 1994, p.17). At the Commonwealth of Independent States (CIS) summit in Minsk (January 1993), Yeltsin committed Russia to encourage greater co-operation between CIS members. He began to advocate that Russia should play a more forceful security role in Central Asia, and said:

> I think the moment has come when responsible international organisations including the UN should grant Russia special powers as a guarantor of peace and stability in the region of the former Soviet Union. Russia has a heartfelt interest in stopping all armed conflicts on the territory of the former Soviet Union (Rashid, 1994, p.226).

On the other hand, for the US and the West, Yeltsin still represented stability in Russia, and it was necessary to support him. The stability of Russia was, for the West, more important than any other regional problem. Yeltsin began to implement new policies, which granted concessions to the nationalists and conservatives. Among these, the Russian 'near abroad' policy directly affected the Caucasus and Central Asia. In his statement in Izvestiya newspaper, the Russian Foreign Minister Kozyrev announced the 'near abroad' policy on 8 October 1993. He emphasised the ethnic conflicts in the former Soviet lands, and claimed that Russia had the legitimate right of military intervention in these Republics. Furthermore, he demanded UN support for a 'gendarme' role for Russia in the former Soviet territory (Yalçın, 1994, p.33). Similarly, in mid January 1994, Kozyrev told a conference of Russian Ambassadors to the CIS and Baltic states that

> The countries of the CIS and the Baltic are the region where Russia's primary vital interests are concerned. They are also the source of fundamental threats to those interests. We must not abandon these regions which have been Russian spheres of interest for centuries. And we must not be afraid of saying this' (Bondarevsky and Ferdinand, 1994, p.52).

The 'near abroad' was the former Soviet Republics, and the 'near abroad policy' stated that because of historical, ethnic, economic, military and strategic ties Russia should have privileged rights and influence in these Republics. Firstly, there was the Russian population in all these Republics. There were over ten million ethnic Russians living in the five Central Asian Republics, 40% of the 25 million Russians living outside Russia were in the 'near abroad'. This was particularly relevant to Kazakstan, 37% of whose population consisted of ethnic Russians according to mid-1993 estimates (Dawisha and Parrott, 1994, pp.xviii-xix).[42] In Russian view, Russian minorities were in danger of becoming second class citizens (Hyman, 1994b, p.61), and this issue became an extremely sensitive one in Russian politics. Throughout 1992, the nationalist press in Russia focused on this issue, and Central Asian authorities were accused of discrimination. 'Russian-speaking hostages' was the theme which was widely exploited during the election campaign in Russia in autumn 1993 and greatly helped the success of Zhirinovsky's party. It was also hotly debated in the State Duma (Bondarevsky and Ferdinand, 1994, p.44).

The second factor which encouraged Russia to formulate its 'near abroad' policy was that Russia was quite legitimately concerned with its economic interests in Central Asia; after all, its entire economy had been based on the same economic system as those of the Central Asian Republics. For example, Uzbekistan's main export, in fact main product, is cotton, and it depends on exporting the cotton to Russia; similarly the Russian textile industry depends on being able to import cotton from Uzbekistan. There was also the matter of energy supplies: Russia was concerned with the question of a 'fair' market price for oil and natural gas. The importance of this was seen when Turkmenistan threatened to cut off natural gas supplies to Ukraine at the end of 1991 and to divert them to Iran and Turkey. This threat forced Ukraine to accept a rise from the old Soviet price of 3 kopeks per cubic metre to 80 kopeks - the price on which the Turkmen leaders insisted. In fact even the new price was still only half of the world market price. Although an agreement was signed between Turkmenistan and Ukraine in which the former agreed to supply the latter with gas, the only way of transporting the gas was via the old trans-union pipeline which fed the Eastern part of Russia. The system was set such that in return for the consumption of gas by the Russian population, Russia sent an equivalent amount of its own gas to Ukraine from a source further west. Therefore, if Turkmenistan had stopped its supplies to Ukraine, this meant in practice ending gas supplies to Russian consumers in the East; in that case, Russia itself would have to implement the cut to Ukraine (Bondarevsky and Ferdinand, 1994, pp.52-53).

Another core Russian interest was related to transportation. Russia wanted to have unrestricted access to rail links between Europe and Asia at cheap prices. Russia had to ensure that as much trade as possible continued to flow between Europe, the Middle East and the Far East via Russia. In order to be able to continue its protective economic interest, Russia needed adequate political stability in those Republics, and by its 'near abroad' policy it aimed to control the region (Bondarevsky and Ferdinand, 1994, p.43).

Thirdly, Russia also regarded Central Asia as an important place for its security, and it did not want any other outside power to establish itself in Central Asia. Russia was concerned over the control of Kazakstan's nuclear weapons and worried about the possible threat of 'Islamic fundamentalism'. Moscow assumed that it would be more convenient to try to control possible infiltration, from places such as Afghanistan, across the shorter southern borders of the former Central Asian Republics than across their much longer boundary with Russia (Bondarevsky and Ferdinand, 1994, p.43).

After mid-1992 Russia returned to Central Asia and began to fill the gap. For example, Russia intervened in the foreign relations of the Central Asian Republics. One such incident happened in July 1992 when four Central Asian states and Azerbaijan joined the Economic Co-operation Organisation (ECO) (Kazakstan had become a temporary associate member) which had originally comprised only of Turkey, Iran and Pakistan (Bondarevsky and Ferdinand, 1994, p.41-42). However, Russia warned the Central Asian Republics that membership of the ECO and membership of the CIS were not compatible. Yalçın (1994, pp.34-35) argued that also because of Russian pressure, the planned second summit of the Presidents of Turkish-speaking Republics in Baku on 20 January 1994 was cancelled. After these developments, at the Ashkabat conference of the CIS (in December 1993), Yeltsin suggested giving dual citizenship to all ethnic Russians living outside Russian territory. This was refused nearly unanimously as it was seen as an important instrument for Russia to intervene in the domestic affairs of the other Republics (Yalçın, 1994, pp.34-35). Turkmenistan was an exception because 'Niyazov announced that Turkmenistan intended to introduce this concept into its legal and political system' (Bondarevsky and Ferdinand, 1994, p.45). Furthermore, during his address to the nation for the New Year (1994), Yeltsin stated: 'We are so inextricably linked by a common history, economy and single fate that living separately is simply not for us. Our people will not allow it' (Hyman, 1994b, p.64). This was a clear indication of Russian intentions with regard to the newly independent republics. However, this situation was acceptable for the West and the US, which sought stability in the region.

Meanwhile, the Caucasus had been suffering from war and instability since 1988, and the conflicts worsened after the end of the USSR. The Conference on Security and Co-operation in Europe (CSCE) and Turkey failed to resolve the disputes. On the other hand, under the leadership of Russia, the Commonwealth of Independent States's (CIS) troops intervened and some stability was brought to the region. This was a proof of the existence of a Russian sphere of influence in the region (Yalçın, 1994, p.34). Therefore, for the West it was a reasonable solution to leave responsibility for the stability of the region to Russia.

After Russia formulated the policy of the 'near abroad', it found suitable political conditions in the Central Asian Republics. Nearly all the leaders of Central Asian Republics were formerly middle ranking or local chiefs of the old Communist Party structure and had traditionally looked up to Moscow; they were traditionally part of the old Soviet Communist system and they were rather unwilling to break away from Moscow. Unsure of their new stance in their Republics, the leaders did not want to lose or risk their political powers. An important factor that affected the attitudes of the Central Asian leaders towards Moscow, was Turkey's promotion of substantive reforms in these newly independent Republics because the regimes in the Turkic republics were anxious about the real intentions of Turkey (Robins, 1993, p.601). One can argue that, in particular, Turkish support for the opposition (Elchibey) in Azerbaijan's 1992 elections encouraged Central Asian leaders to develop close relations with Russia, and contributed to their anxieties about their own positions.

At the global level, at the end of 1991, the Russian federation with its large territory was still an important actor in world politics. After the end of the USSR, Soviet nuclear weapons were divided between four states, this meant that there were four states in the former Soviet territory with nuclear weapons. To be able to control nuclear weapons, the West wanted to see nuclear weapons under the control of one power rather than four (Russia, Belarus, Kazakstan and Ukraine). Therefore, the West encouraged the three Republics to sign an agreement transferring the weapons to Russia. To these pressures, Belarus gave a positive answer. Then, after US encouragement - a guarantee was given to Kazakstan, and aid was promised - Kazakstan also agreed to transfer its weapons. Ukraine initially consented to sign the agreement, but later on, because of pressure from its parliament, it used the issue as a bargaining tool. However it was understood that after some concessions Ukraine would also give up the weapons, and thus it became clear that Ukraine would not be a nuclear threat either (G. Kut, 1994, pp.9-10). The West and the US preferred to see Russia as a partner rather than having to deal with these three states which had not established their stability. This was an indication of the ratification of Russian influence in the former USSR by the West. It may have promoted the stability of the region; however, it meant at the same time returning the region to Russian hegemony. The US was interested in the nuclear weapons on Kazak soil in order to prevent the spread of nuclear weapons. However after the Kazak agreement to transfer these weapons to Russia, the US began to regard the Caucasus and Central Asia in terms of Russian domestic stability. This was an indication of the decline of US support for the Turkish model. Another reason was that, the US was not able to give adequate economic support to Russia, and problems related to economic and political reforms created a suitable basis for the rise of the neo-communist parties. In order to prevent such a development, and to keep Russian markets open, the US supported Yeltsin. This also meant that the US would not support the Turkish Model.

Developments in 1992-1993 showed that competition was not between Turkey and Iran but rather between Russia and Turkey. However, as Blank suggested, it was too difficult for Turkey to compete with Russia, and there were not enough reasons for the US to support Turkey in this competition (G. Kut, 1994, p.19).[43] Russia was largely trying to please its people who were not happy with the political and economic reforms, and tried to use foreign policy as an instrument to satisfy public opinion and expectations. On the other hand Turkey's intentions were also pragmatic. As Acar Okan, advisor to the Turkish Prime Minister (in 1993) emphasised, Turkey wanted to see these Republics as independent members of international institutions and a part of the international community as they would be Turkey's natural allies in international relations.[44] This is an important issue for Turkish governments who see Turkey as a country which has no real allies (except maybe for Pakistan) as proven in the case of the Cyprus crisis of 1974 and in the case of the Kurds where Turkey's supposed allies regard separatist terrorist activities as liberation rather than terrorism.[45]

It is possible to argue that at the beginning of 1994, Russia managed to establish closer relations with the Central Asian states. Islam Karimov, the President of Uzbekistan, paid a formal visit to Moscow on 2-3 March 1994 and important agreements were signed between Uzbekistan and Russia on economic and military issues. The frontier between Turkmenistan and Afghanistan was already under Russian control after an agreement signed between Niyazov and Yeltsin in December 1993 in Ashkhabad. Another extremely important event in relations between Russia and Central Asia was Nazarbayev's visit to Moscow at the beginning of April 1994. During this visit, agreement was achieved on a number of political, economic and social problems. Maybe the most important of these was the agreement for joint use of the Baikonur cosmodrome. In return, Russia would pay Kazakstan $115 million annually. In practice, this meant the creation of a Russian base on Kazak territory. Anatoly Adamyshin, the first deputy Russian foreign minister, also held talks in Tehran with leaders of the Tajik opposition on the opening of peace talks with the Tajik government in March 1994 (Bondarevsky and Ferdinand, 1994, pp.50-51). The re-emergence of Russian control over the region was an important development which would have substantial impact on the situation in Afghanistan and Tajikistan, and constituted an important barrier for Turkey and other states which wanted to establish close relations with the Turkic Republics.

Turkey's growing influence in the area was regarded as dangerous by Russia as expressed by Vladimir Starikov, a Russian diplomat in Armenia: 'We think Russia would benefit from expanded Armenian-Iranian relations. We realise that Turkey is trying to penetrate the Republics of the former Soviet Union. This Turkish penetration has to be limited' (Rashid, 1994, p.212). Russia had its own reasons for this persistent Turcophobia. There are fifteen million Muslims in the Russian Federation, most of whom are of Turkic origin. After the end of the USSR, at a time when people were re-embracing religion and searching for their ethnic identity, in June 1992 a World Congress of Tatars was held in Kazan. Apart from economic and strategic issues, Russia feared a pan-Turkist development within its own territory. Apart from separatism in the Caucasus, it is claimed that 'separatism was growing even in the Yakut-Sakha Autonomous Republic (whose inhabitants are of Turkic origin) in the east' (Bondarevsky and Ferdinand, 1994, pp.51-52).

Re-emergence of Pan-Turkism

Among other factors, possibility of re-emergence of pan-Turkism because of Turkey's active policies can be regarded as a factor which also played a role in the decline of Western support for the Turkish Model.[46] Some circles in the West, argued that Turkey was trying to create a 'Commonwealth of the Turkic-Speaking World' as an alternative to the EU. It was assumed that this was Turkey's reaction to its exclusion from the European Union. It was also foreseen that if Turkey followed this policy with determination it would undermine her European attachment, and transform the country into an 'independent regional superpower' (Sander, 1994, p.37). Therefore, it can be argued that the West assumed that continuation of Western encouragement for Turkey and the Turkish Model could lead to the re-emergence of Turkey as a pan-Turkist state in the region. It was thus necessary for the West to reconsider its support for the Turkish Model.

Meanwhile, Turkish policies towards the Turkic Republics exceeded the boundaries of transferring the Turkish Model. Especially after the periodical meetings of the Presidents of the Turkic Republics and Turkey, the West started to worry about a Pan-Turkist development. Although most of the politicians and bureaucrats advocate Pan-Turkism in Turkey, official policy always refuses these claims. For example: President Turgut Özal repudiated the claim of one of his Ministers (Ercüment Konukman in January 1990) that 'several states in the Soviet Union and in China will be under the Turkish flag in the next century' (Hyman, 1994c, p.16).

However, the speeches of the Turkish officials were controversial, probably showing a change in spirit and attitude with the realities of the times. For example, Prime Minister Demirel visited all five Republics in April 1992, and in Alma Ata gave a speech to an audience of excited Kazaks. He underlined that a great Turkic world had emerged, stretching from the Adriatic to the Pacific rim, and that 'this place is our fatherland. Both our history and our culture begin from here' (Rashid, 1994, pp.210-211). During Demirel's visit to Central Asia, Ankara announced that a summit meeting of Turkic states would take place in Istanbul in the autumn of 1992. More importantly, Demirel publicly acknowledged that some form of association of independent Turkic states was a realistic option (Winrow, 1992, p.110). However, Demirel denied Pan-Turkist accusations. 'We are not Pan-Turkist', he said in an interview,

All we want is that these countries should be standing on their own feet. In the last one thousand years, the people of central Asia have never gathered under one government. Let us have several governments, and having the same culture, the same language, then all of us are happy.[47]

Demirel declared that 'in Central Asia we are the emissaries of Europe. We are Europeans who are taking European values to Central Asia. We want to remain Europeans'. He denied pan-Turkist claims and stated, 'Pan-Turkism, the goal of uniting all Turkic-speaking nations, is Utopian' (Hyman, 1994c, p.16).[48] Similar statements were made by other Turkish decision-makers. For example; aware of Pan-Turkist-Islamist accusations, Turkish Foreign Minister Çetin pointed out: 'We harbour neither pan-Turkic nor pan-Islamic illusions which are bankrupt ideologies of the pre-First World War years' (Çetin, 1992, p.12). The first summit, which gathered the Presidents of the Turkic Republics, was opened by President Özal in Ankara on 30 October 1992. At this summit, Özal appealed to the Presidents 'to make the twenty-first century that of the Turks'. He announced that such a summit would take place every year. When he died in April 1993 just after a tour of Central Asia, as Rashid (1994) pointed out, he was mourned by tens of thousands of people from Alma Ata to Baku. Summits among the presidents of the Turkic Republics take place every year. However, because of the revolution in Azerbaijan in the summer of 1993, the new regime - maybe, as noted above, because of Russian pressure - did not allow the planned second meeting in Baku.[49] Apart from these meetings, Turkish investment in the education of students from these Republics was also an important development.

It may be argued that all these developments alarmed the West about Turkey's real intentions, and contributed to the decline in Western support for the Turkish Model. Although Turkey tried to persuade the West with these official statements that Turkey was not Pan-Turkist, and that in contrast she was bringing Western values to the Central Asian Republics, the Western fear of re-emergence of Pan-Turkism was a factor which negatively affected Western support for the Turkish Model.

Problems Within the Model Itself[50]

As discussed in the first chapter, Turkey's most outstanding problem has been the treatment of ethnic and religious minorities. Kurdish separatism, although on the agenda since 1984, worsened instead of being solved after 1991. Furthermore, it became an international issue on the agenda not only of the Middle East but of world politics. Apart from separatism in the East, Turkey began to face another fatal unrest after 1991 in the form of Alawite dissatisfaction with the state. The Alawite demands for rights from the Turkish state, and their threat to cause new problems, similar to those created by the PKK, if their demands are not met, have been very important. Problems related with the minority issues not only limited Turkish foreign policy, but they also weakened the economy. The fact that the Turkish Model could not cope with minority issues in Turkey, raised questions as to how the same Model would cope in Central Asia and the Caucasus, where the issues related to ethnic and religious minorities are even more complex. Even if there were no other factors, a Turkish Model which struggled to maintain national unity and prevent a civil war, accompanied with the criticisms the situation received from the West, would have convinced the Presidents of the Turkic Republics that maybe Turkey was not the country to take as a sample.

Conclusion

Although the importance of Turkey for the West declined after the end of the USSR as the East-West confrontation ended and the West no longer needed Turkey as a bulwark against the Soviet Union, subsequent developments such as the Gulf War, the war in the Balkans and the emergence of new Muslim Republics in the Caucasus and Central Asia proved that Turkey was still an important partner of the West and the US. Specifically, after the Muslim Republics of the former Soviet Union declared their independence, there was a fear that an Iranian model could replace the old communist system, and Turkey's presence in the region was regarded as representing the West. After Turkey's role in the Gulf War[51] and realising the fragile condition of new Central Asia, in the eyes of the West, Turkey suddenly emerged as an invaluable partner in preserving regional political stability and preventing Iran from extending its influence, and its particular brand of Islamic fundamentalism throughout the area. Once peripheral Turkey therefore found itself in the centre of a region vacated by the overpowering presence of the Soviet Union in the Balkans and Caucasus. This implied new foreign policy horizons for Turkey in the post-Cold War situation. Meanwhile, the dissolution of the Soviet Union led to the independence of the Central Asian Turkic states, and Turkey was regarded as being in a position to show these republics the way.[52]

There were some assumptions and reasons behind Western promotion and support for the Turkish model. This chapter suggests that these are as follows: Firstly, it was assumed that with the end of USSR, a power vacuum was created in Central Asia. In this respect Turkey and Iran have usually been mentioned as rival powers. Iran represented an anti-Western and Islamic regime; on the other hand, Turkey represented democracy (multi-party system), secularism, the free market economy and more importantly closeness to the West. Therefore, the Western fear of Islam, the presence of Iran, geographically, culturally and historically close to the region, and the fear that the Muslim republics could adopt the Iranian model was the main reason that determined Western support for the Turkish model.

Secondly, although Western democracies are the origin of the Turkish model and well established compared to the Turkish one, the Turkish model became popular because of the common culture between Turkey and the Turkic Republics. As Özal[53], Demirel, Nurmemedov[54], Yolcuoğlu[55] and several others have pointed out, there was a suitable cultural (linguistic and religious) base for a close relationship and for the Turkish model.

Thirdly, with the collapse of the USSR, the Turkic republics have been trying to reform their centrally controlled economies, and a fresh example could be helpful for their transformation. In this sense, the Turkish experience in economic transformation after 1980 (following the 24 January decisions) was a fresh and successful example of a transformation from a centrally controlled economy to a market economy.

These were the main reasons that determined Western support for the Turkish model. However, a few years later, western knowledge of the region and its economic, cultural and strategic issues increased, and new developments took place. In turn, the West and the US reconsidered their initial assumptions and policies and reduced their support for the Turkish model, if they did not end it completely. Again there were some important reasons behind the decline in western support for the Turkish model. This chapter suggests that these are as follows: Firstly, after understanding the real conditions of the region, the West realised that although Iran had some geo-strategic advantages in the region, mainly for geographical reasons, it had significant handicaps as well. Primarily, although

Iran is an Islamic state, in contrast to the initial western assumptions, the effect of Iran in the Turkic republics has been very limited. This is mainly because there is a divide between Shiite and Sunni Muslims, and a hostile attitude between these two sects. Iran is a Shiite state; on the other hand the majority of the population of the Turkic states is Sunni, except the Azeris. Iran's influence even over the Azeri population is very limited, as Azeris are Turkic and Iran also has an ethnic Azeri population of some 20 million living in the north of the country, and is worried about the possible unification of these peoples. Iran has been looking mostly for possible co-operation in economic fields, after being isolated by the West. Therefore Iran's policy was pragmatic and realist rather than adventurist and the main reason behind Western support for the Turkish model diminished.

Secondly, after the collapse of the USSR, it was assumed that Russia did not want to regain control over the former Soviet territory. Many analysts talked about a power vacuum created in the region by the end of the USSR. However, especially after 1993, Russia clearly announced its intention of regaining control over the former Soviet territory with its 'near abroad' policy. Russia had some reasons as justifications of her policy. There were economic and security reasons, as Russia wanted to control nuclear power and did not want to see a rival power settled in the former Soviet territory. The 25 million ethnic Russians living outside Russian territory also encouraged Russia to control the former Soviet territory in order to guarantee their civil rights. In 1994 Russia signed several agreements with the Turkic republics and Russian bases reopened in the region. This was not a terrible development for the West, who preferred to deal with one nuclear power in the region rather than four, and was seeking the stability in the region, which Russia could provide. Therefore, in contrast to Turkish expectations, the West allowed Russia to implement the 'near abroad' policy as if it was Russia's legitimate right to control former Soviet territory. Western support for the Russian policy in the Turkic republics was a negative development for western support for the Turkish model, as the two are irreconcilable.

Thirdly, some Turkish policies and declarations by Turkish officials and their heavy-handed policies suggested that there was a danger of Pan-Turkism. Further support for the Turkish model might have encouraged this trend, and therefore support for the Turkish model declined in order to prevent the possible creation of a Pan-Turkic union.

Finally, when the Turkish model became popular, Turkey was involved in an undeclared war in SouthEastern Anatolia costing several lives every day. Since 1991, this problem has not been solved but has worsened: it has negative effects on the Turkish economy and Turkish foreign policy. In addition to this, Turkey faced another fatal crisis in the form of Alawite dissatisfaction, which threatened the unity of Turkey and required the reformation of the Turkish Model. Thus, the problems with the Turkish Model itself have rendered it undesirable for the West as a Model to be promoted.

Meanwhile, in a short period of time the Turkic States began to join international institutions, transform their economies into market economies, and establish close relations with the West directly and not via Turkey.[56] Although democratic reforms were taking place slowly, these developments and the fragile stability which was provided by the new regimes was sufficient for the West and Western companies. Hence, the Turkish Model became unnecessary and too risky for the West to support.

Notes

1   As early as in 1989, Graham Fuller prepared a report for the Rand Corporation which emphasised the importance of the Turkish model for the Muslims of the ex-Soviet Union (*Personal interview with Professor Hasan Koni*, Ankara, 30 March 1996).

2   *Personal interview with William Hale*, London, 29 June 1995.

3   Here, it should be remembered that Özal labelled the economic transformation that took place under his administration after 1980, as the 'Turkish Model'. He argued that the Turkish experiment was a good example for the USSR. See Yapı Endüstri Merkezi Yayın Bölümü, *(1991), SSCB Pazarında Türkiye*, Istanbul, March.

4   *Financial Times*, 21 May 1992.

5   *The Middle East*, August 1992, p. 30.

6   *Sunday Telegraph*, 9 August 1992.

7   See also, G.E. Fuller and I.O. Lesser, (1993), *Turkey's New Geopolitics*, Westview Press, Oxford.

8   See also, A. Rashid, (1994), *The Resurgence of Central Asia: Islam or Nationalism?*, Zed Books, London, p. 209.

9   *International Herald Tribune*, 14 February 1990.

10   *D. Telegraph*, 1 February 1993.

11   *Jane's Defence Weekly*, 18 April 1992.

12   *The Economist*, 26 December 1992 and 8 January 1993.

13   For example, see *Financial Times*, 21 May 1992, with the headline 'Horizon shifts to Central Asia', also, see *Guardian*, 3 April 1992.

14   *Financial Times*, 17 May 1993.

15   *The Washington Post*, 10 February 1992.

16   *Sunday Telegraph*, 29 November 1992.

17   *Middle East*, July 1992, pp. 5-6.

18   Mainly because of these handicaps, in the 1980's some analysts were even suggesting alternative models such as the Korean model, the Mexican model, Neo-Ottomanism, etc, for Turkey to follow, but surprisingly the Turkish Model itself became popular a few years later. For example, see D. Barchard, (1985), *Turkey and the West*, Routledge & Kegan Paul Ltd., London, pp. 89-93.

19   *Personal Interview with Maria Bennigsen Broxup*, London, June 1995; see also J. Laber, (1992), 'Balanced on the Golden Horn', *The Washington Post*, February 9; *Jane's Defence Weekly*, 18 April 1992, p. 649. Analysts like İnan, Devlet, Hale, Mango and Koni underlined the same point as well.

20   India was another country which feared the possible rise of Islamic fundamentalism. See M.H. Nuri, (1992/1993), 'India and Central Asia: Past, Present and Future', *Regional Studies*, Winter, pp. 86-88; For fear of radical Islam, see also J. Miller, (1993), 'The Challenge of Radical Islam', *Foreign Affairs*, vol. 72, no. 2; L.T. Hadar, (1993), 'What Green Peril?', *Foreign Affairs*, vol. 72, no. 2.

21   *The Economist*, (1991), 'Turkey: Star of Islam, survey', 14 December, p. 3.

22   For example, Cemil Çiçek, a Minister of State in Özal's cabinet and currently a member and an MP of Virtue party, believes that 'Islam outside Turkey is becoming more radical gradually. They are causing serious troubles in their societies, they seek to establish states according to Sharia laws, and it is becoming more difficult to control these groups every passing day. The typical example of these is Algeria. Naturally, if radical Muslims take power, the interests of the West will be undermined. Developments in Iran and Algeria, and also the picture in the Middle East determined by some acting groups supported by such states like Iran, Libya and Algeria, seriously frightened the West' (*Personal Interview*, Ankara, December 1994).

23   For example, Ertuğrul O. Çırağan, retired Ambassador and Foreign Policy Advisor to the Democratic Left Party, singled out Iran as a country which wants to export its fundamentalist regime to Central Asia. (*Personal Interview with Ertuğrul Çırağan*, Foreign Policy advisor of Democratic Left Party, Ankara, 1996).

24   For Iran's role in the Afghan conflict and the possible role of Afghanistan for the region, including Central Asia, see R.B. Rais, (1992), 'Afghanistan and Regional Security After the Cold War', *Problems of Communism*, May - June.

25   For example, see A. Apostolou, (1992), 'New Players in an old Game', *The Middle East*, July, no. 213, pp. 5-6; C.R. Saivetz, (1994), 'Central Asia: Emerging Relations with the Arab States and Israil', in H. Malik, (ed.), *Central Asia: Its Strategic Importance and Future Prospects*, Macmillan Press, London, pp. 312-313; O.M. Smolansky, (1994), 'Turkish and Iranian Policies in Central Asia', in H. Malik, (ed.), Central Asia: Its Strategic Importance and Future Prospects, *op. cit.*, pp. 292-293; S.A. Parsons, (1993), *Central Asia the Last Decolonization*, The David Davies Memorial Institute of International Studies, Occasional Paper no. 4, London, p. 8; T. Karasik, (1993), *Azerbaijan, Central Asia, and Future Persian Gulf Security*, Rand, Santa Monica, p. viii; Nuri, *op. cit.*, p. 91; A. Kortunov and E.L. Wiegand Fellow, (1992), 'Strategic Relations between the Former Soviet Republics', *Backgrounder*, The Heritage Foundation, April 17; R. Israeli, (1994), 'Return to the source: the republics of Central Asia and the Middle East', *Central Asian Survey*, vol. 13, no. 1, pp. 22-23; K. Gharabaghi, (1994), 'Development strategies for Central Asia in the 1990s: in search of alternatives', *Third World Quarterly*, vol. 15, no. 1, p. 115.

26   *International Herald Tribune*, 14 February 1990.

27   An example for this positive attitude is the results of a survey conducted by me in the summer of 1993 among 289 students who came to Turkey from the Turkic Republics through cultural agreements. Around 97% of the surveyed students agreed with the statement that Azeri, Turkmen, Uzbek, Kazakh, Kirgiz, and Turks of Turkey were of Turkic origin (option-a). They also supported the idea that relations between Turkey and the Turkic Republics should increase. Also during personal interviews, the Ambassadors of

Azerbaijan and Turkmenistan in Ankara (*Personal Interviews in 1996*), and the councillor at the Kirgiz Embassy in Ankara (*Personal Interview*; Ankara: 28 December 1994), underlined the common culture that makes the Turkish Model desirable for them, although some of the sentiments they expressed can only be interpreted as politeness to a host country.

28 See H. Güler, (1990), *Sovyetler Birliğindeki Türkler*, Türkiye Diyanet Vakfı Yayınları, Ankara; T. Akyol, (1989), *Azerbaycan Kafkaslar ve Ötesi*, Burak Yayınları, Istanbul; Y. Toker, (1992), *Büyük Uyanış*, Toker Yayınları, Istanbul.

29 Furthermore, Pipes regarded Turkey as a model for all Muslim states, not only for the Turkic republics (Pipes, 1994, p. 85). Therefore, a general competition between Turkey and Iran was emphasised, and not only in Central Asia. See D. Pipes, (1994), 'Islam's Intramural Struggle', *The National Interest*, Spring.

30 In a personal interview with Andrew Mango, he underlined the French model as an origin of the Turkish model (*Personal interview with Andrew Mango*, London, June 1995).

31 *Personal interview with Cemil Çiçek*, former State Minister and currently an MP, Ankara, December 1994.

32 *Time*, 10 February 1992, p. 19.

33 *Newspot*, 9 April 1992, p. 2.

34 *Washington Post*, 12 February 1992.

35 *The Wall Street Journal*, 14 February 1992.

36 *The Economist*, 25 February 1992, p. 70; *Economist*, 14 December 1991.

37 *Newspot*, 21 May 1992, p. 3.

38 *Personal interview with Annaguli Nurmemedov*, Under-secretary of the Turkmen Ambassador in Ankara, Ankara, 11 June 1993.

39 For Turkish and Iranian foreign policies towards Central Asian Republics, see A. Vassiliev, (1994), 'Turkey and Iran in Transcaucasia and Central Asia', in A. Ehteshami, (ed.), *From the Gulf to Central Asia: Players in the Great Game*, University of Exeter Press, Exeter.

40 *World Press Review*, November 1991.

41 For example, O. Sander, (1994), 'Turkey and the Turkic world', *Central Asian Survey*, vol. 13, no. 1, p. 37; MEI, 7 February 1992, p. 11; K. İnan, (1995), *Hayır Diyebilen Türkiye*, Timaş Yayınları, Istanbul, p. 71; *Jane's Defence Weekly*, 18 April 1992, p. 650; P. Robins, (1994), 'The Middle East and Central Asia', in P. Ferdinand (ed.), *The New Central Asia and its Neighbours,* Pinter Publishers, London, p. 63.

42 It is stated in the source that figures are mid-1993 estimates from the Bureau of the Census, Centre for International Research.

43 See S. Blank, (1993), *The Eastern Question Revived: Russia and Turkey Contend for Eurasia*, Orta Asya Orta Doğu ile Tanışıyor Konferansına sunulan tebliğ, 12-14 October 1993, Tel Aviv.

44 *Personal interview with Acar Okan*, Ankara, 1993.

45 This was underlined by several politicians during my personal interviews. For example, Abdülkadir Aksu, ex-Interior Minister and currently an MP, Necati Bilican, ex-General Director of Security, ex-Governor of the Emergency Region of South East Anatolia, and Cemil Çiçek, ex-Minister of State and currently an MP, they all stressed foreign support and in particular the position of the West was criticised as a supposed ally. These people claimed that the West supported the PKK in one way or another.

46 About Pan-Turkism, see J.M. Landau, (1995), *Pan-Turkism: From Irredentism to Cooperation*, Indiana University Press, Indiana; P. Copher, (1992), 'Turkey's Grey

Wolves: Key to Central Asia?', *Security Intelligence*, Supplement, Wednesday, 19 August.

47   *International Herald Tribune*, 24 March 1992.

48   Similarly, in another interview, after emphasising that Turkey is not pan-Turkist, he (Demirel) repeated: 'as Turks we can take European values to those countries' (*Financial Times*, 7 May 1993).

49   'Just before the contract (with a consortium of Western oil companies led by BP) was to be signed, however, a rebel military commander armed with Russian weapons staged a coup that brought Heidar Aliyev back to power, who had been a KGB general and a member of the Soviet Politburo. Shortly afterwards, Russia-based Lukoil joined the oil negotiations with Western companies... Russian ambassador, Valter Shonia said the following; "We have had 200 years of co-operation with Azerbaijan. Any politician denying the reality of Russian power is not going to remain long in office", pointing to the fall of the pro-Turkish President Abulfaz Elchibey in 1993's coup'. (The Economist Newspaper Limited, (1994), 'Russian Pressure on Azerbaijan' in *Foreign Report*, London, 14 July).

50   See Chapter One.

51   Bush himself pointed this out in his speech at Ankara Esenboğa airport: 'When Saddam Hussein invaded Kuwait, Turkey acted courageously to ensure that aggression would not stand. And as the whole world knows, the international coalition could not have achieved the liberation of Kuwait without Turkey's pivotal contributions'; see 'President George Bush's speech at Ankara Esenboğa Airport, 20 July 1991', *Turkish Review*, vol. 5, no. 25, Autumn 1991, p. 104.

52   *Financial Times*, 21 May 1992 and *MEI*, February 1992, p. 11.

53   The former President of Turkey, Turgut Özal, pointed out that to establish multiple relations there are suitable historical and cultural bases among Turks. For his declarations related with this issue, see Chapter Two and *Dünya*, 6 November 1992.

54   *Personal interview with Annaguli Nurmemedov*, Chancellor at the Turkmen Embassy in Ankara, Ankara, 11 June 1993.

55   *Personal interview with İsmail Yolcuoğlu*, Chancellor at Azerbaijan's Embassy in Ankara, Ankara, June 1993.

56   See subtitle 'The Decline of the Desire to Adopt the Turkish Model' in Chapter Four.

4   Reactions of the Turkic Republics to Turkey and the Turkish Model

Introduction

In this chapter reactions of the Turkic Republics to the Turkish Model and to Turkey will be considered. To this end, first, the collapse of the USSR and the emergence of the Turkic Republics will be briefly outlined. Second, by referring to the statements made by the Presidents of the Turkic Republics, the initial reactions of each Republic to the Turkish Model and to Turkey will be analysed. Third, possible factors which caused the Turkic Republics to decline the Turkish Model will be discussed. In this chapter, the period from the independence of the Turkic Republics to the end of 1993 will be the focus of our discussion, although to clarify certain points, this time limit will sometimes be ignored. It should be noted that the aim of this chapter is not to analyse the economic, political and cultural problems of the Turkic Republics and their foreign policies in depth. Although some information related to these issues will be provided, the main objective of this chapter is to document the reactions of the Turkic Republics to the Turkish Model and to Turkey.

Emergence of the Turkic Republics

The rule of Gorbachev[1] was a milestone in the process of Soviet collapse. After Gorbachev became the General Secretary of the Communist Party on 11 March 1985, he attempted to reform the Soviet political and economic system, however Gorbachev's six-year struggle ended in failure. As Rutland (1992, pp.207-208) explains, his reforms led not to the revival of the Soviet system, but to its disintegration. Gorbachev's failure to embark upon serious economic reform was one of the most important reasons for this lack of success. When Gorbachev preferred to begin with political rather than economic reforms, his political liberalisation spiralled beyond his control and his economic reforms never really materialised. On 18 December 1990, shortly before his resignation, Prime Minister Nikolai Ryzhkov bluntly stated that 'In the form originally conceived, perestroika has failed' (Rutland, 1992, p.200).

At first, Gorbachev did not accept the existence of a nationality question in the USSR. According to the 1961 Party Programme, which was still valid on Gorbachev's accession, ethnic differences would diminish and ultimately disappear as social and economic standards throughout the USSR improved. Gorbachev's report to the 27th Party Congress in February 1986 referred to the Soviet nationalities policy as an 'outstanding achievement of Socialism' which had 'done away for ever' with national oppression and inequalities of all kinds. According to Gorbachev, an indissoluble friendship among the Soviet nations had been established (White, 1991, p.168), that is, the nationality problem had been solved and a new type of Soviet citizen created. It was on the evening of Saturday July 1, 1989 that Gorbachev first admitted and emphasised the colossal danger of nationalism, when he made a broadcast appeal that underlined the danger of nationalism for perestroika, and the importance of the integrity of the USSR to the Soviet people as a whole (Sheehy, 1989, pp.1-3). Gorbachev's admission was confirmation of the fact that the 'nationality question' had become the third most important element in Soviet social life, along with the economic reforms and democratisation of the political and legal system (Krupnik, 1989, p.69). However, Gorbachev's reforms (Glasnost and Perestroika) had assisted nationalist movements by providing them with suitable conditions to flourish (Armoğlu, 1988, p.230; Mandelbaum, 1992, p.171). The nationalist and separatist movements started to emerge stealthily, because after glasnost a degree of freedom was given to the nationalities and some positive democratic developments took place. The level of media restriction declined, and issues such as the activities of the Communist Party, the Stalinist terror and matters related to nationalities began to be discussed openly. The media law passed in 1990 permitted almost anyone, including individual citizens, to develop their own media outlets; it also abolished censorship and forbade the authorities from interfering in the work of journalists (Tolz, 1992, pp.4-5).[2] This freedom and developments in communications technology enabled the Soviet people to become familiar with the outside world and increased their political and economic demands.[3] This process accelerated the disintegration of the USSR, because the main reason, which was keeping the nationalities together, was the fear of the central authority. When Gorbachev removed this fear, although he did not expect it, the Soviet Union began to dissolve (Armoğlu, 1988, p.230; Bal,

1996b, p.111).

After Gorbachev assumed power, the first important expression of nationalism was in Kazakstan following the nomination of Gennadi Kolbin, an ethnic Russian, to replace Dinmukhamed Kunaev as Party First Secretary in 1986. The demonstrations by Crimean Tatars in Red Square were also important; but for the most part, Soviet nationality disputes started publicly in the Summer of 1987 in the Baltic states. Gorbachev sought to pre-empt nationalist pressures in the Baltic states since the spring of 1988 by legitimising the ventilation of many nationalist demands and promising a much larger degree of cultural and economic autonomy (Ra'anan, 1990, p.65). After 1988, the independence movements in Caucasia and the Baltic states increased political tension. But this time, against conflicts between ethnic groups in Caucasia and other independence movements, the Soviet government used its army: on 19 January 1990 the Red Army entered Baku and the Azeri independence movement was suppressed (Aslan, 1992, pp.22-25). However, these suppressions were unable to halt the disintegration of the USSR. [4]

Gorbachev tried to establish a new federation and save the USSR; he pointed out the necessity of 'a new union treaty', which would replace the treaty of 1922 on which the USSR had been established. The new treaty would guarantee real economic and political sovereignty for the republics (White, 1991, pp.174-175). On August 19, 1991, a day before President Gorbachev was due to sign a new Union Treaty with representatives of the Republics comprising the USSR, the hard-liners in the army and Communist Party apparatus staged a military coup. The coup attempt failed and with it went the last vestige of communist power in the Soviet Union. The Communist Party was suspended and the plotters arrested, and all Republics of the Soviet Union declared formal independence.[5] Although Gorbachev tried desperately to resurrect the USSR in a different shape, as a federation of independent nations, by the end of 1991, the USSR was disbanded[6] and he himself had lost his post as the Soviet president.

In the process of the disintegration of the former USSR, the role of the attempted coup of August 1991 should be emphasised. The coup was a reaction to political and economic collapse, and to the failure of Gorbachev's policies. However, instead of preserving the Soviet state, this attempted August coup against Gorbachev gave greater impetus to the disintegration of the USSR (Dawisha and Parrott, 1994, p.21; Devlet, 1993, p.138). On 8 December 1991, Russia, Belarus and the Ukraine established the Commonwealth of Independent States (CIS) (Hosking, 1992, pp.497-

498)[7] which provoked dissatisfaction among the Central Asian Republics. After the establishment of the CIS by these three Slavic republics, the Presidents of the Central Asian Republics met in Ashkhabad, the capital of Turkmenistan. Saparmurad Niyazov (President of Turkmenistan), Islam Karimov (President of Uzbekistan), Askar Akayev (President of Kirgizstan), Nursultan Nazarbayev (President of Kazakstan) and Rahman Nabiyev (President of Tajikistan) represented their Republics at the meeting. The presidents decided to apply to Join the CIS on the condition that they should enjoy equal status as founder members. On 17 December 1991, Mikhail Gorbachev and Boris Yeltsin, (leader of Russia), met and agreed that the USSR would officially end on 31 December 1991. The request of the Central Asian Republics to be founder members of the CIS was welcomed by the Russian Federation, Belarus and Ukraine. On 21 December 1991, a meeting took place in Alma Ata, the capital of Kazakstan. Gorbachev was not allowed to attend the meeting, which was attended by Russia (Boris Yeltsin), Ukraine (Leonid Kravcuk), Belarus (Stanislav Suskevic), Kazakstan (Nursultan Nazarbayev), Turkmenistan (Saparmurad Niyazov), Uzbekistan (Islam Karimov), Azerbaijan (Ayaz Mutalibov), Tajikistan (Rahman Nabiyev), Armenia (Levon Ter-Petrosyan), Moldova (Mirca Snegur) and Kirgizstan (Askar Akayev). Lithuania, Estonia and Latvia did not attend, while Georgia attended with observer status. At the end of the meeting, it was announced to the world that the CIS had been established and the USSR had ended; in this sense the USSR can be said to have ended even before the date decided by Yeltsin and Gorbachev. Gorbachev announced his resignation in a TV program on 25 December 1991 (Dawisha and Parrott, 1994, pp.21-22; Devlet, 1993, p.138).[8]

As Sheehy suggested, it must be noted that although there is the possibility of a second disintegration within the Russian Federation as it includes 21 ethnic republics (Sheehy, 1993, pp.34-40), Russia still has the will to control other nations and to establish a state similar to USSR (Nahaylo, 1992, p.15).[9] For example, after the August coup, but before the disintegration, the Russian Secretary of state (after November 1991, First Deputy Prime Minister) Gennadii Barbulis suggested that 'Russia should declare itself the legal successor to the Soviet Union, take control of all Union structures on Russian territory, transfer all Soviet nuclear weapons to Russia, transform the Soviet Army into a Russian Army, and dictate terms for the control of inter-republican trade' (Tolz, 1993, pp.41-46). In 1993, some groups such as the National Salvation Front and Civic Union were still suggesting that Russia should control the lands of the former Soviet Union (Tolz, 1993, pp.41-

46).

Following the collapse of the Soviet Union, the analyst claimed that the collapse of the USSR was significant in world history as it marked the end of the last empire. The end of the USSR had tremendous impact on international relations; the classic two superpower-oriented bipolar international system and the struggle between communism and capitalism ended, the international system changed and only the US remained as a superpower (Valenta, 1995, p.77; Nitze, 1990, p.11). For some, instead of a new world order, the world had entered a period of disorder.[10] Others argued that a multipolar system similar to that of the 19th century and the beginning of the 20th century would follow soon, and the rise of Japan and Germany (or the EU) could be taken as indicators of this trend (Waltz, 1993, pp.44-79).

Six out of fifteen newly independent Republics of the ex Soviet Union were Muslim in belief and five of these were also Turkic in origin, namely Azerbaijan, Kazakstan, Kirgizstan, Uzbekistan and Turkmenistan. They were immediately referred to as the Turkic Republics especially in Turkey. Like most others, these Republics were not expecting the quick collapse of the USSR, and neither were they ready for the challenges ahead. This was expressed by Saparmurad Turkmenbashi (Niyazov) (no date, p.13-14), the President of Turkmenistan when he said:

> Of late, the consciousness of the people has undergone dramatic changes. Only yesterday most of the people could not even imagine living outside the empire, and today they cherish 'independent Turkmenistan'. It is the feeling of national pride and dignity that has become overwhelming. Today it has become a special honour to be a citizen of Turkmenistan.... However the fears caused by the empire, the inferiority complex deeply-rooted in the minds of the people, are still there. In view of this, one of the topical issues of today is reshaping the spiritual mind-set and looking for new ways to give impetus to trends of revival.

After the independence, it has not been possible for the Republics to be truly and totally independent of Russia. The Turkic Republics are members of the CIS under the leadership of Russia. As Olcott (1992b, p.120) suggested, it seems that Russia's presence in Central Asia is constant, and even with the formation of national armies Russia will remain an overshadowing military and economic power. The Ambassadors of Turkey in Uzbekistan, Kazakstan and Turkmenistan claimed that although the USSR collapsed, Russia still plays a vital role in this area and to some extent controls these Turkic Republics.[11] Also, as mentioned in the third chapter, Russia is concerned to defend the rights of the Russian minorities living in the area through what is called Russia's 'near abroad' policy[12], which creates new pressures on the Turkic Republics.

Because the economy of the former Soviet Union was centrally controlled, the economies of the newly independent Republics are interdependent. The interregional economic links of the USSR, though damaged, remained after the independence: South Kazakstan still got its electricity from Kirgizstan, while northern Kazakstan helped service Siberia's energy grid; Turkmenistan still sent part of its oil to Russia to be made into jet fuel. While each nation continued to depend on its neighbours' basic inputs - fuel, energy and raw materials - the co-ordinating structures that regulated such commerce shrank or disappeared entirely. Central Asian republics are struggling to have complete control of their economies (Olcott, 1992b, p.109).

The role of Russia in the cultural values of the Turkic Republics of Central Asia is important as well. In the 1990s, around fifty million people live in Central Asia, and around twelve million of them are European descendants of nineteenth and twentieth century settlers. The Russians in Central Asia see themselves as citizens of a remote part of a Russian-dominated state. This is especially true for the northern part of Kazakstan. Many Russian nationalists believe that the Slavic northern part of Kazakstan should be absorbed by Russia (Olcott, 1993, pp.49-50). On the other hand, Central Asians would like to regard themselves as superior to the Russians, and would like to be proud of their history and cultures. In their search for identity and nationhood, they see their civilisations as older and richer, the legacy of Genghis Khan and the Golden Horde, who ruled Russians for 250 years. For example, as Olcott (1993, p.50) pointed out, they snickered when Gorbachev incorrectly referred to the thousand-year-old Russian state. To them, as Annaguli Nurmemedov, the Under-secretary of Turkmen Embassy in Ankara, pointed out in a personal interview, Russians occupied and colonised their land.[13] Although some of the people have positive attitudes towards Russians, in general it can easily be said that there is mostly hostility between the native peoples and the Russians.[14] Similarly, Nurmemedov pointed out the improbability of returning to a federation like the former USSR; but he added that the Turkic Republics did not know what to do.[15]

It is not easy to escape the linguistic and cultural influence of Russian and Russia in the area. For most of urban Central Asia and for most professionals, Russian is still an indispensable language (Naby, 1994, p.35). For example, in Uzbekistan the Russian-language daily Pravda Vostoka was still the most popular newspaper in 1992, and its circulation (127,039) was greater than the circulations (67,460) of the three newspapers published in the

Uzbek language (Uzbekistan Avazi, Turkistan, Uzbekistan Edebiyati ve Sanati) (Hayit, 1993, p.83). Russian speakers outnumber Kazak speakers by three to two in Kazakstan (Olcott, 1993, p.50). Although USSR ended, Russian language is still used in formal relations in the republics. However, it can be argued that use of the Russian language does not mean Russification. In fact, as Gitelman noted, a non-Russian who uses the Russian language may be hostile to Russians, and may insist on maintaining a non-Russian identity (Gitelman, 1983, p.38); in fact, the disintegration of the USSR can be regarded as proof of this. Although the Russians and the native peoples have been living together for more than a century, this period is regarded as a nightmare by the majority of Muslims in these Republics, as proven by several revolts [e.g. the Basmachi (Hiro, 1994, p.338)] against the Russians. The Russian language is spoken by most of the Muslim people, and for example Kazakstan's 'national poet', Olzhas Suleymenov, writes only in Russian (Higgins, 1992). But there are opposite trends: these Republics have made their national languages their official languages and are trying to speak them. For example, Turkmenbashi, (no date, p.28) said: 'It is our duty to teach our children our native language, with no distinction between those who are talented and those who have no talent at all'.

Although the term 'Turkic Republics' is used to refer to Azerbaijan, Kazakstan, Uzbekistan, Turkmenistan and Kirgizstan, it is extremely difficult to regard the Turkic Republics as a single entity, and they also regard themselves as different and their social and cultural characteristics are diverse.[16] As will be emphasised below, the Osh events in Kirgizstan and Uzbek attacks on Meskhetian Turks in the Fergana Valley were among the indications of this diversity, and differences (Winrow, 1992, p.103).[17] After the clashes in the Fergana Valley, 40,000 Meskhetian Turks immigrated to Azerbaijan from Uzbekistan. The Meskhetians had been deprived of their property and had suffered heavy losses in the fierce inter-ethnic clashes with the Uzbek population (Nadein-Raevski, 1992, p.125). Furthermore, even in a historical sense these Turkic peoples regard themselves as different from each other.[18] The boundaries of the Central Asian Republics are by no means settled issues. For example, in addition to boundary claims on Uzbekistan as their ancient city is now in the borders of Uzbekistan, Tajikistan's leaders also have pretensions to a small piece of Kirgizstan; Turkmenistan fears both Uzbekistani and Iranian territorial claims; Uzbekistan, which borders all the others, lays claim to the city of Turkestan, now in Kazakstan, where the tomb of the twelfth century Sufi poet Ahmed Yasavi draws thousands of pilgrims annually (Olcott, 1993, p.51; King,

1992, p.7). As Osh events suggested the Osh region demand autonomy from Kirgizstan and finally integrate with Uzbekistan.

The tribal structure of the Central Asian societies raises questions as to how unity even among the peoples of the same ethnic origin and of the same religion could be established. In all central Asian Republics ties to family, tribe, clan, and locality are far stronger elements of the social fabric than in more developed societies. The flag of Turkmenistan contains five stars, each representing one of the principle tribes of the country (Dawisha and Parrott, 1994, p.148). Three major political groups correspond to clan-based geographic divisions in Kirgizstan as well (Olcott, 1993, pp.55-56). There are cases where the people of one Republic in fact comprise of separate groups, which could be a potential cause of conflicts in the future.[19] For example, in Azerbaijan there are groups such as the Tats, Talyshs, Kurds and Lezgins. In fact, on 21 June 1993, Ali Ikram Humbetov declared that he had established 'the Talysh-Mugan Republic' within the lands of Azerbaijan (called the Lenkoran region). After Humbetov realised that he could not realise his aim, he escaped to Iran on 23 August, 1993 (Lenkeranlı, 1993, pp.30-31).[20]

When the Turkic Republics declared their independence they were immediately faced with mainly two alternative offers to transform their economic and political systems. These were the Turkish Model supported by the West, and the Iranian model (Apostolou, 1992, pp.5-6). The Economist underlined this issue as: 'Turkic states must decide whether to turn to Turkey and its Westernised, secular Islam, or to the richer, more purist-Muslim of Saudi Arabia or Iran'.[21] As Hyman (1994a, p.25) emphasised, Turkey's image rather than Iran's was more potent for all of the Turkic-speaking peoples of Central Asia. On the surface Turkey was a developed, populous country, had developed a strong industrial base and had managerial expertise and industrial know-how. Turkey was also a secular state boasting a relatively successful market economy, a member of major Western institutions such as NATO and the Council of Europe and a big trading partner with the European Community (EC). And no doubt, the assumed cultural and linguistic closeness helped to make Turkey more attractive. This argument is supported by Dr. Anvarbek Mokeev, Under-secretary at the Kirgiz Embassy in Ankara. He emphasised the closeness between Anatolian Turks and Central Asian Turks in ethnicity, language, religion, culture, and history, and that they were psychologically more interested in the Turkish Model and 'therefore although there are several other models such as the Taiwan Model, the Japanese Model, the German

Model and the Kuwaiti Model, the Turkish Model looks the most suitable and close to us'.[22] Mango, on the other hand, mentioned the existence of a romantic admiration for Turkey in the Turkic Republics, and that this admiration exists at all levels of society. For example, when he spoke to Azeris in Turkish, they welcomed him warmly and regarded him as a friend.[23] This warmth towards Turkey, was also seen in the initial reactions of the Presidents of the Republics. For example, Islam Karimov regarded Demirel, the Prime Minister of Turkey, as an older brother, and President Akayev of Kirgizstan regarded Turkey as the star of the Turkic world. Therefore, apart from Turkey's attraction because of its secularism, market economy and closeness to the West (politically), more importantly Turkey's cultural closeness to the Turkic republics should be highlighted as a factor that encouraged the Turkic Republics to welcome Turkey and the Turkish Model.[24] Akyol (1989, pp.11-16) pointed out that the people of Azerbaijan believed that they were brothers of the Anatolian Turks, and at their demonstrations carried the Turkish banner and pictures of Atatürk as well as their own flag. The opinion poll conducted by the Institute of Law and Philosophy at the Azerbaijan Academy of Sciences showed that 43% of Azerbaijani Turks wanted Azerbaijan to establish closer relations with Turkey rather than Iran.[25] As the Union of Turkish Chambers and Bourses (TOBB)'s assessment survey suggested, it is necessary to note that Azerbaijani people were more pro-Turkish than other Turkic peoples were. Uzbeks, Turkmens and the Kirgiz also felt close to Anatolian Turks. The same survey found that Kazaks were the people least interested in Anatolian Turks. As several authors and politicians have argued, the newly emerging Turkic states initially looked positively on Turkey and the Turkish Model.[26] The same sentiments were expressed by Annaguli Nurmemedov, Under-secretary at the Turkmen Embassy in Ankara[27] and Ismail Yolcuoğlu, Under-secretary at the Azeri Embassy in Ankara.[28]

The Rise of Turkey and the Turkish Model in the Turkic Republics

For the leaders of the Turkic republics, Turkey was an obvious and, at first glance, attractive Model for emulation, much like an 'older brother' in president Karimov's words, as it seemed to incorporate features of both the East and the West (Olcott, 1996, p.26). The Presidents of the Turkic states were quick to recognise the importance of Turkey and, within a month of their independence in mid-December 1991, they visited Ankara (Hiro, 1994, p.69). Although the Turkic Republics have significant differences in terms of geopolitical position, historical experience, social, economic and political structures, they have common features such as common cultural values and ethnic origins. Additionally, they are the heirs of the USSR, and the importance of Russia in their domestic and foreign policy cannot be overlooked; there is the continuing presence of authoritarian tendencies; they all are in the process of state and nation-building; they struggle to be part of the international community; and they experience the problems of transforming their economies into market economies and integrating with the world economy; and finally they lack diplomatic personnel and experience. It should be stressed that in these Republics especially in the first years of independence it is difficult to talk about the process of foreign policy-making, as the Presidents tend to make foreign policy decisions alone. The role of the Parliament and the Foreign Ministry is limited. Another important fact that is that the leaders of the Turkic Republics did not anticipate their independence and the Republics were therefore unprepared for independence. In an interview with Anthony Hyman, Bakhadir Abdurazakov, a former Soviet Ambassador from Uzbekistan, said:

> Independence and freedom seemed impossible to imagine only a short time ago. It was too repressive a system ever to permit free expression of nationalist views for independence of the non-Russian nationalities. The disintegration of the empire was God's gift. Really, it is enough to make one believe... In reality, we still have only a nominal independence. It has to be made real.[29]

Azerbaijan

Between 1918 and 1920 Azerbaijan was an independent state; it became part of the Soviet Union in April 1920, as the Azerbaijan Soviet Socialist Republic. In 1990-1991, Azerbaijan supported the idea of a new union treaty and announced its willingness to sign one. It participated in the referendum concerning the preservation of the USSR, which took place in March 1991. 75.1% of eligible voters participated in this referendum and according to the official results, 93.3% of the electorate voted for a 'renewed federation'. The referendum became a demonstration of qualified support for the preservation of the USSR. During the failed August coup, when the State Committee for the State of Emergency (SCSE) sized power in Moscow, Mutalibov issued a statement which seemed to demonstrate support for the coup. Despite continued protests from the Popular Front of Azerbaijan (PFA), which called a poorly-supported general strike on 3 September 1991, the elections for the

Presidency proceeded, although they were boycotted by the opposition, with the result that Mutalibov was the only candidate, and received, according to official results, 84% of the vote.[30] On October 18, 1991, Azerbaijan declared its independence, at the same time adopting a new constitution making itself a presidential Republic.[31] According to the figures of 1989 Soviet Censuses data, Azeris consist of the majority in their republic (83%). The rest of the population consist of Russians (6%), Armenians (6%), Lezghins (2%), others (4%).[32] However because of war with Armenia, the proportion of the Russian and Armenian population declined in the following years.

During the reign of President Mutalibov, Azerbaijan signed the Alma Ata declaration (21 December 1991) to become a member of the CIS. After mass demonstrations, Mutalibov resigned on 6 March 1992, and the first free presidential elections took place on 8 June 1992. Ebulfaz Elchibey, leader of the Azerbaijan Popular Front, became the President of Azerbaijan (Mihmandarlı, 1993, p.4). During his administration, membership of the CIS was not ratified in the Azeri parliament.

In the first year of its independence, apart from general problems such as establishing the new state and transforming the centrally controlled economy to a market economy, Azerbaijan encountered a more serious problem: the war over the Nagorno-Karabakh issue with Armenians which, as Azeri Ambassador in Ankara Mehmed Nevruzoglu Aliyev and his Under-secretary Zakir Hasimov pointed out, constituted the most important obstacle and priority in Azeri domestic and foreign politics. The war forced more than a million people to migrate, and nearly twenty percent of Azeri territory (including Nagorno-Karabakh) was occupied by Armenians. Azeris believe that all the problems in the country are connected to the war, and that if this problem is solved everything will improve.[33] On 10 December 1991, in a referendum, the residents of Nagorny Karabakh voted overwhelmingly for independence; the Azerbaijani authorities considered the poll irregular.[34] In Elchibey's view, the Karabakh issue was more than a national cause, and was related with the independence of Azerbaijan. He argued that Russia never intended to leave Caucasia, and that through this war Russia was weakening both Azerbaijan and Armenia and trying to bring Azerbaijan to her knees. He claimed that a government which refused to cooperate with Russia had little chance of success in the Karabakh conflict. Later developments confirmed Elchibey's claim: when Heydar Aliyev became President and accepted co-operation with Russia, the military situation stabilised, as Russian support for the Armenians declined. This development seems to offer support to the Azeri claim that Russia used the war to persuade Azerbaijan to be a member of the

CIS (Ş. Kut, 1994, pp.246-247).

Turkey became the first country to recognise Azerbaijan, and Azerbaijan reacted warmly. As an example of this, in January 1992 Ayaz Mutalibov visited Turkey.[35] 'We want Turkey to represent us to the outside world' said Hasan Hasanov, the Prime Minister of Azerbaijan.[36] Furthermore, Salih Mehmedov, advisor to the Azeri parliament and an academic at Baku University, said 'If the Turkish world is a body, Turkey is its eyes and brain (Uludağ and Mehmedov, 1992, p.108). A similar attitude was shown by the Azerbaijani Deputy Parliament Speaker, İsa Gambar. He attended the inauguration of the Atatürk Dam, the key unit of the South-eastern Anatolian Project on 25 July 1992, and said that Turkey's development was regarded as development in their own country, adding that Azerbaijan was pleased with the moral, political and economic support offered to it by Turkey, and that when it became a strong nation it would never forget Turkey's support.[37]

In the positive reaction of Azerbaijan to Turkey and the Turkish Model, cultural ties and ethnicity played an important role more so than the other Turkic Republics. The statements of President Elchibey, a Turkic nationalist, were an extreme example of this closeness. In an interview Elchibey's said: 'In the past, there was only one independent Turkish state, it was the Anatolian Turks who were our symbol for independence... We have fifty million Turkish brothers in Anatolia....' (Toker, 1992, p.61). He also explained that they had chosen Turkey as a Model for their state. Statements made by Azeri politicians such as 'enemies of Turkey are our enemies too' give some idea about their attitudes towards Turkey (Pipes and Clawson, 1993, p.135). These statements suggest that the initial reactions of Azeri politicians were very positive and emotional towards Turkey.

The promotion of the Turkish Model, as Elchibey's statement quoted above suggests, was welcomed by Azerbaijan. Elchibey was not alone in stressing the importance of the Turkish Model for Azerbaijan. The third Economy Congress was held in İzmir between 4-7 June 1992, and Azerbaijani Prime Minister Rahim Huseyinov participated in the Congress. In his speech, he said: 'We will try to make Azerbaijan a rich country by benefiting from the experiences of developed countries. Turkey is the most important Model for us. We expect Turkey's support'.[38] Heydar Aliyev, also participated in this congress. He noted that instead of losing time trying to find methods to develop his country he would rather take the Model of Turkey, and said:

> Turkey has progressed more than all other Turkish and Muslim peoples and become a modern country. Therefore, it is not necessary for us to seek another model. The best example for the Nakhichevan Autonomous Republic is Turkey.[39]

Azerbaijan put Turkey at the top of its foreign policy priorities. For example, in the Ankara summit among the Presidents of the Turkic republics and Turkey in October 1992, President Özal put forward the idea of a Turkish common market; in contrast to the other Republics, Azerbaijan welcomed this offer (Ş. Kut, 1994, p.253; Zinin and Maleshenko, 1994, p.112). Because of the Karabakh conflict, the Elchibey administration tried to sign a security treaty with Turkey, but Turkey did not want to do so. In this, Demirel's attitude was important. He preferred to solve the problem through international institutions. If it had been the Özal government, the result might have been different since Özal advocated a more active policy on the Nagorno-Karabakh conflict. Demirel insisted that the policy of his government was to stay out of the conflict and to use diplomatic means to try to halt the fighting. 'Our policy is not to broaden the war', Demirel said, 'but to make it smaller'.[40] When the Minsk group was organised in the Conference on Security and Co-operation in Europe (CSCE), including Russia, the US, Azerbaijan, Armenia and Turkey among other states. Turkey argued that the CSCE principles were the main guarantee of Azerbaijan, and that a solution to the Karabakh conflict would be reached in this way. However Azerbaijan did not regard this as satisfactory, and disappointment was seen on the Azeri side. Turkey's agreement to sell electricity to Armenia; denial of helicopters to Elchibey (to evacuate people from the Armenian-occupied Kelbajer) were also to cause disappointment for Azerbaijan and especially for Elchibey, who had all along been a fervent Turkic nationalist (Hiro, 1994, p.74), and who had tried to limit Azeri relations with Iran and Russia. When after a coup Elchibey was forced to move to Nakhichevan, he was asked whether he had any expectations from Turkey, and he replied: 'I wanted two printing houses and four helicopters, but they did not give them. What can I ask for after this?' (Ş. Kut, 1994, pp.249-252).

As Hiro suggested, the election of Abulfaz Elchibey as president of Azerbaijan in early June 1992 was a plus for Turkey and a minus for Iran in their competition for influence in Azerbaijan. As mentioned earlier, Turkey had supported Elchibey openly. Elchibey claimed that within the next ten years Iran would disintegrate (Ş. Kut, 1994, p.252), referring to Iranian Azeris living in the North of Iran. Iran on the other hand, much to the disappointment of Azeri Muslims, did not support Azerbaijan in the conflict, but appeared to act as a mediator between Muslim Azerbaijan and Christian Armenia, brokering cease-fires. It is even claimed that in the Azeri-Armenian war Iran supported Armenia, weakening the Azeri position in the war (Ş. Kut, 1994, p.252).

Elchibey's impotence in the face of Armenian military superiority undermined his position at home. In this failure, it is claimed that Turkey's reluctance to help Elchibey played a vital role;[41] Elchibey's power and prestige were undermined within Azerbaijan, and this was followed by a coup by Huseinov and Aliyev's presidency, and Azerbaijan adopted a more co-operative policy towards Russia again. Following this, Geydar Aliyev became president, parliament ratified Azerbaijan's membership of the CIS, and Azerbaijan signed the Common Security Treaty.[42] After Aliyev took power he started to follow a more moderate policy towards Russia. This was mainly because he regarded Russia as the main power of the region, and believed that without co-operation with this power it was difficult to survive in this region. Therefore Aliyev's expectations and his foreign policy were more realistic than Elchibey's. This development did not mean that Turkey was no longer important for Azerbaijan, but that Azerbaijan had started to follow a more pragmatic and realistic policy by balancing relations with Russia, Turkey, the CIS and Iran. In contrast to Elchibey, Aliyev started to follow a more careful policy towards Iran as well.

Azerbaijan welcomed the multi-party system of the Turkish Model and after the resignation of Mutalibov in March 1992, democratic elections took place in June and the leader of the Azerbaijan Popular front, became president. As of January 1993, twenty-two parties were registered. Milli Müsavat Partisi (National Equality Party), Milli İstiklal Partisi (National Independence Party), Yeni Azerbaijan Partisi (New Azerbaijan Party) and Sosyal Demokrat Parti (Social Democrat Party) were the main parties. Also some parties such as Taliş Halk Partisi (Talish People Party), Lezgi Demokrat Partisi (Lezgin Democrat Party) and Kürt Beraberlik partisi (Kurdish Unity Party) were established but Justice ministry did not register them as they were established on ethnic base (İncioğlu, 1994, pp.110-115). Although Elchibey ran on a democratic platform, war with Armenia and harsh criticism of opposition hindered him from conducting democratic reforms (Dawisha and Parrott, 1994, p.154; İncioğlu, 1994, p.109).

It should be underlined that the fact that the majority of the Azeri population is Shiite did not bring Azerbaijan close to Iran. In contrast, Azerbaijan preferred the Turkish secular model (Ahrari, 1994, p.533). Because of their secular education during the Soviet era, Azeri politicians and intellectuals felt close to secularism[43], and feared that Iran would export its fundamentalism (Ş. Kut, 1994, p.252). Mehmed Aliyev Nevruzoglu, Azeri ambassador in Ankara, underlined the main principles of Azerbaijan state ideology as democratic, secular, seeking to achieve a market economy, to establish peaceful relations with all other states and to obtain Western technology. He said: 'our number one objective in foreign policy is to save our lands and strengthen our independence'.[44] Zakir Hasimov, Under-secretary at Embassy of Azerbaijan in Ankara, underlined that they approved of the secularism of the Turkish model[45] and had established their new state according to this principle.

At the beginning of February 1992, the Azerbaijani government decided to abandon the Cyrillic alphabet (adopted in 1937) and revert to the Latin alphabet[46] (which had been used from 1922-37 (Fierman, 1991, pp.75-76; Hiro, 1994, p.69; Öner, 1997, p.207). Nevruzoğlu, the Ambassador of Azerbaijan in Ankara, emphasised this and said 'we are not changing our alphabet, but we are turning back to our alphabet that we used between 1922 and 1938. We were the first to adopt the Latin alphabet in the Turkic world'.[47] Azerbaijan's adoption of the Latin alphabet was regarded as a success of Turkey's and the Turkish Model by some sources.[48] However, as Nevruzoglu and Hasimov said, because of the war and financial obstacles it has not been possible to put this decision into full practice. It is gradually being introduced in Azerbaijan, for example, it is used in some schools, some books are published in the Latin alphabet, and the names of streets are written in it as are some newspaper headlines.[49] As a future objective, Hasimov was optimistic even about a common language for Turkic peoples, but he believed that 'our children can achieve this'.[50] Azerbaijan also positively responded to Prime Minister Demirel's invitation, and Azerbaijan sent 1,293 student for higher education and 310 student for secondary education in the 1992-1993 education term.[51]

Azerbaijan also wanted to transform its centrally controlled economy to a market economy. It initiated the move towards a market economy in June 1991 when laws on the bases of economic development and Legislation were passed on land privatisation, taxation and the establishment of a central Bank.[52] In doing this, Azeri Ambassador Nevruzoglu in Ankara expressed similar desires in emotional terms:

> Turkish people are our brothers. Their mentality is like ours, their culture is like ours, their civilisation is like ours, that is to say if Turkey succeeded in this (market economy), we can successfully achieve a market economy by following Turkey. For example, the mentality and the appearance of European people can be different, but the Turks are the same as us.[53]

He added that war had hindered Azerbaijan from privatising its economy.[54] The process of transition to market economy was slowed by political uncertainty and ineffectiveness. Reform was further impeded by the political disruptions of 1993, with war distracting resources and increasing the refugee problem.[55] Initially the Azeris expected huge economic support from Turkey, but these expectations were unrealistic as Turkey's power and its economy are limited, and in fact the Turkish economy was experiencing serious problems.

Kazakstan

On 10 December 1991, the Kazak Soviet Socialist Republic became the Republic of Kazakstan. Nursultan Nazarbayev supported the unity of the USSR and Gorbachev's initiatives to keep the Soviet states together, by opposing the August coup against Gorbachev and struggled to prevent the disintegration of the Soviet Union (Nazarbaev, 1992, pp.129-131). He regarded the meeting between Russia, Ukraine and Belarus in Minsk, at which the foundation of the CIS was established, as dangerous (Ş. Kut, 1994, p.259). However, after the three Slav Republics established the CIS on 8 December 1991, Kazakstan declared her independence on 16 December 1991. Kazakstan was the last of the former Soviet Republics to declare its independence after the Soviet Union had effectively collapsed. On 21 December 1991, Kazakstan joined the CIS as a founder member.[56] Nursultan Nazarbayev was elected as President in December 1991, in an election where no other candidates were allowed to stand.[57]

Kazakstan was treated as an entity separate from Central Asia in the Soviet regionalization. After independence, the Kazak leadership was anxious to reassert Kazakstan's Central Asian credentials. At the Central Asian Summit in January 1993, it was agreed that the Soviet term of Middle Asia, which had excluded Kazakstan, should be replaced by 'Central Asia', which would include all five states of the region (Dannreuther, 1994, p.42). After its independence Kazakstan became, in the eyes of many commentators, the most important state in Central Asia, mainly because, after the disintegration of the USSR, Russia, Kazakstan, Ukraine and Belarus inherited nuclear weapons from the former USSR, and thus Kazakstan attracted the attention of the world. A total of 1,410 ex-Soviet nuclear warheads were based in Kazakstan - 370 on cruise missiles aboard Bear bombers at the Semipalatinsk air base, and another 1,040 on the 104 multi-warhead SS-18 missiles at the Derzhavinsk and Zhangiz-Tobe missile bases.[58] Kazakstan also had an underground testing range, one of the world's two largest space launch complexes, a missile testing range, and the world's only operational ground-based weapons laser (Dunn, 1992, p.15).

Kazakstan was pressurised to de-arm as the West and the US did not want to see nuclear weapons controlled by many small states. President Nazarbayev reassured Douglas Hurd, the British foreign secretary, that Kazakstan would abide by international arms control agreements.[59] During an interview with the Times, Nazarbayev said

> Russia, Ukraine, Belarus and Kazakstan signed a document placing their nuclear weapons under a single command, with the stipulation that if the weapons ever had to be used, they would only be used with the consent of all four states. We all recognise the agreement between the US and the Soviet Union on tactical nuclear weapons. In fact, there are no longer any tactical nukes on the territory of Kazakstan. They will be destroyed in Russia because the facilities for dismantling them are located there.[60]

Similarly, in his visit to the US, Nazarbayev promised to become a non-nuclear state and claimed he had been guaranteed US support if attacked by an aggressor.[61] It should be remembered that Nazarbayev's control over the army and the missiles was notional. A statement by a Russian officer at the Headquarters of the 40th Army in Alma Ata confirms this argument. He said: 'Moscow could put them on lorries and have them out of Kazakstan within days'.[62]

Another factor that made Kazakstan the most important state of Central Asia was that even without nuclear weapons, the vast territory of Kazakstan and its critical geo-strategic position between China and Russia gave the country special importance. With its 2,717,300 sq. km (1,048,880 sq. miles) area Kazakstan was second in size only to Russia in the old union. Because of this strategic position, and its population of 17 million, Kazakstan claims to be a bridge between Asia and Europe - a similar claim to that made by Turkey (Ş. Kut, 1994, pp.254-255). An additional factor that made Kazakstan important in Central Asia was its great resources, for example, its unexploited oil reserves.

During the early days Kazakstan's importance was generally accepted, and a former Soviet Ambassador from Uzbekistan, Bakhadir Abdurazakov, said 'Kazakstan has emerged, controlling nuclear weapons and having natural regional ambitions'.[63] Some authors claimed that 'Kazakstan fully intends to be a major world power, one of the three to emerge from the former Soviet Union, along with Russia and Ukraine. It is the only Muslim ex-Soviet republic with a chance of doing so' (Dunn, 1992, p.15).

On the other hand, Kazakstan faced new challenges. Although it had rich resources, these were not properly exploited. But far more important than this, as will be further discussed below, while most of the new Republics were made up of the ethnic group from which they took their name, the Kazaks were not the majority in their Republic. As Olcott pointed out, 'this fact more than any other has limited the scope of Kazakstan's national revival, and is sure to influence the course of Kazak politics as Kazakstan develops as an independent state' (Olcott, 1994, p.313; Dunn, 1992, p.15).

During one of his speeches, the Kazak President Nazarbayev listed the foreign policy priorities of Kazakstan as, respectively; relations with Russia and the CIS, relations with China; Mongolia; India; Pakistan and other neighbouring states of the region; relations with the West (respectively, the US, Europe and Japan), and finally relations with Turkey and Iran (Ş. Kut, 1994, p.255).

Mainly because of its large Russian minority, relations with Russia are essential for Kazakstan. The number of ethnic Russians, mainly living in Northern Kazakstan, is nearly equal to that of ethnic Kazaks: as the Table 4.1 shows 38% of the Kazak population was Russian, while 40% was Kazak according to 1989 Soviet Census Data. However, just as the Russians have been leaving Kazakstan, Kazaks living in other parts of the former USSR and elsewhere have, since its collapse, been moving to Kazakstan at an increasing rate. The Kazak birth rate is far higher than that of the Russians; over 80% of all teenagers in the country are Kazaks. Therefore it is possible to argue, as Dannreuther does, that in the near future the majority of the population will consist of ethnic Kazaks (Dannreuther, 1994, p.44).[64] There are positive evidences as according to mid-1993 estimates Kazaks increased to 41.9% while Russians declined to 37% (Dawisha and Parrott, 1994, pp.xviii-xix).[65] Further more, in 1994 Kazaks increased to 44% while Russians declined to 36% and in 1995 Kazaks increased to 46% while Russians declined to 35%.[66]

Table 4.1 **Ethnic Composition of the Central Asian Republics and Azerbaijan According to Soviet Census Data-1989 (%)**

National Groups/ Republics	A	Ka	Ki	U	Tur	Ta
Russians	6	38	22	8	10	8
Uzbeks	-	2	13	71	9	24
Kazaks	-	40	-	4	3	-
Azeris	83	-	-	-	-	-
Tajiks	-	-	-	5	-	62
Kirgizs	-	-	52	-	-	1
Turkmens	-	-	-	-	72	-
Tatars	-	2	2	2	-	2
Uighurs	-	1	-	-	-	-
Ukrainians	-	5	3	-	1	-
Germans	-	6	2	-	-	-
Karakalpaks	-	-	-	2	-	-
Lzghians	2	-	-	-	-	-
Armenians	6	-	-	-	-	-
Others	4	6	7	7	6	4

A: Azerbaijan, Ka: Kazakstan, Ki: Kirgizstan, U: Uzbekistan, Tur:Turkmenistan, Ta: Tajikistan

Source: Daria Fane, 'Soviet Census data, union republic and ASSR, 1989', in Ian Bremmer and Ray Taras, eds, Nation & Politics in the Soviet Successor States, New York: Cambridge University Press, 1993, pp.550-60.

Because of the ethnic composition of the population of Kazakstan, there is a possibility of ethnic conflict unless careful policies, which please all sides are followed. Some Russians, including the former Vice President Alexander Rutskoi, have asserted that Moscow should protect Russian speakers everywhere, with force if necessary. 'It's potentially very dangerous': said Galina Staravoitova, Russian President Boris Yeltsin's former adviser on national questions. 'Ethnic fighting could ultimately strengthen the hand of Moscow conservatives who want to restore a Russian-led Soviet empire'. The arch-rightist Russian politician Vladimir Zhirinovsky, a native of Alma Ata, the capital of Kazakstan, even threatened to unleash a nuclear holocaust on Kazakstan which he called a colonial hinterland. On the other hand, many Kazaks consider Russians as a fifth column, with loyalties to Moscow, not to Alma Ata. 'I do not think that Russians have a historical place here,' Khasen Kazha-Akhmen, leader of

Zheltoksan, a Kazak nationalist group is reported to have said (Pope, 1993, p.44). These hostile attitudes suggest that Kazakstan remains vulnerable to ethnic tensions. In 1992, the President's Foreign Affairs adviser, Gani Kasimov, was reported to have said 'Kazakstan could degenerate into 1,000 Yugoslavias. Not immediately, but the danger is there'.[67]

It should be emphasised that ethnic Russians are more educated than the ethnic Kazaks and the number of ethnic Russians working in industry is reported to be ten times larger than that of ethnic Kazaks.[68] Therefore, it was predicted that if ethnic Russians moved from Kazakstan, Kazakstan's economy and industry would face serious problems.[69] For example; the Soviet nuclear test site in the middle of the Kazak steppes, was run by Russians (Zagalsky, 1993, p.17). Also Russia wanted the ethnic Russians to stay where they were, because their migration to Russia would be a burden on Russia. Moreover, presence of ethnic Russians in these Republics helped Russia to implement its policy of 'near abroad'.

President Nazarbayev, although a Kazak, is popular among Russians and has been anxious to maintain close economic ties with Russia. He has also been keen to stop the migration of Russians from Kazakstan. His fear has been that the break-up of the old Soviet Union could release latent Kazak nationalism and upset the country's delicate ethnic balance.[70] On the other hand, Kazakstan, like Ukraine, reacted sharply when Boris Yeltsin suggested that Russia might lay claim to Russian-majority regions inside neighbouring Republics (Dunn, 1992, p.16). While reacting angrily to Russian claims, Nazarbayev explained his policy by saying,

> Kazakstan is the most ethnically mixed of the republics. The emigration policy of the Soviet authorities in recent years created problems. To be frank, it was probably a sly way of carrying out a policy of Russification. I would even say we have an advantage because Kazaks have learned over generations to live together with other peoples. My policy is one of common sense: do not give priority to any ethnic group. If the trash of ethnic conflict is not introduced from the outside, nothing will happen here.[71]

Kazakstan wanted to use nuclear weapons as a guarantee of its territorial integrity (Dannreuther, 1994, p.43), and Nazarbayev wanted some sort of guarantee from the West and the US against Russia because of the large number of ethnic Russians living in the country.[72] Another instrument Nazarbayev wanted to use against Russia was the Turkic-Muslim peoples in the Russian Federation. As if Nazarbayev wanted to point out to the Muslim-Turkic peoples within the Russian Federation, on 19 August 1992, to Russia's clear alarm, Nazarbayev engineered a Kazak-Tatar-Baskir summit, meeting with President Mintimer Shaimiyev of Tatarstan and Murtaza Rakhimov, chairman of the regional parliament of Bashkortostan (formerly Bashkiria) in the city of Uralsk in Kazakstan. The meeting was concluded with a trilateral economic agreement, and the leaders issued a joint statement which revealed the importance they attached to their common Muslim identity and stressed that they would like to mend the economic ties broken when the Soviet Union disintegrated. The implicit warning to Russia was that the Muslim and Turkic presence extended into the Russian Federation itself, and there could be no easy separation of the two worlds (Dannreuther, 1994, p.46).[73]

Apart from Russia, as Nazarbayev's statement indicates, China is also an important country for Kazakstan, mainly because the two countries share a large common border (1700 kilometres). In the early 1990s, China entered the Kazak market to the extent that more than half of Kazak imports were from China. However the main reason that makes China important for Kazakstan is that the Kazaks regard China as a threat to their security (Dannreuther, 1994, p.64).

In comparison with the other Turkic Republics, Kazakstan's reaction to Turkey and the Turkish Model was relatively cool. As mentioned above, Turkey is near the bottom of Kazakstan's foreign policy priority list (Ş. Kut, 1994, p.262). Several reasons can be given for the greater caution and cooler reaction of Kazakstan. Firstly, as underlined above, Kazakstan inherited nuclear weapons from the USSR, and its territory (2,717,300 sq. km) is the largest among the Turkic republics. Kazakstan is also rich in natural resources. Mainly for these reasons the world in general, and the Western world in particular, were very much interested in Kazakstan since the early days. This gave Kazakstan a feeling that it was superior to the other Central Asian Republics, and affected its reaction to Turkey in a negative way. The second factor is related to the delicate composition of the Kazak population. It can be argued that in order not to disturb the large ethnic Slavic groups in Kazakstan, the Kazak leadership deliberately behaved cautiously towards Turkey and did not welcome Turkey and the Turkish Model enthusiastically. The third factor can be valid for all Turkic peoples, and that is the Kazak people were not willing to have another big brother, and feared that Turkey might seek to play this role. Kazaks believe that their country's geo-strategic position is sufficient to make it a regional power.

The Kazaks, like other Turkic peoples, expressed their desire to develop its relations with Turkey. This argument was supported by the statements of President Nazarbayev. Nazarbayev was asked in an interview by the

Washington Times, 'Do you see Kazakstan looking more to the North, to Russian and European traditions, or to the South and the Islamic traditions that lie deep in your roots'? Nazarbayev's reply was,

> As you know, Kazaks are Muslims. And historically Kazaks belong to a Turkic group of people. The Soviet states have separated us from maintaining a relationship with those cultures and those peoples, so naturally we are inclined toward Turkey and the southern Muslim states.[74]

It is important to note that Nazarbayev paid his first official visit to Turkey on 25 September 1991 after the unsuccessful August coup in Moscow (Ataöv, 1992, p.105). During this visit, the Turkish and Kazak sides agreed within the Cultural Co-operation Agreement that the tombs of Seyh Ahmed Yasavi and his teacher Hodja Aslan Baba in the city of Turkestan in South Kazakstan would be repaired by Turkey. When Kazakstan declared its independence on 16 December 1991, the Turkish parliament recognised Kazakstan only 30 minutes after the declaration of independence.[75] The Kazak President attended the Ankara summit of the Presidents of the Turkic Republics in October 1992, showing that Kazakstan regarded itself as a Turkic Republic and wanted to improve its relations with Turkey and the other Turkic Republics. However, at this summit when Özal proposed a Turkish common market, Nazarbayev did not welcome this offer enthusiastically. On this issue, Nazarbayev said:

> Now, a Turkish common market is a subject of secondary importance. Above all, a unity should be achieved among the Republics created by the disintegration of the USSR. A Turkish common market among Turkey and the Turkic Republics is not a totally impracticable subject. But we are more interested in the Black Sea Economic Project of President Turgut Özal. To say only Turks can join a market can bring benefit to no one.[76]

Although Nazarbayev was positive about economic co-operation, he emphasised that he did not support groupings based on religion and ethnicity.[77]

In general, Kazakstan wanted to improve relations with Turkey but not close its options. In the first half of 1992, Kazaks signed twelve joint venture projects with foreigners. It was argued that Turkey was important for Kazakstan as they wanted to connect to Europe via Turkey by recreating the Silk Road. To bring this idea from theory to practice, Kazakstan organised a meeting in Alma Ata on 22-24 April 1992, at which the opening of a Trans-

Asia railway was proposed, arguing that the Silk Road had become important again and that this road would belong to the Turks.[78] Also, in reshaping itself, Kazakstan expressed that it thought highly of the example of Turkey.[79] For example, President Nazarbayev told foreign visitors that the country would follow the Turkish or the South Korean Model of development.[80]

As an advocate of secularism, Nazarbayev's interviews with journalists suggested his desire for democracy. For example, he replied to a Time question by saying, 'We want to enter the democratic world like any other state. Now is the time for the West to help us'.[81] However, democracy in Kazakstan where both the ethnic and religious mix was volatile, was not easy to implement. After the August coup, Nazarbayev abolished the Communist Party on 7 September 1991. In October 1991, he established the People's Congress of Kazakstan Party, which supports him. After the Kazakstan Communist Party was abolished, the Socialist Party was born which had its first congress on 16 March 1992, and announced that it would unite all democratic powers. In general this party supported Nazarbayev as well (Dunn, 1992, pp.17-18).[82] Nazarbayev contained nationalist movements such as the Alash movement, whose members did not wish to see Russians in Kazakstan, and who advocated a revival of Islam. Alash was not allowed to register as a political party, and some leading members were sent to jail on charges of insulting the President and disturbing the peace after a fracas in Alma Ata's mosque in December 1991.[83] Chan Young Bang, a Korean economist who advised the Kazak President, supported the 'conservative' politics of Nazarbayev for reasons of economy. 'Careful observation shows that it may be virtually impossible to accomplish the reform under democratic institutions' he said, 'I am not advocating dictatorship, but you need a strong leadership. It's a tragic phenomenon, of course: reform under democratic conditions is ideal, but in practice it is simply impossible' (Pope, 1993, p.44).

After independence, religion became an important issue for Kazakstan as well. On this issue the president of the Republic said: 'I am asked very often who Kazaks are. I answer, Kazaks are Muslims first and foremost' (Zagalsky, 1993, p.22). However, because of the ethnic composition of Kazakstan twenty four religious persuasions were practising in Kazakstan; in 1993 there were 581 mosques, Christian Orthodox churches, synagogues, and 95 more were under construction (Zagalsky, 1993, p.22). Islamic radicalism appeared in the region after the dissolution of the USSR, and Nazarbayev was concerned by the growth in Islamic fundamentalism in nearby Tajikistan.[84] Nazarbayev's statement during his trip to Delhi in 1992, to the effect that his country rejected religious extremism, enabled the Indian leaders to regard Kazakstan as a potential ally in countering Islamic radicalism.[85] Although Nazarbayev mentioned Islamic fundamentalism in the region, he claimed that there was no base in Kazakstan for Islamic fundamentalism and that therefore he did not regard Islam as dangerous for Kazakstan. Nazarbayev answered a question by the Times 'How great is the danger here from Muslim fundamentalism?' by saying,

> Islam has much stronger roots outside Kazakstan. Buddhism never completely vanished, nor did Islam fully took root here. Kazaks are not as fervent about their religion. There is much value in Islamic culture, just as there is in Christianity, and we are opening more cultural institutions to satisfy people's religious needs. But you should know that fundamentalism is unacceptable to us.[86]

Again, answering a question from the Washington Times in 1992, Nazarbayev said that

> Once again, we have no basis for fundamentalism in Kazakstan. The predominant religions in Kazakstan are Islam and Christianity. The percentage will be something like 40 percent Kazaks (who are Muslims), 35 percent Russians, and we've also got 8 percent Germans. This will be altogether about 85 percent. What remains includes several hundred other nationalities. So, if you can imagine, the layout itself proves that all the existing religions in Kazakstan must be equal and coexist peacefully... and it is certainly more complicated in a place like Uzbekistan, or Turkmenistan. I think Kazakstan and Kirgizstan adhere least of all to the area of fundamentalism.[87]

Kazakstan did not regard Iran as a country which promoted fundamentalism and which posed a danger to Kazak interests. In his interview with the Washington Times, Nazarbayev said,

> I recently met with Mr. Rafsanjani. He tried to tell me that they were not trying to disseminate Islamic ideas. They are not trying to encourage fundamentalism. So I suggested to him that we now do something so that the world develops trust in Islamic countries. I also told him that, in actual point of fact, that on the part of Islam the last 200 years, Islam has not been the one who initiated catastrophic wars. Usually the initiators were the Christian states. Even though you can still cite some local conflicts. So I suggested that all the Muslims shall work out such a policy that they will actually prove the absence of fundamentalism from the Islamic states.[88]

Nazarbayev's statements suggested that Kazakstan did not regard Islam as dangerous, and that 'people should be able to think what they want, they should be able to believe in the religion they want'.[89] He also stressed that fundamentalist Islam had not much chance, and that 'Turkey's secularism is also a Model for us'.[90] In answer to a Washington Times question on this issue, Nazarbayev said:

> According to our legislation, there is no state religion in Kazakstan. Every religion is equal and they are separated from the state. Kazakstan is a multinational state. And, side by side, there exist many religions. That is why there is no basis for fundamentalism there. I on my part will take every measure to prevent fundamentalism there. Kazakstan is also trying to exercise our influence on other Muslim states of the former Soviet Union. So that we'll go in the same direction. I think that a very quick introduction of Western values as well as a very powerful Western economic presence in Kazakstan is a guarantee to keep from fundamentalism.[91]

Kazakstan did not welcome hasty adoption of a Latin alphabet to replace Cyrillic. Nazarbayev again was careful in expressing his thoughts on the matter: 'Using the Latin alphabet will further draw us near to the Western world. In fact, there used to be a Latin alphabet in our country. We are carrying out a common study with the Turkish Ministry of Culture on this issue'.[92] However, Kazakstan never intended to change its alphabet. In addition to economic and practical reasons, the large Russian population in Kazakstan would never allow this change. On the other hand Kazakstan welcomed the opening of a Kazak-Turkish University in the town of Turkestan, under the name of 'Ahmed Yesevi Üniversitesi', and of Turkish schools. Kazakstan also responded positively to Turkey's offer and sent 1,109 students for higher education and 169 students for secondary education in the 1992-1993 education term.[93]

Nazarbayev's statements showed a careful approval of the Turkish Model in economy. 'We want to implement a free market economy. The only Model we have is Turkey', President Nazarbayev told Turkish newspaper Cumhuriyet in early December, 1991.[94] Giving his reasons, Nazarbayev said: 'The economic development that Turkey made within a short time attracts us'.[95] But at the same time, he looked to Asia for economic models, and appointed a Korean-American economist to advise him.[96] However, Nazarbayev was careful not to leave Turkey out either, and when asked about his adviser, he said: 'The only state in front of us is Turkey. South Korea is close to us. But our historical ties with Turkey and Turkish success, in the short term necessitates that we give priority to Turkey'.[97]

In theory Kazakstan welcomed the basic characteristics of the Turkish

Model such as close relations with the West; separation of state and religion (which was not difficult); eagerness to transform its economy to a market economy. Kazakstan made similar claims like Turkey, such as being a bridge between Asia and Europe emphasising its strategic position in the region (Olcott, 1996, p.32). The Kazak parliament adopted Kazakstan's first constitution as an independent state on January 28, 1993. This constitution confirmed Kazak as the state language and recognised Russian as the Republic's lingua franca. Although Russian is not the official language, the new constitution gives special status to Russian as 'the social language between peoples'. According to this constitution, the President has to have a fluent command of the Kazak language. The constitution describes Kazakstan as a 'democratic, secular and unitary state and grants full rights to all citizens'.[98]

Kirgizstan

Kirgizstan declared its sovereignty on 12 October 1990, and after the August Coup, on 31 August 1991, its independence. Askar Akayev was elected as president, unopposed on October 13, 1991, and the Communist Party was banned (Akiner, 1994, p.85).[99] Although the majority of the population of Kirgizstan consists of ethnic Kirgiz (52%), as shown in table 4.1 above, according to the 1989 census there are large numbers of Russians (22%) and Uzbeks (13%). Kirgiz increased 52.4% while Russians and Uzbeks declined to 21.5% and 12.9% respectively according to mid-1993 estimates (Dawisha and Parrott, 1994, pp.xviii-xix). Another source gave the figures for 1994 as follows; Kirgiz 52.4%, Russians 20.9%, Uzbeks 12.7%, Ukrainians 2.4%, others 12.6%.[100] This fragile composition of the population of Kirgizstan requires careful policies similar to those of Kazakstan. There is evidence that ethnic conflicts could easily arise. For example, a violent confrontation erupted between Kirgiz and Uzbeks at the border town of Osh in the Ferghana Valley in 1990; the violence was started by a land dispute. Osh had been incorporated into Kirgizstan in 1924, although Uzbeks formed a majority of the population, and Uzbeks had begun to demand the establishment of an Uzbek autonomous region in Osh Oblast. On 4 June 1990 at least 11 people died and more than 200 were injured, a state of emergency and a curfew were declared, and the border between Uzbekistan and Kirgizstan was closed, but the violence escalated. Order was not restored until August 1991. According to official reports, 230 people died in the violence, but unofficial sources claimed that over 1000 people were killed. The state of emergency was not lifted until November 1991.[101] To underline the degree of danger, a researcher at the Academy of Sciences in Kirgizstan said: 'A civil war is inevitable if nothing is done to solve the ethnic tensions'.[102]

The former Foreign Minister of Kirgizstan, Roza Otunbayeva, listed the foreign policy priorities of Kirgizstan as; relations with the US and Europe, relations with neighbouring states like China, Kazakstan, Uzbekistan and Tajikistan and relations with Turkey. As a factor, which affects Kirgizstan's foreign policy, she underlined that Kirgizstan is landlocked and has no access to the sea (Ş. Kut, 1994, p.263). Like Kazaks, the Kirgizs regarded China as a threat to their security with whom they share a 100km border. Kirgizstan also regarded Uzbekistan as a threat to its security as there is a large number of ethnic Uzbeks (as mentioned above) living in Kirgizstan. However, the democratic policies of Akayev have softened ethnic tension, and since independence, no fighting similar to the Osh events has taken place. However in the summer of 1992, the newspaper Vesti reported that there were calls for vengeance, along with demands that the towns of Osh, Uzgen and Alaba be annexed to Uzbekistan. Some of the ethnic Russians have departed to Russia since the independence and the possibility of a conflict between Uzbeks and Kirgizs has not been a good example for them. However, Kirgizstan has not so far been involved in any border disputes with neighbouring Republics (Doepfner, 1992, p.11).

After the declaration of independence Kirgiz president Akayev paid an official visit to Turkey on 22 December 1991. Özal, who welcomed Akayev at the airport, declared in front of the press that Turkey recognised the independence of Kirgizstan. Akayev then made a speech in which he said: 'Our aim is to recreate the ties which were broken during the communist period with our sister Turkey, and to improve our relations in all aspects'.[103] When he visited the president of the Turkish Grand National Assembly, Hüsamettin Cindoruk, Akayev explained that he was trying to establish a democratic state in Kirgizstan and wanted to use the experience of Turkey. Later on, he visited Süleyman Demirel, then Prime Minister of Turkey. Demirel gave him the letter proving Turkish recognition of Kirgizstan's independence, and Akayev then declared: 'It is a great happiness that our independence is recognised by Turkey, which is the centre of all Turkic peoples. Turkey is the morning star that guides the path of the Turkic Republics'.[104] Akayev described Turkey's role as important, providing a Model of a secular state which looks 'more to the West than to the Islamic world'. In the new Kirgizstan too, he declared, there would be religious tolerance and Islam would determine customs and traditions but not laws and social structures (Doepfner, 1992, p.10). Akayev explained the main features of the new Kirgizstan as democracy, secularism, respect for human rights, and the establishment of a state based on law. He emphasised that they were respectful of Islam but opposed fundamentalism. He said: '...we take Turkey as a Model in terms of state institutions'.[105] Anvarbek Mokeev, Under-secretary at the Kirgiz Embassy in Ankara, similarly emphasised the importance of the Turkish Model for Kirgizstan. He emphasised Turkey's successful economic transformation and democratisation of its social structure, and underlined strong ties between Turkey and Kirgizstan in terms of ethnicity, culture, language, religion and history. Because of these factors, he said, they wanted to use the Turkish Model, not completely, but as a general guide. He also regarded Turkey and the Turkish Model as an instrument to understand the West and Western culture. He underlined the fact that Kirgizstan had opened its first Embassy in Turkey, which showed Kirgiz interest in Turkey.[106]

In contrast to other Central Asian Republics (especially Uzbekistan and Turkmenistan), Kirgizstan welcomed the democratic character of the Turkish Model as well. In fact, Kirgizstan is known as the most democratic and open republic of Central Asia (Ş. Kut, 1994, p.263). It has also been called the 'trend-setter in the dismantling of the communist system'.[107] If this is so, then no doubt the personality of Akayev played a role. Two months after he was elected President (October 1990), Akayev permitted the founding of political parties, and the Kirgiz capital was renamed Bishkek (instead of its Soviet appellation, Frunze). Very soon after the failed Moscow coup Akayev banned the Communist Party, which no longer exists in Kirgizstan under any name (Doepfner, 1992, p.9). In 1992, there were two main parties in Kirgizstan; the Free Kirgizstan Party and the Asaba Party. The Free Kirgizstan Party was a central, mass-based party which made no distinctions between ethnic groups. Asaba, on the other hand, was a nationalist party, both politically and economically. It wanted to recreate the Kirgiz identity (İncekara, 1993, p.9). Nationalists attacked Akayev's policies. For example, Akayev three times vetoed a land reform bill which said: 'the land belongs to the Kirgiz people'. The opposition claimed that Russians had the greater wealth and could more easily afford to buy the state businesses which were being auctioned.[108] Deputies who had sympathy to Communism tried to sabotage the government's push for democratisation whenever possible, sometimes joined forces with nationalist politicians in order to do so (Doepfner, 1992, p.10). The US became the first country to open an Embassy in Bishkek which can be regarded as a reward to Kirgizstan because of its democratic reforms. Turkey became the second country to set up a full diplomatic mission in the Spring of 1992 (Doepfner, 1992, p.9).

Another important policy of Akayev was in his desire to make his country permanently neutral in order to keep its independence and distance from regional conflicts, and maintain its economic and political reforms. On this issue, he said: 'We want to be granted the international status of permanent neutrality. We want to be politically like Switzerland, but in the heart of Asia'. He was keen to emphasise that he only aspired to have relations with democratic and secular West when he said:

> We understand perfectly well that there is a struggle for influence going on in Central Asia. We're looking for partners among the free democratic nations which espouse private property, the priority of human over national rights, and a civil society.[109]

Kirgizstan welcomed the secular character of the Turkish Model and, in order to teach moderate Islam to its people, wanted religious help from Turkey. For example, Kirgizstan asked Turkey to build a mosque in Bishkek, and wanted religious books.[110] Akayev is firmly against Islamic fundamentalism, and said there was no danger of it since the Kirgizs were nomads until this century and Islam never took strong root.[111] Because of the adoption of secularism, political parties based on religion were banned in Kirgizstan, and the country was portrayed as a secular bulwark against Islamic fundamentalism by Tursunbek Cingisev, Prime Minister of Kirgizstan.[112]

Kirgizstan reacted positively to the Turkish offer of adopting a Latin based alphabet. Kirgizstan demanded printed Latin alphabets and a printing house.[113] Anvarbak Mokeev explained that Kirgizstan wanted to replace the Cyrillic alphabet with the Latin alphabet, but that because of economic problems it was difficult to bring this from theory to practice. He emphasised that Turkey's help was essential, but that Turkey had its own problems. Furthermore, he even advocated the development of a common written language based on Anatolian Turkish in the long term.[114] However, given the ethnic make up of the country, and its economic problems this would have been very difficult. Indeed Kirgizstan never changed its alphabet from Cyrillic. Kirgizstan also welcomed Turkey's offer and sent 384 students for higher education and 344 students for secondary education in the education term of 1992-1993.[115]

After declaring independence, Kirgizstan demonstrated a clear willingness for the transformation from a centralised economy to a market economy. The Kirgiz Prime Minister, Cingisev, arriving in Turkey to attend the inauguration of the Atatürk Dam in July 1992, said that Turkey's economic progress was very meaningful for the entire Turkic world.[116] Similarly, at the third Economy Congress held in İzmir between 4-7 June 1992, Deputy President Kulov of Kirgizstan said: 'We are now studying Turkey's economic system in detail, in order to join forces. We will soon change to a free market economy, and we want extensive co-operation with Turkish businessmen'.[117] Kirgiz Foreign Minister Roza Otunbayeva also stressed that Turkey was important for Kirgizstan as an economic partner and economic model (Ş. Kut, 1994, p.267). Akayev wanted to establish a market economy with all its rules, including a ban on monopolies, denationalisation, incentives for creating new businesses, and provisions for bankruptcies and liquidations. The International Monetary Fund, in an effort to rescue the country's modest economy, established an austerity program projected to cost 400 million dollars in its first year (1992). Although its potential was limited, Turkey in order to establish better relations volunteered an assistance of 75 million dollars (Doepfner, 1992, p.10).[118] Kirgizstan became the first Central Asian former Soviet republic to leave the rouble zone and adopt its own currency (the som) in May 1993.[119] This was a further assertion of its independence and commitment to liberalise its economy.

Askar Akayev is a liberal and a former academic, and therefore differs from the other leaders of Central Asia who are all former Communist Party bosses. Although Akayev was a department head of the local Communist Party's Central Committee between 1986 and 1987 he was never an apparatchik.[120] In 1992, he showed signs of reforming the system by positive measures. For example, he set up a special fund to train the native Kirgiz to take over high positions in the commercial and industrial sectors. He also wanted them to be able to take over the running of small shops and restaurants.[121] Like in Kazakstan, Russians make up half the capital's population and around a quarter of the country's. Following the independence as mentioned above although some Russians moved back to Russia, Akayev wanted them to stay in Kirgizstan, and help to keep the industry and the civil service running.[122] He expressed his wish when he said 'I am against emigration. I want to keep the Russians, Jews, and other minorities. We've just set up two national-cultural autonomous districts for the Germans'.[123]

Thus, Kirgizstan welcomed all the main characteristics of the Turkish Model; secularism, a market economy, a democratic system and closeness and co-operation with the West, without committing itself to following a Model.

Turkmenistan

On 27 October 1991, the Supreme Soviet declared the country independent the day after 94.1% of the voters opted for independence in a national referendum, and the Republic of Turkmenistan was born. On 21 June 1992, Turkmenbashi (Niyazov) was re-elected unopposed as president, receiving 99.5% of the votes in an election where he was the sole candidate.[124] Turkmens are the majority in their republic; as Table 4.1 shows, 72% of the population of Turkmenistan consists of Turkmens. The proportion of ethnic Russians was 10% (but this proportion was about 40 percent in the Turkmen capital[125]) and the proportion of ethnic Uzbeks was 9%. In 1993, proportion of Turkmens increased to 73.3%, while Russian's declined to 9.8% (Dawisha and Parrott, 1994, pp.xviii-xix).[126] 1995 figures are as follows; 77% Turkmens, 9.2% Uzbeks, 6.7% Russians.[127] These figures suggest that Turkmenistan does not have an ethnicity problem similar to that of Kazakstan. After independence, Turkmen leadership did not want ethnic Russians to leave the country, but tried to persuade them to stay in Turkmenistan. This was mainly because of the contribution of the Russian minority to the economy as skilled workers. In fact in 1993, Russia and Turkmenistan signed an important agreement, which gave dual citizenship to the ethnic Russians as an incentive for them to stay in Turkmenistan.[128]

Following the dissolution of the USSR, although Turkmenistan became a founder member of the CIS[129] on 21 December 1991 at the Alma Ata meeting, it began to distance itself from the other CIS countries. In May 1992, at a meeting of CIS heads of state in Tashkent, Turkmenistan was not a signatory of the collective Security Agreement, and in January 1993, at another such meeting held in Minsk (Belarus), Turkmenistan, Moldova and Ukraine did not sign a charter on closer economic and political co-operation. The reason was that Turkmenistan was afraid that this charter would lead to a new state similar to the USSR. President Turkmenbashi (Niyazov) often emphasised that he regarded the CIS as primarily a consultative body. At an address to his people, Turkmenbashi (no date, p.9) said:

> Turkmenistan recognises the Commonwealth of Independent States to be a consultative body rather than a governing one. To accept it as a governing body would mean that we accept it to be a state. And this would be a contravention of the notion of Turkmenistan as an independent state.

Although Turkmenistan opposed regional integration, it developed close relations with Russia. Turkmenistan was willing to develop her relations with

Russia in terms of bilateral relations rather than under the banner of the CIS, because Türkmenbashi believed that it would be difficult to retain independence under the banner of the CIS, and the CIS could give no guarantee against threats posed by other members of the CIS. Türkmenbashi opposed the idea that the CIS could become a political or military unity. Turkmenistan wanted to defend herself through bilateral military co-operation and security agreements with Russia. A five-year co-operation agreement has been signed with Moscow, as well as a mutual defence pact to allow the estimated 100,000 ex-Soviet troops to stay in Turkmenistan 'under joint control' (Pope, 1992, p.14). These agreements are important for Turkmenistan, as it regarded Uzbekistan as dangerous because of the later's regional hegemony. There is another issue that could cause disputes in the region: the river Amu Darya, which runs via Turkmenistan to the Aral Sea. The sharing of this river's water could be a cause of disputes.[130] Turkmenistan plans to fully control its territory with its own army by the year 2000. Turkmenbashi, (no date, p.15) said:

> Now we are confronted with a new challenge - the creation of our national army. Today we can confidently state that by the year 2000 the territory of Turkmenistan will see no foreign armed forces and by that time we shall have a united army of Turkmenistan.

This negative attitude towards regional co-operation can be explained mainly by two reasons. First, until the republic became independent, Moscow exploited Central Asia largely as a resource store, carting away cotton, natural gas, oil, silk and gold to factories in Russia and other republics (Levine, 1992). Turkmenistan is rich in resources: it has ten trillion cubic metres of proven natural gas reserves and 213m tonnes of proven oil reserves, according to the government, and produces 5m tonnes of oil and condensate a year (Levine, 1992). With massive gas reserves, and two-thirds of it desert with camels drifting over the occasional sand dune, Turkmenistan could comfortably pass at first glance for an Arab Gulf state (Pope, 1992, p.14). Turkmenistan's richness in resources played an important role in colouring Turkmen policy towards regional co-operation in Central Asia. 'Nobody likes to share his riches', said Foreign Minister Kuliev. 'For a long time the resources of Turkmenistan were exploited by others. It is time for Turkmenistan to use these for itself' (Pope, 1992, p.14). Ş. Kut (1994, p.272) suggested that because of its rich natural resources Turkmenistan believes that it can attract the West. Secondly, Turkmenistan has a small population and therefore it fears being absorbed by the bigger republics. This fear also played an important role in Turkmenistan's cool attitude towards the CIS.

On the other hand, Turkmenistan became a member of the Economic Co-operation Organisation (ECO) in 1992. Turkmenistan was protective about its rich natural resources, and ambitious (Dannreuther, 1994, p.37). When Turkmenistan refused close economic co-operation within the CIS, in terms of investment and the marketing of natural gas, Turkey and the West were regarded as some of the main foreign policy priorities of Turkmenistan (Ş. Kut, 1994, p.272). After Turkmenistan declared its independence Turkey became the first country to recognise it and to open an embassy in Turkmenistan; and Turkmenistan in return opened its first Embassy in Turkey (Saray, 1993b, p.69). Saparmurat Turkmenbashi also paid his first visit abroad to Turkey on 2 December 1991 (Toker, 1992, p.165). As a preparation for Turkmenbashi's visit, Turkmenistan Foreign Minister Avdi Kuliyev came to Turkey. Apart from asking Turkey to recognise Turkmenistan he said: 'We are two nations originating from the same ancestors. Neither of us has lost our languages. Turkey is technologically a developed country. We, on the other hand, are backward in this field' (Toker, 1992, p.166). Following this, Turkmenbashi and his seventy delegates spent four days in Turkey. During this visit, several agreements were signed related with economic, commercial, scientific and technical co-operation, communications and regular flights between Turkey and Turkmenistan were installed.[131] While returning from Turkey to Turkmenistan, Turkmenbashi said:

> We are expecting many things from Turkey. Firstly we want to be recognised by Turkey. We want to exploit Turkmenistan's natural resources with Turkey. I explained in Turkey that we would give citizenship and soil to those who want to come to Turkmenistan from Turkey. We not only regard Turkey as a gate open to the West, but with its big potential we regard Turkey as a partner which will show the path to the Turkmen economy.

He added that

> It is possible to establish a Turkic Common Market. The idea of pure pan-Turkism brings more harm than benefit to us. The idea of economic and cultural unity of people of Turkic origins, and division of wealth among themselves, concerns everybody including me. Political unity is a utopia for me. During my visit to Turkey, I heard the same thing and I am happy to hear that.[132]

These statements suggest that after the disintegration of the USSR, Turkmenistan regarded Turkey as a strong relative country that will help

Turkmenistan in the transformation of its economy and establishment of a new state.

Saparmurad Turkmenbashi was inaugurated as president in June 26 1992, after he had gained 95.5 per cent of the votes in the national elections.[133] In December 1991 the Turkmen Communist Party changed its name to the Democratic Party of Turkmenistan. A government-sponsored opposition party, the Peasant Justice Party, was formed in July 1992. All other political parties are banned.[134] President Turkmenbashi claimed to be promoting multi-party democracy under the umbrella of the former Communist Party. According to Turkmenbashi, veteran communists could rally into a Communist Party, while secretaries of rural district Communist Party Committees and secretaries of Regional Communist Party Committees formerly responsible for the agricultural sector could launch their own Peasants' Party. Other communists could join the Democratic Party headed by Turkmenbashi.[135] The Democratic Party believes that it can 'represent and protect the interests all working people'. The Peasant Party fully supports the chairmen of the Democratic Party, President Turkmenbashi, according to the Peasant Party's own chairman Bairamov (a member of the local Academy of Sciences).[136] It is reported that opposition figures were arrested in Turkmenistan before US Secretary of State James Baker's visit.[137] All the republic's mass media have been monopolised by the ruling party.[138] Multi-party democracy was dismissed in the press as a Jewish invention, while the interior minister called for the introduction of public whipping and executions, pillories and the parading of criminals in cages (Warren, 1993a). A new constitution concentrating power in President Turkmenbashi's hands came into effect on 18 May 1992.[139] Because of the ban on opposition parties and his control over the media, Turkmenbashi, the former head of the Communist Party, has been accused of being a dictator.[140]

Although other characteristics of the Turkish Model such as secularism, market economy, are welcomed by Turkmenistan, the Turkmen leadership is reluctant to adopt the multi-party system aspect of the Turkish Model. In his address to the people of Turkmenistan, Türkmenbashi (no date, p.6) was cautious on this issue:

> Our ultimate goal is to build a democratic secular state in our native Turkmenistan, and in the immediate future - to join the group of most advanced nations. The goal of today - by the year 2000 - is to achieve complete independence in all spheres; to do away with strife, the legacy of the empire; to profoundly develop the economic, social and political potential which would

enable us to catch up with the developed nations.

He (no date, pp.15-16) explained the process of democratisation as

Our choice is to build a democratic state. We are determined to achieve this objective with the gradual introduction of democracy. What does this gradual transition to democracy mean? It means that during the period of transition the democratic principles shall be introduced with no haste and on a step by step basis with a still larger role of the state preserved in all aspects of life. Control over the mass media will be established.

Hence, Turkmen leadership argued that premature political pluralism would threaten the nation's stability, emphasised the need for a transition period and stressed the barriers in front of establishing full democracy immediately. During his visit to Turkey on 2 December 1991, Turkmenbashi said:

Turkmenistan has unequal conditions. For the present time, to eliminate economic crises is the most important point. With the dissolution of the USSR, we are living through a transition period. This period brings anarchy and uncertainty together. We cannot achieve any of our expectations, unless we successfully pass this transitional period.[141]

When asked about his country's poor human rights record and its lack of democratic structures, he said: 'Turkmenistan has the highest regard for human rights. It is the supreme human right to live in stability and without war'.[142] By this he suggested that in the current environment the immediate introduction of more freedom and a multi-party system could potentially lead to conflict in Turkmenistan.

One should keep in mind that Turkmenistan has strong tribal divisions within the country, and rivalry between tribes is regarded as the strongest threat to stability in Turkmenistan (Pope, 1992, p.14).[143] In order to show the importance of tribes in Turkmen life it is noted that 'at the opening of the academic year at the Turkmen state University, students were allocated rooms without regard to their rayon or Oblast. But only a short time later only people from the same villages occupy the same rooms' (Nissman, 1994, p.384). Pointing to this danger, Türkmenbashi (no date, p.21) said; 'To have our state united in future we must completely eradicate the epidemic habit of talking about tribal relationships. No matter what tribes we come from, we remain the sons of the one big family of Turkmenistan'. Most of the claims of Türkmenbashi are not speculation but realities of Turkmenistan, and one can argue as Türkmenbashi did that in a society in which clan ties are very strong, political parties would be established on the basis of clans, and their rivalries could even reach the level of a civil war. Therefore, it is argued that they should first reach the level of a nation state: the importance of clans should be undermined and other factors like religion and nationhood (consciousness of being Turkmen rather than a tribe member) should increase. In the transition period, Turkmenbashi, (no date, pp.17-18) advocated the necessity of strong state power. He said:

> During the first stage of the transitional period control over the mass media will be established to prevent any possible conflicts between the ethnic groups and tribes residing here. The experience of the neighbouring states shows that the publications about land disputes would inevitably give birth to nationalistic aspirations, and the feeling of loyalty to one's own tribe; and this eventually caused strife. Since the way we have chosen is a democratic one we fully agree on the issue of a multi-party life. However, within the period of transition we should stay very cautious as far as the multi-party issue is concerned, as well as opposition

The weakest and rather amusing argument of the Turkmen leadership for not installing democracy has been that the Turkmen people are not psychologically ready for a multi-party system, and that authoritarianism suited the Turkmen character. For example; 'People will be emotionally and psychologically unready to make the right choices for another ten years' said Boris Shykhmyradov, a deputy Prime Minister (Warren, 1993a). Turkmenbashi, (no date, pp.16-17) rejected accusations such as totalitarianism against his rule, which he defended by saying:

> One of the US Senators recently told me: 'We have already lived 200 years as a democratic state. However, I cannot say that we have yet built a democratic society'. And our one-year old state which emerged after seventy years of a totalitarian system is expected to have already established an ideal democracy. The transition from the socialist system to the market economy - from the totalitarian regime to democracy - needs time. The attempt to establish a state of ideal democracy within a day, a year or even five years cannot but be described as adventurous. Where the people are not prepared, and where there are no prerequisites, any attempt to establish a democratic society may not only be a dangerous adventure but may also bring about the dictatorship of anarchy, civil war and strife between clans and tribes. Eventually it may result in the loss of human lives and in the loss of independence. What is mostly needed today is patience, and democracy will be triumphantly and gradually established in Turkmenistan.

Although Turkmenbashi rejected the quick introduction of a multi-party system, it is argued that free electricity, gas and water supplies for all citizens from January 1993 helped to strengthen Turkmenbashi's position as a leader. The lack of a free press and the government's restriction of the opposition prevented the emergence of public criticism. However, the resignation in August 1992 of the Minister of Foreign Affairs, Abdy Kuliyev, was apparently a reaction to the growing 'personality cult' associated with Turkmenbashi (Warren, 1993a).[144]

In terms of the Turkish Model, another important attitude of Turkmenbashi should be highlighted. Like Karimov, Turkmenbashi was an admirer of Atatürk. He discarded his Russified family name (Niyazov) and now calls himself Turkmenbashi, 'leader of all the Turkmens', in self-conscious imitation of Kemal Atatürk, 'Father of the Turks' (Rüesch, 1994, p.28; Pope, 1992, p.14; Warren, 1993b). This shows that Türkmenbashi takes Atatürk as an example. The Turkmen press praises the president's foresight and compares him with Kemal Atatürk, and in 1992 there was even a collective farm in Turkmenistan named after Turkmenbashi, which reminded one of the farm in Ankara named after Atatürk.[145] Therefore, one can argue that his understanding of the Turkish Model is different as he approves of Atatürk's one-party rule and claims, as Atatürk did, that the conditions are not ready for a multi-party system. No doubt, the signs of the personality cult around Atatürk in Turkey must have encouraged him, such as freely scattered statues, portraits, and road names.

Turkmenbashi underlined the importance of Islam and spiritual values for the development of Turkmenistan. The main indicator of this was that in 1992 Turkmenbashi became the first Central Asian leader to perform the hajj (Rüesch, 1994, p.29).[146] On the subject of religion, he said:

> The spiritual wealth of our people must have its specific features. Let us take the issues relating to religion. We stated before that the society we are building is not socialist, communist or Islamic. Islam gives to a person invaluable spiritual wealth. We deeply cherish the great ideas underlying it, which are the expressions of candour, piety and a clear conscience. It is natural that our state has created all favourable conditions for believers. Now everyone is free to profess any religion. No one has the right to prevent anyone from worshipping, or from observing fasting. At the same time one must not determine the state policy through religion. The point is that religion is not a policy but the power which makes the heart and conscience of a person clear. Under the constitution religion is separated from the state. It also means that we are building a secular state (Turkmenbashi, no date, pp.22-23).

In Turkmenistan, instead of regarding religion as a potential danger for the country, Turkmenbashi regarded Islam as a factor that strengthened his position, because he wanted to make use of a more conservative version of Islam which stresses respect for the status quo.[147] This fact is evident for example in when he concluded his address to the people of Turkmenistan saying; 'By way of concluding my address to my dear and respected people, to members of the Khalk maslahat I say: May Allah multiply your efforts. May Allah give us strength in our great undertakings for the good of the people' (Turkmenbashi, p.31). Turkmenbashi's warm attitude towards Islam should not be misinterpreted and regarded as a basis for the Iranian model. In 1992 there was worried criticism in the state-run press about the disorder in neighbouring Tajikistan, which roused Islamic nationalist opposition in Uzbekistan. Perhaps for this reason, Turkmenbashi made some expensive promises, including free water, gas and electricity for every home by the beginning of 1993 (Pope, 1992, p.14). As stated in the third chapter, Annaguli Nurmemedov, under-secretary at the Turkmen embassy in Ankara, said: 'Iranian fundamentalism cannot come to us. Their people are Shiite, our people are Sunni. Our people do not trust their Mullahs'.[148] On the other hand, partly for geographic reasons Turkmenistan and Iran established good relations: Turkmenistan has reached number of transport, banking and trade agreements with Iran. The deal, agreed during a visit in 1992 by Iranian president Akbar Hashemi Rafsanjani to the former Soviet republic considerably expanded Iran's economic influence in the region. Under the agreement, a joint banking and customs system would be established between Turkmenistan and Iran. Road and rail links would be completed. According to Mohsen Nurbakhsh, Iranian finance minister, the 500 million dollars (282 million sterling) cost of the railway would be primarily borne by Iran. This was in addition to 50 million US dollars of Iranian credits to Turkmenistan announced in May 1992. A second project to build a gas pipeline from Turkmenistan to Iran had also been agreed, Nurbakhsh said. A deal for the purchase of 19 billion cubic metres of Turkmen gas by Iran has been signed, with plans to expand this once the pipeline was completed. According to Nurbakhsh, some of this gas would be used in Iran, and some exported to the West and Turkey.[149] Because of these relations some circles, including Velsapar[150], have argued that Turkmenbashi was approaching Iran because of his fear of democracy. Velsapar said: 'The president is afraid of Tehran, but the fear of democracy is driving him into the arms of Iran'.[151] However, as Herzig emphasise Iran did not concentrate on exporting its regime but rather on improving economic relations.[152] Anyhow, it would be difficult, if not impossible to impose a Shiite regime on a Sunni population. Therefore, one must argue that it is not necessary to search for a sinister motive in the close relations between Iran and Turkmenistan. On the other hand, it can not be denied that the democratic record of the Turkmen president has not been a good one.

The Turkish offer of the Latin alphabet was welcomed by Turkmenistan (Rüesch, 1994, p.29).[153] During the visit by the Turkish Minister of Culture Fikri Sağlar to Turkmenistan, the president of Turkmenistan, Saparmurat Turkmenbashi, told a Turkish delegate that '... in the near future we will begin to use the Turkish (Latin) alphabet... we will use the alphabet and the Turkish books that you brought'.[154] Turkmenbashi (no date, p.28) believed that to use the Latin alphabet would bring Turkmen people spiritually closer to the civilised world. Therefore, on 12 April 1993, Turkmenistan's parliament decided that after a transformation period, Crillic alphabet would be abandoned and Latin alphabet would be adopted. Turkmens planned to adopt Latin alphabet by the year 2000 gradually.[155] Turkmenistan also positively responded to Turkey's offer and sent 1,185 students for higher education and 519 students for the secondary education in the education term of 1992-1993.[156]

Turkmenistan, like the other Turkic Republics, is trying to transform its centrally planned economy into a market economy. Turkmenistan regarded Turkey as a Model for this transformation, and Turkmenbashi wanted Turkey to be a partner of Turkmenistan and show the path.[157] In his address to the people of Turkmenistan, Turkmenbashi (no date, p.10) made it clear that he was

> Interested in the economic experience gained by the advanced countries of the world. However, we do not Model on any reform of any state, nor do we try to implant it in full into the realities of Turkmenistan. The reform of the economy of Turkmenistan is based on the national traditions of the people, it is unique, it does not resemble any reform undertaken by any people or any country. Its basic feature is the development of economic life through the development and encouragement of small and middle business strata, the education of a class of entrepreneurs, the class of the rich, the encouragement of foreign investments, rather than the establishment of large enterprises.

In the transition period, Turkmenbashi (no date, p.10) underlined the role of the state thus:

> During the transitional period in which we live we deem it vitally important to

have a strong power and state control over all economic transformations. As we move from the planned centralised economy towards a market one, from public property to private property, from socialist emulation towards market competition, we will be a state which will hold and supervise privatisation issues, as well as pricing. The reforms in question shall be effected stage by stage, gradually and progressively.

These statements suggest that Turkmenistan welcomed the market economy aspect of the Turkish model. Turkey also offered 75 million dollars of Eximbank credits to Turkmenistan. When Turkmenbashi visited Turkey between 2-6 December 1991, it was agreed to transport Turkmen petrol and natural gas through Turkey and export it to Turkey and Europe.[158] Turkmen officials said that they were keen on a 3 billion US dollar, 26bn cubic metres per year pipeline through Iran, then to Turkey and on to Europe. However, Turkey favoured an alternative route: under the Caspian sea, through Azerbaijan and then Georgia or even Armenia. But Turkmen officials believed that the war in the Caucasus was likely to continue for some time and they did not trust Azerbaijan any more than they did Iran. Turkey was eager to exclude Iran for fear of having an Iranian hand on anything of strategic importance (Pope, 1992, p.14). In late 1992, the two countries reached an agreement to co-operate on the eventual construction of a pipeline to convey natural gas from Turkmenistan to Europe via Turkey.[159] The Turkish-Turkmen Work Council was established in 1992 to help to improve economic relations.[160]

Uzbekistan

Uzbekistan was formed as a Union republic of the USSR in 1924. The Republic declared its sovereignty in 1990 and became independent on 1 September 1991. The Communist Party was renamed the People's Democratic Party, and Karimov became its leader. Islam Karimov became president, receiving 86% of the vote, on 29 December 1991.[161] In contrast to Kazakstan's position, the population of Uzbekistan mostly consists of Uzbeks (71%), with a Russian population of 8%;[162] but half of the population of Tashkent is made up of Russians, Ukrainians and other Europeans. According to the New York Times, in 1992, these minorities backed Karimov because they believed he would protect them from both Islamic fundamentalists and Uzbek nationalists. Uzbekistan's 45,000 Jews also generally supported President Karimov.[163] However, since independence, ethnic Russians have been departing to Russia, and therefore the proportion of ethnic Russians in the population of Uzbekistan has been decreasing. Its proportion of the population in 1993 was probably closer to 6%.[164] Uzbek nationalism has always been strong and this does not encourage the Russians to stay.[165]

It was argued that apart from Kazakstan, Uzbekistan was the prime candidate for being the regional power of Central Asia (Kırımlı, 1997, pp.54-55). Kazakstan was regarded as a Republic, which could easily fall into civil war because of its ethnic composition. Uzbekistan, on the other hand seemed to have lesser ethnic problems. Apart from the newly discovered oil fields, the figures showed Uzbekistan as the world's third-largest cotton grower and seventh-biggest gold producer (Boulton, 1992). The Independent argued that as the most populous country in Central Asia, and the historic centre of Turkestan, Uzbekistan's self-appointed role as a regional power could strongly affect the direction of the other Turkic Republics, determining whether they followed the path of democracy, Islamic fundamentalism or dictatorship.[166]

After the independence, Uzbek foreign policy was totally controlled by the President Islam Karimov who listed the foreign policy priorities of Uzbekistan as the countries of the CIS, Russia, Central Asia and Kazakstan, the Muslim East, the countries of the Asian Pacific domain, Turkey, other Muslim countries, Asian states like China and India, the newly industrialised countries of South East Asia and the US, and developed states like Germany, Spain, France and Italy (Ş. Kut, 1994, p.268).[167] While in general Uzbekistan is regarded as a threat by neighbouring republics mainly because of Uzbek chauvinism and large Uzbek population (Kırımlı, 1997, p.54), as authorities in the American Embassy in Tashkent claimed that Uzbekistan regard only Russia as a threat and Kazakstan as a rival power in Central Asia as other republics such as Turkmenistan, Tajikistan and Kirgizstan are too weak to compete with Uzbekistan (Ş. Kut, 1994, p.271).[168] On the other hand, Uzbekistan regarded the developments in Tajikistan as dangerous for its own security. Karimov feared that if radicals gained control of the Tajik state, it would be possible for them to interfere in the domestic politics of Uzbekistan through the latter's ethnic Tajik population, spreading radical ideas and even claiming certain regions from Uzbekistan. However, Kerimov's efforts to ensure that Tajikistan's brand of ethnic, clan and religious strife did not spread across the border included a widespread suppression of his own political opponents, mostly secular democrats.[169] Uzbekistan took an active role in the fight against the opposition in Tajikistan. In December 1992, an Uzbek helicopter was shot down in Tajikistan, revealing the extent of covert Uzbek support for the return to power of a neo-communist regime. Uzbek warplanes and, some believe, ground forces took an active part as an alliance of Islamic radicals and democrats was forced out of the capital, Dushanbe.[170]

Although Karimov did not put Turkey at the head of Uzbekistan's foreign policy priorities list, he mentioned that he regarded Turkey as an example for his Republic in terms of economic reforms, the balance between religion and state, and the experience of overcoming ethnic and cultural difficulties. He regarded the Turkish example as useful in establishing their state (Kerimov, 1992, p.30). Lesser (1992, pp.18-19) suggested that because of the ethnic and linguistic links between the Uzbeks and Turks, Uzbeks were attracted by the Turkish model.

Karimov visited Turkey between 22-24 December 1991 and in his speeches and declarations described the path that Uzbekistan would follow. 'As the state of Uzbekistan, we are taking Turkey as an example in all its aspects. We will establish the state from A to Z by taking Turkey as a model. If Turkey supports us, no one can enslave the Uzbeks'.[171] He also said: 'I announce to the whole world that my country will go forward by the Turkish route. We have chosen this road and will not turn back'.[172] He emphasised that Uzbekistan did not welcome Iran. In fact, in contrast to the Kazaks, Uzbekistan criticised Iran for supporting fundamentalists and regarded Iran as dangerous for its security. On this subject, Karimov said:

> There are hands and offers from all world states and also from Saudi Arabia and Iran. But we say Turkey. The principles of Atatürk are parallel to those we want to install in Central Asia. I am an admirer of Atatürk. I hope the Central Asian peoples will succeed where Atatürk succeeded in Turkey.[173]

Similar statements were made by a former Soviet Ambassador (in Cairo, Kabul, Dacca, and Mogadishu) from Uzbekistan, Bakhadir Abdurazakov, such as;

> Our friendship with Turkey is very close. Its envoy was the first to give in his credentials, although the US Embassy actually opened before Turkey's. The Turkish Embassy in Tashkent opened at the time of Süleyman Demirel's state visit in April 1992. For us, Turkey represents a successful modern and secular society. With Iran we are polite, but much still divides us in ideas and the place of religion in society.[174]

He also emphasised that Uzbekistan wanted to establish close relations with the West, saying 'We want Western advice at a difficult time in our history. We do not ask for bread and meat, as others do - in fact, we have huge potentials here. Its not charity we are asking for from the West, after all, but the best technology and a partnership'.[175]

Karimov's reaction to ideas of a Turkish common market and Turkish unity was not negative. He said:

> I am on the side of the unity of the Turkic people. I support the idea of a unified Turkic people, this unification must take place. Instead of political unification, economic unification can be established; you could call this a Turkic Common Market. If unification is possible for Slavs, it must be possible for Central Asian peoples, and this unification must include Azerbaijan and Turkey.[176]

Another important indicator of Uzbekistan's warm welcome to Turkey and the Turkish Model was that Karimov gave his country's Foreign Ministry headquarters to Turkey to use as its embassy.[177] These points suggested that Turkey enjoyed unrivalled prestige in Uzbekistan because of ethnic links with Central Asia and because of its economic success. Turkey was regarded as a model.

Although the constitution of Uzbekistan, adopted on December 8 1992, declares Uzbekistan to be a multi-party democracy, Uzbekistan has been rather reluctant to establish a multi-party system and follow the multi-party aspect of the Turkish model[178], in fact Uzbekistan is the least changed of the Republics from the Soviet period. President Karimov has tried to keep matters under his sole control.[179] In Uzbekistan, stability has been obtained at the price of repressing almost all dissent, inside and outside Karimov's administration. Newspapers have been closed on just the hint of criticism. The Uzbek government believes that at this stage to give freedom and establish a multi-party system would be dangerous for the interests of Uzbekistan. For example, in 1992, Ilhan Zakhirov, an official in the Foreign Ministry, argued that democracy was a luxury for Uzbekistan at that stage, saying

> Our relations with America are very low, because our administration does not allow freedom to criticise as in Moscow. Their diplomats try to teach us, but our traditions are different.... Our people are very kind, but it is very dangerous to give things like democracy. We do not have practice in being a democratic state.[180]

Apart from the Tajik war and the threat of Islamic fundamentalism, Safaev, who became the Uzbek foreign minister in February 1993, said it was vital that Russia's 'enormously complicated' political, economic and ethnic problems did not spill over into all-out conflict. Russian nationalism, and the internal threat of Islamic fundamentalism, were potential 'mortal dangers' for Uzbekistan. The Foreign Minister said there were difficulties in establishing all the processes of democracy in such a short time. Uzbekistan, however, was the only Central Asian state which had a presidential election with more than one candidate. Apart from Islam Karimov, Muhammed Salih, leader of the Erk party, was a candidate in 29 December 1991 election and Salih received 12% of the votes.[181] In 1992, the Financial Times reported that Karimov believed that Uzbekistan was in a period of transition between the old regime and democracy, and that this would take time. He saw his style of government as a buffer between growing Muslim fundamentalism and Western-style democracy. Karimov was trying hard to develop business ties, with special emphasis on secular Turkey.[182] Similarly, a former Soviet Ambassador from Uzbekistan, Bakhadir Abdurazakov, underlined the lack of experimentation in democracy in Uzbekistan. He said that 'It took the peoples of the Western countries two centuries to reach their present state of democracy and freedom, with the experience of civil wars, bloody revolutions and counter-revolutions'. He added:

> But we in Central Asia have set ourselves the task of building up democracy by peaceful methods on the basis of civil agreement. A gradual process of transition is inevitable. The indispensable condition for success in this is the preservation of civil consensus and inter-ethnic peace.[183]

Similarly, Jamal Kemal, president of the Uzbek Writers' Union, said: 'We are telling the opposition, please wait some years. We have no proper army. We have no strong borders. Help us build an independent state. First we must have independence, then democracy'.[184]

The US encouraged Uzbekistan to adopt a multi-party system. In December, 1991, the Bush administration announced the establishment of diplomatic relations as a reward for Kazakstan and Kirgizstan who had taken the offer and seemingly adopted democratic principles. In the following months, the US opened Embassies also in Uzbekistan and Turkmenistan. The main reason was not because their human rights record had improved, but simply the US wanted to try to monitor the changes on the ground.[185] Secretary of State James A. Baker visited Moldova, Armenia, Azerbaijan, Turkmenistan, Tajikistan and Uzbekistan in February 1992.[186] On this trip, Baker appealed to Central Asian leaders in Azerbaijan, Turkmenistan, Tajikistan and Uzbekistan to abide by a set of ten principles of democracy and human rights in exchange for US diplomatic recognition. Baker added: 'The US has diplomatic relations with many countries, although we disagree with their lack of political and economic freedom, where we use those relations to push for greater economic and political reform'.[187] The opposition in

Uzbekistan explained to Baker that the country remained a totalitarian state, but they wanted the US to extend formal diplomatic recognition as a means of helping the democracy movements. For example, 'politically we have no freedom at all', said Abdurahmin Pulatov, co-chairman of the opposition movement Birlik. 'The totalitarian regime has been destroyed in Moscow, but in Tashkent it continues to exist. I think that the sooner diplomatic relations are established, the better it will be for those forces which do not have democratic freedoms', said Pulatov, whose nationalist-oriented group was recognised but barred from elections. During Baker's visit, Karimov declared that he would abide by Baker's principles such as commitment to free elections, respect for human rights and minorities and establishment of free markets.[188] After Baker's visit the US became the first foreign country to establish an Embassy in Tashkent (Boulton, 1992).

In contrast to the statements of Karimov, the multi-party system was not established in Uzbekistan by 1993, and as Veli Ahmed Sadur, a Tatar academic and an important member of the Islamic Renaissance Party, suggested, Uzbekistan became the most authoritarian republic in Central Asia.[189] In its annual human rights report, issued in January 1993, the US State Department said that Uzbekistan was 'responsible for significant human rights abuses... The regime's heavy-handed control of the political process... is a major impediment to further progress and left in doubt its commitment to democratisation'. The report also stressed that 'despite government denials, the frequency of assault on opposition political figures, with the assailants never being apprehended, suggested government involvement'.[190] In an interview with Asal Azamova of Moscow News, Abdurakhim Pulatov, the leader of the opposition movement Birlik, explained the governmental repression, and claimed that his movement was repressed under the name of fundamentalism although it was not a religious organisation.[191] Pulatov's co-chairman of the democratic nationalist Birlik Popular Movement was thrown out of his university job as an 'enemy of the state'. In early December 1992, just days after the Uzbek parliament adopted a new constitution committed to multi-party democracy and human rights, Birlik was banned.[192] It is argued that authoritarian tendencies in Central Asia are related with the political culture rather than practical reasons. For example, Dawisha and Parrott argue that 'Just as Central Asia did not undergo a social revolution similar to Russia's in 1917, during the past five years it has not experienced a democratic revolution similar to the one occurring in Russia and several other post-Soviet states' (Dawisha and Parrott, 1994, p.147).

In comparison with the other Republics, Islam is stronger in Uzbekistan.

Apart from Turkish religious aid, Saudi Arabia, Iran, Kuwait, Libya and Egypt have sent Korans and other religious books to the headquarters of the Religious Board in Tashkent, and helped to build new mosques and seminaries. Islam Karimov's speeches stressed his respect for Islam. For example, after his victory following the elections on 29 December 1991, Karimov made a point of swearing his oath on the Koran and has since tried to avoid confrontation with Islam.[193]

Karimov made a point of criticising Iran and Iranian fundamentalism often. On one occasion he said:

> Uzbekistan is a place in which Islam is strong for historical reasons. We do not think that Islam will cause a big threat in Uzbekistan. The majority of our people are in favour of secularism. We do not interfere in anybody's religious freedom, but we do not allow fundamentalism to get Uzbekistan into its claws.[194]

This argument is supported by several other people as well; Dedehan Hassanov, who was banned from registering an Islamic revival party, said: 'God gave us Islam so we could live decently and not steal'. But he believes it is still too early to create an Islamic state and denies that Iran is a model, saying that Iranians are Shiite Muslim 'fanatics' whereas the Uzbeks are Sunni (Boulton, 1992). Similarly, Nazirov, mayor of Samarkand, said: 'The people do not want to go backwards. They want progress, not fundamentalism'.[195]

In the case of alphabet reform, although initially Uzbekistan considered both Arabic and Latin alphabets, it later decided to adopt the Latin alphabet, which strengthens the relations between Turkey and Uzbekistan. At the same time, the adoption of the Latin alphabet brought Uzbekistan closer to the West. On this issue Karimov said: 'In the case of the alphabet, we will make a decision between the Arab and Latin alphabets. Our preference will be on the side of the Latin alphabet'.[196] Uzbekistan also positively responded Turkey's offer and sent 1,124 students for higher education and 270 students for the secondary education in the term of 1992-1993.[197] However, in contrast to other republics, Uzbekistan called most of its students back to Uzbekistan. In the 1992-93 Academic year 1120 students, and in the 1993-94 academic year 244 students were called back to Uzbekistan. Uzbekistan was disturbed by the activities of the Uzbek opposition in Turkey and believed that most of Uzbek students held meetings with Uzbek opposition (Muhammed Salih) (Çarıkçı, 1997, p.767).

Uzbekistan, on the other hand, welcomed the market economy aspect of the Turkish Model. As noted above, in his visit to Ankara in December 1991, Karimov clearly stated that Uzbekistan would make use of Turkey's experience in economic transformation from a centrally controlled economy to a market economy. In fact, Abdurazakova emphasised that the rough plan of transition to the free market and implementation of radical economic reforms was worked out by the Uzbek leadership long before the state visit to Turkey.[198] Apart from trying to increase profits from natural resources, the ruling People's Democratic Party (former Communist Party) began taking steps towards introducing a market economy. But, as in other former Soviet republics, the measures met resistance. Price liberalisation in January 1992 provoked student riots (Boulton, 1992).[199]

Although the portion of Russians is not high, the importance of them in Uzbek economy is much greater. Similar to Kazakstan, the agrarian sector of the Uzbek economy still employs mainly the local population (53 percent of the number of Uzbeks of working age), whereas a mere 2.5 percent of ethnic Russians are engaged in agriculture. The picture is the opposite in industry, which employs 33 percent of Russians and 11 per cent of Uzbeks.[200] Therefore, the presence of Russians in Uzbekistan and peaceful relations between Uzbeks and Russians are essential, otherwise the Uzbek economy and efforts for market economy can be badly damaged. In the process of transition to a market economy, as a major producer of gold and cotton, Uzbekistan is already keen for foreign investors to help process more of its wealth internally rather than export raw materials (Boulton, 1992).

It is possible to say that Uzbekistan welcomed some of the aspects of the Turkish Model such as secularism, market economy and closeness to the West. But, although the multi-party democracy aspect of the Model was nominally welcomed, in practice it has not been accepted and the authorities claim that for the sake of 'stability', implementation of democracy has been delayed. Karimov stated that he was an admirer of Atatürk and wanted to follow Atatürk's path, and if taken literally, this suggests that for some time there will not be a multi-party system in Uzbekistan. Hence, one could call Uzbekistan an authoritarian state where a multi-party system will be adopted only when the situation becomes ready according to the authorities. This is clear from the constitution of December 8, 1992, which strictly separated Islam and the state, but also envisaged a centralised presidential system, with power centralised in the hands of President Karimov.

The Decline of the Desire to Adopt the Turkish Model

It is clear that during the first year of their independence, the Turkic Republics in general welcomed the Turkish Model in differing degrees of enthusiasm and regarded Turkey as a relative country which could help them economically, politically and culturally. The Turkic Republics were interested in the 'Turkish road to the West' and regarded Turkey as a gateway to the West (Griffiths, 1993, p.77). This short period, which lasted about two years was a time when emotions ran high and optimism was at its peak. After emotional visits and mutual declarations, the leaders of the Turkic Republics gradually began to realise the limitations of Turkey. In turn, their desire for the Turkish Model and their unrealistic expectations from Turkey were replaced by realism and pragmatism, and also by the personal ambitions and limitations of their Presidents. They did not abandon the Turkish Model completely, but their desire for this Model declined and they began to say that they wanted only the good parts of the model. They did not deny their special relations with Turkey on issues such as education and Turkish commercial activities in the Republics.[201] In contrast to the initial statements of the Presidents, the Turkic Republics began to mention the existence of other models that could suit them better, such as the Indonesian Model, the Malaysian Model, the Chinese Model and so on (Salih, 1993, pp.14-17).[202] The reasons for the decline of the Turkic republics' desire for the Turkish Model can be grouped as follows.

After the reciprocal visits it became obvious to the leadership of the Turkic Republics that Turkey had limitations economically and politically. The greatly increased access to the world at large after the first year of independence, showed them how far the 'Turkish Model' lagged behind other economies. There were disappointing limits to the amount of unsecured investment money that Turkish businessmen were willing to direct to the region. The Turkic Republics were no longer inclined to view the Turkish standard of living as a long-term final goal (Olcott, 1996, p.27). On the other hand, although the Turkic Republics initially regarded the Turkish Model as a social and economic miracle, when they visited Turkey they found a country beset with inflation, unemployment and almost as many other problems as their own Republics. Therefore, in some respects they realised that they were not worse off than Turkey, and maybe even better. In Akiner's words: 'The Central Asians now realise there isn't as much money in Turkey as they had expected. Academics come back from Turkey and say there are few scientists of comparable quality to those at home. They see Istanbul and Ankara and then they see the Turkish villages and say 'we're not much worse off'.[203] Same sentiments were expressed by Anvarbak Mokeev, Under-secretary at the Embassy of Kirgizstan in Ankara, who explained that they had realised that

Turkey had its own problems and therefore they would avoid unrealistic expectations from Turkey.[204] While accusing the Soviet system of colonialism, at the same time he emphasised high education level and development of infrastructure as positive aspects of Soviet rule. He also stressed that students who came from the Turkic Republics to Turkey for education should study in fields which were not good in their native countries. He claimed that medical schools were better in Kirgizstan than in Turkey, and therefore Kirgiz students in Turkey should not attend medical faculties, but rather faculties of business administration, international relations, economics, banking and hotel management.[205]

Turkish support for the Azerbaijan Popular Front alienated the leaders of the Turkic Republics from Turkey. One of the implications of Turkish support for the Azeri opposition was that the leaders of the other Turkic Republics became sceptical about Turkey, as they saw that in the case of Azerbaijan Turkey supported the opposition, but not the ruling elites, who were in the same position as them. Therefore, they wondered whether Turkey, in the long term, would support the opposition in their own republics as well, causing them to lose power. For example, in Turkmenistan there was worried criticism in the state-run press about the victory of the pan-Turkist Popular Front in Azerbaijan (Pope, 1992, p.14). During the Elchibey period, the leaders of the Central Asian Republics were anxious of the political movements taking place in Azerbaijan, fearing that unrest might reach their own Republics, and therefore they did not even want to establish close relations with Azerbaijan, or take sides in the Azeri-Armenian conflict (Ş. Kut, 1994, p.253).

Yet, as well as failing to find a solution to the Azeri-Armenian conflict, Turkey also failed to keep Elchibey in power. The position of Elchibey was important, as Turkey had supported him during the election campaigns and he in turn had distanced Azerbaijan from Moscow's orbit and turned to Turkey. However, Elchibey, the democratically elected president, was overthrown by a coup in 1993. Turkey supported the opposition but, in the end, failed to keep Elchibey in power, and this revealed to the Republics that Turkey's support or hostility was not so important as Turkey was too weak to compete against Russia in the region. Therefore, Turkey's initial image as a strong, developed sister state was badly undermined after the fall of Elchibey.

Another contributing factor was that the leaders of the Turkic Republics understood that the Turkish Model did not operate perfectly even in Turkey.[206] There were problems related to ethnic and religious minorities, and there was an undeclared war in South East Anatolia costing several lives every day. More over, Turkey's heavy-handed approach in these matters was not approved by the West. This realisation alienated the leaders of the Turkic Republics from the Turkish Model, because the composition of the peoples of the Turkic Republics were even more vulnerable than that of Turkey. Also there were several religions and many sects within these religions in the region. The problems in Turkey made it clear to Central Asian leaders that this Model did not operate well even in Turkey.

There were also questions as to politically how stable Turkey really was. Up to 1991, there was a remarkable stability in Turkish politics, with the Motherland Party in power since 1983. But after 1991, Turkey saw much more instability in its domestic political system, in particular as a result of economic crises and increasing separatist movements. This in turn damaged the image of Turkey in the world and in the Turkic Republics.

Apart from realising the limitations of Turkey, the leaders of the Turkic Republics learned about the international system and its power centres. They became more realistic about the world in general and their expectations of Turkey in particular. For example, Hasimov appreciated Turkey's efforts to end the Azeri-Armenian conflict, and regarded Turkey's efforts as satisfactory, saying Turkey was not expected to intervene militarily.[207] On the other hand, Elchibey had tried to sign a security co-operation agreement with Turkey. Later it was realised that Turkish military intervention was difficult because of Turkey's position: on the one hand it was trying to enter the EU, which would not welcome Turkish intervention in the Azeri-Armenian conflict, and neither would the US, as an ally of Turkey, welcome it. On the other hand, Grachev, Russian Defence Minister, declared that an intervention in the conflict could start a third world war. The Turkic Republics realised that Russia was still a military superpower and did not seem set to abandon former Soviet territory. The Russian impact limited the actions of the Turkic Republics in international relations.[208] After realising these facts, the Republics started to follow more cautious and less emotional policies.

Of course, the role of the West can not be overlooked in the decline of the Turkish Model from favour. Although the West energetically supported the Turkish Model and promoted it to the Turkic Republics, after realising that its initial assumptions such as an Iranian threat, instability in the area and a new power vacuum were wrong and sometimes exaggerated and misleading, the West decreased its support for the Turkish Model. The complicated ethnic make up of the Republics played an important role in this decision as well. Although using the common denominators of ethnicity, common language, and religion had seemed like a good idea at the time, it became apparent that it had the potential danger of provoking nationalist, if not racist feelings in the

Republics, and lead to unrest. Moreover, Turkey was not a good Model in terms of providing solutions to ethnic and religious unrest.

All the Republics wanted to establish close relations with the West, and asked the West to invest in their Republics, because they realised that the developed states of the West, as well as the Pacific, were in a better position than Turkey to give economic help. Therefore, after realising that the West no longer promoted and supported the Turkish Model, they stopped talking about the Turkish Model and their interest both in the Model and in Turkey declined. In contrast to initial expectations, instead of using Turkey as a mediator, the Turkic Republics realised that they could establish direct relations with the West and the US. The West as well, very soon realised that they did not need a third party in the middle. As Olcott emphasises, Turkey's strategy of becoming a 'bridge' faltered because of a general lack of interest on the part of Western investors (Olcott, 1996, p.26). The knowledge and formation about these Republics in the West had increased dramatically over a very short period of time. Above everything else, they did realise that on most occasions Turkey did not have any more insight into these Republics than they did. Languages were not as close as previously assumed, and not readily mutually understandable to an untrained ear. The best example of the situation was when interpreters had to be used during the meetings of the Turkic Presidents, and Russians at that. Common culture was possible but doubtful because after seventy years of Soviet rule, and living without any contact with each other, Turkey and the Turkic Republics did not share much. The West also realised the differences between Sunni Islam in Turkey and the traditionally more sectarian tradition of Islam, for example, in Uzbekistan. For Kazakstan and Kirgizstan religion never posed a problem because of historical and traditional reasons. When these facts were combined with all the other negative indicators against Turkey, the West could do without Turkey in the formulation of their policies towards the Turkic Republics.

The attitude of Turkey towards the Republics also played a role to hasten the decline of interest in Turkey. Turkic Republics did not want a new 'big brother' in the shape of Turkey just when they were trying to get rid of Russia. 'We are not looking for a big brother' said Azerbaijan's Prime Minister, Hassan Hassanov. 'We had a big brother in the past and we do not need a new one!' (Tabrizi-Sabri, 1994, p.154). Although Turkey stated that it did not want to act as a big brother, the Turkic Republics were sensitive on this issue. After seventy years of Soviet domination of their region, the leaders of the Turkic Republics were eager to avoid constructing deliberate or inadvertent dependency relationships with foreign partners. After the first few months,

Turkey's talk of being Central Asia's elder brother made many of the region's leaders nervous (Olcott, 1996, p.27). Turkey gave the impression that it failed to understand the sovereignty and dignity of the other Turkic Republics. For example: while Uzbekistan offered its foreign ministry to Turkey for use as a Turkish embassy, Turkey gave an ordinary three floor apartment house with no garden. When Karimov visited Turkey he was shocked by the place offered for the Uzbek embassy and then a suitable building site offered to Uzbekistan for buildings to be built as an Uzbek Embassy. This was a clear indicator that Turkey initially regarded itself superior to the Turkic republics and despised them, which in return negatively affected their attitudes towards Turkey. Another issue is related with the languages of these republics. Turkish linguists and politicians usually regard languages of these republics as dialects of Turkish (Arat, 1992, pp.59-69; Turan, 1990, pp.50-55).[209] Some Turkish scholars even suggested them to adopt Anatolian Turkish as a base to achieve common language (Karaörs, 1994, p.63). However, as Marie Bennigsen Broxup pointed out, these republics regard their languages as independent languages and they are disturbed by the Turkish side's attitude.[210]

Table 4.2   Survey Among Turkic Students (İzmir, June-July, 1993); Distribution of Students According to Turkic Republics

Nationality	Number	%
Turkmen	116	39.86
Azerbaijanian	11	3.78
Kirgiz	11	3.78
Uzbek	39	13.40
Kazak	16	5.49
Unknown	98	33.67
Total	291	100.00

An education exchange programme was one of the main developments in relations with Turkic republics. However, students from Turkic republics came to Turkey for education, faced some difficulties. Initially some organisational problems occurred while these students were locating different Universities and high schools.[211] Secondly, scholarships offered by Turkey to these students were not regarded as satisfactory by students. In a survey conducted by me, while only 47 (16.26%) students regarded services and scholarships offered by Turkey to them as sufficient, 242 (83.73%) students regarded them as insufficient.[212] As mentioned above the Uzbek government called most of the students to Uzbekistan as the Uzbek government believed that they held meeting with Uzbek opposition in Turkey. Furthermore, as Anvarbak Mokeev, Under-secretary at the Embassy of Kirgizstan in Ankara, pointed out in the same way, Turkic Republics realised that in some fields of education they are not much worse off Turkey.[213] Thus realisation of the limits of Turkey in the educational field as well as other fields affected their attitudes towards Turkey and the Turkish Model in a negative way.

The role of Russia is also important in this decline of the Turkish Model. In the post-Soviet era the leaders of the Turkic Republics recognised the substantial common interests between themselves and Moscow. Because nearly all the new leaders were occupying important places in the old Communist Party structure, and they had positive attitudes towards Moscow. Therefore it was difficult for them to break away from Moscow. Additionally, they did not want to lose their own political power inside their Republics. In many ways it was a problem of lack of democratic experience and training. The other reason which encouraged close relations with Russia was related to security: both the leaders of the Turkic Republics and the leaders in Moscow saw Islamic fundamentalism as a threat. The most notable case of this was Tajikistan. They wondered whether by any chance the spread of fundamentalist movements and unrest to their republics.[214] This factor also affected the reactions of the Turkic republics to the Turkish Model in the long term.

Conclusion

With the end of the USSR, the fifteen republics of the former Soviet Union became independent. Six of these newly independent republics had an overwhelmingly Muslim population, and five of them were regarded as Turkic Republics because of their Turkic heritage. After the end of the USSR, the newly independent Republics tried to reform their political and economic systems. Two alternative models of development were thought to be open to them: the Turkish Model and the Iranian Model. The reactions of the Turkic Republics to these Models were heavily affected by the cultural environment of these Republics. Primarily, Turkey had ethnic, and linguistic links, as languages of the same family were spoken by the peoples of the Turkic Republics; and religious links, as the majority of the populations of the Turkic Republics were Muslim and specifically Sunni like Turkey.

Mainly because of this cultural environment, the peoples of the Turkic Republics felt a closeness towards Turkey and therefore reacted positively to the Turkish Model. This affinity towards Turkey existed even among the leadership of the Republics; and judging by their statements it is possible to argue that they welcomed the Turkish Model enthusiastically. On several occasions they stated that they would follow this Model, which had been promoted to them by the West and Turkey, and would not turn back. All of them welcomed certain characteristics of the Turkish Model - secularism, the market economy, and closeness and co-operation with the West - but, as Mango suggested, the democratic aspect of the Turkish Model was generally not welcomed[215], especially by Uzbekistan and Turkmenistan, where opposition movements were repressed. Although the Kazak regime was not as authoritarian as these two, and Kazakstan and Kirgizstan have taken the lead in instigating democratic reforms (Kampfner, 1992), in Kazakstan, nationalist parties were not allowed to be registered, as the Kazak leadership was afraid of alienating ethnic Russians. Karimov and Niyazov (Turkmenbashi) took the example of Atatürk, and therefore wanted to follow the Turkish Model of 1920, which featured a single party under the strong leadership of Atatürk. Both of these leaders appreciate Atatürk and admire him; mainly for this reason, Niyazov adopted the name 'Turkmenbashi' (leader of Turkmens) which is very similar to that of 'Atatürk' (father of Turks).[216] Kırgizstan and Azerbaijan, on the other hand, welcomed the democratic aspect of the Turkish Model as well as the other aspects.

However, after emotional statements and reciprocal visits, the Turkic Republics realised the limitations of Turkish power and understood that the Turkish Model did not operate perfectly even in Turkey. In particular, Turkish support for the opposition (the Azerbaijan People's Front) in Azerbaijan and the success of Elchibey alienated the Turkic Republics from Turkey. Therefore, after the initial emotional welcome for Turkey and the Turkish Model, the Turkic Republics became more realistic, and their interest in the Turkish Model declined rapidly after the end of 1992.

Notes

1   For the Gorbachev era, see S. White, (1991), *Gorbachev and After*, Cambridge University Press, Cambridge; D.W. Spring, (1991), *The Impact of Gorbachev*, Pinter Publishers Limited, London; B. Meissner, (1988), 'Gorbachev's Socio-Political Programme', *Aussenpolitik*, no. 4, pp. 376-390; B. Miessner, (1990), 'Gorbachev in a

Dilemma: Pressure for Reform and the Constellation of Power', *Aussenpolitik*, no. 2, pp. 118-134; H. Teltschik, (1989), 'Gorbachev's Reform Policy and the Outlook for East-West Relations', *Aussenpolitik*, no. 3, pp. 201-214; R.G. Kaiser, (1991), 'Gorbachev: Triumph and Failure', *Foreign Affairs*, vol. 70, no. 2. pp. 160-174. For Soviet history, see G. Hosking, (1992), *A History of the Soviet Union*, Fontana Press, London.

2   For general information about the media under Gorbachev, see W. Laquer, (1990), *Stalin. The Glasnost Revelations*, Macwell Macmillan International, Oxford.

3   *Personal interview with Selçuk Alkın*, a member of the administrative committee of the Azerbaijan Culture Society, Ankara, 19 July 1993.

4   For nationalist movements, see J.A. Armstrong, (1992), 'Nationalism in the Former Soviet Empire', *Problems of Communism*, January-April, pp. 121-133.

5   The Economist Intelligence Unit, (1994), *Russia, Country Profile 1993-1994*, London, p. 4; For the August coup also see M. Mandelbaum, (1992), 'Coup de Grace: The end of the Soviet Union', *Foreign Affairs*, vol. 71, no. 1; M. Carnovale, (1992), 'In the Wake of a Failed Coup: Moscow and the Fate of the Union', *The International Spectator*, vol. 27, no. 1, pp. 47-67.

6   Economic failure was mentioned as having played a vital role in the collapse of the Soviet Union by the diplomats I interviewed. For example, İsmail Yolcuoğlu, ex-Counselor at the Embassy of Azerbaijan in Ankara, pointed out that the main reasons for the collapse of the USSR were first, the oppression of the nations and the lack of democracy in the society, and second, the unsuccessful economy. He claimed that if people had known these problems and considered them, they would have been able to predict the time of the collapse of the USSR. (*Personal interview with İsmail Yolcuoğlu*, Counselor at the Embassy of Azerbaijan in Ankara, Ankara, 10 June 1993). Dulat Kuavisen, Third Secretary responsible for political affairs at the Embassy of Kazakstan in Ankara, similarly underlined economic problems and the lack of democracy in the society as the main causes of the decline of the former Soviet Union. (*Personal interview with Dulat Kuavisen*, third secretary responsible for political affairs at the Embassy of Kazakstan in Ankara, 10 July 1993). About the impact of economy in the disintegration of former USSR see for example; White, *op. cit.*, pp. 100-103; İ. Ergun, (1992), 'Kollektif Sistemden Piyasa Ekonomisine Geçiş Sorunları', in *Türkiye Modeli ve Türk Kökenli Cumhuriyetlerle Eski Sovyet Halkları*, Yeni Forum, Ankara, p. 109; J. Smith and E.F. Green, (1989), 'The Dilemma of Reform in the Soviet Union' in W.G. Miller, (ed.), *Toward A More Civil Society*, Harper & Row Publishers, London, pp. 125-127; İ. Uludağ and S. Mehmedov, (1992), *Sovyetler Birliği Sonrası Bağımsız Türk Cumhuriyetleri ve Türk Gruplarının Sosyo-Ekonomik Analizi Türkiye ile İlişkiler*, TOBB, Istanbul, p. 9; N. Mihmandarlı, (1993), *Azerbaycan*, KEIB/BDT Araştırma Dizisi, no. 6, İstanbul Ticaret Odası Yayın no. 15, Istanbul, p. 1.

7   *Time*, 23 December 1991, p. 13.

8   Sabah Gazetesi, (1992), *Kırgızistan*, Türki Cumhuriyetler Dizisi, pp. 12-13.

9   For Russian nationalism, see RFE/RL Research Institute, (1988), 'Russian Nationalism Today', *Radio Liberty, Research Bulletin*, Special Edition, 19 December.

10   For example, see T.G. Carpenter, (1991), 'The New World Disorder', *Foreign Policy*, no. 84, pp. 24-39.

11   *Zaman*, 18 June 1992.

12   For the 'near abroad' policy see Chapter Three.

13   *Personal interview with Annaguli Nurmemedov*, Under-secretary at the Turkmen Embassy

in Ankara, Ankara, 11 June 1993.

14   In the survey conducted by the author of this book among the Turkic students in Turkey, around ten percent of Turkic students showed their positive attitudes towards Russians. However, answers of ninety percent of the students suggested that there were hostile attitudes between Turkic people and Russians in general. The same survey showed that over 86% of the Turkic students disagreed with the statement, 'in the future, by integrating with Russians and other minorities, the Turkic Republics will be under Russian sovereignty, as they were in the USSR'. Also, over 92% of the students said that they did not miss Soviet rule.

15   *Personal interview with Annaguli Nurmemedov*, Under-secretary at the Turkmen Embassy in Ankara, Ankara, 11 June 1993.

16   For the cultural and ethnic environment of Central Asia and the Caucasian peoples, see M. Mesbahi, (1994), *Central Asia and the Caucasus after the Soviet Union*, University Press of Florida, Gainesville; R. Conquest, (1970), *The Nation Killers*, Macmillan, London; C.W. Hostler, (1993), *Turks of Central Asia*, Praeger, London; S.P. Poliakov, Translated by Anthony Olcott, (1992), *Everyday Islam*, M.E. Sharpe, London; A. Bennigsen and C. Lemercicer-Quelquejay, Translated by O. Türer (1988), *Sufi ve Komiser, Rusyada İslam Tarikatları*, Akçağ Yayınları, Ankara; A. Bennigsen and M. Broxup, (1983), *Islamic Threat to the Soviet State*, St. Martin's Press, New York; A. Bennigsen, Translated from Russian to Turkish by Selim Taygan, (1984), *SSCB'ndeki Müslümanlar*, Vali Yayınları, Ankara; S. Zenkovsky, (1960), *Pan-Turkism and Islam in Russia*, Harvard University Press, Cambridge; H.C. D'encausse, Translated by A. Teşen, (1992), *Sovyetlerde Müslümanlar*, Ağaç Yayıncılık Ltd. Şti., Istanbul; S. Zaim, (1993), *Türk ve İslam Dünyasının Yeniden Yapılanması*, Yeni Asya Yayınları, Istanbul; M. Saray, (1993), *Azerbaycan Türkleri Tarihi*, Nesil Matbaacılık ve Yayıncılık San. ve Tic. A.Ş., Istanbul; A.V. Malashenko, (1993), 'Islam Versus Communism', in D.F. Eickelman, (ed.), *Russia's Muslim Frontiers*, Indiana University Press, Indianapolis; S.A. Panarin, (1994), 'The Ethnohistorical Dynamics of Muslim Societies within Russia and the CIS', in M. Mesbahi, (ed.), *Central Asia and the Caucasus after the Soviet Union*, University Press of Florida, Gainesville; A. Higgins, (1992), 'Kazakhs in thrall to a colonial past', *The Independent*, 14 April; Z. Gitelman, (1983), 'Are Nations Merging in the USSR' *Problems of Communism*, September-October; E. Naby, (1994), 'The Emerging Central Asia: Ethnic and Religious Factions', in M. Mesbahi (ed.), *Central Asia and the Caucasus after the Soviet Union,* University Press of Florida, Gainesville; A.G. Frank, (1992), *The Centrality of Central Asia*, VU University Press, Amsterdam; J. Critchlow, (1992), 'Will There Be a Turkestan?' *RFE/RL Research Report*, vol. 1, no. 28; D. Hiro, (1994), *Between Marx and Muhammad*, Harper Collins Publishers, London; M.B Olcott, (1993), 'Central Asia's Political Crisis', in D.F. Eickelman (ed.), *Russia's Muslim Frontiers,* Indiana University Press, Indianapolis; N. Devlet, (1993), *Çağdaş Türkiler*, Ek Cilt, Doğuştan Günümüze Büyük İslam Tarihi, Çağ Yayınları, Istanbul.

17   For inter-ethnic conflicts in Central Asia, see A. Kamilov, (1992), 'Internal Conflicts in Central Asia: Social and Religious Perspectives', in K. Rupesinghe, P. King and O. Vorkunova, (eds), *Ethnicity and Conflict in a Post-Communist World*, St. Martin's Press, New York, pp. 141-151; T. Saidbaev, (1992), 'Inter-Ethnic Conflicts in Central Asia: Social and Religious Perspectives', in Ethnicity and Conflict in a Post-Communist World, *op. cit.*, pp. 151-171.

18   *Personal Interview with İsmail Yolcuoğlu*, Under-Secretary at the Azeri Embassy in Ankara, Ankara, 10 June 1993.

19   *Türkiye İktisat*, April 1993, p. 4.
20   Lenkeranlı claims that this was a Russian plot against Elchibey.
21   *The Economist*, 21 February 1992, p. 47.
22   *Personal interview with Dr. Anvarbek Mokeev*, Under-Secretary at the Kirgiz Embassy in Ankara, Ankara, 28 December 1994.
23   *Personnel Interview with Andrew Mango*, London, 29 June 1995.
24   For example, see *Financial Times*, 21 May 1992, *Middle East*, July 1992, no. 213, p. 5-6; A. Yalçın, (1994), 'Tarih Perspektifinden Orta Asya'nın Geleceği', *Avrasya Etüdleri*, vol. 1, no. 1, 1994, p. 38, T. Akyol, (1990), *Azerbaycan Sovyetler ve Ötesi*, Burak Yayınları, Istanbul, pp. 12-13; H. Güler, (1990), *Sovyetler Birliğindeki Türkler*, Türkiye Diyanet Vakfı Yayınları, Ankara; Y. Toker, (1992), *Büyük Uyanış*, Toker yayınları, Istanbul.
25   *Zaman*, 20 July 1992, p. 5.
26   For example, see A. Apostolou, (1992), 'New Players in an old Game', *The Middle East*, no. 213. pp. 5-6; *Financial Times*, 21 May 1992; Akyol, *op. cit.*; Toker, *op. cit.*; Güler, *op. cit.*
27   *Personal interview with Annaguli Nurmemedov*, Under-secretary at Embassy of Turkmenistan in Ankara, Ankara, 11 June 1993.
28   *Personal interview with İsmail Yolcuoğlu*, Under-secretary at Embassy of Azerbaijan in Ankara, Ankara, 10 June 1993.
29   *The Middle East*, March 1993, p. 18.
30   Europa Publications Limited, (1992), *Eastern Europe and the Commonwealth of Independent States*, London, p. 452.
31   The Economist Intelligence Unit, *(1993), Country reports, Georgia, Armenia, Azerbaijan, Kazakstan, Central Asian Republics, 3ʳᵈ quarter 1993*, London, p. 8.
32   See Table 4.1.
33   *Personal interview with Mehmed Aliyev Nevruzoğlu*, Azeri Ambassador in Ankara, Ankara, 3 January 1995 and *Personnel Interview with Zakir Hasimov*, Under-Secretary at the Azeri Embassy in Ankara, Ankara, 3 January 1995.
34   Europa Publications Limited, *(1994), Eastern Europe and the Commonwealth of Independent States 1994*, London, p. 147.
35   *Times*, 28 January 1992.
36   *Independent*, 21 December 1991.
37   *Newspot*, 30 July 1992.
38   *Newspot*, 18 June 1992.
39   *Ibid.*
40   *The Washington Post*, 19 March 1992, p. 17.
41   For example, see G. Kut, (1993), 'Elçibey'in sonu Türkiye modelinin sonudur', *Cumhuriyet*, 24 June, p. 2; C. Çandar, (1993), 'Azerbaycan veya 21. Yüzyıla Elveda', *Sabah*, 22 June.
42   *Tashkent*, May 1992.
43   *Personal interview with Andrew Mango*, London, 29 June 1995.
44   *Personal interview with Mehmed Aliyev Nevruzoğlu*, Azeri Ambassador in Ankara, Ankara, 3 January 1995.
45   *Personal interview with Zakir Hasimov*, Under-secretary at Embassy of Azerbaijan in Ankara, Ankara, 3 January 1996.
46   *Newsweek*, 3 February 1992, p. 24; *Independent*, 27 April 1992, Hiro, *op. cit.*, p. 69.
47   *Personal interview with Mehmed Aliyev Nevruzoğlu*, Azeri Ambassador in Ankara, Ankara, 3 January 1995.

48   *Times*, 28 January 1992.
49   *Personal interview with Mehmed Aliyev Nevruzoğlu*, Azeri Ambassador in Ankara, Ankara, 3 January 1995.
50   *Personal interview with Zakir Hasimov*, Under-secretary at Embassy of Azerbaijan in Ankara, Ankara, 3 January 1996.
51   See Table 2.12.
52   The Economist Intelligence Unit, *(1993), Country Profile, Georgia, Armenia, Azerbaijan, Central Asian Republics, 1992-1993*, London, p. 45.
53   *Personal interview with Mehmed Aliyev Nevruzoğlu*, Azeri Ambassador in Ankara, Ankara, 3 January 1995.
54   *Ibid.*
55   Eastern Europe and the Commonwealth of Independent States 1994, *op. cit.*, p. 153.
56   The Economist Intelligence Unit, (1993), *Country Report, 3rd quarter 1993, Georgia, Armenia, Azerbaijan, Kazakstan, Central Asian Republics*, London, p. 10.
57   *Ibid.*
58   *Guardian*, 19 May 1992.
59   *Times*, 22 January 1992.
60   *Time*, 6 April 1992, p. 15.
61   *Guardian*, 19 May 1992.
62   *Times*, 26 March 1992.
63   *The Middle East*, March 1993, p. 18.
64   Dannreuther claimed that 'As early as the year 2000, Kazakhs could constitute over 50% of the country and form an absolute majority'.
65   It is stated in the source that 'Figures for population ... are mid-1993 estimates from the Bureau of the Census, Centre for International Research'.
66   TIKA, (1995), *Kazakistan Ülke Raporu*, Ankara, p. 7; *Eurasian File*, no. 90, January 1998, p. 2.
67   *The Economist*, 5 December 1992.
68   Sabah Gazetesi, (1992), Kazakistan, Türki Cumhuriyetler Dizisi, p. 18.
69   *The Economist*, 7 March 1992.
70   *The Economist*, 7 March 1992.
71   *Time*, 6 April 1992, p. 15.
72   *New York Times*, 16 May 1992.
73   *Times*, 24 August 1992.
74   *The Washington Times*, 20 May 1992.
75   Sabah Gazetesi, (1992), *Kazakstan*, Türki cumhuriyetler dizisi, p. 11.
76   *Ibid*
77   *Dünya*, 6 November 1992.
78   Sabah *Gazatesi, (1992), Kazakistan*, Türki cumhuriyetler dizisi, p. 18.
79   *Moscow News*, 22 March 1992.
80   *Times*, 26 March 1992.
81   *Time*, 6 April 1992, p. 15.
82   TİKA, (1995), *Kazakistan Ülke Raporu*, Ankara, p. 13.
83   *The Economist*, 7 March 1992.
84   *Times*, 24 August 1992.
85   *Moscow News*, 22 March 1992.
86   *Time*, 6 April 1992, p. 15.
87   *The Washington Times*, 20 May 1992.

88   *Ibid.*
89   Sabah Gazetesi, (1992), *Kazakistan*, Türki cumhuriyetler dizisi, p. 12.
90   *Independent*, 21 December 1991.
91   *The Washington Times*, 20 May 1992.
92   Sabah Gazetesi, (1992), *Kazakstan*, Türki cumhuriyetler dizisi, p. 1.
93   See Table 2.12.
94   *Independent*, 21 December 1991.
95   Sabah Gazetesi, (1992), *Kazakstan*, Türki cumhuriyetler dizisi, p. 11.
96   *The Economist*, 7 March 1992.
97   Sabah Gazetesi, (1992), *Kazakstan*, Türki cumhuriyetler dizisi, p. 11.
98   *IHT*, 29 January 1993.
99   Country Report, 3rd quarter 1993, Georgia, Armenia, Azerbaijan, Kazakstan, Central Asian Republics, *op. cit.*, p. 12; Sabah Gazetesi, (1992), *Kırgızistan*, Türki cumhuriyetler dizisi, p. 13.
100 TİKA, (1995), *Kırgızistan Ülke Raporu*, Ankara, p. 7.
101 Eastern Europe and the Commonwealth of Independent States 1994, *op. cit.*, pp. 382-383; *Times*, 24 March 1992.
102 *Times*, 24 March 1992.
103 Sabah Gazetesi, (1992), *Kırgızistan*, Türki cumhuriyetler dizisi, p. 13.
104 *Newsweek*, 3 February 1992, p. 23; Sabah Gazetesi, (1992), *Kırgızistan*, Türki cumhuriyetler dizisi, p. 14.
105 Sabah Gazetesi, (1992), *Kırgızistan*, Türki cumhuriyetler dizisi, p. 14.
106 *Personal interview with Dr. Anvarbek Mokeev*, Under-secretary at the Kirgiz embassy in Ankara, Ankara, 28 December 1994.
107 D. *Telegraph*, 11 June 1993.
108 *Guardian*, 15 March 1992.
109 *Guardian*, 15 March 1992.
110 Sabah Gazetesi, (1992), *Kırgızistan*, Türki cumhuriyetler dizisi, pp. 14-15.
111 *Guardian*, 15 March 1992.
112 *The Economist*, 20 February 1993.
113 Sabah Gazetesi, (1992), *Kırgızistan*, Türki cumhuriyetler dizisi, p. 14.
114 *Personal interview with Anvarbek Mokeev*, Under-secretary at the Kirgiz Embassy in Ankara, Ankara, 28 December 1994.
115 See Table 2.12.
116 *Newspot*, 30 July 1992.
117 *Newspot*, 18 June 1992.
118 For Turk-Eximbank's credits see Chapter Two.
119 *Times*, 11 May 1993 and F. *Times*, 11 May 1993.
120 *Guardian*, 15 March 1992.
121 *Times*, 24 March 1992.
122 D. *Telegraph*, 6 April 1992.
123 *Guardian*, 15 March 1992.
124 Country Report, 3rd quarter 1993, Georgia, Armenia, Azerbaijan, Kazakstan, Central Asian Republics, *op. cit.*, p. 16; 'Turkmenistan', in Eastern Europe and the Commonwealth of Independent States 1994, *op. cit.* pp. 661-662.
125 F. *Times*, 24 December 1993.
126 It is stated in the source that 'Figures for population ... are mid-1993 estimates from the Bureau of the Census, Centre for International Research'.

127 TİKA, (1996), *Türkmenistan Ülke Raporu*, Ankara, p. 14.
128 *F. Times*, 24 December 1993.
129 For Saparmurad Turkmenbashi's ideas about the CIS, see S. Niyazov, (1993), 'Our Policy Towards the CIS', *Revival*, October, no. 1.
130 For the Aral lake and water issue and affects of cotton production, see P.M. Carley, (1989), 'The Price of the Plan: Perceptions of Cotton and Health in Uzbekistan and Turkmenistan', *Central Asian Survey*, vol. 8, no. 4.
131 Sabah Gazetesi, (1992), *Türkmenistan*, Türki cumhuriyetler dizisi, pp. 13-14.
132 *Cumhuriyet*, 18 December 1991.
133 *Moscow News*, 5 July 1992.
134 Country Report, 3rd quarter 1993, Georgia, Armenia, Azerbaijan, Kazakstan, Central Asian Republics, *op. cit.*, p. 16.
135 *Moscow News*, 23 February 1992.
136 *Moscow News*, 5 July 1992.
137 *Moscow News*, 23 February 1992.
138 *Ibid.*
139 Country Report, 3rd quarter 1993, Georgia, Armenia, Azerbaijan, Kazakstan, Central Asian Republics, *op. cit.*, p. 16.
140 IHT, 12 May 1993.
141 *Cumhuriyet*, 18 December 1991.
142 *Times*, 29 January 1994.
143 For the main tribes of Turkmens; see TİKA, (1996), *Türkmenistan Ülke Raporu*, Ankara, p. 18.
144 'Türkmenistan', in Eastern Europe and the Commonwealth of Independent States 1994, *op. cit.*, p. 663.
145 *Moscow News*, 5 July 1992.
146 *S. Telegraph*, 24 January 1993.
147 *S. Telegraph*, 24 January 1993.
148 *Personal interview with Annaguli Memedov*, Under-secretary of the Turkmen Embassy in Ankara, Ankara, 1993.
149 *Financial Times*, 14 May 1992.
150 Ak-Muhammed Velsapar, a leading member of the small opposition movement Agzybirlik in Turkmenistan.
151 *S. Telegraph*, 24 January 1993.
152 For details, see E. Herzig, (1995), *Iran and the former Soviet South*, The Royal Institute of International Affairs, London.
153 *F. Times*, 3 May 1992.
154 Sabah Gazetesi, (1992), *Türkmenistan*, Türki Cumhuriyetleri Dizisi, p. 18.
155 TİKA, (1996), *Türkmenistan Ülke Raporu*, Ankara, p. 95.
156 See Table 2.12.
157 Sabah Gazetesi, (1992), *Türkmenistan*, Türki Cumhuriyetleri Dizisi, p. 23.
158 *Ibid.,* p. 21.
159 'Turkmenistan', in Eastern Europe and the Commonwealth of Independent States 1994, *op. cit.*, p. 664.
160 Sabah Gazetesi, (1992), *Türkmenistan*, Türki Cumhuriyetleri Dizisi, p. 24.
161 Country Report, 3rd quarter 1993, Georgia, Armenia, Azerbaijan, Kazakstan, Central Asian Republics, *op. cit.*, p. 18; TİKA, (1995), *Özbekistan Ülke Raporu*, Ankara, p. 12.
162 See Table 4.1.

163 *The New York Times*, 17 February 1992, p. 7.

164 The Econonmist Intelligence Unit, (1994), *Country Profile, Georgia Armenia Azerbaijan Central Asian Republics, 1993-1994*, London, p. 127.

165 The results of a survey among ethnic Russians showed that in comparison with other Republics ethnic Russians living in Uzbekistan more inclined to move to Russia. 38% of the people surveyed said they had the desire to leave for Russia. 36% of them wanted to stay permanently in Uzbekistan while 26% said 'it is difficult to answer'. For the details of this survey see, J. Dunlop, (1994), 'Russia: confronting a loss of empire', in I. Bremmer and R. Taras, (eds), *Nations and Politics in the Soviet Successor States*, Cambridge University Press, Cambridge, pp. 65-67.

166 *Independent*, 2 January 1993.

167 For Kerimov's ideas, see I. Kerimov, (1992), *Uzbekistan: The Road of Independence and Progress*, Taşkent, Uzbekistan.

168 *The Middle East*, March 1993, p. 18.

169 *IHT*, 16 February 1993.

170 *Independent*, 2 January 1993.

171 Sabah Gazetesi, (1992), *Özbekistan*, Türki Cumhuriyetleri Dizisi, p. 9.

172 *Independent*, 21 December 1991; 'The presidents of several of the Republics have waxed lyrical in praise of the 'Turkish Model'. 'I announce to the world that my country will go forward by the Turkish route', said Uzbek president Islam Kerimov'. (*Newsweek*, 3 February 1992, p. 23; *S. Times*, 19 January 1992).

173 Sabah Gazetesi, (1992), *Özbekistan*, Türki Cumhuriyetleri Dizisi, p. 9.

174 *The Middle East*, March 1993, p. 18.

175 *Ibid.*

176 Sabah Gazetesi, (1992), *Özbekistan*, Türki Cumhuriyetleri Dizisi, pp. 9-10.

177 *D. Telegraph*, 31 March 1992.

178 Country Report, 3rd quarter 1993, Georgia, Armenia, Azerbaijan, Kazakstan, Central Asian Republics, *op. cit.*, p. 18.

179 *The Wall Street Journal*, 6 November 1992.

180 *Ibid.*

181 TİKA, (1995), *Özbekistan Ülke Raporu*, Ankara, p. 12; *Independent*, 27 March 1993.

182 *S. Telegraph*, 5 April 1992.

183 *The Middle East*, March 1993, p. 18.

184 *Independent*, 2 January 1993.

185 *D. Telegraph*, 31 March 1992.

186 *The New York Times*, 17 February 1992, p. 7.

187 *IHT*, 17 February 1992.

188 *Ibid.*

189 *Personal interview with Veli Ahmed Sadur*, a Tatar academic, Leicester, 1993.

190 *F. Times*, 26 January 1993. I should note that in Ankara, although I was able to hold interviews with representatives of the other Republics at their Embassies, the Uzbek representatives refrained from talking to me, and eventually suggested that I should leave my questions with them and that they would convey their answers by post but I did not receive any statements from them.

191 For the whole of the interview, see A. Azamova, (1992), 'Do Muslims need democracy?', *Moscow News*, 27 September.

192 *Independent*, 2 January 1993; For the repression of the opposition and human rights problems in Uzbekistan, see *Guardian*, 10 April 1993; *Moscow News*, 22 March 1992;

Moscow News, 29 September 1992; *F. Times*, 26 January 1993; *Independent*, 12 December 1992; A. Azamova, (1993), 'Prisoners of Conscience: silent cry for help', *Moscow news*, 15 January; 'Uzbekistan's former vice-president Shukrullo Mirsaidov believed that the authorities should end economic and political dictatorship'. (A. Azamova, (1992), 'The prohibitive cost of dictatorship', *Moscow News Weekly*, no. 40, 4 October).

193 *D. Telegraph*, 31 March 1992; TİKA, (1995), Özbekistan Ülke Raporu, Ankara, p. 12.

194 Sabah Gazetesi, (1992), *Özbekistan*, Türki Cumhuriyetleri Dizisi, p. 9.

195 *Independent*, 14 October 1992.

196 Sabah Gazetesi, (1992), *Özbekistan*, Türki Cumhuriyetleri Dizisi, p. 9; For language planing in Uzbekistan see W. Fierman, (1991), *Language Planning and National Development*, Mouton de Greyter, New York.

197 See Table 2.12.

198 *The Middle East*, March 1993, p. 18.

199 For details of the student revolts, see *IHT*, 18 January 1992; *IHT*, 21 January 1992; *Moscow News Weekly*, no. 5, 1992 and 2 February 1992, p. 5.

200 *Moscow News*, 1 March 1992.

201 *Personal interview with Andrew Mango*, London, 29 June 1995.

202 Muhammed Salih is the leader of the Erk Democratic Party in Uzbekistan. In his article, he emphasised Uzbek regime's interest in the Chinese Model rather than the Turkish Model.

203 *Independent*, 3 April 1992; See also, S. Akiner, (1993), *Central Asia: New Arc of Crisis?*, Royal United Services Institute for Defence Studies, London, p. 57.

204 *Personal interview with Anvarbek Mokeev*, Under-secretary at the Kirgiz Embassy in Ankara, Ankara, 28 December 1994.

205 *Ibid.*

206 See Chapter One.

207 *Personal interview with Zakir Hasimov*, Under-secretary at Embassy of Azerbaijan in Ankara, Ankara, 3 January 1996.

208 *Personal Interview with Ertuğrul O. Çırağan*, Retired Ambassador, and currently foreign policy adviser to the Democratic Left Party (DSP), Ankara, 1996.

209 For a general knowledge about Turkish Language see also, Reşid Rahmeti Arat, (1987), *Makaleler*, Türk Kültürünü Araştırma Enstitüsü, Ankara.

210 *Personal Interview with Marie Bennigsen Broxup*, Editor of Central Asian Survey, Quarterly Journal, London, June 1995.

211 For the details of these problems, see A. Arslan, (1994), *Türk Cumhuriyetleri ve Türk Topluluklarından Türkiye'ye Gelen Öğrenciler (1992-1993)*, Yay Ofset, Istanbul.

212 For Distribution of Students According to Turkic Republics, see Table 4.1.

213 *Personal interview with Anvarbek Mokeev*, Under-secretary at the Kirgiz Embassy in Ankara, Ankara, 28 December 1994.

214 *Personal interview with William Hale*, London, 29 June 1995.

215 *Personal interview with Andrew Mango*, London, 29 June 1995.

216 It is said that Niyazov first considered adopting the name 'Atatürkmen', before adopting 'Türkmenbaşı'.

5 Conclusion

The term 'Turkish Model' is used to refer to the model of development and government in Turkey whose characteristics are secularism in a Muslim society, a market economy, closeness and cooperation with the West, and a multi-party system. During the 1991-92 period, when politicians, academics and the media talked about the Turkish model, they in fact underlined these principles, and pointed out to Turkey as the only Muslim state which featured all these principles in its system.

The Turkish Model was initially designed by Atatürk between 1923-1938. The state was established on a secular basis therefore the Sultanate and the Caliphate were abolished and the principle of secularism was inserted into the 1924 constitution, with an amendment made in 1937 accompanied by various social reforms. Significantly, Atatürk turned Turkey's face to the West and this became one of the basic characteristics of the Turkish Model. After the Second World War, Soviet demands pushed Turkey towards the West in real terms. Turkey joined NATO, and Turkish membership of Western institutions such as the Council of Europe, the OECD, and its associate membership of the EC, strengthened Turkey's closeness to the West.

In 1946, the Democrat Party was established, and it came to power after its victory in the 1950 election. This meant the end of the one-party rule which had existed since the establishment of the Republic. Western states encouraged Turkey towards this change, as well as the dissatisfaction among the masses of the population with the RPP. This was a success for Turkish democracy, and after this development the multi-party system became one of the important features of the Turkish Model.

In the economic field, after the 24 January 1980 decisions, liberal economic policies were applied to the economy. This marked the end of the import substitution strategy as a means of industrialisation. Instead, a free market mechanism was adopted and state intervention in the economy was reduced, and the economy opened to the outside world. With these policies, the Turkish economy was transformed from being closed, agricultural and non-competitive to being market-oriented, liberal and rapidly industrialising. Thus, in the 1990s Turkish experience in economic transformation and the market economy constituted other characteristics of the Turkish Model.

Although the Turkish Model has achieved all of the above, it has handicaps as well. Turkish democracy was interrupted three times by the Turkish military (in

1960, 1971, and 1980) although since 1983, Turkey has been governed by civil rulers. More importantly, since 1984 Turkey has been involved in an undeclared war in its own territory (in South-East Anatolia) because of Kurdish separatism. This has certainly been the most important problem facing Turkey and the Turkish Model, because it undermined the popular image of the Turkish Model, and it negatively affected the Western attitude as well as that of the Turkic Republics towards Turkey. Unless a solution is found, in the long term, apart from harming the Turkish economy, it might cause a civil war between Turks and Kurds, as well as creating problems for Turkey's future relations with the West and the Turkic Republics. On the other hand, although at present Alawite dissatisfaction as a religious minority group does not constitute a concrete danger for Turkey and the Turkish Model, it appears to be a potential source for crisis. The Alawites are not satisfied with the Turkish Model and demand changes in it. They want recognition of their identity and state support for the continuation of their culture. All these problems point to the fact that the Turkish Model has been unable to create a democratic civil society.

The West, including the US, supported and promoted the Turkish Model to the Turkic Republics. Western and US decision-makers declared on several occasions that the Turkish Model was an ideal path for the newly independent Muslim Republics of the Caucasus and Central Asia. There were some assumptions and reasons behind this Western promotion and support for the Turkish Model.

Firstly, it was assumed that with the end of the USSR, a power vacuum had been created in Central Asia, as it was believed that Russia did not desire to control former Soviet territory and had vacated the region. Who would fill this gap? In this respect Turkey and Iran were mentioned as rival powers. Iran represented an anti-Western and Islamic regime; on the other hand, Turkey represented democracy, secularism, the free market economy and more importantly closeness to the West. The Turkish Model was seen as an important asset and instrument by the West to overcome the power vacuum created by the dissolution of the USSR. Therefore, the Western fear of Islam, the presence of Iran, geographically, culturally and historically close to the region, and the fear that the Muslim Republics could adopt the Iranian model was the main reason that strongly encouraged the West to support the Turkish Model.

Secondly, although Western democracies are the origin of the Turkish Model and are still stronger than it, the West supported the Turkish Model and put it forward as an ideal path instead of putting forward Western Models, because Central Asians mostly had Turkic origins, and the assumption was that years of communism probably had not drastically altered these Turkic origins and cultures.

Therefore it was assumed that there was positive public opinion in these Republics towards Turkey. In other words, the assumption was that it would be easier for the Muslim republics to follow the path of a country with which they felt affinity and shared a common culture. Therefore the alternatives for models would be either Iran or Turkey, but not Western democracies. The Turkish transition from monarchy to a semi-dictatorial leadership to a multi-party system was seen as the closest experience to that of the new republics as well.

Thirdly, after the collapse of the USSR, the Turkic Republics had to reform their centrally controlled economies, but they had no experience of free trade and the requirements of a market economy did not exist in the Republics. Therefore, a fresh example could be helpful for their transformation. In this sense, the Turkish experience in economic transformation after 1980 (following the 24 January decisions) was a fresh and successful example of a transformation from a centrally controlled economy to a market economy. Therefore, apart from other characteristics, Turkey's success in economic transformation was a factor which encouraged the West to support the Turkish Model.

These were the main reasons that determined Western support for the Turkish model. However, it is difficult to interpret this support as Western confirmation of the maturity of the Turkish Model. Instead, the Turkish model was usually used as a symbol of the principles (secularism, market economy, cooperation with the West and a multi-party system) mentioned at the outset of this conclusion. In turn, it was assumed that the adoption of these principles by the Turkic Republics would be in the interests of the West as well as Turkey.

After the first year of these republics' independence, Western knowledge of the region and its economic, cultural and strategic issues increased, and new developments took place. In turn, the West and the US reconsidered their initial assumptions and policies and ended their support for the Turkish Model. Again there were some important reasons behind the decline in Western support for the Turkish Model.

Firstly, after understanding the real conditions in the region, the West realised that although Iran had some geo-strategic advantages in the region, it had significant handicaps as well. Primarily, although Iran is an Islamic state, in contrast to the initial Western assumptions, the effect of Iran in the Turkic Republics was very limited. This is mainly because there is a divide between Shiite and Sunni Muslims, and a hostile attitude between these two sects. Iran is a Shiite state; on the other hand the majority of the population of the Turkic states is Sunni, except for the Azeris. Iran's influence even over the Azeri population is very limited, as Azeris are Turkic and their nationalistic feelings are strong. Also, Iran has an ethnic Azeri population of some twenty million living in the north of the country, and is worried about the possible unification of these peoples. It must also be pointed out that, maybe because it realised its limits in the region, in contrast to Western expectations, Iran did not become involved in a struggle to export its regime to the Turkic Republics. In fact it has been looking for possible cooperation in economic fields, after being isolated by the West. Therefore Iran's policy was pragmatic and realistic rather than adventurist. This was a surprise for the West: the danger of the Iranian model in the Turkic Republics was the main reason which led the West to promote the Turkish Model to the region as a counter-ideology. Therefore, because of Iran's pragmatic policy, the main reason behind Western support for the Turkish Model diminished.

Secondly, after the collapse of the USSR Russia initially gave priority to domestic affairs, and it was assumed that Russia did not want to regain control over the former Soviet territory. Most people therefore talked about a power vacuum created in the region by the end of the USSR. However, especially after 1993, Russia clearly announced its intention of regaining control over the former Soviet territory known as the 'near abroad' policy, Russia justified her policy in three ways. There were economic reasons, as the Russian economy depended on the other Republics (and vice versa); security reasons, as Russia wanted to control nuclear power and did not want to see a rival power settled in the former Soviet territory. Around 25 million ethnic Russians living outside Russian territory also encouraged Russia to control the former Soviet territory in order to guarantee their civil rights. In 1994, Russia signed several agreements with the Turkic Republics and Russian bases reopened in the region. This was not a terrible development for the West, which preferred to deal with one nuclear power in the region rather than four, and was seeking the stability in the region which Russia could provide. Therefore, in contrast to Turkish expectations, the West allowed Russia to implement the 'near abroad' policy as if it was Russia's legitimate right to control former Soviet territory. Western support for Russian policy in the Turkic Republics was a negative development for Western support for the Turkish Model, as the two are irreconcilable.

Thirdly, promotion of the Turkish Model was an instrument of Western foreign policy, and after about a year it became clearer that the Turkic Republics were not adopting fundamentalism, there was in fact no power vacuum but rather stability in the Republics in general, all the Turkic republics welcomed the main characteristics of the Turkish Model, although in practice there were still problems. Therefore, in terms of Western policy, promotion of the Turkish Model had played its role successfully by attracting the interests of the Turkic Republics towards the West instead of the Islamic Middle East, especially Iran. This meant that since the Turkish Model had played its part there was no longer the need for further support of the Turkish Model. Furthermore, it might have side effects as well, because some Turkish policies and declarations by Turkish officials suggested that there was a danger of pan-Turkism for the West. Further support for the Turkish Model might have encouraged this trend, and therefore support for the Turkish Model declined in order to prevent the creation of a pan-Turkic union.

Finally, although the Turkish Model became popular after the end of the USSR, Turkey was involved in an undeclared war in South-East Anatolia costing several lives every day. Since 1991, this problem has not been solved but has worsened: it has negative effects on the Turkish economy and Turkish foreign policy. In addition to this Turkey faced another fatal crisis in the form of Alawite dissatisfaction, which also threatens the unity of Turkey and demands reform of the Turkish Model. These two problems are crucial for Turkey and constitute an important part of the current Turkish political agenda. The effects of these crises on Turkey played a negative role in terms of Western support for the Turkish Model.

In general, in the 1990s Turkey did not expect the rapid collapse of the USSR, and thus was not ready for the new situation. However, when the USSR disintegrated, the Turkish side welcomed its end and the creation of the Turkic Republics. This reaction was strongly affected by the fact that the Anatolian Turks and the population of the Turkic Republics are of the same origins, and there are cultural and linguistic connections. Turkey's position in the post-Cold War era affected Turkish reactions as well; mainly, Turkish refusal by the EU, isolation on crucial issues like Cyprus and Kurdish separatism, and attempts to find new arguments proving it was still important for the West and global politics, played vital roles in the enthusiastic Turkish reaction to the end of the USSR and the emancipation of the Turkic Republics. Turkey regarded the Turkic Republics as natural allies who could support the Turkish position on international issues. During the Cold War, Turkey was important as a bulwark against the Soviet Union for Western security. As a member of NATO, Turkey defended 37 percent of the common borders with the Communist block (Warsaw Pact) and maintained the second-largest army in NATO. However, with the end of the Soviet Union, the confrontation between West and East also ended and old hostilities motivated by ideological and military competition were replaced by new friendships. This new situation meant that Turkey was no longer an important partner for the West (including the US), as a buffer against the Soviet Union. On the other hand, Turkey's political leadership wanted to convince the Western powers that Turkey still occupied an important strategic position in global politics and was still important to the West. Therefore, Turkey was also anxious to try to find an agenda with which it could approach the post-Cold War situation. The emergence of the Muslim Republics as independent states provided Turkey with a means of showing she was still important for the West, because Western promotion of the Turkish Model provided Turkey with new instruments; it meant a ratification of Turkey's strategic position in the region after the Cold War, enabling Turkey to claim that it was still important for the West and world politics. The second instrument that Western promotion of the Turkish model provided for Turkey was that although almost all levels of Turkish society were interested in the issue and welcomed the developments, they were sceptical because of accusations of pan-Turkism and pan-Islamism ideologies, which were usually regarded as threats to world peace. Neither did they want to frighten Russia, which remained a superpower militarily, or the West, which never welcomes pan-Turkism and pan-Islamism. While the Turkish side (in general) was sceptical and tried to find new arguments and formulate Turkish policy towards the Turkic Republics, Western (especially US) promotion of the Turkish Model gave a good opportunity to the Turkish government and everybody in Turkey, who wanted to have close ties with the Turkic Republics. This idea was welcomed by Turkish politicians and the Turkish government, mainly because it offered a solution to the problem of finding an overall framework for Turkish policy. Now it was easy to establish close relations with the Turkic Republics without frightening Russia or the West, and without being accused of pan-Turkism or pan-Islamism.

Turkish politicians, parties, intellectuals, the media and public welcomed the end of the USSR. Although the Turkish left was sceptical at first, later on they changed their minds and also welcomed the developments. However, Marxists and the Kurdish left were the exception to this enthusiastic welcome. Turkish Marxists were determined to adhere to their cause, claiming that although the Soviet model had collapsed the communist ideology had not, and underlined the continuing presence of China and Cuba as socialist states. On the other hand, after the end of the USSR the Kurdish side turned completely towards separatism. The reaction of different levels of Turkish society - parties, elite, the media and public - affected each other and Western (statements of politicians and the media) support for Turkey affected Turkish society in general; for example, the enthusiastic statements of Turkish leaders about the Turkish world affected public opinion, and therefore Turkish people started to believe that a Common Market or Community of Turkic states would be established. On the other hand, the West's proposal of the Turkish Model, and interpretations by the foreign and domestic media such as a 'new Turkic world was born' or that 'Turkey is becoming a superpower' affected Turkish politicians and encouraged them to make such enthusiastic statements. Public opinion, in its turn, encouraged Turkish politicians to take active steps to solve the Azeri-Armenian conflict; furthermore, the Turkish public called for military intervention in the conflict.

After the end of the USSR, Turkey started to take active steps and recognised the Turkic Republics - becoming the first country to do so. Although Turkey declared that it was not involved in competition with any other country, it also shared the Western view of the threat of Iranian export of its regime and therefore, as a secular, Western-oriented state, wanted to prevent Iran from doing this. The Turkish International Cooperation Agency (TICA) was established to regularise relations between Turkey and the Turkic Republics, and the first summit between the presidents of Turkey and the Turkic Republics took place in Ankara in October 1992. Although Turkish resources are limited and Turkey has internal problems, Turkey gave credits to the Turkic Republics, helped them to modernise their telecommunications, and encouraged them towards economic reforms. However, the most important developments took place in the field of cultural relations. Turkey welcomed 6729 Turkic students in 1992. They attended Turkish universities, and were regarded as a bridge for future relations between Turkey and the Turkic Republics. Turkish 'Avrasya TV' started to broadcast to the Turkic Republics. Turkish help was also important in the field of religion as Turkey wanted to export its model of moderate Islam. The Turkish Presidency of Religious Affairs sent books and Imams to the Turkic republics; students from the Turkic world came to Turkey for religious education. These students were financed and educated by the Turkish Presidency of Religious Affairs. Apart from the state, the Turkish private sector has been active in the educational field: Turkish businessmen opened colleges in every Republic which represented the Turkish culture, moderate Islam and the ideals of Atatürk. Turkish as well as English is taught to the students, and these colleges have been welcomed by the Turkic Republics since they offered education above regional standards. Another important issue was the adoption of the Latin alphabet by the Turkic Republics. Turkey advocated that this was essential to integrate with the world and to adopt the Turkish Model. In 1993 the Turkic Republics agreed to adopt the Latin alphabet. On the other hand, Iran advocated the Arabic alphabet, which was not welcomed by any of the Turkic republics; only Central Asian Republic welcomed this offer was Tajikistan.

The initial reactions of the Turkic Republics to the Turkish Model were strongly affected by the cultural environment of these Republics. Primarily Turkey has ethnic links, as a majority of the population of the Turkic Republics is of Turkic origin; linguistic links, as languages of the same family are spoken by the majority of the peoples of these republics; and religious links, as a majority of the population of the Turkic Republics believe in Islam, specifically the Sunni sect which is dominant in Turkey. Although two-thirds of the Azeri population is Shiite, this does not create any crucial problems for Turkey, because national feeling is stronger than religious feeling among the Azeri population. Furthermore, there is a degree of hostility between Azerbaijan and Iran. Mainly because of this cultural environment, the peoples of the Turkic Republics feel closeness towards Turkey and therefore they reacted positively to the Turkish Model. This admiration and affinity towards Turkey existed even amongst the leadership of the Republics, which initially welcomed the Turkish Model enthusiastically. On several occasions they stated that they would follow this Model, which had been promoted to them by the West and Turkey, and claimed that they would not turn back. Another factor that strongly affected the initially warm reaction to the Turkish Model was that when these republics declared their independence, they were to some extent unaware of the realities of the Turkish situation: because of the lack of communication with the outside world during the Soviet era, they assumed that Turkey was powerful, economically and politically perfect, had no problems and was ready to help them establish their new states. All of them welcomed the aspects of the Turkish Model related to secularism, the market economy and closeness and cooperation with the West, but the democratic aspect of the Turkish Model was generally not welcomed, especially by Uzbekistan and Turkmenistan, where opposition movements were repressed. Although the Kazak regime was not as authoritarian as these two, and Kazakstan and Kirgizstan have taken the lead in instigating democratic reforms, in Kazakstan, nationalist parties were not allowed to be registered, as the Kazak leadership was afraid of alienating ethnic Russians. Karimov and Turkmenbashi took the example of Atatürk, and wanted to follow the Turkish Model of 1920's, featuring single-party rule and the strong leadership of Atatürk. Both of these leaders appreciate and admire Atatürk; mainly for this reason Niyazov adopted the name 'Turkmenbashi' (leader of Turkmens) which is very similar to that of 'Atatürk' (father of Turks). Kirgizstan and Azerbaijan, on the other hand, welcomed the democratic aspect of the Turkish Model as well.

However, after emotional statements and reciprocal visits by the Turkish side and the Turkic Republics, the latter realised the limitations of Turkish power and understood that the Turkish model did not operate perfectly even in Turkey. When the leaders of the Turkic Republics came to Turkey, they witnessed high inflation, unemployment, separatist activities in South-East Anatolia and sectarian demands by Alawites from the Turkish state. The greatly increased access to the world at large after the first year of independence, showed them how far the 'Turkish Model' lagged behind other economies. In contrast to initial assumption, the Turkic Republics understood that the Turkish standard of living could not be a long-term final goal for them, as the Turkish Model was not a social and economic miracle. There was not as much fund in Turkey as they had expected. Therefore, all the Republics wanted to establish close relations with the West, and asked the West to invest in their Republics, because they realised that the developed states of the West, as well as the Pacific, were in a better position than Turkey to give economic help. After realising that the West no longer promoted and supported the Turkish Model, Turkic republics stopped talking about the Turkish Model and their interest both in the Model and in Turkey declined. In contrast to initial expectations, instead of using Turkey as a mediator, the Turkic Republics realised that they could establish direct relations with the West and the US. The West as well, very soon realised that they did not need a third party.

The role of the Turkish involvement in Azeri domestic politics can not be overlooked in the decline of the Turkish Model from favour. Turkish support for the opposition (the Azerbaijan People's Front) in Azerbaijan and the success of Elchibey, alienated the Turkic republics from Turkey and encouraged them to approach Russia, since those in power were afraid that they might lose their posts if the opposition became strong through receiving help from Turkey. For example related with this, Uzbekistan called, most of the students who were sent to Turkey for education, back to Uzbekistan as Uzbek leadership believed that these students held meetings with the Uzbek opposition in Turkey. Additionally, the fact that Turkey supported the opposition in Azerbaijan but, in the end, failed to keep Elchibey in power, revealed to the Republics that Turkey's support or hostility was not so important as Turkey was too weak to compete against Russia in the region. Thus, Turkey's initial image as a strong, sister state was badly undermined after the fall of Elchibey. Above all these reasons, the Turkic Republics did not want to have a new big brother after just getting rid of the old one, and therefore worried about that Turkey could play the role of big brother over the new Republics. Some enthusiastic statements by Turkish politicians gave impetus to these worries, and in return, this helped the Turkic Republics to lose interest in Turkey and the Turkish Model. Therefore, after the initial emotional welcome for Turkey and the Turkish Model, the Turkic Republics then became more realistic and sceptical, and although they have not abandoned the Turkish Model they have begun to say they want only the good aspects of the model, and to emphasise that Turkey is not perfect. Thus, their interest in the Turkish Model declined after 1992.

One can argue that the West achieved almost all its objectives by promoting the Turkish Model, as the Turkic Republics welcomed secularism, the market economy and cooperation with the West. In the case of democracy, all the Republics said that they wanted to establish a democratic multi-party system, but some of them (especially Turkmenistan and Uzbekistan) are reluctant to embark on democratic reforms as they claim they need time to do so. In general, they refused the Iranian model, and there is no instability in the Turkic Republics that could threaten Western business interests. For Turkey's part, there was a degree of success, as Turkey also wanted to stop Iran and advocated the principles noted above. The adoption of these was only a partial success for Turkey, however, as Turkey had broader expectations and wanted to expand its economic, cultural and political influence under the banner of the Turkish Model. In the cultural field Turkey has had some success, and in terms of politics it managed to coordinate the summits among the leaders of the Turkic Republics and Turkey. But in general Turkey was not ready for the role it wanted to play. Because, it is economically weak and itself tries to attract Western investment and needs Western capital and technology, politically it is experiencing ethnic and religious minority problems and is involved in an undeclared war within its borders. Therefore, Turkey can be regarded as partly successful, as almost all the principles advocated by Turkey and the West were adopted to a degree by the Turkic republics, despite the fact that its more ambitious projects such as Özal's initiative of a Turkic common market failed. Turkish analysts and commentators continue to regard the period between 1991-92 as a time of 'missed opportunity' for Turkey, however given the reality of the domestic political conditions and World politics, it is clear that Turkish enthusiasm for 'leadership' was more utopian than realist.

Bibliography

Books and Articles:

Abramowitz, M. I. (1993), 'Dateline Ankara: Turkey After Özal', *Foreign Policy*, no. 91, Summer.

Ahmad, F. (1969), *The Young Turks: The Committee of Union and Progress in Turkish Politics 1908-1914*, Oxford.

Ahmad, F. and Ahmad, T.B. (1976), *Türkiye'de çok Partili Politikanın Açıklamalı Kronollojisi (1945- 1971)*, Bilgi yayınları, Istanbul.

Ahrari, M. E. (1994), 'The dynamics of the new great game in Muslim Central Asia', *Central Asian Survey*, vol. 13, no. 4.

Akçura, Y. (1991), *Üç Tarz-ı Siyaset*, Türk Tarih Kurumu Yayınları, Ankara.

Akiner, S. (ed.) (1991), *Cultural Change and Continuity in Central Asia*, Kegan Paul, London.

Akiner, S. (1993), *Central Asia: New Arc of Crisis*, Royal United Services Institute for Defence Studies, Whitehall Paper Series, London.

Akiner, S. (1994a), 'Central Asia: An Overview of Kyrgyzstan, Tajikistan, Turkmenistan and Uzbekistan', in *Eastern Europe and the Commonwealth of Independent States 1994*, Europe Publications, London.

Akiner, S. (ed.) (1994b), *Political and Economic Trends in Central Asia*, British Academic Press, London.

Akiner, S. (1995), *The Formation of Kazakh Identity: From Tribe to Nation-State*, Royal Institute of International Affairs, London.

Aksoy, M. (1993), 'Kalkınma ve Kürtçülük Meselesi', *Yeni Forum*, vol. 14, no. 289.

Akun, Ö.F. (1992), 'İkinci Abdülhamit'in Kültür Faliyetlerine Bazı Dikkatler', *İkinci Abdulhamid ve Dönemi Semposyum Bildirileri*, Seha Neşriyat ve Ticaret A.Ş., Istanbul.

Akyol, C. (1993), 'Terrörle Mücadelede Yapılan Yanlışlar ve Doğrular', *Yeni Forum*, vol. 14, no. 295.

Akyol, T. (1989), *Azerbaycan Sovyetler ve Ötesi*, Burak Yayınları, Istanbul.

Algül, H. (1991), *Bir fazilet Devletinin Kuruluşu*, Nil Yayınları, Izmir.

Ali, A.S. (1993), 'Prospects of Cooperation with Central Asian States', *Pakistan Horizon*, April.

Altuğ, Y. (1988), 'Soviet Union's Foreign Relations from the Beginning Until the End of Second World War: 1917-1945', *Siyasal Bilgiler Fakültesi Dergisi*, vol. 43, no. 3/4.

Altuğ, Y. (1991), 'Atatürk and the Building of a Modern Nation State', *Turkish Review*, vol. 5, no. 25.

Anadol, C. (1995a), *Alparslan Türkeş, MHP ve Bozkurtlar*, Kamer Yayınları, Istanbul.

Anadol, C. (1995b), *Alparslan Türkeş, Olaylar Belgeler Hatıralar ve MHP*, Burak Yayınevi, Istanbul.

Andican, A.A. (1993), '21. Yüzyılda Doğru Türkistan Cumhuriyetleri', *Yeni Forum*, vol. 14, no. 291.

Antonius, G. (1938), *The Arab Awakening*, Hamilton, London.

Apostolou, A. (1992), 'New Players in an Old Game', *The Middle East*, no. 213.

Arat, R.R. (O.F. Sertkaya ed.) (1987), *Makaleler*, Türk Kültürünü Araştırma Enstitüsü, Ankara.

Arat, R.R. (1992), 'Türk Lehçe ve Şiveleri', in *Türk Dünyası El Kitabı, cilt. II*, Türk Kültürünü Araştırma Enstitüsü, Ankara.

Aren, S. (1995), 'Yeni Bir Dünya Yeni Bir Sosyalism', *Yeni Türkiye*, vol. 1, no. 3.

Armaoğlu, F. (1988), *20.Yüzyıl Siyasi Tarihi 1914-1980*, Türkiye İş bankası Kültür Yayınları, Ankara.

Armstrong, J.A. (1992), 'Nationalism in the Former Soviet Empire', *Problems of Communism*, January-April.

Armsttrong, H. C. (1939), *Grey Wolf*, Penguin Books, Harmondsworth.

Arslan, A. (1994), *Türk Cumhuriyetleri ve Türk Topluluklarından Türkiye'ye Gelen Ögrenciler (1992-93)*, Yay Ofset, Istanbul.

Arter, D. (1993), *The Politics of European Integration in the Twentieth Century*, Dartmonth Publishing Company, Hants.

Aslan, Y. (1992), *Azerbaycan'ın Bağımsızlık Mücadelesi*, Yağmur Basın Yayın, Ankara.

Aslan, Y. (1993), 'Azerbaycan'da Sovyet Oyunu', *Yeni Forum*, July.

Ataöv, T. (1992), 'Turkey's Expanding Relations with the CIS and Eastern Europe', in C.H. Dodd (ed.), *Turkish Foreign Policy*, Eothen Press, Huntington.

Atasayar, K. (1992), '3. İktisat Kongresinin Ardından', *İşveren*, no. 6.

Atila E. (1993), 'Turkey and the European Community in the Changing Post-War International System', in C. Balkır and A.M. Williams (eds), *Turkey and Europe*, Pinter Publishers Ltd, London.

Avcıoğlu, D. (1989), *Türklerin Tarihi, V Volumes*, Tekin Yayınları, Istanbul.

Ayata, A. (1993), 'Ideology, Social Bases, and Organizational Structure of the Post-1980 Political Parties', in A. Eralp, M. Tunay and Birol Yeşilada (eds), *The Political and Socioeconomic Transformation of Turkey*, Praeger, London.

Ayata, S. (1993), 'The Rise of Islamic Fundamentalism and Its Institutional Framework' in A. Eralp, M. Tunay and Birol Yeşilada (eds), *The Political and Socioeconomic Transformation of Turkey*, Praeger, London.

Aybet, G. (1992), 'Turkey in its Geo-Strategic Environment', in *Rusi & Brassey's Defence Yearbook 1992*, Royal United Services Institute, London.

Aybet, G. (1994), *Turkey's Foreign Policy and Its Implications for the West: A Turkish Perspective*, Royal United Services Institute for Defence Studies, Whitehall Paper Series, London.

Aydın, A. (1997), 'Orta Asya Petrolü Üzerine Zor Bir Senaryo: Hazar-Akdeniz Mega Projesi', *Yeni Türkiye*, vol. 3, no. 15.

Azamova, A. (1992a), 'Do Muslims need democracy?', *Moscow News*, 27 September.
Azamova, A. (1992b), 'The prohibitive cost of dictatorship', *Moscow News Weekly*, no. 40, 4 October.
Azamova, A. (1993), 'Prisoners of Conscience: silent cry for help', *Moscow News*, 15 January.
Baharçiçek, A. (1993), *The Impact of Recent Major Changes in International Politics for Turkey's Security Interests*, Ph.D. Thesis submitted to Nottingham University, Nottingham.
Bal, İ. (1996a), 'European Union, Turkic Republics and Turkish Dilemma', *Pakistan Horizon*, vol. 49, no. 1.
Bal, İ, (1996b), 'Instruments of Soviet Control in the Central Asia', *Eurasian Studies*, vol. 3, no. 2.
Bal, İ. (1996c), 'Yusuf Akçura, Üç Tarz-ı Siyaset ve Üç Tarz-ı Siyasetteki Türkçülük'ün Varsayımları Üzerine Yorumlar', in A. Yuvalı, M. Ergunşah, M. Keskin and A. Öztürk (eds), *Türkiye Cumhuriyeti Devletinin Kuruluş ve Gelişmesine Hizmeti Geçen Türk Dünyası Aydınları Sempozyumu Bildirileri (23-26 May 1996)*, Erciyes Üniversitesi Türk Dünyası Araştırmaları Merkezi Yayınları, Kayseri.
Bal, İ. (1997a), 'The Turkish Model: the place of the Alawites', *Central Asian Survey*, vol. 16, no. 1.
Bal, İ. (1997b), 'Orta Asya ve Batının Dış Politika Aracı Olarak Türk Modeli', *Yeni Türkiye*, vol. 3, no. 15.
Banuazizi, A. and Wein, M. (eds) (1994), *The New Geopolitics of Central Asia*, Indiana University Press, Bloomington.
Barchard, D. (1985), *Turkey and the West*, Routledge & Kegan Paul, London.
Barchard, D. (1990), 'Muslims, be men not mice', *The Spectator*, 10 February.
Başbuğ, H. (1984), *İki Türk Boyu, Zaza ve Kurmancılar*, Ankara.
Baykara, N. (1992), 'Türk Devletleri Ekonomik Birliği', *Gözlem Dergisi*, 15 September.
Bender, C. (1991), *Kürt Tarihi ve Uygarlığı*, Kaynak Yayınları, Istanbul.
Bennigsen, A. (1984), *SSCB'ndeki Müslümanlar*, (Translated from Russian into Turkish by Selim Taygan), Vali Yayınları, Ankara.
Bennigsen, A. and Broxup, M. (1983), *Islamic Threat to the Soviet State*, St. Martin's Press, New York.
Bennigsen, A. and Lemercicer-Quelquejay, C. (1988), *Sufi ve Komiser, Rusyada İslam Tarikatları* (Le soufi et le commissaire, Les confréries musulmanes en URSS, translated into Turkish by Osman Türer), Akçağ yayınları, Ankara.
Beşikçi, İ. (1990), *Bir aydın, Bir Örgüt ve Kürt sorunu-Belgeler*, Istanbul.
Bilge, S.A. (1983), 'Turkey's Long Quest for Security Ends with First Enlargement of the Alliance', *NATO Review*, vol. 31, no. 3/4.
Birand, M.A. (1986), *Emret Komutanım*, Milliyet Yayınları, Istanbul.
Birand, M.A. (1990), *Türkiye'nin Ortak Pazar Macerası, 1959-1990*, Milliyet Yayınları, Istanbul.

Blank, S. (1993), *The Eastern Question Revived: Russia and Turkey Contend for Eurasia*, Orta Asya Orta Doğu ile Tanışıyor Konferansına sunulan tebliğ, 12-14 October 1993, Tel Aviv.

Bondarevsky, G. and Ferdinand, P. (1994), 'Russian Foreign Policy and Central Asia', in Peter Ferdinand (ed.), *The New Central Asia and Its Neighbours*, Pinter Publishers, London.

Boulton, L. (1992), 'Painful and protracted birth of a nation', *Financial Times*, 8 May.

Bowder, G. M. (1977), 'Turkey At the Crossroads', *The World Today*, vol. 33, no. 5.

Bozgeyik, B. (1993), *İslam Birliği Üzerine Oynanan Oyunlar*, Timaş, Istanbul.

Bozkurt, R. (1992), 'Bağımsız Devletlerle İlişkilerde Fırsat ve Tehlikeler', *Istanbul Sanayi Odası Dergisi*, vol. 27, no. 315, 22 May.

Bozkurt, V. (1992), *Türkiye ve Avrupa Topluluğu*, Ağaç Yayıncılık Ltd. Şti., Istanbul.

Bölükbaşı, S. (1993), 'Turkey Challenges Iraq and Syria: The Euphrates Dispute', *Journal of South Asian Middle Eastern Studies*, vol. 16. no. 4.

Brown, J. (1989), 'The Military and Society: The Turkish Case', *Middle Eastern Studies*, vol. 25.

Brown, J.M. (1992), 'Parliament comes back to life', *Financial Times*, 21 May.

Bumke, P. (1989), 'The Kurdish Alevis- boundaries and perceptions' in A. Andrews (ed.), *Ethnic Groups in the Republic of Turkey*, Weiesbaden.

Carley, P.M. (1989), 'The Price of the Plan: Perceptions of Cotton and Health in Uzbekistan and Türkmenistan', *Central Asian Survey*, vol. 8, no. 4.

Carnovale, M. (1992), 'In the Wake of a Failed Coup: Moscow and the Fate of the Union', *The International Spectator*, vol. 27, no. 1.

Carpenter, T.G. (1991), 'The New World Disorder', *Foreign Policy*, no. 84.

Connelly, D.A. (1994), 'Black Sea Economic Cooperation', *RFE/RL Research Report*, vol. 31, no. 26.

Conquest, R. (1970), *The Nation Killers*, Macmillan, London.

Copher, P. (1992), 'Turkey's Grey Wolves: Key to Central Asia?', *Security Intelligence*, Supplement, Wednesday, 19 August.

Coşkun, A. (1997), 'Türk Dünyası ve Komşularımızla İlişkiler', *Yeni Türkiye*, vol. 3, no. 15.

Critchlow, J. (1992), 'Will There Be a Turkestan?' *RFE/RL Research Report*, vol. 1, no. 28.

Çandar, C. (1993a), 'Elçibey İçin İleri', *Sabah*, 19 June.

Çandar, C. (1993b), 'Azerbaycan veya 21. Yüzyıla Elveda', *Sabah*, 22 June.

Çarıkcı, E. (1997), 'Türk Cumhuriyetlerinde Ekonomik Gelişmeler ve Türkiye'nin Katkıları', *Yeni Türkiye*, vol. 3, no. 15.

Çetin, H. (1992), 'Turkish Security Structures of Changing Continent - a Turkish view', *NATO Review*, no. 2.

Çetin, H. (1995), 'Türkiye'nin Dış Politika Öncelikleri', *Yeni Türkiye*, no. 3.

Çiller, T. (1995), *Türkiyem*, DYP Yayınları, Ankara.

D'encausse, H.C. (1988), *Islam and the Russian Empire*, I.B.Tauris & Co. Ltd., London.

D'encausse, H.C. (1992), (Translated into Turkish by A. Teşen), *Sovyetlerde Müslümanlar*, Ağaç Yayıncılık Ltd. Şti., Istanbul.

Dannreuther, R. (1994), *Creating New States in Central Asia*, The International Institute for Strategic Studies, Adelphi Paper, London.

Dawisha, K. and Parrott, B. (1994), *Russia and the New States of Eurasia*, Cambridge University Press, Cambridge.

Demirel, S. (1992), 'Newly-Emerging Centre', *Turkish Review*, Winter.

Demirel, S. (1995), '21. Yüzyılın Eşiğinde Türkiye'nin Dış Politikası', *Yeni Türkiye*, vol. 1, no. 3.

Demirer, M.A. (1994), 'Temmuz Ayından Sıcak Mesajlar', *Yeni Forum*, vol. 15, no. 303.

Denktaş, R. (1995), 'Kıbrısta Son Durum', *Yeni Türkiye*, vol. 1, no. 3.

Derin, F.Ç. (1992), 'Osmanlı Devletinin Siyasi Tarihi', in *Türk Dünyası El Kitabı vol. I*, Türk Kültürünü Araştırma Enstitüsü, Ankara.

Deringil, S. (1989), *Turkish Foreign Policy During the Second World War: An Active Neutrality*, Cambridge University Press, Cambridge.

Deringil, S. (1992), 'Turkish Foreign Policy Since Atatürk', in C.H. Dodd (ed.), *Turkish Foreign Policy*, The Eothen Press, London.

Devlet, N. (1993), *Çağdaş Türkiler*, Ek Cilt, Doğuştan Günümüze Büyük İslam Tarihi, Çağ Yayınları, Istanbul.

Directorate General of Press & Information of the Turkish Republic, (1990), 'Southeastern Anatolia Project (GAP)', *Turkish Review*, vol. 4, no. 20.

Directorate General of Press & Information of the Turkish Republic, (1993), *Turkey*, Ankara.

Directorate General of Press & Information of the Turkish Republic, (1993), 'Turkish Republic on its 70th Anniversary', *Turkish Review*, vol. 7, no. 32.

Doepfner, A. (1992), 'Kirgizstan Moves Toward Democracy', *Swiss Review of World Affairs*, October.

Doğan, A. (1997), 'Orta Asya Ülkelerinin Dış Pazarlara Açılımı ve Ekonomik İşbirliği Teşkilatının (ECO) Rolü', *Yeni Türkiye*, vol. 3, no. 15.

Doğan, Y. (1993), 'Azerbaycan'ı Türkiye Kaybetti', *Milliyet*, 20 June.

Doğan, Y. (1993), 'Ankara Darbecilerle flort ediyor', *Milliyet*, 22 June.

Down, E.C. (1986), *The Origins of Arab Nationalism*, Columbia University, Middle East Institute.

Duke, S. (1996), 'The Second Death (or the Second Coming?) of the WEU', *Journal Of Common Market Studies*, vol. 34, no. 2.

Duman, H. (1993), *Türk Cumhuriyetleriyle Kültürel İşbirliği*, Enformasyon ve Dokumentasyon Hizmetleri Vakfı, Ankara.

Duna, C. (1988), 'Turkey's Peace Pipeline', in J.R. Starr and D.C. Stoll (eds), *The Politics of Scarcity*, Westview Press, London.

Dunlop, J. (1994), 'Russia: confronting a loss of empire', in I. Bremmer and R. Taras (eds), *Nations and Politics in the Soviet Successor States*, Cambridge University Press, Cambridge.

Dunn, M.C. (1992), 'Kazakhstan: Nuclear-Armed Giant of Central Asia', Soviet Commonwealth, The Estimate, *The Washington Times*, Supplement: 1-10 Friday.

Ecevit, B. (1984), 'Türk Milleti ve Türkiye', *Nokta Dergisi*, 11-17 June.

Ecevit, B. (1993), 'Türk Halk Tasavvufu İnanç Özgürlüğü ve Laiklik, *Çağrışım Dergisi*, June.

Effendi, M.Y. (1994), 'Letter to the Editor', *Central Asian Survey*, vol. 13, no. 4.

Elekdağ, Ş. (1993), 'Şaşkınlığın Daniskası', *Milliyet*, 27 June.

Enayat, H. (1982), *Modern Islamic Political Thought*, Macmillan, London.

Eralp, A. (1993), 'Turkey and European Community', in A. Eralp, M. Tunay and B. Yeşilada (eds), *The Political and Socioeconomic Transformation of Turkey*, Praeger, London.

Eraslan, C. (1992), 'İkinci Abdül Hamit'in İslam Birliği Siyaseti ve Eğitime Etkileri', in *İkinci Abdülhamid ve Dönemi Semposyum Bildirileri*, Seha Neşriyat ve Ticaret A.Ş., Istanbul.

Erbakan, N. (1991), *The Just Economic System*, Refah Partisi Yayınları, Ankara.

Erbakan, N. (1995), 'Türkiye'nin Dış Politikası Nasıl Olmalı', *Yeni Türkiye*, vol. 1, no. 3.

Ercilasun, A.B. (1992), 'Resmi Dil Türkçedir', *Türk Kültürü*, vol. 30, no. 348.

Erdoğan, M. (1993), 'Türkiye 'de Demokrasiye Geçiş Deneyimi (1945-1950)', in *Türkiye - Azeraycan ve Orta Asya Cumhuriyetlerinde Democracy ve Piyasa Ekonomisine Geçiş Süreci*, Yeni FORUM Uluslararası 2. Sempozyumu 16-23 November 1992, Bakü, Azerbaycan, Yeni Forum A.Ş., Ankara.

Erer, T. (1990), *Kürtçülük Meselesi*, Istanbul.

Ergun, İ. (1992), 'Kollektif Bir Sistemden Piyasa Ekonomisine Geçiş Sorunları', in *Türkiye Modeli ve Türk Kökenli Cumhuriyetlerle Eski Sovyet Halkları*, Yeni Forum, Ankara.

Erkanlı, O. (1973), *Anılar... Sorunlar... Sorumlular*, Baha Matbaası, Istanbul.

Eroğlu, F. (1994), 'Güneydoğuda Siyasi çözüm arayışlarının ideolojik kökenleri', *Türk Yurdu*, vol. 14, no. 78.

Europa Publications Limited, (1992), *Eastern Europe and the Commonwealth of Independent States*, London.

Europa Publications Limited, (1994), *Eastern Europe and the Commonwealth of Independent States*, London.

Fierman, W. (1991), *Language Planning and National Development*, Mouton de Greyter, New York.

Finkel, A. and Hale, W. (1990), 'Politics and Procedure in the 1987 Turkish General Election', in A. Finkel and N. Sırman (eds), *Turkish State, Turkish Society*, Routledge, London.

Frank, A.G. (1992), *The Centrality of Central Asia*, VU University Press, Amsterdam.

Fraser, G. (1988), 'Enver Pasha's Bid for Turkestan 1920-1922', *Canadian Journal of History*, vol. 23, no. 2.

Fuller, G. E. (1993), 'The fate of the Kurds', *Foreign Affairs*, vol. 72, no. 2.

Fuller, G. E. and Lesser, I.O. (1993), *Turkey's New Geopolitics*, Westview Press, Oxford.

Gankovsky, Y.V. (1994), 'Russia's Relations with the Central Asian States since the Dissolution of the Soviet Union', in H. Malik (ed.), *Central Asia: Its Strategic Importance and Future Prospects*, Macmillan Press, London.

Gerger, E. (1989), *Tanzimattan Avrupa Topluluğuna Türkiye*, İnkilab, Istanbul.

Gharabaghi, K. (1994), 'Development strategies for Central Asia in the 1990s: in search of alternatives', *Third World Quarterly*, vol. 15, no. 1.

Gitelman, Z. (1983), 'Are Nations Merging in the USSR', *Problems of Communism*, September-October.

Goldberg, D.T. (1992), 'The semantics of race', *Ethnic and Racial Studies*, vol. 15, no. 4.

Gökalp, Z. (1992), 'Türkler'le Kürtler', *Küçük Mecmua*, no. 1, Diyarbakır.

Gökalp, Z. (translated into English by Robert Devereux) (1968), *The Principles of Turkism*, E.J. Brill, Leiden.

Gökdemir, A. (1995), 'Yirmibirinci Asrın Milletimize Vaad Ettiği İmkanlar', *Yeni Türkiye*, vol. 1, no. 3.

Göyünç, N. (1992), 'Türk-Kürt ilişkileri', *Yeni Forum*, vol. 13, no. 274.

Griffiths, S.I. (1993), *Nationalism and Ethnic Conflict: Threats to European Security*, Oxford University Press, Oxford.

Gunder, M.M. (1994), 'The Changing Kurdish Problem in Turkey', Research Institute for the Study of Conflict and Terror, London.

Gülensoy, T. (1994), 'Türkiyede Kürdoloji Araştırmaları', *Azerbaycan*, vol. 43, no. 296.

Güler, H. (1990), *Sovyetler Birliğindeki Türkler*, Türkiye Diyanet Vakfı Yayınları, Ankara.

Güner, A.O. (1995), 'Rusya'nın Panislavism İdeolojisi ve Türk Dünyası', *Yeni Türkiye*, vol. 1, no. 3.

Gürler, Y. (1992), 'Kürtlerin Türk Kültürü İçindeki Yeri', *Yeni Forum*, vol. 13, no. 274.

Güvemli, O. (1992), 'Bağımsız Devletler Topluluğu içinde Türk Topluluklarının Ekonomik durumu', *Istanbul Sanayi Odası Dergisi*, vol. 27, no. 315.

Güzel, H.C. (1995), '21. Asır Türk Asrı Olacaktır', *Yeni Türkiye*, vol. 1, no. 3.

Hacıoğlu, M. (1992), 'Dünyada Yeni bir Güç Dengesi Oluşuyor', *Istanbul Sanayi Odası Dergisi*, vol. 27, no. 315.

Hadar, L.T. (1993), 'What Green Peril?', *Foreign Affairs*, vol. 72, no. 2.

Haim, S.G. (1976), *Arab Nationalism*, London.

Hale, W. (1981), *The Political and Economic Development of Modern Turkey*, Croom Helm, London.

Hale, W. (1990), 'The Turkish Army in Politics, 1960-73', in A. Finkel and N. Sırman (eds), *Turkish State Turkish Society*, Routledge, London.

Hale, W. (1992), 'Turkey, the Middle East and the Gulf Crisis', *International Affairs*, vol. 68, no. 2.

Halefoğlu, V. (1991), 'The importance of the Soviet Union for Turkey', *Turkish Review*, vol. 5, no. 24.

Hanioğlu, Ş. (1986), *Osmanlı İttihat ve Terakki Cemiyeti ve Jon Türkler 1889-1902*, Istanbul.

Hardman, W.M. (1990), *Kemalism: Evolution or Revolution*, A Dissertation Submitted to the Faculty of the School of Arts and Sciences of the Catholic University of America in Particular Fulfillment of the Requirements For the Degree Doctor of Philosophy, Washington.

Haurani, A. (1970), *Arabic Thought in the Liberal Age*, London.

Haurani, A. (1991), *A History of the Arab Peoples*, Faber and Faber Limited, London.

Hayit, B. (1993), 'Vatanımı Ziyaret Ettim', *Türk Dünyası Araştırmaları*, no. 83.

Henze, B.P. (1992), *Turkey: Toward the Twenty-First Century*, Rand Corporation, Santa Monica.

Heper, M. and Evin, A. (ed.) (1988), *State, Democracy, and the Military: Turkey in the 1980s*, Gruyter, New York.

Herzig, E. (1995), *Iran and The Former Soviet South*, Royal Institute of International Affairs, London.

Heyd, U. (1950), *Foundations of Turkish Nationalism*, Luzac & Compony Ltd. and The Harvill Press Ltd, London.

Higgins, A. (1992), 'Kazakhs in thrall to a colonial past', *The Independent*, 14 April.

Hilav, S. (1992), 'Düşünce Tarihi 1908-1980', in M. Tuncay, C. Koçak, and others (eds), *Türkiye Tarihi Çağdaş Türkiye cilt. 4*, Cem Yayınevi, Istanbul.

Hindle, T. (1993), 'Young Turks', in *The World in 1994*, The Economist Publications, London.

Hiro, D. (1994), *Between Marx and Muhammad*, Harper Collins Publishers, London.

Hohmann, H.H., Meier, C. and Timmermann, H. (1993), 'The European Community and the Countries of the CIS: Political and Economic Relations', *The Journal of Communist Studies*, vol. 9, no. 3.

Hosking, G. (1992), *A History of the Soviet Union*, Fontana Press, London.

Hostler, W.C. (1957), *Turkism and The Soviets*, George Allen & Unwin Ltd., London.

Hostler, W.C. (1993), *The Turks of Central Asia*, Praeger, London.

Hulagu, M. (1993), 'İngiliz Belgelerinde Pan - Islamism ile İlgili Bir Rapor', *Türk Dünyası Araştırmaları*, no. 85.

Hunter, S. (1992), 'The Muslim Republics of the Former Soviet Union: Policy Changes for the United States', *The Washington Quarterly*, Summer.

Hunter, S. (1994), 'Azerbaijan: search for identity and new partners', in I. Bremmer and R. Taras (eds), *Nations & Politics in the Soviet Successor States*, Cambridge University Press, Cambridge.

Huntington, S. (1993), 'The Clash of Civilizations', *Foreign Affairs*, Summer.

Hussain, R.S. (1992), 'Political Economy of Pak Relations with CARs', *Regional Studies*, Autumn.

Hyman, A. (1994a), 'Central Asia and the Middle East', in M. Mesbahi (ed.), *Central Asia and the Caucasus after the Soviet Union,* University Press of Florida, Gainesville.

Hyman, A. (1994b), *Political Change in Post-Soviet Central Asia,* RIIA, London.

Hyman, A. (1994c), *Power and Politics in Central Asia's New Republics,* Research Institute for the Study of Conflict and Terrorism, London.

Israeli, R. (1994), 'Return to the source: the republics of Central Asia and the Middle East', *Central Asian Survey,* vol. 13, no. 1.

İnalcık, H. (1992), 'Osmanlı İmparatorluğu'nda Kültür ve Teşkilat', *in Türk Dünyası El Kitabı, vol. I,* Türk Kültürünü Araştırma Enstitüsü, Ankara.

İnan, A. (1971), *M. Kemal Atatürk'ten Yazdıklarım,* Istanbul.

İnan, K. (1989), 'The South-East Anatolian Project: A Perspective for Future Investors', *Turkish Review,* vol. 3, no. 15.

İnan, K. (1993), *Dış Politika,* Ötüken yayınları, Istanbul.

İnan, K. (1995a), 'Dış Politika', *Yeni Türkiye,* vol. 1, no. 3.

İnan, K. (1995b), *Hayır Diyebilen Türkiye,* Timaş Yayınları, Istanbul.

İncekara, A. (1993), *Kırgızistan,* Istanbul Ticaret Odası, Istanbul.

İncioğlu, N. (1994), 'Yeni Türk Cumhuriyetlerinde Toplumsal Bölünmeler, Siyasal Güçler ve Yeni Siyasal Yapılanma', in B.E. Behar (ed.), *Bağımsızlğın İlk Yılları,* Kültür Bakanlığı Yayınları, Ankara.

Kafesoğlu, İ. (1992), *Türk Milli Kültürü,* Boğaziçi Yaınları, Istanbul.

Kaiser, R.G. (1991), 'Gorbachev: Triumph and Failure', *Foreign Affairs,* vol. 70, no. 2.

Kalalaycıoğlu, E. and Sarıbay, Y. (ed.), (1986), *Türk Siyasal Hayatının Gelişimi,* Beta Basım Yayım Dağıtım A.Ş., Istanbul.

Kamilov, A. (1992), 'Internal Conflicts in Central Asia: Social and Religious Perspectives', in K. Rupesinghe, P. King and O. Vorkunova (eds), *Ethnicity and Conflict in a Post-Communist World,* St. Martin's Press, New York.

Kampfner, J. (1992), 'Seeds of Islam find a place to flower amid veils and vigilantes', *D. Telegraph,* 31 March.

Karamısır, S. (1994), *Türkiye'nin Siyasi Meseleleri,* Osmanlı Araştırmaları Vakfı, Istanbul.

Karaosmanoğlu, A.L. (1988), 'Turkey and the Southern Flank: Domestic and External Context', in J. Chipman (ed.), *NATO's Southern Allies,* Routledge, London.

Karaosmanoğlu, A.L. (1992), 'Türkiye 'de Demokrasinin Uluslararası Koşulları', in *Türk Modeli ve Türk Kökenli Cumhuriyetlerle Eski Sovyet Halkları,* Yeni Forum A.Ş., Ankara.

Karaosmanoğlu, A.L. (1993), 'Officers: Westernization and Democracy', in M. Heper, A. Öncü and H. Kramer (eds), *Turkey and the West,* I.B. Tauris & Co Ltd, London.

Karaörs, M. (1994), 'Türk Dilinin Birliği Bütünlüğü ve Söz Varlığı', *Yeni Forum,* vol. 15, no. 296.

Karasik, T. (1993), *Azerbaijan, Central Asia, and Future Persian Gulf Security*, Rand, Santa Monica.

Karayalçın, M. (1995), 'Yeni Ufuklar ve Türkiye', *Yeni Türkiye*, vol. 1, No. 3.

Karluk, R. (1992), 'Yeni bağımsızlığını kazanmış Türk Cumhuriyetlerinin serbest piyasa ekonomisine geçişinde alınması gereken tedbirler ve öneriler', *Istanbul Sanayi Odası Dergisi*, vol. 27, no. 315.

Kartay, Hami. 'The Past, Present and Future of Turkish Industry', *Turkish Review*, Spring 1989, vol. 3, no. 15.

Keddie, N.R. (1972), *Sayyid Jamal ad-Din 'al-Afghani'*, University of California Press, London.

Kedourie, E. (1966), *Afghani and Abduh*, Frank Cass & Co. Ltd., London.

Kerimov, I. (1992), *Uzbekistan: The Road of Independence and Progress*, Uzbekistan, Taşkent.

Kesic, O. (1995), 'American-Turkish Relations at a Crossroad', *Mediterranean Quarterly*, Winter.

Keskin, M. (1990), 'Güneydoğu Anadoluda Türk devletleri', *Türk Yurdu*, vol. 10, no. 37.

Kırımlı, M. (1997), 'Uzbekistan in the New World Order', *Central Asian Survey*, vol. 16, no. 1.

King, P. (1992), 'The Future of the Soviet Union: Deconstruction versus Disintegration', in K. Rupesinghe, P. King and O. Vorkunova (eds), *Ethnicity and Conflict in a Post-Communist World*, St. Martin's Press, New York.

Kinross, P. (1993), *'Atatürk The Rebirth of a Nation'*, Weidenfeld & Nicolson, London.

Kirzioğlu, F. (1968), *Kürtlerin Türklüğü*, Ankara.

Kitapçı, Z. (1988), *Türkistanda İslamiyet ve Türkler*, Nur Basımevi, Konya.

Kocabaş, S. (1993), 'Birinci Dünya Harbinde Araplar Üzerine İngiliz Oyunları', *Türk Dünyası Tarih Dergisi*, no. 74.

Koçak, C. (1992), 'Siyasal Tarih 1923-1950', in M. Tunçay, C. Koçak, H. Özdemir, K. Boratav, S. Hilav, M. Katoğlu, A. Ödekan and S. Akşin (eds), *Çağdaş Türkiye 1908-1980*, Cem Yayınevi, Istanbul.

Kortunov, A. and Fellow, E.L.W. (1992), 'Strategic Relations between the Former Soviet Republics', *Backgrounder*, The Heritage Foundation, April 17.

Kozlu, C. (1994), *Türkiye Mucizesi için Vizyon Arayışları ve Asya Modelleri*, Türkiye İş Bankası Kültür Yayınları, Ankara.

Kozlu, C. (1995), 'Diplomaside Yeni Cephe... Doğu Asya', *Yeni Türkiye*, vol. 1, no. 3.

Kösoğlu, N. (1990), *Türk Dünyası Tarihi ve Türk Medeniyeti Üzerine Düşünceler*, Ötüken Neşriyat A.Ş., Istanbul.

Krupnik, I.I. (1989), 'Mulitnational Society', *Soviet Anthropology & Archeology*, Winter.

Kuniholm, B.R. (1980), *The Origins of the Cold War in the Near East: Great Power Conflict and Diplomacy in Iran, Turkey, and Greece*, Princeton University Press, New Jersey.

Kuniholm, B.R. (1991), 'Turkey and the West', *Foreign Affairs*, vol. 70, no. 2.

Kuran, E. (1992), 'Osmanlı İmparatorluğunda Yenileşme Hareketleri' in *Türk Dünyası El Kitabı cilt. I*, Türk Kültürünü Araştırma Enstitüsü, Ankara.

Kurşun, Z. (1992), *Yol Ayırımında Türk-Arab İlişkileri*, İrfan Yayınevi, Istanbul.

Kut, G. (1993), 'Elçibey'in sonu Türkiye modelinin sonudur', *Cumhuriyet*, 24 June.

Kut, G. (1994), 'Yeni Türk Cumhuriyetleri ve Uluslararası Ortam', in B.E. Behar (ed.), *Bağımsızlığın İlk Yılları*, T.C. Kültür Bakanlığı, Ankara.

Kut, Ş. (1994), 'Yeni Türk Cumhuriyetlerinin Dış Politikaları', in B.E. Behar (ed.), *Bağımsızlığın İlk Yılları*, Kültür Bakanlığı Yayınları, Ankara.

Küçük, C. (1992), 'İkinci Abdül Hamit'in Dış Politikası', in *İkinci Abdülhamid ve Dönemi Semposyum Bildirileri*, Seha Neşriyat ve Ticaret A.Ş., Istanbul.

Laber, J. (1992), 'Balanced on the Golden Horn', *The Washington Post*, 9 February.

Laffan, B. (1992), *Integration and Co-operation in Europe*, Routledge, Oxford.

Landau, J.M. (1981), *Pan-Türkism in Turkey*, C. Hurst & Company, London.

Landau, J.M. (1990), *The Politics of Pan-Islam*, Clarendon Press, Oxford.

Landau, J.M. (1995), *Pan-Turkism: From Irredentism to Cooperation*, Indiana University Press, Indiana.

Laquer, W. (1990), *Stalin. The Glasnost Revelations*, Macwell Macmillan International, Oxford.

Lenczowski, G. (1980), *The Middle East in World Affairs*, Cornell University Press, London.

Lenkeranlı, M.H. (1993), 'Azerbaycanı Bölmeye Yönelik Rus-İran Müşterek Seneryosu: Taliş-Mugan Cumhuriyeti', *Azerbaycan*, no. 294.

Lesser, A. (1992), 'The Bridge-Builders', *The Jerusalem Report*, 12 March.

Levine, S. (1992), 'Bartering for the riches of cash-starved Türkmenistan', in *F. Times*, 8 July.

Lewis, B. (1951), 'Recent Developments in Turkey', *International Affairs*, vol. 27, no. 3.

Lewis, B. (1961), *The Emergence of Modern Turkey*, London.

Lewis, G. (1974), *Modern Turkey*, Benn, London.

Lough, J. (1993a), *Russia's Influence in the `Near Abroad': Problems and Prospects*, Conflict Studies Research Centre The Royal Military Academy Sandhurst Camberley, Surrey.

Lough, J. (1993b), 'Defining Russia's Relations with Neighbouring States', *RFE/RL Research Report*, vol. 2, no. 20.

Louis, R. (1984), *The British Empire in the Middle East 1945-1951, Arab Nationalism, the United States, and Postwar Imperialism*, Clarendon Press, Oxford.

Mackenzie, K. (1981), *Turkey Under the Generals*, Conflict Studies, London.

Malashenko, A.V. (1993), 'Islam Versus Communism' in *Russia's Muslim Frontiers*, Dale F. Eickelman (ed.), Indiana University Press, Indianapolis.

Malik, M.J. (1992), 'The `great game' begins', *Asia-Pacific Defence Reporter*, June-July.

Mandel, R. (1990), 'Shifting centres and emergent identities: Turkey and Germany in the lives of Turkish Gastarbeiter', in D.F. Eickelman and J. Piscatori (eds), *Muslim Travellers*, Routledge, London.

Mandelbaum, M. (1992), 'Coup de Grace: The end of the Soviet Union', *Foreign Affairs*, vol. 71, no. 1.

Mango, A. (1992), 'European Dimensions', *Middle Eastern Studies*, vol. 28, no. 2.

Mango, A. (1993), 'The Turkish Model', *Middle Eastern Studies*, vol. 29, no. 4.

Mardin, Ş. (1989), *Jon Türklerin Siyasi Fikirleri 1895-1908*, İletişim Yayınları, Istanbul.

Matthews, K. (1993), *The Gulf Conflict and International Relations*, Routledge, London.

Mcdowall, D. (1992), *The Kurds; A Nation Denied*, Minority Rights Publications, London.

Mcghee, G. C. (1954), 'Turkey Joins the West', *Foreign Affairs*, vol. 32, no. 4.

Meissner, B. (1988), 'Gorbachev's Socio-Political Programme', *Aussenpolitik*, no. 4.

Meissner, B. (1990), 'Gorbachev in a Dilemma: Pressure for Reform and the Constellation of Power', *Aussenpolitik*, no. 2.

Mesbahi, M. (1993), 'Russia and the Muslim states: change or continuity?', *Central Asian Survey*, vol. 12, no. 2.

Mesbahi, M. (ed.) (1994), *Central Asia and the Caucasus after the Soviet Union*, University Press of Florida, Gainesville.

Mihmandarlı, N. (1993), *Azerbaycan*, KEIB/BDT Araştırma Dizisi, no. 6, İstanbul Ticaret Odası Yayını, no. 15, Istanbul.

Miller, J. (1993), 'The Challenge of Radical Islam', *Foreign Affairs*, vol. 72, no. 2.

Moosa, M. (1988), *Extremist Shi'ites: The Ghulat Sects*, Syracuse University Press.

Müftüler, M. (1993), 'Turkey and European Community: An Uneasy Relationship', *Turkish Review*, Autumn.

Mütercimler, E. (1993), *Türkiye - Türk Cumhuriyetleri İlişkiler Modeli*, Anahtar Kitaplar Yayınevi, Istanbul.

Naby, E. (1994), 'The Emerging Central Asia: Ethnic and Religious Factions', in M. Mesbahi (ed.), *Central Asia and the Caucasus after the Soviet Union*, University Press of Florida, Gainesville.

Nadein-Raevski, V. (1992), 'The Azerbaijani-Armenian Conflict: Possible Path towards Resolution', in K. Rupesinghe, P. King and O. Vorkunova (eds), *Ethnicity and Conflict in a Post-Communist World*, St. Martin's Press, New York.

Nahaylo, B. (1992), 'Ukraine', *RFE/RL Research Report*, vol. 1, no. 39.

Nazabaev, N. (1992), *Without Right and Left*, Class Publishing, London.

Nissman, D. (1994), 'Türkmenistan: Searching for a National Identity', in I. Bremmer and R. Taras (eds), *Nations & Politics in the Soviet Successor States*, Cambridge University Press, Cambridge.

Nitze, P.H. (1990), 'America: An Honest Broker', *Foreign Affairs*, vol. 69, no. 4.

Niyazov, S. (1993), 'Our Policy Towards the CIS', *Revival*, no. 1.

Nuri, İ. (1977), *Kürtlerin Kökeni*, Istanbul.

Nuri, M.H. (1992/1993), 'India and Central Asia: Past, Present and Future', *Regional Studies*, Winter.

Okyar, O. (1980), *Cumhuriyet Dönemi Türkiye Ekonomisi*, Akbank Yayınları, Ankara.

Okyar, O. (1993), 'Türkiye'de Sistem Arayışı (1930-1980) ve Sonuçları', in *Türkiye-Azerbaycan ve Orta Asya Cumhuriyetlerinde Demokrasi ve Piyasa Ekonomisine Geçiş Süreci*, Yeni Forum Uluslararası İkinci Sempozyumu 16-23 October 1992, Bakü Azerbaycan, Yeni Forum A.Ş., Ankara.

Olcott, M.B. (1992a), 'Central Asia's Post-Empire Politics', *Orbis*, Spring.

Olcott, M.B. (1992b), 'Central Asia's Catapult to Independence', *Foreign Affairs*, vol. 71, no. 3.

Olcott, M.B. (1993), 'Central Asia's Political Crisis', in D.F. Eickelman (ed.), *Russia's Muslim Frontiers*, Indiana University Press, Indianapolis.

Olcott, M.B. (1994), 'Kazakhstan: a republic of minorities', I. Bremmer and R. Taras (eds), *Nations & Politics in the Soviet Successor States*: Cambridge University Press, Cambridge.

Olcott, M.B. (1996), *Central Asia's New States*, United States Institute of Peace Press, Washington.

Orga, İ. (1958), *The Rise of Modern Turkey*, Robert Hale Limited, London.

Orhonlu, C. (1992), 'Türkiye Cumhuriyeti Tarihi', in *Türk Dünyası El Kitabı, vol. 1*, Türk Kültürünü Araştırma Enstitüsü Yayınları, Ankara.

Orkun, H.N. (1987), *Eski Türk Yazıtları*, Ankara.

Öner, M. (1997), 'Ortak Türk Alfabesi Hakkında Bazı Notlar', *Yeni Türkiye*, vol. 3, no. 15.

Özal, T. (1991a), *SSCB Pazarında Türkiye*, Yapı Endüstri Merkezi Yayın Bölümü, Istanbul.

Özal, T. (1991b), *Turkey in Europe and Europe in Turkey*, K. Rustem & Brother, Nicosia.

Özcan, A. (1992), *Pan-Islamism; Osmanlı Devleti Hindistan Müslümanları ve İngiltere 1877-1914*, İsam Yayınları, Istanbul.

Özgüden, D. (1988), *The Extreme-Right in Turkey*, Info-Turk, Brussels.

Öztürk, M. (1992), 'Doğu Anadolu meselesinin tarihi boyutları Üzerine bazı görüşler', *Türk Yurdu*, vol. 12, no. 55.

Öztürk, M.O. (1993), *Ordu ve Politika*, Gündoğan Yayınları, Ankara.

Panarin, S.A. (1994), 'The Ethnohistorical Dynamics of Muslim Societies within Russia and the CIS', in M. Mesbahi (ed.), *Central Asia and the Caucasus after the Soviet Union*, University Press of Florida, Gainesville.

Parmaksızoğlu, İ. (1983), *Tarih boyunca Kürt Türkleri ve Türkmenler*, Ankara.

Parsons, S.A. (1993), *Central Asia the Last Decolonization*, The David Davies Memorial Institute of International Studies, Occasional Paper no. 4, London.

Perinçek, D. (1995), 'Güneyli Dış Politikası', *Yeni Türkiye*, vol. 1, no. 3.

Pevsner, L.W. (1884), *Turkey's Political Crises*, Praeger, New York.

Pipes, D. (1994), 'Islam's Intramural Struggle', *The National Interest*, Spring.

Pipes, D. and Clawson, P. (1993), 'Ambitious Iran, Troubled neighbours', *Foreign Affairs*, vol. 72, no. 1.

Poliakov, S.P. (1992), (Edited with an introduction by Martha Brill Olcott, Translated into English by A. Olcott), *Everyday Islam*, M.E. Sharpe, London.

Pope, H. (1992), 'Türkmenistan: Kuwait on the Caspian', in *Middle East International*, 10 July.

Pope, V. (1993), 'Back to the future in Central Asia', *U.S. News & World Report*, 8 March.

Ra'anan, U. (1990), *Gorbachev's USSR*, Macmillan, London.

Rais, R.B. (1992), 'Afghanistan and Regional Security After the Cold War', *Problems of Communism*, May-June.

Rashid, A. (1994), *The Resurgence of Central Asia: Islam or Nationalism?*, Zed Books, London.

Rasonyi, L. (1988), *Tarihte Türklük*, Türk Kültürünü Araştırma Enstitüsü, Ankara.

RFE/RL Research Institute, (1988), 'Russian Nationalism Today', *Radio Liberty, Research Bulletin*, Special Edition, 19 December.

Rısvanoğlu, M. (1994), *Saklanan Gerçek vol. 1 and 2*, Tanmak Yayınları, Ankara.

Robins, P. (1991), *Turkey and the Middle East*, Pinter Publishers, London.

Robins, P. (1993), 'Between Sentiment and Self-interest: Turkey's policy toward Azerbaijan and the Central Asian States', *Middle East Journal*, vol. 47, no. 4.

Robins, P. (1994), 'The Middle East and Central Asia', in P. Ferdinand (ed.), *The New Central Asia and its Neighbours*, Pinter Publishers, London.

Rouleau, E. (1993), 'The challenges to Turkey', *Foreign Affairs*, vol. 72, no. 5.

Rowley, G. (1993), 'Multinational and National Competition for Water in the Middle East: Towards the Deepening Crisis', *Journal of Environmental Management*, vol. 39, no. 3.

Rupert, J. (1992), 'Dateline Tashkent: Post-Soviet Central Asia', *Foreign Policy*, no. 87.

Rustow, A. (1976), 'İkinci Meşrutiyette Meclisler', *Güney-Doğu Avrupa Araştırmaları Dergisi*, no. 4-5.

Rutland, P. (1992), 'Economic Crises and Reform', in S. White, A. Pravda and Z. Gitelman (eds), *Developments in Soviet and Post-Soviet Politics*, Macmillan, London.

Rüesch, A. (1994), 'Fear of Democratization in Türkmenistan', *Swiss Review of World Affairs*, January.

Rywkin, M. (1994), *Moscow's Lost Empire*, M.E. Sharpe, Newyork.

Sabah Gazetesi, (1992), *Azerbaycan*, Türki Cumhuriyetler Dizisi.

Sabah Gazetesi, (1992), *Kazakistan*, Türki cumhuriyetler dizisi.

Sabah Gazetesi, (1992), *Kirgizistan*, Türki Cumhuriyetler Dizisi.

Sabah Gazetesi, (1992), *Özbekistan*, Türki Cumhuriyetleri Dizisi.

Sabah Gazetesi, (1992), *Türkmenistan*, Türki cumhuriyetler Dizisi.

Sadak, N. (1949), 'Turkey Faces the Soviets', *Foreign Affairs*, vol. 27, no. 3.

Sagadeev, A. (1993), 'Russia and the great power ideology', *Central Asian Survey*, vol. 12, no. 2.

Saidbaev, T. (1992), 'Inter-Ethnic Conflicts in Central Asia: Social and Religious Perspectives', in K. Rupesinghe, P. King and O. Vorkunova (eds), *Ethnicity and Conflict in a Post-Communist World*, St. Martin's Press, New York.

Saivetz, C.R. (1994), 'Central Asia: Emerging Relations with the Arab States and Israel', in H. Malik (ed.), *Central Asia: Its Strategic Importance and Future Prospects*, Macmillan Press, London.

Salih, M. (1993), 'From the Turkish Model to the Chinese Model', *BITIG Journal of the Turkish World*, October.

Sander, O. (1993), 'Turkish Foreign Policy: Forces of Continuity and of Change', *Turkish Review*, Winter.

Sander, O. (1994), 'Turkey and the Turkic World', *Central Asian Survey*, vol. 13, no. 1.

Saray, M. (1987), *Gaspıralı İsmail Bey*, Türk Kültürünü Araştırma Enstitüsü, Ankara.

Saray, M. (1993a), *Azerbaycan Türkleri Tarihi*, Nesil Matbaacılık ve Yayıncılık San. ve Tic. A.Ş., Istanbul.

Saray, M. (1993b), *Türkmen Tarihi*, Nesil Matbaacılık ve Yayıncılık San. ve Tic. A.Ş., Istanbul.

Satterthwaite, J.C. (1972), 'The Truman Doctrine: Turkey', *The Annals*, vol. 401, May.

Seferoğlu, Ş.K. (1993), 'Türkmen ve Kürt Türkleri', *Türk Kültürü*, no. 243.

Seferoğlu, Ş.K. (1994), 'Hocam Fındıkoğlu ve Bölücülük-3', *Yeni Forum*, vol. 15, no. 299.

Sekban, M.Ş. (1970), *Kürt Sorunu*, Istanbul.

Sezer, D.B. (1992), 'Threat Perceptions in Southern Europe: The Case of Turkey', in L. Valki (ed.), *Changing Threat Perceptions and Military Doctrines*, Macmillan Press, Basingstoke.

Sheehy, A. (1989), 'Gorbachev Addresses Nation on Nationalities Question', *RFE/RL Report on the USSR*, 14 July.

Sheehy, A. (1993), 'Russia's Republics: A Threat to Its Territorial Integrity?', *RFE/RL Research Report*, vol. 2, no. 20.

Sırma, İ.S. (1990), *İkinci Abdülhamid'in İslam Birliği Siyaseti*, Beyan Yayınları, Istanbul.

Sindi, A.M. (1978), *The Muslim World and Its Efforts in Pan-Islamism*, A Ph.D. Dissertation Presented to the Faculty of the Graduate School University of Southern California.

Smith, J. and Green, E.F. (1989), 'The Dilemma of Reform in the Soviet Union' in W.G. Miller (ed.), *Toward A More Civil Society*, Harper & Row Publishers, London.

Smolansky, O.M. (1994), 'Turkish and Iranian Policies in Central Asia', in H. Malik, *Central Asia: Its Strategic Importance and Future Prospects*, Macmillan Press, London.

Soysal, İ. (1991), '70 Years of Turkish Soviet Political Relations', *Turkish Review*, vol. 5, no. 24.

Söylemez, Y. (1992), 'Turkey: Western or Moslem', *Turkish Review*, Autumn.

Spring, D. W. (1991), *The Impact of Gorbachev*, Pinter Publishers Limited, London.

Sultan İkinci Abdülhamid, (1984), *Siyasi Hatıratım*, Istanbul.

Sümer, F. (1992), 'Osmanlılar ve Türkler', *Türk Dünyası Tarih Dergisi*, no. 75.

Sümer, F. (1992), *Oğuzlar*, Türk Dünyası Araştırmaları Vakfı, Istanbul.

Şen, F. (1993), 'Black Sea Economic Cooperation: A Supplement to the EC?', *Aussen Politik*, vol. 44, no. 3.

Şerafettin T. (1990), *Türk Kültür Tarihi*, Bilgi Yayınevi, Ankara.

T.C. Başbakanlık Hazine ve Dışticaret Müsteşarlığı, (1993), *Avrupa Topluluğu ve Türkiye*, Avrupa Topluluğu Koordinasyon Genel Müdürlüğü, Ankara.

Tabrizi-Sabri, G.R. (1994), 'Azerbaijan and Armenian Conflict and Coexistence', in A. Ehteshami (ed.), *From the Gulf to Central Asia New Players in the New Great Game*, University of Exeter Press, Exeter.

Taubman, W. (1982), *Stalin's American Policy, From Entente to Detente to Cold War*, W.W. Norton and Company, New York.

Teltschik, H. (1989), 'Gorbachev's Reform Policy and the Outlook for East-West Relations', *Aussenpolitik*, no. 3.

The Economist, (1991), *Turkey: Star of Islam*, 14 December.

The Economist Intelligence Unit, (1993), *Georgia, Armenia, Azerbaijan, Central Asian Republics, 1992-1993, Country Profile*, London.

The Economist Intelligence Unit, (1993), *Georgia, Armenia, Azerbaijan, Kazakhstan, Central Asian Republics, 3rd quarter 1993, Country reports*, London.

The Economist Intelligence Unit, (1993), *Turkey, Country Profile 1993-1994*, London.

The Economist Intelligence Unit, (1993), *Turkey, Country Profile, 1992-93*, London.

The Economist Intelligence Unit, (1993), *Turkey, Country Report 4th quarter 1993*, London.

The Economist Intelligence Unit, (1994), *Georgia Armenia Azerbaijan Central Asian Republics, 1993-1994, Country Profile*, London.

The Economist Intelligence Unit, (1994), *Russia, Country Profile 1993-1994*, London.

The Economist Intelligence Unit, (1994), *Turkey, Country Profile, 1993-94*, London.

The Economist Newspaper Limited, (1994), 'Russian Pressure on Azerbaijan' in *Foreign Report*, London, 14 July.

Timur, T. (1991), *Türkiye'de Çok Partili Hayata Geçiş*, İletişim Yayınları, Istanbul.

Togan, S. (1992), 'Piyasa Ekonomisine Geçiş Süreci ve Türkiye'nin Tecrübeleri', in *Türkiye Modeli ve Türk Kökenli Cumhuriyetlerde Eski Sovyet Halkları*, Yeni Forum AŞ., Ankara.

Toker, Y. (1992), *Büyük Uyanış*, Toker Yayınları, Istanbul.

Tolz, V. (1992), '*Russia*', *RFE/RL Research Report*, vol. 1, no. 39.

Tolz, V. (1993), 'The Burden of the Imperial Legacy', *RFE/RL Research Report*, vol. 2, no. 20.

Tunay, M. (1993), 'The Turkish New Right's Attempt at Hegemony', in A. Eralp, M. Tunay and B. Yeşilada (eds), *The Political and Socioeconomic Transformation of Turkey*, Praeger, London.

Tunaya, T.Z. (1986), 'Osmanlı İmparatorluğundan Türkiye Büyük Millet Meclisi Hükümeti Rejimine Geçiş', in E. Kalaycıoğlu and A.Y. Sarıbay (eds), *Türk Siyasal Hayatının Gelişimi*, Beta Basım Yayım Dağıtım A.Ş.,Istanbul.

Tuncay, H. (1978), *Ziya Gökalp*, Toker Yayınları, Istanbul.

Tuncay, M., Koçak, C., Özdemir, H. and others (eds), (1992), *Çağdaş Türkiye 1908-1980*, Cem Yayınları, Istanbul.

Turan, A. (1992), 'Kürt Tarihi ve Uygarlığı', *Yeni Forum*, vol. 13, no. 273.

Turan, İ. (1986), 'Silahlı Kuvvetler, Koalisyonlar ve Bakanların Özellikleri', in E. Kalaycıoğlu and A.Y. Sarıbay, (1986), *Türk Siyasal Hayatının Gelişimi*, Beta Basım Yayım A.Ş., Istanbul.

Turgut, M. (1992), 'Kürtçe Konuşan vatandaşlarımızın Sayısı meselesi', *Yeni Forum*, vol. 13, no. 277.

Turkmenbashi, S. (no date), *Address to the peoples of Türkmenistan*, Nurol Matbaacılık A.Ş, Ankara.

Türk İşbirliği ve Kalkınma Ajansı, (1994), *Türk Cumhuriyetlerinin tanışma ve yakınlaşmasında basının rolü konferansı, 20-21 October 1993, Istanbul*, Konferanslar Dizisi 4, Ankara.

Türk İşbirliği ve Kalkınma Ajansı, (1995), *Kazakistan Ülke Raporu*, Ankara.

Türk İşbirliği ve Kalkınma Ajansı, (1995), *Kırgızistan Ülke Raporu*, Ankara.

Türk İşbirliği ve Kalkınma Ajansı, (1995), *Özbekistan Ülke Raporu*, Ankara.

Türk İşbirliği ve Kalkınma Ajansı, (1996), *Türkmenistan Ülke Raporu*, Ankara.

Türk İşbirliği ve Kalkınma Ajansı, (1999), *Türkmenistan Ülke Raporu*, Ankara.

Türkdoğan, O. (1993a), 'Türkiye'de Etnik Gruplar', *Türk Dünyası Tarih Dergisi*, vol. 7, no. 78.

Türkdoğan, O. (1993b), 'Terör olayının sosyo-pskolojik nedenleri', *Türk Yurdu*, vol. 13, no. 71.

Türkeş, A. (1985), *Dokuz Işık*, Burç Yayınları, Eskişehir.

Türkeş, A. (1995), 'Önsöz', in C. Anadol, *Alparslan Türkeş, MHP ve Bozkurtlar*, Kamer Yayınları, Istanbul.

Türkeş, A. (no date), *Temel Görüşler*, Bizim Ocak Kitap kulübü, Ankara.

Uludağ, İ. and Mehmedov, S. (1992), *Sovyetler Birliği Sonrası Bağımsız Türk Cumhuriyetleri ve Türk Gruplarının Sosyo-Ekonomik Analizi Türkiye ile İlişkiler*, TOBB, Istanbul.

Uzun, A. (1996), 'Türk Devlet ve Tolulukları ile İlgili Eğitim Faaliyetlerimiz', *Bilig*, no. 1.

Uzunyaylalı, T.M. (1990), *Avrupa Topluluğu İslam ve Türkiye*, Doğu Ajans Yayınları, Istanbul.

Valenta, J. (1995), 'Coping with the Red-Brown Spirit in the Post-communist Countries', *Issues & Studies: A journal of Chinese Studies and International Affairs*, vol. 31, no. 1.

Vali, F.A. (1971), *Bridge Across the Bosporus the Foreign Policy of Turkey*, The Johns Hopkins Press, London.

Vali, F. A. (1972), *The Turkish Straits and NATO*, Hoover Institution Press, California.

Vassiliev, A. (1994), 'Turkey and Iran in Transcaucasia and Central Asia', in A. Ehteshami (ed.), *From the Gulf to Central Asia: Players in the Great Game*, University of Exeter Press, Exeter.

Veremis, T. (1992), 'Greek-Turkish Relations and the Balkans', in *The Southeast European Year Book 1991*, Hellenic Foundation for Defence and Foreign Policy, Athens.

Waltz, K.N. (1993), 'The Emerging Structure of International Politics', *International Security*, vol. 18, no. 2.

Warren, M. (1993a), 'Turkmens suffer unkindest cult', *S. Telegraph*, 24 January.

Warren, M. (1993b), 'Grateful Turkmens extend rule of their benevolent dictator', *D. Telegraph*, 31 December.

Weekes, A.S. and Weekes, R.V. (1978), 'Turks, Anatolian' in R.V. Weekes (ed.), *Muslim Peoples*, Greenwood Press, London.

White, S. (1991), *Gorbachev and After*, Cambridge University Press, Cambridge.

Winrow, G.M. (1992), 'Turkey and Former Soviet Central Asia: National and Ethnic Identity', *Central Asian Survey*, vol. 11, no. 3.

Winrow, G.M. (1995), *Turkey in Post-Soviet Central Asia*, Royal Institute of International Affairs, London.

Wohlstetter, A.J. (1994), 'Rus emparyalizmi hortlarken batı bocalıyor', *Yeni Forum*, vol. 15, no. 298.

Xiaodong, Z. (1992), 'Central Asia on the Rise', *Beijing Review*, 3-9 August.

Yalçın, A. (1992a) 'Ülkede iç savaş ortamı varmı?' *Yeni Forum*, vol. 13, no. 275.

Yalçın, A. (1992b), 'Ülkenin ve devletin bölünmezliği', *Yeni Forum*, vol. 13, no. 276.

Yalçın, A. (1992c), *Türkiye Modeli ve Türk Kökenli Cumhuriyetlerle Eski Sovyet halkları*, Yeni Forum Dergisinin 16-19 Eylül tarihinde düzenlediği sempozyuma sunulan bildiriler, Yeni Forum A.Ş., Ankara.

Yalçın, A. (1992d), 'Türk Modeli' Kavramı ve Türkiye'nin İktisadi Kalkınmasındaki Bazı Özellikler', *Yeni Forum*, vol. 13, no. 283.

Yalçın, A. (1993a), 'Türk modeli kavramı ve Türkiye'nin iktisadi kalkınmasındaki bazı özellikler' in *Türkiye Azeraycan ve Orta Asya Cumhuriyetlerinde Demokrasi ve Piyasa Ekonomisine Geçiş Süreci*, Yeni Forum Uluslararası 2. Sempozyumu 16-23 October 1992 Bakü, Azerbaycan, Yeni Forum A.Ş., Ankara.

Yalçın, A. (1993b), 'Terrörle mücadelede Doğru teşhis ve strateji', *Yeni Forum*, vol. 14, no. 295.

Yalçın, A. (1994), 'Tarih Perspektifinden Orta Asya'nın Geleceği', *Avrasya Etüdleri*, vol. 1, no. 1.

Yalçıntaş, N. (1990), 'Turkey and the European Community', in H. Korner and R. Shams (eds), *Institutional Aspects of Economic Integration of Turkey in to the European Community*, Verlag Weltarchiv Gmbh, Hamburg.

Yerasimos, S. (1991), 'Türkiye, Sahnenin önünde geçen bir yıl', in H. Bayri (ed.), *Yaşadığımız Dünya 1992*, Metis Yayınları, Istanbul.

Yeşilada, B.A. (1988), 'Problems of Political Development in the Third Turkish Republic', *Polity*, vol. 21, no. 2.

Yetkin, Ç. (1993), 'Atatürk milliyetçiliği ve terrör', *Yeni Forum*, vol. 14, no. 286.

Yılmaz, A. (1993), 'Sosyal Bütünleşme, Ayrımcılık ve Türkiyede etnik Sorun', *Yeni Forum*, vol. 14, no. 294.

Yılmaz, B. (1994), 'Turkey's new role in international politics', *Aussen Politik*, no. 1.

Yusuf, S. (1997), 'Türkiye'nin Türk Dünyasındaki Ekonomik Girişimleri', *Yeni Türkiye*, vol. 3, no. 15.

Yülek, E. (1997), 'Türki Cumhuriyetler ile İşbirliğinin Geliştirilmesi', *Yeni Türkiye*, vol. 3, no. 15.

Zagalsky, L. (1993), 'Finding Its Own Way', *Bulletin of the Atomic Scientists*, October.

Zaim, S. (1993), *Türk ve İslam Dünyasının Yeniden Yapılanması*, Yeni Asya Yayınları, Istanbul.

Zaralı, (1986), *Anap Üzerine Tezler*, 11.Tez. no. 2.

Zeine, N.Z. (1958), *Arab-Turkish Relations and the Emergency of Arab Nationalism*, Beirut.

Zeine, N.Z. (1966), *The Emergence of Arab Nationalism*, Khayats, Beirut.

Zenkovsky, S. (1960), *Pan-Turkism and Islam in Russia*, Harvard University Press, Cambridge.

Zinin, Y.N. and Maleshenko, A.V. (1994), 'Azerbaijan', in M. Mesbahi (ed.), *Central Asia and the Caucasus after the Soviet Union*, University Press of Florida, Gainesville.

Documents (Governmental Reports, Party Leaflets, Unpublished Materials)

'President George Bush's Speech at Ankara Esenboğa Airport, 20 July 1991', *Turkish Review*, vol. 5, no. 25, Autumn 1991.

'TOBB Türk Cumhuriyetleri İnceleme ve Araştırma Gezisi', (12-21 April 1992), an unpublished report prepared by TOBB.

20-21 October 1993 Türk Cumhuriyetlerinin Tanışması ve Yakınlaşmasında Basının rolü Konferansı Sonuç bildirgesi.

21 Soruda Adil Düzen, (Ankara: Refah Partisi Yayınları).

24 Aralık 1995 Refah Partisi Seçim Beyannamesi (Özet), (Ankara: Refah Partisi Yayınları).

24 Aralık 1995 Seçimi Refah Partisi Sloganları, (Ankara: Refah Partisi Yayınları, 1995).

Ambassador Ümit Arık, head of TICA (Turkish International Cooperation Agency), '*Yeni Uluslararası Düzen, Türk is Politikası, Bağımsız yeni Türk Devletleri ve Türk İşbirliği, Kalkınma Ajansı*', an unpublished document from the archives of TICA.

An unpublished note on the Soviet economy at the beginning of 1990 prepared by Şevket Özügergin, Consultant responsible for Trade and Economy at the Turkish Embassy in Moscow, April 1990.

Ankara Declaration (Ankara Bildirisi), Ankara, unpublished, Foreign Ministry, 1992.

Başbakanlık Basın Merkezi, (1995), 'Tansu Çiller'in Rektörler Toplantısında Yaptığı Konuşma, (19 March, 1995)', in *Avrupa ile Bütünleşiyoruz, Gümrük Birliği*, Ankara.

Bekir Nebiyev, Azeri Linguist (Professor), his speech, in *Sürekli Türk Dili Kurultayı*, (Ankara: Kültür Bakanlığı, Özel Dizi, 1992).

Bugüne Kadar Başkanlığımızca Soydaşlarımıza Sunulan Hizmetler. An unpublished note prepared by the Presidency of Religious Affairs.

CHP-SHP Bütünleşme genel Kurulu, Ana İlkeler ve Temel Hedefler Bildirgesi, (Ankara: CHP Yayınları, 18 February 1995).

Cumhurbaşkanı Sayın Süleyman Demirel'in Türk İşbirliği ve Kalkınma Ajansı'nın Üçüncü Çalışma Yılının Başlangıcında 'Günümüzde Avrasya' Konulu Toplantıda Yaptıkları Konuşma, (14 Eylül 1994), (Ankara: TIKA, 14 September 1994).

Cumhuriyet Halk Partisi Çalışma Raporu, (Ankara: 27. Olağan Kurultay 9-10 Eylül 1995).

Demokratik Sol partinin 1995 Seçim Bildirgesi Özet, (Ankara: DSP Yayınları, 1995).

Durmuş Fikri Sağlar, 'Kültür Bakanı Durmuş Fikri Sağlar' in *Sürekli Türk Dili Kurutayı*, (Ankara, Kültür Bakanlığı Yayınları, no. 1413, 1992).

Güvercin, DSP Genel Merkezi Haber Bülteni, 5 August 1994.

Hazine ve Dış Ticaret Müsteşarlığı İhracatı Geliştirme Etüd Merkezi, Dış Ticaret Elemanı Eğitim Programı 2-10 Mart 1992, '*Yeni Türk Cumhuriyetleri ile Ticari İşbirliği Olanakları*' by H. Gültekin Köksal.

Kamil Veliyev, Azeri Linguist (Professor), his speech, in *Sürekli Türk Dili Kurultayı*, (Ankara: Kültür Bakanlığı, Özel Dizi, 1992).

Milli Eğitim Bakanlığı Yurtdışı Eğitim Genel Müdürlüğü, (1993), *Milli Eğitim Bakanlığı ve Türk Dünyası*, Prepared by Zeki Alan, Ankara.

Milli Görüşün İktidardaki Hizmetleri (1974-1978), (Ankara, Refah Partisi Yayınları).

President Turgut Özal's address at the 'European Studies Centre Global Panel', 9 April 1991, *Turkish Review*, Spring 1991, vol. 5, no. 23.

Refah Partisinin Anayasa Değişikliği Uzlaşma Teklifi, (Ankara: Refah Partisi Yayını).

The number of the TV Channels in Turkey, were taken from the High Council of Radio Television (RTÜK) on April 7, 1997.

The speech by the Head of the Foreign Policy Institute, Seyfi Taşhan, delivered at the meeting organised by the Royal Institute of International Affairs on 13-14 January 1992, 'Turkey from marginality to centrality', *Turkish Review*, vol. 6, no. 27, Spring 1992.

The speech of the Kazakh representative, *Sürekli Türk Dili Kurultayı*, (Ankara: Kültür Bakanlığı, Özel Dizi, 1992).

Tünegün Kasymbegov, adviser to the Kirgiz president, his speech, in *Sürekli Türk Dili Kurultayı*, (Ankara: Kültür Bakanlığı, Özel Dizi, 1992).

Newspapers And Other Media Sources

Cumhuriyet, 18 December 1991.
Cumhuriyet, 6 July 1992.
Cumhuriyet, 9 July 1992.
Cumhuriyet, 14 July 1992.
Cumhuriyet, 21 September 1992.
Cumhuriyet, 20 June 1993.
Cumhuriyet, 22 June 1993.
Cumhuriyet, 28 June 1993.
Cumhuriyet, 17 July 1993.
Cumhuriyet, 18 July 1993.
D. Telegraph, 31 March 1992.
D. Telegraph, 6 April 1992.
D. Telegraph, 1 February 1993.
D. Telegraph, 11 June 1993.
Denge Kurd Newspaper, October 1993.
Dünya, 27 April 1992.
Dünya, 6 November 1992.
The Economist, 18 June 1987.
The Economist, 14 December 1991.
Financial Times, 3 May 1992.
Financial Times, 14 May 1992.
Financial Times, 21 May 1992.
Financial Times, 26 January 1993.
Financial Times, 7 May 1993.
Financial Times, 11 May 1993.
Financial Times, 17 May 1993.
Financial Times, 24 December 1993.
Guardian, 15 March 1992.
Guardian, 3 April 1992.
Guardian, 19 May 1992.
Guardian, 10 April 1993.
Hürriyet, 14 July 1992.
Hürriyet, 5 May 1993.
Hürriyet, 28 June 1993.
Hürriyet, 12 July 1993.
International Herald Tribune, 14 February 1990.
International Herald Tribune, 18 January 1992.
International Herald Tribune, 21 January 1992.
International Herald Tribune, 17 February 1992.
International Herald Tribune, 13 March 1992.
International Herald Tribune., 24 March 1992.

International Herald Tribune, 29 January 1993.
International Herald Tribune, 16 February 1993.
International Herald Tribune, 12 May 1993.
Independent, 21 December 1991.
Independent, 3 April 1992.
Independent, 27 April 1992.
Independent, 25 May 1992.
Independent, 14 October 1992.
Independent, 12 December 1992.
Independent, 2 January 1993.
Independent, 27 March 1993.
Independent, 6 July 1993.
Le Monde, 17 June 1993.
Milliyet, 20 May 1992.
Milliyet, 9 July 1992.
Milliyet, 30 May 1993.
Milliyet, 12 June 1993.
Milliyet, 24 June 1993.
Milliyet, 28 June 1993.
Milliyet, 27 November 1993.
Milliyet, Konda Büyük Araştırması, 2 March 1993.
Moscow News, 23 February 1992.
Moscow News, 1 March 1992.
Moscow News, 22 March 1992.
Moscow News, 5 July 1992.
Moscow News, 29 September 1992.
New York Times, 16 May 1992.
Newspot, 4 June 1981.
Newspot, 12 March 1992.
Newspot, 9 April 1992.
Newspot, 7 May 1992.
Newspot, 21 May 1992.
Newspot, 18 June 1992.
Newspot, 30 July 1992.
Newspot, 3 December 1992.
Newspot, 11 March 1993.
Newspot, 19 August 1994.
Official Gazette, 17 November 1991.
Radikal, 18 December 1996.
Radikal, 19 December 1996.
Radikal, 20 December 1996.
S. Telegraph, 5 April 1992.
S. Telegraph, 9 August 1992.

S. Telegraph, 29 November 1992.
S. Telegraph, 24 January 1993.
S. Times, 19 January 1992.
Sabah, 3 February 1992.
Sabah, 15 October 1992.
Sabah, 17 October 1992.
Sabah, 22 June 1993.
Sabah, 23 June 1993.
Sabah, 18 August 1993.
Sabah, Piar-Galup Araştırması, 9 July 1992.
SWB, ME/1290, A5, 29 January 1992.
SWB, SU/1322, A4/1, 6 March 1992.
SWB, SU/1346, C1/2, 3 April 1992.
Tercüman, 1 February 1992.
Tercüman, 28 September 1992.
The New York Times, 17 February 1992.
The Washington Post, 9 February 1992.
The Washington Post, 10 February 1992.
The Washington Post, 12 February 1992.
The Washington Post, 19 March 1992.
The Washington Times, 20 May 1992.
Times, 22 January 1992.
Times, 28 January 1992.
Times, 24 March 1992.
Times, 26 March 1992.
Times, 26 May 1992.
Times, 24 August 1992.
Times, 11 May 1993.
Times, 29 January 1994.
Yeni Düşünce, 10 September 1993.
Yeni Günaydın, 1 February 1992.
Yeni Hafta, 27 September-3 October 1993.
Yeni Hafta, 4-10 October 1993.
Yeni Hafta, 11-17 October 1993.
Yeni Yüzyıl, 26 December 1996.
Zaman, 24 December 1991.
Zaman, 18 June 1992.
Zaman, 20 July 1992.
Zaman, 4 July 1993.
Zaman, 7 August 1993.

Magazines

2000'e Doğru, July 1992.
İktisat Dergisi, April 1992.
İşveren, Türkiye İşveren Sendikaları Konfederasyonu yayını, no. 6, June 1992.
Jane's Defence Weekly, 18 April 1992.
Jane's Defence Weekly, 18 April 1992.
Moscow News Weekly, no. 5, 2 February 1992.
Newsweek, 3 February 1992.
Security Intelligence, 19 August 1992.
Security Intelligence, Supplement, Wednesday, 19 August 1992.
Tashkent, May 1992.
The Christian Science Monitor, 15-21 May 1992.
The Economist, 15-21 February 1992.
The Economist, 25 February 1992.
The Economist, 7 March 1992.
The Economist, 5 December 1992.
The Economist, 8 January 1993.
The Economist, 20 February 1993.
The Middle East, July 1992.
The Middle East, August 1992.
The Middle East, March 1993.
The Wall Street Journal, 14 February 1992.
The Wall Street Journal, 13 March 1992.
The Wall Street Journal, 6 November 1992.
Time, 13 May 1991.
Time, 23 December 1991.
Time, 10 February 1992.
Time, 6 April 1992.
Tim-se, no. 103, March 1992.
Türkiye Günlüğü, Summer 1992.
Türkiye İktisat, April 1993.
World Press Review, November 1991.
Yeni Forum, May 1992.
Yeni Forum, June 1992.
Yeni Forum, November 1992.
Yeni Forum, July 1993.
Yeni Forum, August 1993.
Yeni Forum, March 1994.
Yeni Forum, May 1994.
Yön, vol. 1, no. 20, 16 October 1994.

TV Programmes

ATV (a Turkish TV channel), 24 September, 1994; Siyaset Meydanı (directed by Ali Kırca); the first TV programme concerning the Alawite people, focusing on their demands from the state and the place of Alawites within Islam was broadcast. During the October 1994, a TV series prepared by Zülfü Livaneli for (ATV Channel) concerning Alawite people and their demands.
TRT Avrasya TV, News at 6.00 p.m., 18.11.1999.

Personal Interviews

Personal interview with Veli Ahmed Sadur, a Tatar academic, (Leicester, 1993).
Personal interview with İsmail Yolcuoğlu, Under-Secretary at the Embassy of Azerbaijan in Ankara, (Ankara, 10 June 1993).
Personal interview with Annaguli Nurmemedov, Under-Secretary at the Turkmen Embassy in Ankara, (Ankara, 11 June 1993).
Personal Interview with Arif Soytürk, Director of Foreign Department of Presidency of Religious Affairs, (Ankara, 21 June 1993).
Personal interview with Acar Okan, Adviser to the Prime Minister, (Ankara, 7 July 1993).
Personal interview with Dulat Kuavisen, third secretary responsible for political affairs at the Embassy of Kazakhstan in Ankara, (Ankara, 10 July 1993).
Personal interview with Selçuk Alkın, a member of the administrative committee of the Azerbaijan Culture Society, (Ankara, 19 July 1993).
Personal interview with Cemil Çiçek, former State Minister and currently an MP, (Ankara, 1994).
Personal interview with Anvarbek Mokeev, Under-Secretary at the Kirgiz Embassy in Ankara, (Ankara, 28 December 1994).
Personal Interview with Abdülkadir Aksu, former Minister of Interior Affairs, (Ankara, 1995).
Personal Interview with Nurmuhammad Hanammov, Turkmen Ambassador in Ankara, (Ankara, January 1995).
Personal interview with Mehmed Aliyev Nevruzoğlu, Azeri Ambassador in Ankara, (Ankara, 3 January 1995)
Personnel Interview with Zakir Hasimov, Under-Secretary at the Azeri Embassy in Ankara, (Ankara, 3 January 1995)
Personal Interview with Necati Bilican, General Director of Security, (Ankara, 5 January 1995).
Personal Interview with Marie Bennigsen Broxup, Editor of Central Asian Survey, quarterly Journal, (London, June 1995).
Personal interview with William Hale, Professor at SOAS, (London, 29 June 1995).
Personal interview with Andrew Mango, (London, 29 June 1995).

Personal Interview with Kamran İnan, Retired Ambassador and former Minister of Foreign Affairs, (Ankara, 1996)

Personal Interview with Ertuğrul O. Çırağan, Retired Ambassador, and currently foreign policy adviser to the Democratic Left Party (DSP), (Ankara, 20 March 1996).

Personal interview with Hasan Koni, Professor at Ankara University, (Ankara, 30 March 1996).

Personal interview with Ayşe Ayata, Professor at Middle East Technical University, (Ankara, 14 May 1996).

Personal interview with Nadir Devlet, Professor at Marmara University, (Kayseri, 24 May 1996).

Surveys Conducted by the Author

1. A Survey was conducted by the author in İzmir, Manisa and Edremit, among 519 Turkish people. (İzmir, Manisa, Edremit, May-July 1993).
2. A Survey was conducted by the author in İzmir among 291 students who came from Turkic republics to Turkey for education. (İzmir, June-July 1993).